AF207820

Endorsements

Credibility is critical in the development and dissemination of management theory and practice. It is generally agreed that requisite organization (RO) and the levels of work and human capability/managerial accountability approach are not widely known and are frequently overshadowed by the latest management fad. Indeed, many organizations that have used requisite concepts to improve their organizations are reluctant to publicize their success for competitive reasons. The end result is that awareness of the effectiveness of the work levels approach is disturbingly low. Therefore, as a service to our readers and to provide some ammunition when attacked with the question, "Who else has used this stuff?" or, "does this stuff work?" we offer a series of endorsements from a variety of knowledgeable individuals who have experience with the work levels concepts. Consider this as grease for the wheels of acceptance.

FROM CEOS....

"My journey began in 1982 when, by chance, I was seated next to Elliott Jaques on a trans-Pacific flight. I had recently moved from an operating role to a headquarters function and he probed my thoughts on the organizational maze which I had come to accept in a large organization. I can remember that this was not the most relaxing flight, but for me it was the most fruitful.

"The journey continued with the application of requisite organization as President/ Managing Director of three subsidiary companies, and as a CEO of two publicly listed global mining and metals companies over a period of twenty years. All these organizations suffered economic and organizational distress to varying degrees. They were widely spread across Australia, USA, Europe and New Zealand and yet the problems and the solutions were the same. Implementation involved a process of internal review and organizational change, asking the very questions that Elliott had posed in our first encounter – How many levels of management are actually needed? – Who is accountable for output at required quality by when? – What are the minimum managerial authorities?

"This executive guide provides many practical insights from an extraordinarily capable group of contributors to guide you, the reader on your own journey."

NICK STUMP
Former CEO Commonwealth Aluminum Corp, Group Executive CRA Ltd,
CEO Comalco Ltd CEO MIM Holdings Ltd

"In my experience, requisite organization continues to provide the best known principles for organizational structure, staffing decisions and management practices. I have found requisite principles equally applicable across multiple cultures and evolving societal norms as well as across a wide range of organizations—those with a social mission as well as those with a profit mission. In my opinion, this compilation of history, theory and application is a 'must-read' for anyone accountable for leading any organization."

W. J. (JOE) PRIVOTT
Formerly President and CEO of Novus International, Inc. a private global specialty chemical company and now CEO of Privotts LC, a management consulting practice..

"Two years ago VON began implementing a requisite organization framework. RO has been instrumental in helping VON Canada, a national organization with 51 branches and almost 16,000 staff and volunteers across the country, to build a structure and process that provides a consistent framework of thinking and language.

"The articles in this book which describe the use of RO in both private and public sectors bring to light the principles and elements that organizations need to consider while implementing RO.

"Although implementation is a time-consuming, systematic process, the benefits of identifying levels of work, spans of control and managerial accountability are extremely beneficial in organizationally complex settings.

"This Executive Guide clearly identifies the ways that RO can effectively aid in the building of strong organizations with strong people."

DR. JUDITH SHAMIAN, RN, PhD., LLD, Sc.D
President & CEO of VON Canada
VON is a not-for-profit charitable organization
and the largest home and community services organization in Canada.

"When I was first introduced to the work of Sir Wilfred Brown and Dr. Elliott Jaques in the early nineties, I had no idea how it would eventually benefit my business successes and how it would transform my beliefs about managing and leading. Requisite organization (RO) is more than theory. It is managerial science that reveals the real leadership principles required for maximum effectiveness in organizations.

"After taking an assignment to transform a business with long-term stagnant growth, I used requisite organization to create a high performance culture with aligned cross-functional accountabilities, supported by capable people in clearly defined roles. By unleashing our people's full capacity to solve problems and fix ineffective systems and processes, the organization delivered double-digit growth in short order and has now sustained that level of growth for four consecutive years. As a result of these RO principles, the managerial-employee relationships are growing stronger, employees feel greater empowerment, and execution has dramatically improved.

"The exciting prospects of allowing employees to utilize their full capability and creativity to achieve an organization's vision is not just possible but becoming an expectation of managerial leadership. This book unveils applications of RO and its impact on employees and on bottom-line results. Through the publishing of this book the Global Organization Design Society is putting its mark on the understanding of management and how to improve organizations. Employees in these organizations and other stakeholders of these organizations will be the ultimate beneficiaries."

RON J. HARDING
President, Mallinckrodt Baker, Inc.

"When I began using requisite organization concepts in my company, we had only 30 employees and everyone reported to me. Now after 18 years of sustained growth and profitability, we have 600 employees and four levels of managers.

"I used requisite organization system concepts and tools to develop my own managerial and enterprise-building capabilities and to design a suitable organizational structure for each growing stage—all within the financial constraints of a small growing organization.

"The requisite concepts that I found most useful were accountability/authority, the time-span of a role, the necessary distance between managerial levels, current applied capability, the clarifying assumptions about why people work, and acceptance of a variety of styles limited only by uncontrollable behaviors.

"It was a bonus that RO concepts also helped me to better understand the structure and functioning of other supplier and client organizations that we relate to in the course of our business."

ALFREDO D'ALESSIO
Founder and CEO
CEITECH, the leading supplier of IT support services to businesses in Argentina

"When an organization is structured correctly, employees know what they are expected to do and perform their tasks efficiently. Each layer of supervisors and managers adds value to the corporation.

"If workers are spending all their time trying to figure out what their bosses want or playing political games, the company ends up with wasted effort. But the right corporate structure helps motivate workers and improve productivity.

"That's been our experience at Sunoco Inc., where we have applied the theories of Elliott Jaques, an internationally recognized expert on corporate hierarchy, to rebuild our organization.

"We suffered from too much bureaucracy, and our costs were too high. Work was getting done, but it wasn't focused on a goal, so Sunoco was not achieving satisfactory financial results.

"The changes at Sunoco have been phenomenal....We rose from the bottom of the industry to first place in return on capital in just 1 year.

"In today's environment, a corporation must restructure all the time. Technology changes, environment changes, consumers change, and your strategy changes. As a result, the work done by employees changes continuously and the organization must reflect the market.

"A corporation should be a dynamic, living organism—not a truncated organization, struggling to survive. By creating an effective corporate structure, a CEO can build a healthy organization that generates value for its shareholders, employees, and customers."

DOUGLAS MACKENZIE
CEO, Suncor Inc. (Canada)
Oil & Gas Journal, Tulsa, OK, September 7, 1992.

OTHER SENIOR MANAGERS...

"I commend the GO Society for its achievements in promulgating the insights of Wilfred Brown, Elliott Jaques and their Brunel University colleagues into *Organization Design, Levels of Work and Human Capability* and ensuring the further development and application of these insights in today's organizations.

"I had the privilege of working with Dr Jaques for over 10 years in my role at CRA Ltd as the Group Executive responsible for Human Resources and believe this period to be one of the most productive and enjoyable experiences of my working life.

"The CEO and I, together with our colleagues on the Executive Committee, worked in partnership with Elliott to test and articulate requisite organization concepts and implementation processes as we overhauled structures and management systems across our Business Units.

"Requisite organization concepts provided us with a Human Resources framework for our business strategies which has resulted in significant and persistent impact on CRA's productivity and profitability.

"May your readers also come to enjoy the benefits of this proven approach to the design and management of productive organizations."

J. T. (JACK) BRADY
Formerly Group Executive for Human Resources with CRA Ltd
—now part of the global miner Rio Tinto PLC

"It [this theory] gave me some tools to better understand that hierarchy did not have to be pejorative – in fact it could add value. If you have less layers of work you can get rid of a hell of a lot of bureaucracy; bureaucracy is about layers of people who don't add value. This is a way of streamlining the decision making....The work we [each] do does have different degrees of complexity.

"We have to have better levels of service and that means we have to have people with accountability and the authority to handle customer needs more directly than in the past....This is no organizational folly: it has a purpose which is about sharpening customer focus."

LES CUPPER
Head of Group Human Resources
Commonwealth Bank, Australia
Australian Financial Review, *BOSS* Magazine, 12 April, 2002.

"I was first exposed to requisite organization (RO) when I was a young production manager working for CRA in the mid 80s. For me the concepts that were being proposed seemed more like simple common sense than a fully integrated management framework, the result of some 30 odd years of study and research. As I progressed through my career I become more interested in the observations of the model at work and the genesis of RO.

"The work of Elliott Jaques and his colleagues is as much a study of the human condition as it is a model for management application in the business world. There are no short cuts in the quest for the design and application of effective management systems in today's competitive world. Understanding levels of work, individual capability and the potential for properly designed and applied management systems is the key to delivering exceptional results. The recognition that people are not simply the most important resource in the business, they are the business, will open up a whole range of new possibilities to management in all fields of endeavor.

"I commend the GO Society for taking on this challenge and for its dedication to making this work accessible to a new generation of business leadership. As the torch is passed to a new generation of leaders, the light that shines forward is a lot brighter as a consequence of their work."

MARK CUTIFANI
Chief Operating Officer
CVRD Inco

"Over the last three years, Securicor has doubled in size, largely through targeted acquisitions. Over 80 percent of our employees now work outside the UK – where different phases of market development, different legislation, unique customer needs and cultural diversity add considerably to the challenges of our leaders. Functioning effectively in this new environment demanded a level of leadership unprecedented at Securicor.

"Our vision and business model demand exemplary leadership within an autonomous, performance-related environment and [with levels of work and capability] we now had insight into what makes an excellent leader within Securicor and a mechanism to identify and assess Securicor leaders of the future."

IRENE COWDEN
Senior Manager and member of the board
taken from "Securicor," *Strategic HR Review*, March 2004
(Securicor has since tripled again in size and is now Group4Securicor.)

"Over the years I've had the opportunity to use requisite organization methods for selection purposes in a number of companies. Again and again I observed how individuals initially assessed to have high potential had in fact over time advanced in the company to more complex roles with greater accountability.

"Four years ago, we at Syngenta Argentina had a strong need to improve our selection and talent pool planning systems. After evaluating alternative methods, we decided to adopt RO concepts and methods.

"Today we are fully satisfied and know that this was the right choice. RO systems provided a clear process that our managers enthusiastically embraced. As a valuable bonus our managers have gained deeper understanding of levels of work complexity, levels of human capability, and managerial accountability."

CRISTINA FRANICHEVICH
Human Resources Manager Latin America South
Syngenta Argentina

THE MANAGEMENT GURUS...

"This [requisite organization] is ... a system." (Deming's highest compliment)

W. EDWARDS DEMING
Letter to Elliott Jaques, December 8, 1990

"Elliott Jaques's work is held widely unrecognized but increasingly will become recognized. The reason is simple. Most of industrial psychology is made up of odds and ends and bits and pieces of studies without a theoretical base and it will become clear that there is an increasing need for conceptual integration. Then Elliott's work will be more widely recognized and used.

"There needs to be an effort to integrate Elliott's work into contemporary psychoanalytic theory because he came out of that tradition and what he's done continues to build on it and expand on it in ways that will build an increasingly sophisticated psychology."

HARRY LEVINSON, Ph.D
Emeritus Clinical Professor of Psychology, Harvard Medical School
Emeritus Chairman of The Levinson Institute

"A very important contribution to the theory and practice of management, containing ideas and techniques that are entirely new ...."

CHESTER I. BARNARD
endorsement of Measurement of Responsibility in *Harvard Business Review*, January 1957

"I was particularly impressed with the links Elliott Jaques made between levels of work, levels of human capability and effective managerial leadership practices. The authors have shown in numerous case studies how companies have implemented these inter-related concepts to develop their staff's human potential and to boost their business results. It is clear that talent is scarce and will become more so in the not too distant future. Any leader who wants to retain and engage the talented members of their team will gain a foothold by reading numerous articles in this book. They provide great insight and they also offer some excellent "how to's.""

"This comprehensive, concept-rich book focuses with brilliant clarity on the neglected area of organizational design from a systems perspective. The book will not simply be read; it will be studied as a text offering innovative insights and practical tools to unleash creativity, boost productivity, improve profitability, and inspire commitment at all organizational levels. It offers ready-to-use guidance opening fresh perspectives to managers and aspiring leaders."

"Requisite Dynamics are essential for a world we don't live in yet, a fluid, constantly shifting set of aspirations and expectations that demand that structural shapes adapt to the demands of these uncommon times. Begin with requisite organizational tools."

Organization Design, Levels of Work & Human Capability

EXECUTIVE GUIDE

SERIES EDITOR
Ken Shepard

EDITORS
Jerry L. Gray
James G. (Jerry) Hunt
Sarah McArthur

WRITING CONSULTANT
E. Forrest Christian

GO Global Organization Design Society

GLOBAL ORGANIZATION DESIGN SOCIETY EDITION, 2007
Copyright © 2007 by the Global Organization Design Society

Published in Canada by the Global Organization Design Society, a not-for-profit corporation incorporated in Ontario, Canada.

www.GlobalRO.org

Library and Archives Canada Cataloguing in Publication

Shepard, Ken; Gray, Jerry L.; Hunt, James G. (Jerry); and McArthur, Sarah; Editors
Organization Design, Levels of Work and Human Capability / Ken Shepard, Series Editor

Cover and book design: Ilona Staples

Includes bibliographic references and index.
ISBN 978-0-9783859-0-3

Printed and bound in Canada.

10 9 8 7 6 5 4 3 2 1

Contents

Part One: Perspectives on the Levels of Work Approach to Organizational Design

Part Two: Enhanced CEO Performance

Dedicated to

Wilfred Brown and **Elliott Jaques**

who laid the foundations for what they intended to become
a unified science-based theory of management.
We are grateful for their creative intention and extraordinary contribution.

And to key staff members at BIOSS,
the Brunel Institute for Organizational and Social Studies,
who collaborated in that era and continue their endeavors
together with their colleagues and disciples in their evolving work.

**David Billis, D. John Isaac, Warren Kinston,
Ian Macdonald, Ralph Rowbottom, and Gillian Stamp**

GO SOCIETY READING SERIES

THE GO SOCIETY READING SERIES IN ORGANIZATION DESIGN

- *Organization Design, Levels of Work, and Human Capability: Executive Guide* (this book)

PLANNED:

- *Design of Government Organizations: Levels of Work and Human Capability*

- *Design of Not-for-Profit Organizations: Levels of Work and Human Capability*

- *Breakthroughs in Management and Organization Design Theory: Contributions of the Levels of Work and Human Capability Approach*

- *Levels of Work and Human Capability: Implications for Society*

- *Teaching / Learning Requisite Organization Theory and Practice in Various Settings*

Why This Book Now?

As the work-levels/managerial accountability paradigm comes into general use, it will produce its own substantial benefits to the individual firm and to society, and will also enhance the power of other major profit generators in the new economy.

Aligning appropriate level of work complexity with human capability levels to support effective managerial accountability seems to be the unrecognized master key to strategic breakthrough, competitive advantage, increased profit margins, better work environments for employees, and a better society.

Foundations for this work-levels approach were developed through a 17-year partnership between Wilfred Brown, long-time Managing Director of Glacier Metal Company, and Dr. Elliott Jaques, its principal scientist and researcher. This approach has proven robust over time, but remains relatively unknown due in part to the fact that early adopters of this approach guarded this competitive advantage as proprietary.

The Global Organization Design Society was formed in 2004 to promote Brown's and Jaques's comprehensive, total system approach. At the GO Society's first world conference in Toronto the following year, participants spoke openly about their levels-based experiences and shared their knowledge to increase awareness and use of these powerful methods around the world.

The Society proudly launches this first book in the GO Reading Series. The series is planned as documentation of the ongoing spread and use of these ideas and as encouragement and guidance to future generations of general managers, practitioners, management educators and researchers.

This book is important now because it describes worldwide successful experiences with a levels-based approach to organization design and management that results in significant increases in employee satisfaction, customer satisfaction, and financial results—averaging 20-30 percent increases in productivity and profitability without new investment.

The work-levels approach raises the value of the organization's human capital. It establishes values and practices that greatly increase effectiveness, leading to pride, and better work climates that attract and retain the best workers.

Of even greater importance in western society, the work itself is a strong source of individual self-respect and respect for others. When its design permits workers to achieve their full potential, the natural effect is not only stronger and more profitable organizations, but also a more vital and robust society.

Many of us have studied those exemplars that pioneered modern profit-driving management systems: Japan's extraordinary success with Total Quality Management, Toyota's Management System, GE's design of the five-level business unit in 1970, GE's identification of high-potential managers beginning in the 1970s and level-based management development program in the 1980s, Motorola's Six Sigma and corporate training systems, and Wal-Mart's strategic IT system linking point-of-sale, supplier, and inventory systems.

Yet when other companies attempt to replicate these breakthrough strategies, implementation success rates are surprisingly low. We believe that successful implementation of each of these systems, as well as other strategic management actions, requires a work-levels-based approach to strategy and organization design.

This requires recognition that both the complexity of work and the capability of people occur at distinct levels, and that responsibility and accountability need to be systematically assigned to people at the right level of capability who are in roles of the right level of complexity.

The approach also provides conditions for greatly increased success rates in implementing profit-generating systems such as Total Quality Management and Six Sigma. Executives who understand work levels know that transitioning an organization from operating under one management model to another often increases the human capability required to design, plan, and implement such a change.

Aligning work complexity with human capability gets the strategic plan off paper and into the organization's practices. And the levels-shifting redesign increases the use of more of the available talent, often shrinking the number of frontline workers while increasing the number at the next higher level.

Although work-levels theory is not widely recognized, its influence may be broader than most appreciate. A delegation from the Nikkeiren, Japan Federation of Employers' Associations, visited and studied Glacier Metal Company in the l960s prior to issuing its report, "Abilities First Principles." By 1979, the concepts and practices of the Glacier personnel assessment and promotion system had been adapted across Japanese firms and then were included in their international operations. We are endeavoring to identify Japanese researchers who can further document the diffusion of these ideas that have contributed to the development of the Japanese juggernaut we frequently study but continue to misunderstand.

In the early 1970s, Fortune 100 executive consultant Walter Mahler read Glacier publications and folded Glacier ideas into his recommendations for the design of GE's talent pool system. This system subsequently identified and developed GE's high-potential future leaders including Jack Welch and the current CEO, Jeffery Imelt. Many appreciate GE as selecting and developing some of the world's best corporate managers and praise GE's famous executive center at Crotonville. However, few realize that Crotonville's curriculum is designed to support effective transition between levels. Mahler also taught these practices at a number of other top ranking corporations.

Additionally, this Glacier-project-inspired work-levels approach to talent pool development is alive and well in the current best-selling book, *The Leadership Pipeline*, by Ram Charan, Stephen Drotter and James Noel, 2001. There is clear documentation of the lineage of the levels work from Wilfred Brown to Walter Mahler to Stephen Drotter.

In the 1980s and 90s, the US Army invested 15 years and Conzinc Riotinto of Australia (CRA, now Rio Tinto) invested 12 years in building high productivity and accountability rooted in work-levels theory in significant parts of their organizations.

With more and more companies using these methods and executives around the world finally willing to share their secret, now is the right time for this book.

Our Audience

This first book in the GO Reading Series is written specifically for private sector CEOs and general managers who want to create highly productive, accountable organizations within which employees thrive in roles that suit their capability. This book will also be useful to director-level managers who support the top-level team.

And of course this book will be of great interest to all students of administration including managers, consultants, and academics who look for a proven, science-based model to underpin their work.

Our Authors

The 32 articles in this book were authored or co-authored by CEOs, consultants, academics, and management educators from seven countries. Most of our authors have extensive experience in the private sector, though we have chosen three leaders of work-levels implementation from government and not-for-profit organizations to illustrate the universal applicability of these concepts.

Our authors are senior professionals who report that the concepts had a major impact on their practice and effectiveness. Some knew and worked with Wilfred Brown and Elliott Jaques in the 1970s at the Glacier Institute of Management (GIM) and at the Brunel Institute for Organizational and Social Studies (BIOSS). Others worked on major projects at CRA and the US Army. Some co-authored articles with Jaques. Many enjoyed personal friendships with Jaques who was generous with his time in mentoring those who sought his counsel. In short, these internationally based authors have been personally and deeply touched by this work and their contacts with Brown and Jaques. They continue in their passion to deepen their understanding and application of this theory.

Our authors, who integrated these concepts into their work, came from a variety of roles and specialties including general management, management consulting, management education and research, strategic planning, human resources, organization development, psychoanalysis, psychology, counseling, social psychology, executive coaching, and engineering.

While one would expect each to build on their own strengths and perspectives to produce a variety of conceptual variations, areas of focus, and process differences in their work, the reader will find there is a significant communality in their approaches based on the foundational concepts you will soon read about in this book.[1]

We appreciate their creative efforts, professional discipline, and good-spirited patience in working with the editors, making revisions, and meeting deadlines to make this book possible.

Our Subject

The primary focus of this book is the private sector executive's relationship to this work-levels-based management system with answers to many commonly held questions.

- What is this management system?
- What problems does it solve, and what opportunities does it seize?
- What are its potential benefits and risks?
- How solid is it? How well conceived, researched, and tested?
- Who else has used it? Anybody in my industry?
- What did they do and how did they do it?
- What makes for a successful project?
- How do we know if we are ready for this?
- Do we have to implement the whole system, or can we do it in pieces?
- How does it relate to other strategic initiatives we may be implementing like Total Quality or Six Sigma?
- How much time and energy will it take?
- What resources are available to help us?

Thus, this book describes the body of ideas based on original insights into levels of work complexity and human capability that Wilfred Brown and Elliott Jaques developed over years of clinical research at the Glacier Metal Company. Their findings evolved into a comprehensive management system that Elliott Jaques called requisite organization. In some parts of the world, it is called by a variety of other names used during the evolution of the theory including The Glacier Project, Time-Span of Discretion, Work Levels, and Stratified Systems Theory (SST).

---

1   Editorial note: Those interested in reading about the the major concepts and their variations in practice can find a glossary of key terms and variations on the GO Society's website in the resources section, www.GlobalRO.org.

This book also deals with implementation experiences by organizations in various sectors, industries, and organization functions around the world, and in both partial and complete projects, in both large and small organizations.

How the Book Is Organized

We endeavored to create a logical sequence to this book for those interested in reading from cover to cover. For others, each article is designed to stand alone so that those with more targeted interests may follow them according to their own priorities.

The book's parts flow as follows:

PART ONE: PERSPECTIVES ON THE LEVELS OF WORK APPROACH TO ORGANIZATIONAL DESIGN

For those unfamiliar with this work-levels-based management system, we have chosen articles by writers with four different perspectives.

- A crisp business overview with examples by a senior business writer and editor of a premier national business magazine.
- Elliott Jaques's own overview summarized from one of his last books, *Social Power of the CEO*, by a management development educator writing for executives in corporate universities.
- An overview and detailed description of an illustrative work-levels project written by senior consultants to orient executives to the system and help them imagine how a sample major implementation might play out.
- A thoughtful overview of the theory and how managers often react to it from their current belief systems written by a senior management professor who speaks widely to executive audiences as well as teaching and supervising doctoral students in the area.

PART TWO: ENHANCED CEO PERFORMANCE

We have included articles in this part that illustrate how CEOs can use this well-designed system to create the sustainable foundation and leverage to achieve their profitability and effectiveness goals.

PART THREE: MAJOR APPLICATIONS OF THE LEVELS OF WORK APPROACH

This part describes several private sector projects in manufacturing, metal processing, pharmaceuticals, and projects in military, charitable, and religious organizations to demonstrate the universality of the principles working as a system.

PART FOUR: PARTIAL APPLICATIONS OF THE LEVELS OF WORK APPROACH

This part demonstrates an array of approaches to using a work-levels perspective in different aspects of organization work including systems design, just-in-time intact work group training, cross-functional teams, design of information technology systems, and employee assistance counseling.

PART FIVE: FITTING THE RIGHT PERSON TO THE RIGHT ROLE AT THE RIGHT TIME

This part provides an overview of the importance of assessing human capability to overall organization effectiveness, the insights and leverage from tracking the individual working journey, and presents a comprehensive web-based software approach to managing the talent pool development process.

PART SIX: THE DYNAMICS OF IMPLEMENTING THE LEVELS OF WORK APPROACH

This part includes a number of interesting perspectives that support the CEO in sizing up and deciding to launch a work-levels-based project including aspects of organizational readiness, the validity and trustworthiness of the approach, and metaphors that communicate the power of the approach.

PART SEVEN: DEVELOPMENT AND DIFFUSION OF LEVELS OF WORK CONCEPTS

This part provides insight into the Brown and Jaques partnership that developed the foundations of this approach, describes the research and diffusion of the approach, and points a path forward.

A Final Word

We believe that the reason so many CEOs and general managers are more interested in finance, acquisitions, innovation, or marketing than in designing and managing the business is because there has been no readily teachable or learnable system of organizational design. Many managers perceive the art of management to be a parade of ephemeral exhortations touted in an ever-renewing shelf of management books.

In contrast to this perception, we believe that the levels of work complexity and human capability approach can deliver sustainable profitability and social well-being. It is a well-developed and tested framework that can be taught, learned, and applied in a reasonable amount of time. The aligned concepts make up an easy-to-learn and flexible diagnostic model that the manager can carry in his or her head and use without dependency on staff specialists.

When given a chance to hear CEOs describe the system and how they have used it, executives capable of systems thinking often perceive the face validity of this management system and are eager to explore it further.

We hope that the CEO voices in this book provide you the opportunity to have that realization yourself.

ACKNOWLEDGEMENTS

The editors are first indebted to Wilfred Brown and Elliott Jaques who collaborated over 17 years applying the principles of action research and scientific method to develop the foundations for this field of work. We also acknowledge the BIOSS staff members that worked with Jaques to refine the theory including David Billis, D. John Isaac, Warren Kinston, Ian Macdonald, Ralph Rowbottom, Gillian Stamp, and others too numerous to mention. Several continue to contribute to on-going GO Society work. Finally we are grateful to those who carried the ideas to every continent, further developing the methods and the variety of applications, and building bridges to related disciplines.

The idea for this book emerged in 1999 at a requisite organization clinic jointly sponsored by Elliott Jaques and Ken Shepard in Toronto and attended by about 70 client managers and consultants from Europe, Argentina, the United States and Canada. Ten volunteered to contribute to and support such a book.

Now eight years later, with the help of many, this book has come to life. When Ken Shepard, the Series Editor, began exploring how to design the project, Marshall Goldsmith, a coach to Fortune 100 CEOs and editor of books for the Peter Drucker

Foundation, provided early guidance. He recommended that Sarah McArthur, a Managing Editor for his books, help the GO Society with theirs. Sarah provided the detailed roadmap, sage advice, project coordination, and quality copy-editing, making sure our abstractions and systems logic would be highly readable by the time-short executive. We appreciate Sarah's professionalism.

The Toronto advisory group that provided early energy for founding the GO Society also provided strong support for the book. Seven of its members committed to write articles and invested the early capital. These included Charlotte M. Bygrave, Ron Capelle, Donald V. Fowke, Herb Koplowitz, Paul McDowell, Ken Shepard, and Paul J. Tremlett.

At this point the GO Society Editorial Board was formed. Jerry L. Gray who had known both Brown and Jaques, and James G. (Jerry) Hunt, who had worked many years on integrating Jaques's concepts in the general leadership literature, both signed on for the book. Each of the editors has reviewed each article draft several times and worked over a year closely coordinating on bi-weekly teleconferences. All pulled their weight. And special thanks goes to Jerry L. Gray who carried a more than double load when the Series Editor was incapacitated for several months.

At this point the authors commited to the project. We appreciate their creative efforts, professional discipline, and good-spirited patience in working with the editors, making revisions, and meeting deadlines to make this book possible. Some authors were executives who related their experience in using requisite organization. We appreciate their courage in overcoming concerns that their colleagues may see them as less objective if they espouse a particular approach to management, or concerns that their revelations may enable competitors to soon copy their successes.

And we are grateful to employees in roles throughout the organization who struggled to understand and to implement these ideas and to provide the feedback and problem solving that in the end made these methods work and worth reporting in this book.

The Rock of Gibraltar during this project was Kenneth C. Craddock. He had been attracted to W. Edwards Deming's systems approach to quality and worked for Deming a number of years until his death. Subsequently he was attracted to Elliott Jaques's systems approach to management and began his nine-year immersion in the Jaques-related literature. Craddock carries the history of the field in his head and advised on the book in many late night calls.

Craddock finished his Fourth Edition of the *Annotated Bibliography on Requisite Organization* in the middle of the book project, and the editorial team plus T. Owen Jacobs gave careful editorial review to the 1000 page magnum opus. This review greatly enriched our understanding of where this book fit in the extensive literature and influenced our work and evolving consensus.

E. Forrest Christian, a professional writer who had studied and written about Brown and Jaques for several years, acted as writing consultant to several authors helping them shape initial interviews, outlines, and Power Point slide presentations into polished articles.

T. Owen Jacobs and Michelle Malay Carter read several articles and provided insights in reshaping the articles and in articulating important points.

David Creelman, a speaker and writer on Human Capital, who had interviewed and written several articles on Elliott Jaques, served as "coffee shop advisor" and provided keen insights.

Kenneth C. Craddock and Herb Koplowitz provided technical review and E. Forrest Christian and David Creelman provided editorial and shaping advice while reading and copy-editing the entire book. Jack Fallow, T. Owen Jacobs, Herb Koplowitz, Sarah McArthur, and George Reilly provided diligent service in final proofreading.

Laurence S. Lyons, Peter S. Robinson, and Melanie Parke advised on the aesthetics of cover and book design. The arduous task of final proofreading was done by Jack Fallow, Herb Koplowitz, T. Owen Jacobs, George Reilly, and the editors.

Special recognition must be given to Ken Shepard and his role in seeing this book come to fruition. There is no doubt among all of the contributors that without Ken's dedication, hard work, perseverance and vision, this book would never have seen the light of day. He supported his vision with action and commitment and was unwavering in his efforts to get the job done. The Society owes Ken an unrepayable debt of gratitude for his role in this book.

MEET THE EDITORS

KEN SHEPARD, PH.D.

Ken Shepard, Ph.D., management consultant, is Principal of the Canadian Centre for Leadership and Strategy and President of the Global Organization Design Society.

As a consultant, Ken specializes in coaching to senior leaders, top management team building, strategy formulation and implementation, organizational design, and installing effective accountability structures and management practices.

Ken held management positions in business, government, and not-for- profit organizations. He was program director at the Niagara Institute, a Canadian leadership center providing executive development for private sector, government, and labour executives and he designed and led national consultations on complex societal issues. He also served as Assistant Professor of Management at Pepperdine and Loyola Marymount universities, and lectured at the University of Pennsylvania and the University of Southern California.

Ken co-founded the Global Organization Design Society in 2004 and has served as its first president since then.

JERRY L. GRAY, PH.D.

Dr. Jerry L. Gray is Dean Emeritus and Senior Scholar at the I. H. Asper School of Business at the University of Manitoba. He taught management and organizational behavior at the University of Manitoba from 1970-2004. He was appointed Dean in 1996 and held the CA Manitoba Endowed Chair in Business Leadership. Dr. Gray also taught at the Glacier Institute of Management and was Visiting Professor at the Owen Graduate School of Management at Vanderbilt University in 1979-81. In 2003 he was named a "Leader in Management Education" by PriceWaterhouseCoopers and *The National Post*.

Dr. Gray has published four books in the areas of organizational behavior and supervision, and articles on organizational design, employee motivation, leadership, and management development.

Now retired from the University of Manitoba, Dr. Gray is a director of two public companies, and five non-profit organizations and is a Founding Board Member of the Global Organization Design Society. As president of J.L. Gray & Associates Ltd., a consulting firm specializing in human resource development, Dr. Gray has consulted with major corporations in North America.

In the editor's words—My Life with Requisite: "I encountered the work of Elliott Jaques and Wilfred Brown as a graduate student at Southern Illinois University in 1966. I learned the concepts as a research assistant to Fremont A. (Bud) Shull, Jr., who organized a symposium on the concepts, and from Bud's colleague, John McCarty, a consultant then working to implement the theory at Allen Industries. I spent part of 1967 at the Glacier Institute of Management (GIM) doing my thesis, working with Derek Newman in his consulting, and teaching and taking courses at GIM—some taught by Wilfred Brown and Elliott Jaques. It was an experience of a lifetime!

"My keen interest persisted and I've used every opportunity to incorporate the concepts into my research, textbook writing, and teaching. My 1974 book, *The Glacier Project: Concepts and Critiques,* presented the basic concepts in one volume, as well as some of the critical views of that era. I was pleased that both Brown and Jaques gave permission to use their writings in the book, knowing that there would be critical articles as well.

"As my career interests evolved, my continuing interest in the concepts manifested in my teaching and my consulting practice. Over the years I have taught literally thousands of students and executives about the concepts, including over 2,000 MBA students in the Canada, the US, China, and Thailand.

"In my consulting, I believe that the time-span of discretion concept is the most powerful analytical tool a consultant can have, almost regardless of the consulting assignment. Conducting a time-span analysis of roles reveals critical information about tasks, task complexity, authority relationships, and so on.

"When I heard Jaques use the phrase "trust-inducing organization" with regard to his system, it occurred to me that the fundamental purpose of requisite concepts supported a fundamental value of my own—the importance of psychological, social, and financial justice in organizations. And as if I needed further proof, the fundamental causes of dysfunctional behavior in organizations became clear. So the bottom line for me is that requisite concepts can be a major causal factor in creating trust-inducing organizations."

JAMES G. (JERRY) HUNT

James G. (Jerry) Hunt, Ph.D. University of Illinois at Urbana-Champaign, Paul Whitfield Horn Professor of Management, former department chair of management and Director of the Institute for Leadership Research at Texas Tech University.

In the editor's words—My Life with Requisite: "While completing my Ph.D. in 1966, I became quite interested in recent work reporting differences in leadership and leadership results at various organizational levels in a study involving one of our faculty members. Upon degree receipt, I accepted a position at Southern Illinois University at Carbondale, received a research grant from the National Institute of Mental Health and a summer fellowship at the University of California at Berkeley. I worked on multiple-level leadership for both the grant and fellowship and published a number of manuscripts, none of which had much theory. However, neither I nor very few others that I knew about, had much theory to guide such multiple-level work. Organizational levels was a topic that was mentioned not infrequently in empirical studies of leadership. It was intuitively obvious that there should be differences in leadership predictions and requirements by managerial level, but our knowledge base did not even make it possible to accurately compare levels from one study to the next.

"Then in the early 70s, I organized the first of the eight-volume, biennial leadership symposia series with help from my colleagues at SIU-C. Even so, in spite of Jaques's work reported elsewhere by Jerry L. Gray, I did not make the connection with Jaques. I tended to associate Jaques's writings with other things such as compensation. Sometimes being as multifaceted as Jaques led some of us away from an area that we should have been knowledgeable about.

"As a part of the leadership symposia series I was able to obtain funding from the Army Research Institute through T. Owen Jacobs. Besides funding, I discovered work he was doing with Jaques to be fascinating and to go far beyond anything with which I was familiar. First, the work appeared in article form, then it provided the basis for some books which Jaques co-authored. This research started with the military and the books broadened that to large corporate-type organizations. Jacobs and his colleagues spent a considerable amount of time and effort consulting at the highest levels in the US military and began to provide some systematic empirical data concerning Jaques's theory and levels as applied to the military.

"Along the way, I had a "Eureka" experience and became interested in writing a leadership book that would focus on extensions to Jaques's work on requisite organizations or stratified systems. I completed the book in 1990 using an extended version of Jaques's framework suggested by the earlier work of Jaques and Jacobs. There I attempted a major synthesis with the leadership literature of the day, including charisma and other related writings.

"Shortly after, I teamed with my colleague Bob Phillips and we scheduled a conference and a book to bring together scholars who synthesized their leadership work with that of requisite organization. In combination, the books formed a package designed to help integrate Jaques's work. I believe RO theory, in combination with ideas from the two books and developments since the early 90s, provide a rich conceptual base from which to conduct both consulting and systematic theoretical and empirical management research.""

SARAH MCARTHUR

Sarah McArthur is founder of SDedit, a writing and editing firm based in San Diego, California. Her forte is management, leadership, business, and executive coaching. With nearly 20 years' experience in the publishing field, Sarah has been managing and development editor for more than 15 books. She has played significant roles in the best-selling management classic, *Coaching for Leadership* as well as *Amazon.com*, *USA Today* and *Wall Street Journal* #1 best-seller, *What Got You Here Won't Get You There*.

A sought-after editor and writer, Sarah has worked on numerous books and articles with influential executive coach and best-selling author and editor, Marshall Goldsmith, including *Global Leadership: The Next Generation*, *Coaching for*

Leadership (2e), and *Learning Journeys*. She is currently the editor of the World Association of Business Coaches e-zine, a forum for leadership and management experts and theorists; writing and editing expert for Ethos Consulting; and managing editor of the GO Reading Series. www.sdedit.com

E. FORREST CHRISTIAN

E. Forrest Christian is a professional writer and editor who works with experts to translate their ideas and thoughts into articles, website materials, and books. While educated in the social sciences and broadly read, he's also had career experience in technical roles such as software developer, computer security professional, and business process designer. He has honed his communication skills in positions as trainer, consultant, technical writer, web designer, and project manager.

Project-oriented and multidisciplinary, Forrest has become recognized as an expert in several technical areas, and his writings have been translated into five languages.

Finding and becoming fascinated with the writings of Wilfred Brown and Elliott Jaques in 2003, he read deeply and wrote hundreds of pages of essays for his website, making these complex ideas plain to divers audiences. Through a chain of events, Forrest began supporting a senior requisite organization consultant, then several, then provided video and writing support to the 2005 GO Conference. More recently, he served as writing consultant to the editors and contributors to this book.

Forrest provides writing support to busy practitioners around the world through the wonders of VOIP telephone interviews and email in a number of ways:

- He grows and transforms author insights, experiences, outlines, presentation Power Point slides, or rough first drafts into compelling stories, articles, case studies, and web materials.
- He reshapes, cuts or expands previously published material to meet requirements for new use.

His web writings on RO are available at www.manasclerk.com/blog/.

ABOUT THE CONTRIBUTORS

RICHARD B. D. BROWN

Richard B. D. Brown has been working with the ideas and concepts of Brown and Jaques for more than 30 years, with a firsthand view of this relationship and the burgeoning of the ideas of these two men as his father was Wilfred Brown. Despite initial filial cynicism of their concepts, he is now a complete convert and has been advocating the development of their ideas for many years. He has written more than 25 articles that put their ideas in day-to-day contexts.

CATHERINE G. BURKE

Catherine G. Burke, Ph.D., is associate professor at the University of Southern California, School of Policy, Planning, and Development. Burke's research focuses on organization and systems design, management theory, and leadership, using stratified systems theory and systems leadership theory. She has been a consultant to a number of public, private, and non-profit organizations. She has also served on a corporate board of directors.

CHARLOTTE M. BYGRAVE

Charlotte M. Bygrave is the principal of Bygrave & Associates, where she specializes in helping senior teams develop and implement human resource management and organization development solutions that turn business strategy into action. She has more than 20 years experience as a human resources executive and consultant in multi-national firms in the pharmaceutical, financial services, and high technology industries. As the vice president human resources at Hoffmann La Roche Ltd, Charlotte worked extensively with the senior managers and Dr. Elliott Jaques to implement a reorientation of the organization's structure, staffing, and managerial leadership practices.

PIET L. CALITZ

Piet L. Calitz is managing director of bioss International Limited (bioss). In his global role, Piet is extending the footprint of bioss across divergent host cultures and markets. He has a master's degree in organizational psychology, and has done extensive consulting in organizations in private and public sectors in southern Africa. Piet is especially interested in leadership development in uncertainty and in turbulent times. In addition, he is the author of the meta-competencies matrix, an integrated and unique levels framework for enhancing leadership.

MICHELLE MALAY CARTER

Michelle Malay Carter is a consultant with PeopleFit with 15 years experience in training and organizational development. An author and speaker, her writing has been featured on HR.com, and she served as a visiting lecturer at NC State University.

Her graduate thesis related her experiences using requisite organization principles to create a selection and succession strategy within a national sales department.

STEPHEN D. CLEMENT

Dr. Stephen D. Clement is founder and president of Organizational Design, Inc. (ODI), a Texas-based consulting firm. He has been involved in the application of requisite organizational design principles and concepts for more than 20 years. Steve worked closely with Dr. Elliott Jaques and Sir Roderick Carnegie in a ten-year year collaborative effort at CRA (a major Australian mining company) where many of the principles were first refined and tested in an operational environment. He is currently involved in applying RO-related concepts in several long-term industrial and government studies. He is the co-author of *Executive Leadership: A Practical Guide to Managing Complexity* with Dr. Jaques.

KENNETH C. CRADDOCK

Kenneth C. Craddock is a consultant specializing in requisite organization and in quality. In the early 1990s, he was an assistant to W. Edwards Deming at Columbia University, the man who gave quality to the Japanese. From the mid-1990s, he has researched the organization theory of Elliott Jaques and Wilfred Brown. He has authored an extensive online Annotated Bibliography of works relating to requisite organization theory (downloadable from GlobalRO.org). He holds an MPA [Masters in Public Administration] degree from the JFK School at Harvard and an MA in history from Columbia.

SHEILA DEANE

Sheila Deane is a co-founder and director of PeopleFit Australasia (PFA), a specialist consulting company represented in Australia and the US. Its services focus on mobilizing organizational line managers in self-deployed organization reform using a reference framework of requisite organization principles and practices. PFA provides unique application of RO-based principles and practices to improve the following: cross-organization alignment, teamwork project management, performance management, organization structure, people (HR) systems and talent pool management.

MAURICE DUTRISAC

Maurice Dutrisac is one of the founding partners and the practice leader for strategic planning and organizational design for Mastermind Solutions Inc., a consulting firm established in 1999. Prior to his consulting career Maurice worked for 24 years as an executive for large companies in Canada and the United States. Maurice has an MBA degree from McMaster University.

JULIAN FAIRFIELD

Julian Fairfield began his career in manufacturing. After serving as plant manager, he worked for McKinsey, specializing in strategy and organization and leading the seminal reorganization of CRA, which utilized and expanded on the "levels of work" concept. Author of the book, *Levels of Excellence*, Julian is currently working on a book about the nature of human evolution in terms of how consciousness interfaces with our biology to produce culture(s).

JACK FALLOW

Jack Fallow is a director of the Centre for Organisation Effectiveness Ltd. Previously he was chairman of GasForce ltd, an employee-owned business that he created as a buy-out from British Gas. At British Gas, Fallow held director roles in human resources, customer service, operations and international strategy. Much of his consultancy practice is around practical leadership and sustainability. His interests include the complexity sciences and their relevance to managerial leadership.

DONALD V. FOWKE, FCMC

Donald V. Fowke, FCMC is an experienced consultant in strategy, organization, and people development using the concepts of global organization design. He has assisted in defining business strategy and business plans for companies in a variety of industries, designed organization structures and change management programs to ensure implementation and follow-through on the strategy, assessed executives and managers against the needs of the new roles, and implemented talent pool systems. He has designed compensation to align incentives and felt-fair rewards throughout the organization.

JERRY B. HARVEY

Jerry B. Harvey is Professor Emeritus of Management Science at The George Washington University where he engaged in not teaching for 33 years. Currently he serves as a consultant to a variety of organizations and is working on a book, *Do You Want to Play with Mr. Porter?*

JUDITH HOBROUGH

A graduate of Brunel and London University, Judith Hobrough has worked as a consultant within the area of people and organizational development. She has extensive international experience as well as experience in the management and implementation of projects in both the private and public sectors. A key aspect of her work is concerned with the area of talent management and the identification and development of potential together with effective supporting processes.

T. OWEN JACOBS

T. Owen Jacobs is co-founder and partner of Executive Development Associates, LLC. His work includes research on general officers at the Army Research Institute, and developmental assessment of mid-level officers at the Industrial College of the Armed Forces where he held the Leo Cherne Chair. He is a Fellow of both the American Psychological Association and the Association for Psychological Science.

ELLIOTT JAQUES

Elliott Jaques was research professor of management science, department of management, George Washington University in Washington D.C., and professor emeritus of social science at Brunel University, England. He held an M.D. from Johns Hopkins, a Ph.D. from Harvard, and was a member of the British Psycho-Analytical Society. Dr. Jaques was cited by (then General) Colin Powell for "…his outstanding contribution in the field of military leadership theory and instruction…" He was the author of numerous articles, in one of which he created the concept of the *mid-life crisis*, and more than 20 books, among them *The Life and Behavior of Living Organisms*, published by Praeger Publishers.

JANET LANGFORD KELLY

Janet Langford Kelly's corporate experience with levels of work and requisite organization principles, along with her expertise in corporate law, corporate governance, and the business judgment rule provides her with a unique vantage point in advising boards of directors on accountability, decision authority, and pay for performance systems design.

HERB KOPLOWITZ

Herb Koplowitz, Ph.D., is president of Terra Firma Management Consulting. He works with organizations in every sector helping them become effective, efficient, and trust building. He does this by helping them develop appropriate structure, staffing, and management practices. Herb has worked with requisite organization for 15 years and has trained and lectured on it in the US, Canada, Jamaica, South Africa and India. His clients appreciate his ability to find simplicity and order in complex problems.

GERALD A. KRAINES

Gerald A. Kraines, M.D. is president and chief executive officer of The Levinson Institute, a New England-based management-consulting and leadership-development firm, whose mission is to improve the practice of leadership and realize the human potential of organizations. Also on the faculty of Harvard Medical School, Dr. Kraines is widely known for his expertise on managerial and leadership issues, focused on bringing both scientific knowledge and common sense back to the workplace. His critically acclaimed book, *Accountability Leadership*, was published by Career Press in 2001.

NANCY R. LEE

Nancy R. Lee is president of Requisite Organization Associates Inc., a firm that helps organizations understand and utilize effective structure, staffing, and managerial practices. She has extensive experience as a corporate manager and consultant to senior management. Clients with which Nancy has worked include Citibank, Hoffmann La Roche, IATA, IBM, Kellogg's, MetLife, and the Royal Bank of Canada. Nancy was employed by General Electric, Macy's New York, and Wedgwood. Doubleday and Ballantine Books published her book on management development entitled *Targeting the Top*. She has also written *The Practice of Managerial Leadership*, based on requisite principles, available from www.xlibris.com.

IAN MACDONALD

Ian Macdonald, Ph.D., is managing partner at MAC Associates, Ltd. He was a research fellow at BIOSS working with Elliott Jaques, Gillian Stamp, and others on a wide range of civil service, mental health, and other projects. He has been a consultant to numerous public, private, non-profit organizations, churches, and communities in England, Australia, the US, Canada, Russia, and the Middle East.

ALISTAIR MANT

Alistair Mant is chairman of the Socio-technical Strategy Group (UK). He is an international authority on the development of leadership in complex systems in both the private and public sector. He spends approximately a third of each year in Australasia, where he was born and where his most recent book, *Intelligent Leadership*, remains a best seller. He is Adjunct Professor at the Swinburne University of Technology in Melbourne and a member of the Global Coaching Partnership.

PAUL MCDOWELL

With more than 25 years' experience within the information systems and human resources fields, Paul McDowell's credentials include leadership roles in IT, architectures, data warehousing, large systems integration, software engineering, and program delivery. He has applied the work levels approach to redesigning several executive-level organizations at Canadian top 500 firms. He currently works for BearingPoint Inc., an international management and technology consulting firm at which, as managing director, he heads the financial services technology practice for Canada.

GLENN W. MEHLTRETTER, JR.

Dr. Glenn W. Mehltretter, Jr. is president of PeopleFit®. He is recognized internationally for the tools he has developed to apply RO theory to organizational design, talent management, and cognitive capacity assessment.

He has accumulated 5,000+ data points in matching people to roles, which led to the creation of the PeopleFit Integrity Index, a benchmarking measure for effectiveness in deploying human resource talent.

DWIGHT MIHALICZ

Dwight Mihalicz currently consults for, and is senior vice president of Capelle Associates Inc. His 25 plus years of organization experience includes senior management positions in national and international organizations. In these positions he was involved in the leadership and strategic planning for large-scale, complex projects, such as global redesign and start-up operations. Throughout his career, Dwight has obtained extensive experience in project and change management processes with large organizations. Along with his current position at Capelle Associates, Dwight has maintained directorships in two European-based organizations and is currently immediate past chairperson of UNICEF Canada.

JOHN MORGAN

Rev. John Morgan has a Ph.D. in organizational leadership. His doctoral research was in the field of requisite organization. Senior Pastor of Piñon Hills Community Church (PiñonHillsChurch.Com) in New Mexico, John trains and consults high-capacity leaders through The John Morgan Company. He is author of *Horsepower:*

How Leadership Works and co-author of *How to Discover Your Personal Life Mission: Finding Your Passion and Living Your Dream.*

ANDREW OLIVIER

A decorated Marine officer, Andrew Olivier has worked in the corporate world, built a software company, and had two management consultancies. The Southern African management consultancy in 1998 changed its name to bioss South Africa and in Australia was bioss Australia. Andrew works independently and discretely with high-potential individuals, many of whom are well known public figures. In 2003 he published *The Working Journey.*

ATILIO A. PENNA

Author of books and articles published in Spain, USA, and Argentina, Atilio A. Penna is professor, jury, and director of doctoral dissertations at Buenos Aires, Rosario, Belgrano, and Palermo Universities. Atilio is co-author of the *Theory of the Entrepreneurial Organization Transition* and has created a body of concepts and practices that facilitate the development of the entrepreneur's capability, improve small entrepreneurial organizations, and increase their sustainability. Atilio also manages Atilio Penna and Associates, a consulting firm specializing in small entrepreneurial organizational design and coaching CEOs.

GEORGE REILLY

George Reilly has recently entered semi-retirement after 40 years as a psychologist. His career included educational consulting with handicapped and disturbed children, university vocational and personal counseling, industrial psychology and organizational development with a multi-national mining and smelting company, extensive EAP counseling services, expert witness services to the courts, and extensive psychotherapy services. During the past 30 years, all spheres of his work have been strongly influenced by the principles of requisite organization.

ALEXANDER ROSS

Alexander Ross was long-time editor of *Canadian Business* magazine. He became very interested in Elliott Jaques's ideas, became friends with him, and was in the process of writing a book about Requisite Organization for the business audience when he died unexpectedly.

HARALD SOLAAS

Harald Solaas is a consultant, teacher, and theoretical researcher of RO who lives and works in Argentina where for many years he worked with Elliott Jaques on a large project. He currently holds the Chair of Análisis y Diseño Organizacional at the Universidad de Belgrano, Buenos Aires. His efforts have been focused upon making the potential benefits of RO applications more widely known and available to work organizations in general.

KARL STEWART

Karl Stewart is a mining engineer. He was the group consultant to CRA, Ltd. where he led the development of implementation and system theories to allow managers to bring about positive organizational change. He later successfully applied this work as managing director of Comalco Smelting. Prior to these activities he was the site manager at Weipa Bauxite mine and vice president of human resources of Comalco, Ltd.

PETER TAYLOR

Peter Taylor's consulting work focuses on the development of people and organizations as well as change management. His work has extended across reviewing strategies, changing structures and systems, and evaluating the competencies, qualities and capabilities of people. As a manager, he gained first-hand knowledge of introducing career and performance management systems. With extensive experience using the EFQM Excellence Model, Peter led a team that won the British Quality Foundation annual quality award.

PAUL J. TREMLETT

President and co-founder of *CORE*international, Inc., a management consulting business dedicated to helping executives plan, design, and manage their organizations for outstanding performance, Paul J. Tremlett has an extensive background in complex organization change management, strategic planning, organization restructuring, and management education and training. Paul has helped more than two dozen public and private sector organizations align their work systems to more effectively achieve strategic and operational goals.

MARK VAN CLIEAF

Mark Van Clieaf is managing director of MVC Associates International, a leading consultancy in integrating CEO scorecard design, optimal management structure design, enterprise performance measurement, CEO succession planning and talent management, and executive pay for performance, all linked to value for shareholders and society. His research and consulting on the Five Levels of CEO Work, Five Levels of CEO Capability, and Five Levels of Corporate Governance and the link to shareholder and societal value are recognized worldwide by boards, institutional investors, and the business media.

GEORGE WEBER

A seasoned professional with more than 30 years of progressive experience mainly in the not-for-profit and volunteer sector, George Weber has provided senior-level leadership to large Canadian and global organizations. George is Secretary General Emeritus of the International Federation of Red Cross and Red Crescent Societies, and is currently CEO of the Canadian Dental Association (CDA), a professional membership organization and chairs one of the five major international committees of the FDI World Dental Federation. He has been awarded a number of state and other honors from Canada and other countries.

JOS J. WINTERMANS

An experienced CEO with a record of significant value creation in challenging business environments, Jos J. Wintermans is president and CEO of Cygnal Technologies. Before joining Cygnal, he served as president and CEO of the Sodisco-Howden Group, where he restructured the company to perform better and become the leading distributor of Hardlines and Building Materials for Independent Merchants across Canada; president and CEO of Skyjack Inc.; president and CEO of Rogers CableSystems Ltd; and president, CEO, and member of the board of Canadian Tire Acceptance Ltd.

Organization Design, Levels of Work & Human Capability Executive Guide

Perspectives on the Levels of Work Approach to Organizational Design

Perspectives on the Levels of Work Approach to Organizational Design

This is a management system developed over 50 years of research and practice. There are some new concepts that take some time to understand and a system by its nature takes some time to understand, and even those who have become very familiar with the theory still find new things to learn and appreciate about its application.

At first we thought of starting the book with a single overview article, but subsequently decided to present four overviews from different perspectives; one written by a business magazine writer, one a summary of Elliott Jaques's writing to an executive audience, one by consultants aiming to give executives an overview of implementing RO, and one by an academic and personal friend of Elliott Jaques's who speaks and writes for business audiences. Notwithstanding the four perspectives, all have the same objective—to bring readers up to speed who are not that familiar with the requisite management system.

"The Long View of Leadership" was written in 1992 by **Alexander Ross** for *Canadian Business* magazine, the premier business publication in Canada. Those who know the literature say Ross's article is one of the best short pieces to introduce the system to a new executive reader. In other words, unlike many other journalists and managers, Ross got it right. His brief essay covers the basic concepts and also suggests reasons why the theory is resisted by many managers ("too many people have too many vested interests"). Given that the magazine is targeted at executives, Ross spends considerable time relating success stories, including an emphasis on the success at Canadian Tire Acceptance Corporation, which is covered in greater detail in Part 2 in the article by Jos J. Wintermans and Paul J. Tremlett.

Elliott Jaques published two books in the year before his death in 2003 at the age of 86. One of them was *Social Power and the CEO: Leadership and Trust in a Sustainable Free Enterprise System.* The article "Social Power and the CEO" is a book summary produced by **Business Book Review**, which summarizes business books for its subscribers—largely senior practitioners and corporate universities. The article is an excellent summary of requisite organization concepts. For the executive who is relatively unfamiliar with RO concepts, this article will be a worthwhile introductory exposure.

One of the biggest challenges facing an RO consultant is to explain over 30 books and thousands of research articles to a client in the brief meeting time that consultants often have with their clients. Three experienced RO consultants, **Maurice Dutrisac**, **Herb Koplowitz**, and **Ken Shepard** decided to solve this problem and jointly wrote "Executive Guide to RO-based Organizational Design." The article is a relatively short piece designed for the senior executive reader. After reading the article, the executive would be able to understand the overall system, its concepts, ways to implement it, and the benefits. They wrote this piece and have made it available for use worldwide with attribution.

We conclude this part with **Jerry B. Harvey**'s very readable classic article, "Musings about the Elephant in the Parlor, or Who the Hell is Elliott Jaques?" A Professor Emeritus at George Washington University, author of *The Abilene Paradox* and other popular management books and friend and colleague of Elliott Jaques, Jerry B. Harvey wrote this paper—in his usual humorous and insightful way—to address the issue and frustration of a great theory lying in relative obscurity. So not only does this article present the concepts from a different perspective, but it also deals with the all important question of why it has met so much resistance.

The Long View of Leadership

Alexander Ross

WHAT'S IMPORTANT

Explanation of Jaques's theory by a business magazine writer.

Examples of CEOs and businesses that have successfully used Stratified Systems Theory (SST).

CEO testimonial that SST is a dependable long-term fix.

Why, if SST applications produce such dramatically positive results, Jaques's theories are not more widely known and used.

How teams can undermine managerial leadership.

How "fast trackers" think.

Most people can't think beyond next week. If you can think years ahead, you're the boss—or probably should be. That's the basis of a management theory that's working miracles for its corporate disciples[1].

—Alexander Ross

If your employees don't know who their real boss is, if their pay scales bear little relation to the work they do, if the lower-downs think management is incompetent and the higher-ups are fighting turf wars with each other, help is on the way. Despite what countless consultants have been telling you, setting up teams and quality circles is not an automatic cure for bureaucratic sclerosis. Such democratic solutions are like trying to steer a car by twisting the rear-view mirror back and forth-it may seem to work for a while, but sooner or later you will probably crash, because you're operating under false assumptions. The only lasting solution is to set up clearly demarcated levels of authority and accountability, and to make sure the people at each level of your organization are mentally equipped to do their jobs. That's a drastic oversimplification of the prescription offered by Canadian-born psychoanalyst and management expert Elliott Jaques. His organizational theories, shaped by more than 40 years of on-the-job research, are beginning to revolutionize management thinking around the world. Some admirers believe that Jaques and his Stratified Systems Theory (SST) represent a major intellectual achievement—a comprehensive body of insights that explains organizational behavior the way Adam Smith described economic systems or Sigmund Freud explained the mysteries of the human psyche. Others have dismissed Jaques's work as a form of managerial fascism that arbitrarily slots people into organizational cages. But the handful of companies that have actually applied Jaques's theories have reported almost magical results, including quantum leaps in productivity and profits, and happier, more dedicated employees throughout the organization.

Executives who have applied Jaques's theories say "most of them boil down to common sense."

What Jaques claims to have discovered, at these and other organizations, is that natural hierarchies assert themselves wherever human beings organize themselves to

---

1   Editors' Note: The issue is actually not how far ahead one can think but how far ahead one can work.

This article was originally printed in *Canadian Business*, May 1992. This article is here reprinted in its original form courtesy of CB Media Limited, 70 The Esplanade, 2nd floor, Toronto, Ontario M5E 1R2. To learn more about *Canadian Business*, visit the *Canadian Business* website at: http://www.canadianbusiness.com.

fight or work. "This structuring is true regardless of whether it's a factory in Calcutta, a mine on Bougainville Island in the Solomons, or a mine out in the middle of the Namibian desert," he says. "Everywhere you find the same phenomenon." Much of what Jaques says directly contradicts current management doctrines, which stress the importance of teamwork, employee participation and the removal of management layers. These touchy-feely approaches to management, he argues, aren't merely misguided. They are fundamentally, disastrously, dangerously wrong; and if pursued, they will make North American industry even less competitive than it already is. "Everything is teams, teams, teams," he says. "But we've brought in the teams in ways that have totally undermined the importance of effective managerial leadership. It's total quality management, right?"

And everybody's agreed on this stuff. And as long as this goes on, the Japanese will "knock bloody hell out of us."

Jaques says touchy-feely approaches to management are fundamentally, dangerously wrong!

SST applications have produced such dramatic results that some people can't understand why Jaques is not as famous or fashionable as, say, Tom (*In Search of Excellence*) Peters or W. Edwards Deming, whose statistical theories provided the intellectual underpinnings for the postwar revival of Japanese manufacturing. For one thing, Jaques is primarily a scientist, not a management consultant. Until recently, he has shown little interest in popularizing his work. For another, his stuff is not easy to understand. He has written 16 books that articulate his theories; but almost no one has succeeded in the daunting task of reading all of them. His theories also generate built-in resistance because they sound so, well, undemocratic.

One implication of SST is that people's problem-solving abilities develop through youth and maturity in predictable patterns. This means that each person has an inherent potential for cognitive development and is thus equipped to rise only so high, and no higher, in an organization. Learning and experience will enhance our skills and knowledge, but no amount of positive thinking can change our potential to approach problems in increasingly sophisticated ways. Jaques is basically saying that some people are born with the ability to make CEO—and some aren't. In a culture that is obsessed with self-improvement, that amounts to a major heresy. But the main barrier to acceptance, some of his adherents believe, has been the short-term fixation of North American management. "Jaques is not the instant pudding that

How to measure cognitive levels has been a question that has obsessed Elliott Jaques for much of his career. After successive refinements, he now thinks he's developed a reliable, scientifically valid method. It involves asking the person to discuss some controversial question—such as, say, whether or not to legalize recreational drugs. Some people flatly declare that legalizing marijuana would be wrong. Others might draw historical parallels with Prohibition. Others, the fast-track people, will set up two or three parallel lines of reasoning and are capable of grasping how a multiplicity of possible outcomes might interact with each other.

A trained observer, says Jaques, can spot these cognitive levels by watching for certain conversational cues. And these varying levels of sophistication are expressed as a person's natural time horizon, determining his or her fitness to occupy one or another stratum.

Problem-solving abilities, though, aren't the only determinant of competence, of course. Competent managers must also have the necessary knowledge and skills, have no destructive personality quirks, and must want to be in the roles they occupy. If these conditions are met, subordinates will feel their boss "knows what he's doing", and the boss himself will feel comfortable setting the context for people in the next level down in the hierarchy.

everybody looks for," says Jos Wintermans, president of Canadian Tire Acceptance Ltd., who has used Jaques's SST to reorganize and nearly double the size of his company. "I don't think most managers have the stomach to live it and actually do it, because it's tough slugging. The people who succeed are the ones who have taken five or 10 years, consistently changing their environment."

But Jaques's hour may be about to strike.[2] The Harding Consulting Group Inc., a Miami-based consulting firm with offices in Toronto and Houston, working exclusively within the Jaques context, has produced impressive results that CEOs are beginning to notice. Isolated pockets of support are beginning to surface in consulting firms and executive suites from Louisville, Kentucky, to Melbourne. Some US firms have applied Jaques's theories with such indecent success that for years they wouldn't talk about it publicly, for fear of tipping off their competitors. Now such firms as Whirlpool Corp. in Michigan, and Kentucky-based Commonwealth Aluminium Corp. are beginning to do a little on-the-record boasting. The Toronto

---

2   Editorial Note: This article was written in 1992, and worldwide usage of the methods has expanded significantly since then.

office of Price Waterhouse is exploring how SST can be applied to the hiring process and, in February, sponsored a breakfast lecture by Jaques that attracted about 45 CEOs from major Canadian companies.

So who is Elliott Jaques and what is he telling us? He graduated with a BA from the University of Toronto in 1937, completed his medical degree at Johns Hopkins Medical School in 1941, and took a Ph.D. at Harvard in social relations in 1952. He spent most of the war years as a liaison between the psychiatric units of the British and Canadian armies, working much of the time on officer selection methods. He stayed in Britain after the war, qualifying as a psychoanalyst at the British Psychoanalytical Society. His army work, combined with his clinical studies, gave him a dual interest in how people and organizations develop and interact. His research in human development prompted him to describe "the midlife crisis," a term Jaques invented that has become part of the language. From 1947 until 1965, he spent his mornings seeing seven psychoanalytic patients and his afternoons prowling around the premises of the Glacier Metal Company, an engineering firm that had retained him as a consulting social scientist.

He worked with the company for more than 30 years. It was his laboratory, a living microcosm of organizational behavior. Like a diligent anthropologist, he became an equally familiar presence in Glacier's boardroom and at meetings of the union shop stewards. "My concern," he says, "became how to develop social institutions that can enhance human morality, human effectiveness, human creativity."

That concern enlarged his role from scientific observer to a sort of specialized management researcher. The workers and managers of Glacier helped him shape his theory of stratified systems. Jaques, in turn, helped reshape Glacier into one of the few UK companies that was triumphantly immune to the British Disease—excessive trade unionism and heavy bureaucracy. The company was eventually absorbed into a conglomerate called Associated Engineering. But the managers whom Jaques had helped select and train at Glacier ended up running Associated and seven of its nine subsidiaries.

Since then, Jaques has worked with such diverse organizations as CRA Ltd., the Australian subsidiary of British-based mining conglomerate RTZ Inc.; the Church of England; and the US Joint Chiefs of Staff on organizational matters, and last year received a certificate of appreciation from Gen. Colin Powell for "outstanding contributions in the field of military leadership theory."

Some US firms used SST so successfully they wouldn't talk about it for fear of tipping off their competitors.

Jaques argues that companies get into trouble when the layers on their organizational charts fail to correspond to the natural universal structure, and when hierarchical divisions are blurred so that managers aren't clearly accountable for the work of their subordinates. But his explanation of why organizations need hierarchies, and how they operate, may represent a fundamental advance in our understanding of people and organizations. What, he wondered, was the hidden principle that distinguished one level of hierarchy from another? It was his mates from the shop floor at Glacier who suggested the first clue: it has to do with time.

What defines the level of work in a stratum, he realized, is "the target completion time of the longest task, project or program assigned to that role." At stratum I, the production line or the typing pool, it might take a day to set up a lathe or 20 minutes to type a letter. At higher levels, tasks extend farther in the future: perhaps two years for a sales manager to rebuild a marketing organization or five years for a CEO to turn around a company.

Years of fieldwork also revealed that people in organizations were remarkably unanimous about where the cut-off points should be between one stratum and another: three months for stratum I, one year for stratum II, two years for stratum III, five years for stratum IV, and 10 and 20 years for strata V and IV. The perceived complexity of work within an organization, in other words, does not increase in a consistent way. It is discontinuous, just as water is discontinuous in its progression from solid to liquid to steam. The fact that so many people, in so many different cultures and situations, perceived the hierarchies of their organizations in the same way, persuaded Jaques that he'd stumbled on something fundamental.

The corollary of this notion turned out to be more controversial. If there are natural strata in human hierarchies, there are also people who are naturally meant to occupy them. Some people can't see past their next pay cheque, and usually end up in stratum I. Others, a miraculous few, are endowed with the Churchillian gift to glimpse across the centuries. In between are the rest of us. At any given time in our maturation, the level of sophistication with which we approach problems determines where in the hierarchy we really belong. Jaques has spent decades testing the cognitive abilities of people in various strata, and now believes he can reliably predict their capacity to rise to higher levels. Jaques has identified various levels of cognitive ability ranging from the very concrete ("Hand me that broom") to the very abstract, in which a person is capable of imagining several chains of possible consequences and relating one possible outcome to the others. His research shows, he says, a strong correlation between cognitive ability and time horizons.

The smarter we are at processing information, in other words, the farther we are able to project ourselves into the future. That's the fundamental difference between Archie Bunker and Henry Kissinger—not just intelligence or acquired knowledge, but a measurable, qualitative difference in the way each solves problems, and in the time horizons of the roles in which each feels most comfortable. A Churchill, whose abilities Jaques would characterize as stratum VIII or IX, would probably feel bored running a company such as General Motors Corp. And what usually happens when a CEO's cognitive abilities fail to match the level of hierarchy he occupies is that he shrinks that company down to his own level.

Yes, it sounds glib when stated that baldly. But the theory is being applied with astonishing results. Executives who have gone through the long and painful experience of reorganizing a company along these lines report that much of it boils down to common sense—but that Jaques's theories provide a powerful conceptual framework that validates what many smart CEOs do instinctively anyway. At Toronto-based Suncor Inc., the restructuring cut deep, the pain was pervasive and the results have been impressive. Doug MacKenzie, the executive vice-president in charge of refining and marketing, has worked with the Harding Group since 1989 to restructure the company's Sunoco Group, which runs refinery and retail operations in Eastern Canada. Suncor's operations in Alberta have not been affected. The exercise involved analyzing who was reporting to whom at what level, trimming down the organization from six to five strata, and combining some functions to promote accountability. He has tried to introduce SST concepts throughout the organization, right down to the truck driver level. Despite what MacKenzie calls "all the pain and agony"—they reduced staff overall from 908 to 750—Sunoco was the only major oil company that didn't lose money during the first half of 1991. Sales per employee have increased by 83%. It has become one of Canada's most profitable refining and marketing operations; four years ago it was one of the least profitable. MacKenzie says the reorganization has liberated the energies of people throughout the company. "Jet fuel sales are something I didn't even have a handle on," he says. "And all of a sudden we increased our sales last year by 157%."

Jaques argues that such victories are to be expected when companies achieve "requisite organization"—that is, when their hierarchies correspond to the natural divisions he's identified, and when people at each level clearly understand what's expected of them. A well-run hierarchy allows people to work to their full potential. He bridles at experts who compare the function of modern managers to those of coaches or orchestra conductors, and who to try to replace individual accountability with group responsibility. The aim should not be to abolish or undermine hierarchies, but to make them work more effectively.

Will SST ever become widely accepted? Perhaps not, because it challenges conventional assumptions in so many fields, from compensation policy to personnel testing. Too many fields have too many vested interests in personality tests (useless, Jaques believes), bonusing systems (which he says are disruptive) and office perks. Besides, the Harding Group is virtually the only consulting firm in the world with extensive experience in implementing SST[3], and George Harding believes his company must stay small to avoid diluting the purity of Jaques's theories, which he is convinced will be the conventional wisdom a century from now. "Once you get this stuff in your blood," he says, "you see everything through it. It's a way of understanding work, the world and people."

ABOUT THE AUTHOR

Alexander Ross was long-time editor of *Canadian Business* magazine and is since deceased. He became very interested in Elliott Jaques's ideas, became friends with him, and was in the process of writing a book about Requisite Organization for the business audience when he died unexpectedly.

---

3   Editorial note: Even at the time this article was written, there were numerous consultants around the world with extensive experience in implementing a work-levels/managerial accountability approach to the workplace.

Summary of
"Social Power and the CEO"
by Elliott Jaques

Business Book Review

WHAT'S IMPORTANT

The book *Social Power and the CEO: Leadership and Trust in a Sustainable Free Enterprise System*, was written by Elliott Jaques and published by Quorum Books in 2002. A summary of this book was produced by *Business Book Review* and is reprinted here by permission. It includes the following:

- Summary of requisite organization concepts as seen through the eyes of a professional business writer.

- A focus on how requisite concepts foster leadership and trust in organizations.

- Brief critical analysis of requisite organization.

- Suggested approach for CEOs considering using RO.

Jaques…demonstrates that not only has the bureaucracy naturally evolved with society throughout its "post-tribal" history, but that all attempts to establish a sustainable alternative form have failed. If that is indeed the case, then his advice for fixing its ills deserves some serious consideration.[1]

According to Jaques, everyone's ideas about human nature at work are clouded by serious, invasive misconceptions that have continually fueled the development of ill-advised managerial leadership systems. Drawing on more than 50 years of thought, observation, analysis, and experimentation, *Social Power and the CEO* demonstrates that these shortcomings are not the result of CEO ineffectiveness as many believe, but flow from unclear concepts of managerial accountability and authority; no concepts of vertical or lateral organizational structure; dysfunctional processes for the selection and development of talent, for performance appraisal and merit review, and task assignment; and "trouble-making" compensation systems.

Thus, the work is offered to CEOs, the senior executives who advise them, HR specialists, academics, students, and consultants to demonstrate how Jaques's unique systems of managerial leadership and organization can grow well-organized and effectively led managerial hierarchies that contribute to an economically secure nation and a life of fulfillment for all employees.

Part I: Debunking the Myth of Why People Work

Jaques notes that *work* is defined by *Webster's Dictionary* as "labor, travail, toil, drudgery, grind"; thus, many CEOs believe people work because they have to. It is also believed that the nearer one is to the top of the employment hierarchy, the more satisfaction one gains from being employed. By the same token, it is assumed that the lower one is, the more frustration and dissatisfaction one experiences with work. People at lower levels are viewed as needing supervision, and also needing results-based financial incentives to overcome their lackluster and dispirited attitudes toward their work, which implies that people are paid basic wages/salaries for being less than fully committed to performing their work satisfactorily.

---

1   This article is reprinted in its original form with permission by the copyright holder, *Business Book Review*™. Copyright © 2004 *Business Book Review*, LLC. All rights reserved. ISSN 0741-8132.

Jaques, who defines *work* as "an organism's use of judgment in making the decisions necessary to reach a goal," has found that attitudes and feelings about work are very different from these common assumptions. He contends that everyone needs to be engaged in socially valued work and that employees resent senior management's failure to understand how deeply seated the importance of work is to them. They want work that provides them with the opportunity to exercise their full potential, to receive fair compensation, and to not be subjected to the usual "artificial carrot-and-stick treatment" used to coerce them into doing their jobs.

Despite the deep importance of work to people, and despite the satisfaction gained from having conditions that allow effective collaboration in that work, difficulties in ensuring such cooperation have been a perennial problem in managerial systems, where self-interest and employee rivalry are persistent issues. During the past 50 years or so, attempts have been made to overcome this problem via the introduction of group dynamics training, the use of group decision making, self-managed teams, and various kinds of group and department bonuses and profit sharing. While these approaches may be effective in the short term, they are not sustainable over time because they are in direct conflict with the contract under which all employees have always worked.

Specific provisions aside, this contract is between the employer and the *individual* rather than the group. And, though many believe that any kind of individualistic contract supports and encourages self-directed self-interest, it is Jaques's contention that it does not undermine effective cohesion and collaboration—quite the contrary. He believes that the way to gain social cohesion and effective collaboration within managerial organizations is to clarify and strengthen individually those aspects of accountability, authority, recognition, and reward that govern vertical relationships between managers and subordinates, and horizontal relationships among individuals whose roles demand effective collaboration with each other.

"Everyone's ideas about human nature at work are clouded by ubiquitous, invasive, serious misconceptions. These misconceptions have continuously fueled the development of ill-advised managerial leadership systems."

Part II: Accountability and Authority—a Framework for Leadership

Because accountability and authority are at the heart of all interpersonal relationships, managerial hierarchies gain their success or failure through the success and failure of the working relationships between and among their people. Accountability and authority establish where people stand in relationship to each other, determine who can say what to whom, who *must* say what to whom, and establish who can get whom to do what.

Thus, it is crucial that CEOs model accountability and authority with their senior executive subordinates and require them to do the same with their subordinates. CEOs must understand that people are not employed as groups and cannot be held responsible for working as an accountable group—only the board of directors falls into that category. They must also understand that human behavior in managerial systems is determined by the people systems set by the CEO and the board and not by the psychology or psychopathology of each individual.

It is a property of managerial systems that managers, not subordinates, are always accountable for results. In other words, the salesperson is not accountable for results, the production worker is not accountable for outputs, and the engineer is not accountable for design quality. Individual employees can only be held accountable for their full commitment to carry out assigned tasks. The employee contract is about paying employees a wage/salary for doing their best—for using their full knowledge and best endeavors to carry out assignments. Although they may not always succeed in achieving a specified goal, they must be able to show that they tried their best to do so. Moreover, they must not be given bonus pay for doing their best. To do so is to state that a base salary/wage is for less than full commitment, which undermines managers by handing some of their authority over to an impersonal and dysfunctional payment mechanism. This reduces their accountability and their sense of involvement, and it weakens the relationship between manager and subordinate.

In the meantime, managers must be able to assume that, as a matter of employee contract, their subordinates are always doing their best, and, if this is the case, there is nothing more they can do. Subordinates encounter many unpredictable circumstances, such as flaws in raw materials and component supplies and/or unexpected moves by the competition, which are outside the purview of the individual employee. Thus, it is up to CEOs and managers to deal with such disrupting variables by modifying assignments, modifying methods, making adjustments to cope with unanticipated changes in external conditions, adding resources, giving more time, coaching subordinates, and/or reassigning work.

Because managers set all the operating conditions, and are the ones to be held accountable for work results and the behavior of their subordinates, they need the necessary authority to ensure that they can discharge such accountability. Jaques identifies four that every manager must have in order to be an effective and trustworthy managerial leader.

1. Authority to veto an appointment. The author contends that managers do not need, and should not be given, the authority to hire (the organization, and not the manager, is the employer). However, they should be given the unequivocal authority to turn down any candidates, presented from above, who they believe cannot do the necessary work.

2. Authority to deselect (decide that an unsatisfactory subordinate should be removed from a role) after due process. Managers do not need, and should not be given, the authority to dismiss or fire. Instead, they should have the authority to decide that, if a subordinate is no longer working at the minimum required level of effectiveness, the individual will no longer keep his or her position with that particular manager, but be transferred elsewhere within the organization. If no possible vacancy exists, the individual is terminated with the benefits associated with layoff rather than dismissal.

3. Authority to decide what types of assignments to give to subordinates and not be bypassed by their own managers in this regard.

4. Authority to decide at what level of effectiveness a subordinate is working and what level of merit pay the subordinate should receive.

"Unclarity and incorrect assumptions about managerial accountability and authority are the starting point for dysfunctional people systems."

Accountability and authority cannot exist effectively if the CEO does not have specific and accurate information about the size of the roles two levels down in the organization, the size they should be in order to get the work done, the level of capability (the "size") subordinates must have in order to fill these roles, and their actual level. Job evaluations, thought to be objective measures (because numbers are used to express the final results of various evaluation processes), are inept measures of role size. IQ testing, Myers-Briggs assessments, and other types of intelligence and personality tests also fail to give an objective measure of the size of a person, especially as it relates to the size required for a given level of work in a role. Thus, the author advocates certain time measurements, which he has found to provide a systematic, powerful approach to managerial leadership that overturns a number of greatly limiting and dysfunctional assumptions about work and people.

According to Jaques's findings, an assignment is not just *what* an individual has been directed to do, but it is a "what-by-when" task, which is about "time-span," a simple, direct, objective measure of the size of a role. If two roles have the same time-span, they are the same size, regardless of what is involved in completing them. Moreover, people seem to have a universal view of what constitutes fair pay differentials for different levels of time-span, regardless of country, type of industry/occupation, or actual pay.

Time-span estimates are obtained from the manager, who has identified the longest tasks or sequence of tasks during which he or she relies on the subordinate's judgment in completing them. The range of these periods can be several days at the shop-floor level; months at first-line managerial level; one, two, three, or more years for longer-term development projects at mid-management level; or five, ten, twenty, and more years on long-term goals at the corporate senior executive level.

This simple measure of a role's size has led to a connected measure of the size of the individual (i.e., the largest role an individual has the potential to carry out in work he or she values and for which he or she has gained the necessary knowledge and experience). The time-span of such a role (what Jaques calls the person's *time-horizon*) is the longest time forward that an individual can plan and execute an assignment or reach a goal. Thus, a person can be identified as having a six-month, two-year, or seven-year time-horizon. Moreover, with these formulations of time-span and time-horizon, it is possible for an employee, an employee's manager, and the manager's manager to arrive at a consistent evaluation of the employee's current potential capability, in terms of the highest level of role the employee can perform.

The time-span instrument can also be used to discover the fundamental structure for effective managerial hierarchies. When this structure is applied, it gives the CEO a clear and apparent foundation for effective operations and effective management leadership. Jaques contends that poor organizational structure has two serious consequences: First, because there is a strong tendency to create control systems that reduce managerial judgment as far as possible, a serious loss in managerial effectiveness can result. Second, top management focuses on training, exhortation, and other change efforts as a means of transforming values and attitudes so that people behave and work together differently and more effectively, in line with what they have been given to do as a means of achieving improved organizational functioning.

Jaques contends that the exact opposite is needed. Rather than changing behavior and outlook, it is more effective to develop better managerial leadership systems—in other words, systems that take full advantage of the judgment and decision-making capabilities of managers at all levels, and holds them accountable for results obtained by subordinates under their leadership. A clear and well-structured hierarchical organization is the prerequisite, and it begins with the concept of time-span.

The author notes that time-span boundaries at one day, three months, one year, two years, five years, ten years, and twenty years have great significance for the hierarchical organization structure. Anyone in a role whose time-span falls between the same two adjacent boundaries as the time-span of their manager's role will feel too close to that manager. In other words, this individual will feel as though the manager adds little value to his or her work and does not have the necessary vision to set the context for this work. Any manager with an immediate subordinate whose role is farther down than the next time-span range will feel "pulled down into the weeds," managing tasks that are too short for the manager's role. Finally, any subordinate with a manager whose role has a time-span at any level in the next higher time-span range will feel just the right distance away.[2]

"Understanding the 2-D[3] nature of time leads to the ability to measure prime aspects of human behavior which have until now been taken for granted as non-measurable."

Establishing the right number of basic layers, then, is the first step in building an effective organization. Thus, any CEO who wants to establish an effective managerial leadership system will begin by establishing a structural foundation layered in accord with the time-span framework. All that needs to be done is to measure the time-span of the CEO's role, place it in its proper layer, and count down from there to determine the number of organizational layers (strata) the organization can have. It will then be possible to look down and see a *comprehensible* series of strata, because the work at each stratum will have certain distinctive characteristics, derived from common time-spans and the particular quality and complexity of the work that informs each.

---

2   Editorial note: This paragraph assumes that employee and manager are in roles whose complexity matches their level of capability.

3   Editorial note: Jaques's two dimensions of time were *chronos* (the time that actually elapsed in completing a task) and *kairos* (the length of time a manager intends a task to take).

Jaques notes that CEOs have become infected with the common, yet destructive, assumption that certain qualities, personality traits, and/or competencies are required for certain types of work. However, the author contends that there is no such thing as a "leadership personality"—everyone needs to possess reasonable amounts (not too much and not too little) of sociability, initiative, analytical ability, aggressiveness, optimism, realism, risk taking, honesty, intuition, loyalty, reliability, balance, cooperativeness, etc., in order to work effectively in any position. Thus, once it is recognized that the employment contract implies that reasonable behavior is required, a much simpler and much more valid approach to the evaluation of human capability becomes available. With this method, CEOs will get what they really need—the ability to ensure the placement of the right people, in the right roles, at the right time, at all levels, and in all functions in the organization.

The approach begins with the understanding that there are only four qualities that individuals need in order to be able to function successfully in any given role in a managerial hierarchy:

1. The necessary potential capability or time-horizon (TH), which is a measure of the level of a person's information processing complexity—his or her raw native ability—to match the level of complexity of the role, measured in time-span.
2. The skilled knowledge (K/S) required to function in the role.
3. Sufficient valuing of the work in the role, so as to be fully committed (C) to doing the work.
4. The ability to carry out the required behaviors (RB).

Thus, when people's TH matches the time-span of the role, and they have the appropriate K/S, experience, C, and RB, they are the right people for the right roles, at the right time.

A key CEO function, one that affects every employee and their self-esteem and self-actualization, is the performance appraisal, which Jaques chooses to call the *personal effectiveness appraisal*. He believes that every capable manager, including every CEO, maintains a running evaluation of his or her immediate subordinate. And, he notes that this view is verified by the fact that, universally, managers manipulate performance appraisals on a regular basis so that they align with this intuitive evaluation they make of their subordinates on a daily basis. These assessments exist in the manager's mind, but there has never been a language or a scale for expressing them.

For example, any well-appointed manager knows if an immediate subordinate is functioning satisfactorily in his or her particular time-span role; knows he/she is working as well as someone in the top half of the role or in the bottom half; and knows if the subordinate is working like someone in the top of the top or bottom half, in the middle of the top or bottom half, or in the bottom of the top or bottom half.

This method of appraisal highlights the distinction between performance and personal effectiveness. According to the author, performance defines the subordinate's results, which can be counted objectively. Personal effectiveness, on the other hand, defines how well a subordinate is *judged* to have done in achieving those results. This distinction is of value because, as regards performance, it sharpens people's ability to do their day-to-day work more successfully, and allows them to implement the "early warning task assignment." Because their performance is not being measured in terms of results, subordinates feel they can freely approach their managers when they find it impossible to achieve the assigned results.

"Great managerial leadership derives from the setting of sound strategies and success in carrying out those strategies, and not from any particular personality qualities."

Another important CEO role is the development of the managerial system's mission and strategic plan, which Jaques contends will fail if not implemented according to the systematic planning procedure he advocates. As discussed previously, the operational scale of any managerial system is defined and measured by the time-span established for the role of CEO. This time-span determines the number of organizational layers required and the TH level required of the CEO. Thus, the organization's mission and strategic outreach will always be functions of the greatest time-span and TH of the CEO's role. The bigger the CEO's role, the further into the strategic future he or she must plan. Jaques strongly disagrees with today's conventional wisdom, which says that, because information technology has produced such rapid change, planning for more than one or two quarters ahead is impossible, regardless of mission, strategy, or mid- to long-term objectives. He believes, instead, that though it may be necessary to change and adapt plans more frequently, times-span and TH are the most critical and influential factors.

Many companies create plans for different time periods—the most popular being three to five and, sometimes ten years. In the author's estimation, however, none of these periods is designated according to any fundamental principles for developing a system of optimum planning levels. For example, in stratum VI corporations (most

Fortune 500 companies), a wide variety of tasks are performed, with hourly, day-to-day, week-to-week, month-to-month, year-to-year, and years-ahead time-targets. And, though the CEO has hour-to-hour, day-to-day, and week-to-week tasks, they are different from those same tasks of the shop floor operator or the office clerk, because these shorter tasks are concerned with the company as a whole.

In the CEO's stratum VI role, key corporate goals would be set at twelve years, but key goals for three to five years would also be articulated. In addition, three to four seven-year goals would be set, as part of tactical planning, for carrying out the twelve-year strategy. This sets a point of alignment for each of the CEO's immediate subordinates, for each would be assigned key goals for which they would develop seven-year strategies that are aligned with the CEO's seven-year plan for the whole company. Concurrently, stratum VI executives would find it useful to sort out organizational goals for stratum V in the five-to-ten year range.

The next step involves establishing tactical plans for Strata IV and III at three years (for IV) and at one year (the budgeting level for III). Each of the subordinates would then follow the same cascading planning process so that all managers at every level have an overall strategic thrust that aligns with the CEO's tactical plans, both at stratum IV and lower down.

Compensation practices are of eminent importance for millions of wage/salary earners and their families, for compensation determines standard of living, socio-economic status, economic security, self-esteem, and the distribution of wealth in capitalist nations. Unfortunately, most compensation systems suffer from a host of untenable notions about what constitutes a sound approach. They include the misconceptions that: 1) people should be held accountable for their own results and should receive incentive pay that accords with these results; 2) work is something people are *forced* into in order to survive, so incentives are essential in getting people to give their best efforts; and 3) human labor is a commodity, whose price is bargained for and set according to market forces.

These misconceptions force employees to be self-seeking and grasping, and to cut corners on quality, in order not to lose out in the compensation stakes. Under fairer treatment, however, people are capable of behaving fairly, reasonably, honestly, and cooperatively, even about pay. According to Jaques, it only takes a very simple compensation system to elicit this positive side of human nature—one that involves creating a pay structure that provides an equal pay range for roles of equal complexity, regardless of occupation—the higher the level of complexity, the higher the pay. It also involves holding individuals accountable for being fully committed and paying them within their range at the step that matches their manager's evaluation of their effectiveness.

Given these views of why people work, manager-subordinate accountability, managerial authorities, the nature and measurement of individual capability and individual roles, the appraisal of personal effectiveness, strategic planning and alignment, and compensation, what, then, is managerial leadership?

"The need for short-, mid-, and long-term planning will always exist as a critical factor in successful business regardless of changes in technology."

Jaques contends that because it is part of each employee's employment contract to do his or her best, it is not part of any manager's leadership accountability to motivate or stimulate subordinates to do what they have contracted to do. Thus, CEOs can stop trying to change their behavior so that it conforms to some idealized standard. So-called people or leadership skills are nothing more than the ability needed by leaders to manipulate subordinates into doing what they want them to do in the absence of clear and correct accountabilities, authorities, and managerial leadership practices.

Instead, CEOs can develop sound strategic plans that will allow the achievement of the company's goals, set by the board or by the owner and, like all managers, they should seek the counsel of their subordinates in developing the strategy for successfully achieving these goals. Leading subordinates means giving them assignments that effectively contribute to success and displaying the initiative, flexibility, and adaptability to change direction and adjust assignments in order to overcome any difficulties along the way.

Managerial leadership must also concern itself with the issue of CEO capability—the issue of whether any given CEO has the right level of capability for his or her role, is too big for the role, or is not quite big enough. The degree of match can readily be measured and stated in terms of the role's time-span (which is fixed by the key goals) and the CEO's TH [time horizon]. When TH is shorter than the time-span of the role, the subordinates of these CEOs, many of whom may have capability levels within the same CEO stratum, will find their innovative initiatives being constricted. Moreover, this constriction will work its way down through the organization until the loss of work causes the organization to settle out at the level of the CEO's capability. When CEO TH is in line with the role's time-span, it is the most powerful force possible for overcoming the effects of any shortcomings in managerial structures and practices. And, though all the difficulties may not be resolved, the effective operational leadership can lift employee morale and satisfaction. Finally, if the CEO's TH is greater than the role's time-span, the organization will grow and develop, despite any shortcomings in organizational arrangements. Although the managerial system is not automatically sound, the operational leadership is, and this has a profound effect on employees.

Remarks

Jaques, who is considered one of the most controversial management theorists/consultants in the world (if not the most), is known, among other things, for his contention that "there is no one single, self-established concept in the field of management on which you can build a testable theory." *Social Power and the CEO* offers that theory and demonstrates how it informs the values of the leadership of hierarchical managerial organizations, the values he believed should inform socio-economic life in a sustainable system of democratic free enterprise, and the value of mutual trust between people. And, it makes the case that these values can be made real, practical, and consistent with sound business practices.

It is difficult to imagine that anyone in any arena of the world of business would disagree much with Jaques's view of the state of management theory, or his belief that there is a real need for a system that would allow effective managerial leadership and organization to emerge.

Nonetheless, there are, indeed, compelling reasons to examine Jaques, and examine him closely. First, his theory provides what appear to be valid reasons for the management abuses and poor corporate performances the literature consistently bemoans. Secondly, he provides practical insights into redesigning organizational roles and compensation systems, so that they no longer undermine organizations and the people who must work in them. And, third, he touts bureaucracy as the only structure that truly fits human nature. Although this last reason is a major source of some of the criticism thrown Jaques's way, he demonstrates that not only has the bureaucracy naturally evolved with society throughout its "post-tribal" history, but that all attempts to establish a sustainable alternative form have failed.

If that is indeed the case, then his advice for fixing its ills deserves some serious consideration. In evaluating Jaques's theories and guidelines, readers of this book might take a more objective middle road that avoids blind devotion or blind criticism and test any organizational design by the author's criterion of mutual trust. His message to CEOs is that they must assess managerial systems to ascertain whether they increase mutual trust or increase mutual suspicion. "Organizational structures, selection and career development processes, personal effectiveness appraisal, merit review and compensation systems, methods for evaluating levels of work and levels of capability, that require behaviors that support mutual trust are good for efficiency, good for people, and good for the nation." It is a template for social leadership that organizations themselves can prove or disprove, without further intellectual debate, in the testing ground of their own practical experience.

ABOUT THE AUTHOR

Business Book Review™ is a best in class business book summary service. *Business Book Review* is a key component of the leadership and management development curricula for many Global 500 companies. Its brief but comprehensive synopses of the best business books encourage readership, improve the business intelligence of entire organizations, and support their goals to establish a continual learning environment. Visit www.businessbookreview.com or contact jfayad@businessbookreview.com for more information. *Business Book Review*, LLC1549 Clairmont Road, Suite 203, Decatur, GA 30033.

An Executive's Guide to RO-based Organizational Design

Maurice Dutrisac, Herb Koplowitz, and Ken Shepard

WHAT'S IMPORTANT

- An introduction and overview of requisite organization (RO) written for a CEO reader.

- A CEO's story of his experience leading a full RO implementation process in his organization, including motivations, milestones, and afterthoughts.

- How a CEO reframed intractable problems by using RO concepts to target root issues rather than symptoms.

- A detailed explanation of a simplified eight-step process that a CEO can follow to implement RO.

What the requisite organization-inspired strategic process brought us was not pre-baked strategies but new glasses so we could see and mobilize the levels of capability within and across functions that could make a difference.

—The CEO of Owen Chemicals

Introduction to Requisite Organization Design[1]

Requisite organization (RO) is one of the very few management systems, and certainly the most researched and validated management system that links all aspects of a business to ensure the:

- right organization structure
- right people
- right accountabilities
- right leadership practices

Implementation of RO has led to:[2]

- increased profits of 30 to 200 percent, including 20 percent to 40 percent growth, cost reduction, and increased productivity and market share
- improved customer relations
- greater employee satisfaction and retention

Requisite organization does this by ensuring:

- the optimal number of layers in the structure and well understood cross-functional relationships
- clear roles, accountabilities, and authorities
- leadership roles and practices that help managers become effective leaders and employees to use their full capabilities
- fair performance management and compensation systems
- assessment methods and a talent pool system that identify the best people for hiring and promotion, and supports effective career development and succession planning

---

1 Requisite organization is an integrated management system researched and designed by Dr. Elliott Jaques and described in his book, *Requisite Organization: A Total System for Effective Managerial Organization and Managerial Leadership for the 21st Century*, 1st edition 1989, 2nd edition 1996, 2nd edition amended 1999, Cason Hall, Gloucester, MA; Gower Publications, Aldershot, England, 1991; Arlington, London. The authors produced and staffed public workshops given by Dr. Jaques in Toronto during the 1990s and maintained close relationships with him until his death in 2003. He personally encouraged free use of his concepts as long as full and complete credit was given to his copyrighted material. The major concepts in this article are based on the authors' understanding of Dr. Jaques's teaching and writings.

2   Results are documented in a number of the case studies presented in this book.

CEOs embrace requisite organization because it illuminates mismatches between their strategy, organization structure, and their talent pool. Once evident, mismatches are easily rectified. Below are examples of what CEOs are saying about RO-grounded interventions.

- The North American president of a global appliance manufacturer said, "By applying these concepts at our Canadian subsidiary, we were able to grow sales by 33 percent in two years during a flat market and become the number one appliance company in Canada."[3]
- The CEO of the world's largest electronics distributor stated, "I have been involved in major turnarounds that have succeeded beyond my expectations through using these principles to obtain substantial productivity gains while at the same time achieving growth in sales and margins."
- The owner of a fifth-generation family business observed, "We got a successful transfer to the new generation, and a professional management structure to carry it forward."
- The CEO of a chemical company said, "This system of management gave me and my senior team a very clear plan of what needed to be done with our structure and our people to achieve our vision of growth."
- The controlling shareholder of a consumer packaged goods company said, "We were slipping and competitors were crowding our position. I'm surprised how fast the new organization allowed us to regain our edge and get everybody pulling in the same direction."
- The chairman and CEO of a fast-growing construction and engineering business noted, "Management talent was our Achilles heel, and the system identified our future needs far enough in advance that we could prepare our next generation of leaders to be ready when we needed them."

Around the world over the past 20 years, hundreds of companies have employed key components of requisite organization, including:

---

3   This book also contains an article about how Inglis, a Canadian white goods manufacturer and distributor and subsidiary of Whirlpool, applied requisite organization to good effect.

In Canada—Imperial Oil, Sunoco, Canadian Tire Acceptance*,[4] Beaver Lumber, Hoffmann-LaRoche,* Visa, Swiss Herbal Remedies, a major Ontario utility, two large multi-national resource companies, two of the largest banks, and one of the largest book retailers.

Abroad—Ashland Chemicals, Avery-Dennison, CRA (now Rio, part of Rio Tinto), Commonwealth Industries (Aluminum),* First National Bank of Omaha, Ford Aerospace, Frigidaire Corporation, G & K Services, H. J. Heinz, Johnson and Johnson, Lennox Industries, Mallinckrodt Specialty Chemical, Maxwell Labs, Novus International,* Shell Chemicals, Unilever, United Stationers, Verizon Inc., Visteon, Whirlpool,* and many others.

Executive to Executive

The CEO's Experience of the Requisite Organization Process in Action

We thought it would be helpful to provide a CEO's perspective (using Owen Chemicals, a fictitious amalgam of real-life experiences) of how requisite organization can work to transform the business in a time- and cost-effective manner even in the rush of daily events.

This narrative is in the voice of the CEO of Owen Chemicals, a provider of boutique chemicals to other manufacturers in a rapidly evolving technology sector. The board of directors brought him in to turn around the firm's increasing loss of key accounts.

The eight-step process outlined below is only one of several ways of implementing requisite organization.[5]

STEP ONE: BUILDING THE SENIOR TEAM

"Three years ago, the board perceived that the previous CEO was spending too much time down in the weeds and decided he wasn't capable of leading the company. I had been VP Manufacturing at Owen some years ago, but left when I got a chance to be CEO of a smaller company in the same industry, where I learned to apply requisite

---

4   This book includes articles that describe how companies marked with an asterisk applied requisite organization or related levels of work and human capability concepts to benefit their organization.

5   The eight-step implementation method we present here is our own invention as a simplified means of presenting and writing about levels of work and levels of human capability concepts. The method is only one of a variety of implementation methods in use by executive practitioners and consultants around the world.

organization systems. The Owen board believed I had demonstrated the ability to work on seven-year objectives while keeping the important short-term balls in the air. They believed I had the potential to grow Owen from a stratum V business into a stratum VI company within 10 to 12 years." (Note: stratum is a term meaning level of work complexity, to be more completely defined in the last section of this article.)

"Within the first few months of meeting with customers, employees, and suppliers, I identified a key issue: long-term customers were complaining that the company was not as innovative as our competitors, and that our own product-and-service development initiatives and quality programs did not align with theirs. They indicated that they didn't want to switch suppliers, but said they would have to look around if things didn't change.

"I took a hard look at the level of the roles in the senior team and the capability of the people in those roles. No wonder the customers had been displeased. The VPs for marketing, product development, and HR were all working in roles at stratum III and had little bench strength to do more than run simple processes and fight the all-too-frequent fires.

"I created three new roles at IV and filled them with fully competent stratum IV executives prior to launching a strategic review. I felt I needed good bench strength at stratum IV first to help me design the five- to ten-year future, and then to support my work on it while also working with me on shorter-term, corporate-wide objectives. And while doing that work, they also had to carry accountability for improving their own functions in the two- to five-year time frame. Re-staffing the senior team involved two new appointments and releasing pent-up talent in one that had been micro-managed too long.

"Once I had the right people on board, we were ready to go. Early on I asked the team to spend a day looking at requisite organization as an accountability management framework. After some struggling with the new concepts, each member signed on. I gradually changed meeting formats to include time to be more reflective and to bring in industry competitive data, and I encouraged respectful dialogue and debate. Confident that we had built some good new habits, I decided to invest our time in a complete strategy review."

STEP TWO: DESIGNING CORPORATE STRATEGY
"What made this strategy review different was that I had some new tools. When we

did our external environmental scan of threats and opportunities, we could now assess the stratum capability of our major competitors in each function to understand what we were up against. We learned how to assess what level their quality system worked at and at which level their product development function was designed. And when we did an internal scan of our own strengths and weaknesses, we saw where we had designed each of these functions.

"After benchmarking our competitors on a number of functions, I decided that our best bet was to surpass the competition in strategic customer relations and management. We felt that our customer relationship managers (CRMs) must know our clients' needs before and better than our customers do, and they must be able to devise and deliver new products and services that meet those needs in ways that our customers would not think of. And we needed to establish a Six Sigma quality and innovation program to be able to meet these escalating customer expectations efficiently.

"With the pain of past and potential customer losses and the board's mandate, the senior team was motivated to invest about ten days together over a six-month period to do the strategic thinking. Our reward was a joint commitment to focus on raising the corporate performance by raising the level of two key functions and increasing customer-focused process coordination across functions.

"What the requisite organization-inspired strategy process brought us was not pre-baked strategies, but new glasses so we could see the levels of capability within and across functions that could make a difference. And using these same 'levels' tools, we were able to test our plans for feasibility and troubleshoot our own ability to implement the plans."

STEP THREE: DETERMINING THE STRUCTURE REQUIRED TO IMPLEMENT THE STRATEGY

"Over the next three months, we used RO's efficient interview methods to go beyond our typical organization charts to map how roles were actually working in terms of levels. This explained many of our current problems. I'd been frustrated by my CRMs' lack of innovativeness.

"We had had a quality program, but it never produced much. We seemed to pick the wrong projects. But through these new maps, I saw that the quality manager had been working an entire level too low, at stratum III, and customer-relations staff and quality teams had been working at stratum II. No wonder we had disappointing results.

"Then we studied different ways to improve the structure to support our new strategy. We prepared several options testing new roles at different levels and with different lateral relations. We were not always able to follow the requisite organization theory in a pure way, but the theory helped us predict what may go wrong with our compromises and to plan how to mitigate those issues."

STEP FOUR: DESIGNING THE WORKING RELATIONSHIPS BETWEEN FUNCTIONS

"In the past, even when the product development group came up with something good they seemed to be out of sync with customer service. In fact, we'd get the most juvenile behavior and turf wars. It drove me crazy.

"Now using RO principles, I understand that as CEO at stratum V, I hold the role of anchoring focus on the customer and ensuring redesign of work processes across functions.

"If the product development department thinks the job of customer service is to flog their new features, and customer service thinks it's the job of product development to create the features they ask for, then there is bound to be conflict.

"So I've learned to put substantial effort into designing role relationships to provide for appropriate cooperation between functions and coordination of their work through strategy."

**STEP FIVE: ENSURING YOU HAVE THE PEOPLE YOU NEED IN THE RIGHT ROLES—
NOW AND IN THE FUTURE**
The immediate need to staff for strategy
"Our first and immediate issue was correcting a 35 percent mismatch between our current employees' capabilities and the roles they were assigned to.

"Here communication was extremely important to all employees and especially to those whose roles would be affected. The happy stories involved those who had been trapped in roles below their level of capability, and they were eager for promotions into higher roles. Those who had already been promoted over their heads required great care. Senior managers spoke to these folks explaining that it was management's fault and not theirs, that they had been put in a situation to fail, and that management would do everything they could to find them a job for which they were well fitted. A few were offered transfers to other facilities, and some took early retirement. All in all employees gave management high marks for how we handled this."

Ensuring Talent to Secure Our Future

"Not only did I have to address the immediate threat to market share caused by lack of innovation, but I also needed to be looking into the future to ensure the firm would remain successful.

"Our top team at IV, and even the layer below that at stratum III, are baby boomers. We did a couple of big downsizings in the early 1990s, and we now have a talent gap. In a few years when people start to retire, we're going to have a problem.

"Where the talent pool was thin, RO methods were particularly helpful and time-efficient. We had already in previous steps collected much of the data needed in this phase. In two-level meetings, first with me and my IVs, and then the IVs and their IIIs, we did some just-in-time training in RO's methods to assess information processing ability of subordinates. Through these processes, we soon had our first cut at identifying the people who will mature to stratum IV capability in coming years.

"Generally managers have all of the information they need to make decisions about placing employees in roles. What they need is a language to use to discuss capability and a process to help them move through their decision making quickly. My managers were surprised at how rapidly they came to consensus about an individual's capability. We made sure we put quality time into doing this right and that the process was perceived fair and respectful to all."

STEP SIX: MANAGING PERFORMANCE—ENSURING YOUR MANAGERS ARE SKILLED AT MANAGERIAL LEADERSHIP

"Our managers are all experts in their fields. Our product development managers really know technology. But frankly I don't think they have a clue what it means to be a manager. They've been to the usual courses on leadership, but there is still much missing, and that costs us dearly. I was confident we could get a lot more done and generate 10 to 20 percent more profit without hiring another employee if our managers only made better use of the people they had.

"I used to lament that my product development managers didn't have 'the right managerial stuff,' but that wasn't the problem. Even when the right people were in the right roles (in terms of cognitive capacity, technical skills, and commitment), there was no guarantee that they understood the role of a manager.

"In a three-month period, I first laid out the RO managerial leadership practices for which I would hold all managers accountable. Then, all managers took a three-day training program in those practices, complete with the framework, tools, meeting processes, and role-playing experiences. In the training, managers would learn to direct employees, engaging them in tasks that support strategy and make best use of each employee's capabilities; support employees, coaching them to improve their abilities; and hold their employees accountable, ensuring they work effectively.

"I made sure that the training was tailored to Owen Chemicals' values and strategy."

STEP SEVEN: CEMENTING THE CHANGE BY STRENGTHENING THE ROLE OF THE MANAGER OF MANAGERS

"I was concerned that our managers were not applying what they learned in the management practices trainings.

"From RO principles, I learned that the reason they were not applying their learning was that I was not holding my subordinates accountable for their practices, and my subordinates were not cascading that accountability to their subordinates. When I did hold them accountable for managing well, it was like magic.

"I also needed to make sure that my IVs learned how to carry out their manager-once-removed (MoR) accountabilities down to II. MoRs needed to be trained in how to ensure that the managers below them do their work as managers.

"With regard to my MoR accountability for mentoring and career development of my subordinate-once-removed, I learned to have these interviews to assess talent and help with career development plans without undermining the manager-subordinate relationship.

"I found that the MoR role is a radically new concept for most managers, and senior managers need to be trained to handle this new accountability. It is part of the structural glue that makes strategy execution happen."

STEP EIGHT: BUILDING THE COMPENSATION SYSTEM

"It seemed to make sense to leave redesigning the compensation system until last. I worried about biting that bullet, because pay schemes seem to bring out the worst in people. But I was surprised. We got it done in about six months with little resistance.

"We, like many others, had been using one of the major 'point-based' compensation systems, because of its extensive database to benchmark pay for comparable positions in our geographic area. However, I was unhappy with the amount of time spent in assessing a position and found many managers spent too much time gaming the system.

"We set up the system to pay our employees a base salary depending on the stratum of their role. My staff found research showing that this pay system feels fair to both employer and employee. We decided to pay a yearly bonus on top of that determined by the manager's judgment of how effectively the employee worked above and beyond what their salary paid for."

Some Afterthoughts from the Owen Chemicals CEO

INITIAL RESISTANCE

"At first, some managers saw RO concepts as excessively rational and arbitrarily dependent on individual managerial judgments that could easily be wrong. However, the well-designed and facilitated RO meeting processes tailored to the company's culture and led with respect and compassion soon helped them to appreciate the RO approach as a well-crafted balance of head, heart, and gut.

"Many managers were initially uncomfortable making judgments about people's capability and talking candidly with them about judgments on their work. I helped managers break through their misgivings by providing training and opportunity in peer groups to test, practice, and refine their judgments. Particularly important was their sense that when in doubt about an employee, they would work together to collect new data and test the data in well-crafted mentoring sessions. And employees would always have the benefit of appeal and career discussions with their MoR.

"Finally, a few managers had serious doubts about RO's concepts relating to how human capability matured over a lifetime and how focusing on these limits could discourage employees and might lead to an elitist culture. Again, we learned to apply RO with a good balance of head, heart, and gut; and, with experience, learned that most people already have a sense of their potential and reasonable aspirations. The feared problems rarely occurred.

"As a bonus, the RO process helped managers focus on capability and break through informal, stereotype-based barriers related to gender and ethnicity that had been unfair to employees and costly to the company in terms of lost talent. And we learned to smooth out some of the difficult feedback interviews by providing our managers and MoRs with better training and with hot-line coaching."

"Thirty months in, Owen Chemicals is a very different energized and growing company. First quarter I took personal stock; second quarter, staffed key senior team positions; third quarter, developed senior team consensus around the new strategy; and fourth quarter designed the new structure, including both the vertical and preliminary cross functional relationships. We devoted the next two quarters to staffing the new roles, training, and MoR development—completing most of the change work within 18 months of my arrival. We cleaned up loose ends during the last 12 months, finally completing the compensation work in month 30. We are aligned, excited, and on the move!

"My board was also excited when, after two years, our revenue had increased by 38 percent, expenses decreased by 18 percent, and our profit had doubled."

Reframing Intractable Problems

All executives, at some point, face what they believe to be intractable problems. By targeting root issues rather than symptoms, RO provides a unique perspective that allows for straightforward resolution of seemingly intractable problems. For example, the EVP of HR of a major oil company had to improve the people skills of a highly valued leader:

We tried management by objectives. We tried 360-degree feedback and coaching. We sent him to a two-week leadership program at a blue-ribbon leadership center, and he came back fully committed to change. Yet, within three weeks, he was back to his old, bad habits.

The company could have fired the manager, but that would have meant losing someone the CEO saw as uniquely valuable. The problem couldn't be ignored but the traditional interventions had accomplished little.

Seemingly intractable leadership problems frequently involve good people who alienate their staff by micro-managing, as well as brilliant managers who leave their less brilliant followers bewildered. There are many proffered solutions, from training to one-on-one coaching to management systems like multi-rater feedback. Unfortunately, seldom do any of these work in the long term, but we use them for lack of anything better and because we feel compelled to do something.

Other intractable problems include frequent adjustments of the number of organizational levels, grouping of functions around individuals competing for Hay points, muddle of titles around status norms in an industry, oscillating pulls between centralization and decentralization, and the endless tensions between product, geographic, and functional silos. These are usually "resolved" by re-organizing every few years. Many feel that any fleeting improvements are more than overwhelmed by the costs and disruptions of the changes.

Those who understand RO know that these intractable problems are inevitable reflections of poor organizational structure. Requisite organization provides to executives the context they need to take action upon the root cause of their issues.

Research shows that, on average, 40 to 50 percent of employees report to a manager who is ill-suited to provide them adequate leadership. When manager-subordinate role relationships are wrongly designed, even the most well-intentioned manager will be ineffective and the most dedicated employee will be frustrated. Add to this that approximately 35 percent of employees are in roles that do not match their current capability, and the fact that organizations are successful at all is a testament to our human work ethic.

It is not surprising that most organization design is inadequate, because there is little in the way of solid theory on the subject aside from the large body of work pioneered by Dr. Elliott Jaques. His work is now the topic of hundreds of independent research studies.[6] Jaques studied organizations for 55 years. The roots of his research go back to the now legendary Glacier Metal Company studies begun by the Tavistock Institute in 1948. With the exception of perhaps Peter Drucker's writings, no body of work has this kind of pedigree. Why then is requisite organization theory so little known?

Elliott Who?

Elliott Jaques was so focused on research that he did a poor job of marketing his findings. This, combined with his habit of dismissing the work of academics across the whole range of social sciences as "bunkum," did not serve to win friends or influence people. Nevertheless, the power of his requisite organization concepts, when integrated with effective OD processes for implementation, continues to win quiet adherents as increasing numbers of senior OD-process-savvy consultants incorporate Jaques's concepts into their methods. Because of Jaques's controversial style, many who use his concepts do not

---

6   A complete bibliography of research in the field of requisite organization and its requisite organization base can be downloaded from the Global Organization Design Society's website http://www.GlobalRO.org.

promote him as the father of the theory behind their methodologies, and therefore his theory's influence and application is much broader than most are aware.

A Fortune 500 office supply firm makes extensive use of RO theory, but the EVP of HR says, "I don't even talk about requisite organization except with people like you." A global communications equipment manufacturer used Jaques's theory to take our organizational levels and to broad-band compensation in the late 1980s—a high pay-off innovation that was then picked up by many of the Fortune 100 companies—but you won't find that written up anywhere. One of the big three integrated petroleum companies developed a method for assessing a manager's potential, but unless you know the people who created it you won't know that it is based on Jaques's research.

Despite the lack of visibility and the intellectual challenge Jaques's dense books present, organizations keep implementing work based on RO theory because, as one executive says, "[They] have never found anything better. It's practical, it's useable, and the concepts make sense to line people."

The aforementioned oil company EVP of HR found that trying to fix the personality of the recalcitrant manager was a dead-end. However, by applying requisite organization principles, he was able to design and staff an effective department, and the previous personality and style problems just fell away. With this insight, he went on to redesign additional departments and found a host of other "intractable people/management" problems also vanished.

A Complete Theory

Requisite organization is a complete theory-based design and implementation process.

It starts with an understanding of the complexity of different kinds of work, derives rules for organization structure, looks at how to staff the different layers of the firm, and moves on to issues of setting accountabilities, defining authority, establishing managerial leadership practices, and even establishing fair-pay levels. It presents a rich, consistent, and research-based view of how to structure and manage an organization.

Similarly, using Jaques's concepts to tailor OD processes greatly increases their effectiveness. Facilitation of strategy with careful attention to these principles clears away muddle and points to effective strategies and implementation plans.

Jaques's concepts also multiply the impact of planned participation and training processes. His concepts can align and strengthen many existing organization processes.

The advantage of having a broad consistent framework like RO is that it provides enduring solutions rather than bandages. A systems approach can both explain and remove problems such as:

"Mary is a brilliant sales strategist, but none of her staff members know how to execute her ideas."

"The marketing department is at war with production again. We change the bodies but personality conflicts don't go away."

"Our managers don't have any clear idea of what their role entails."

All these problems are merely outcomes of the wrong accountabilities, the wrong layering, lack of role clarity, or other structural issues. They can all be resolved.

The RO approach appeals to an architectural mindset. It is about building a well-crafted, solid, and efficient infrastructure that can thrive in turbulent times. Structures that Australian mining giant CRA put in place with these methods in the early 1980s are still in place today, despite several changes in leadership and a change in ownership. When a major Canadian bank used RO principles in its personal and commercial client group (17,000 employees), executives were clear they were not just trying to deal with the problem of the week. They were building "a structure that will be in service for at least the next decade." That's a different way of thinking, but that is why Jaques keeps winning adherents. He always was different.

Key Lessons from RO Research

Jaques's research led him to believe there are a number of principles that apply to all organizations in which people manage other people. Those principles fall into three areas: structure, people, and management.

STRUCTURE SUPPORTS STRATEGY

Research shows that the jobs in an organization vary from less to more complex in a series of discrete steps. The job of a manager is not just "more complex" than that of a frontline worker; it is complex in a different way. Similarly, a division manager is not just a bigger job than a first-line manager; it entails new kinds of complexity. The

STRATUM	TIME-SPAN RANGE	TYPICAL ROLES
VIII	50 years plus	Super corporation CEO (Examples: GE, Exxon)
VII	20 – 50 years	International Corporation CEO
VI	10 – 20 years	Group Vice President, International Corporation
V	5 – 10 years	Business Unit President, CEO of mid-sized company
IV	2 – 5 years	General Manager, large plant manager, Vice President
III	1 – 2 years	Line manager, Department Director, senior professional
II	3 – 12 months	Front-line manager, Supervisor
I	up to 3 months	Front-line employee, lead hand

TABLE 1.3.1

discrete steps of complexity are called strata. The number of strata that are appropriate for any given organization depends upon the size and complexity of the organization.

The large Canadian banks all have strategies that require their CEO role to be located at stratum VII, hence requiring six strata of management to support it. In a medium-sized department, there are likely three levels of work complexity—which implies that it makes sense to have only three levels of hierarchy, not more, but not fewer either.

It was Jaques who named these levels "strata", and his genius was in devising a way to measure the complexity of work. He picked up on an idea that one of his early clients presented him; the idea that complexity of work was related to time. Shop floor workers use their discretion to complete tasks assigned over hours, days or a couple of weeks , but that's about it. Their manager will be working tasks that will not be completed for another three months to a year ahead. By the time you get to the CEO of large, complex organizations (IBM, GE, Toyota), they are working to shape the corporation's role in society for decades to come. Table 1.3.1 shows the strata defined in terms of time span.

The concept of stratum allows you to build a structure that supports your strategy in two ways.

First, you can specify the stratum that your strategy requires for each role. There is a tremendous and measurable difference between a VP marketing at stratum III, capable of designing advertising and promotional materials, and one at stratum VI, who can work to build your global brand in a planned way over the next 12 years. Place the role too low and your strategy will fail. Place it too high and you will be wasting money on an over-qualified VP who is likely to expand the marketing department beyond where it is needed for your strategy.

Second, more than 50 years of research and experience make it clear that employees want to be managed by a manager one stratum above them. A manager at the same stratum as you makes you feel like they are breathing down your neck. One who is two or more strata above you feels too distant; managers two levels up do not want to slow down to coach you. Usually we see managers who micro-manage or who are too aloof as having a personality problem. In truth, these problems are merely symptoms of a poorly designed structure.

THE SELECTION AND DEVELOPMENT OF PEOPLE TO WORK WITHIN THE STRUCTURE
When selecting a candidate for a role, whether a CEO or the frontline worker, it is important to find someone who is willing to do the work and has the necessary skills. But most important, they must have the cognitive capacity needed for the role. *Cognitive capacity* is an individual's ability to handle complexity, their mental horsepower, and it is critical for two reasons. First, while most of us gain in this dimension as we mature, there does not seem to be any way to accelerate its growth—you can't fix someone's cognitive capacity by sending him on a training course. Second, cognitive capacity is what allows an individual to succeed in a role at a given stratum.

The board may desire to expand against stratum VI competitors and choose a strategy at VI or perhaps VII. It must therefore select a CEO capable of executing the strategy at VI or VII. Boards not using the Jaques system have no way to reliably distinguish a stratum VI-capable CEO from one capable at V.

In one recent example, a stratum V-capable CEO of a Canadian subsidiary installed a requisite system and was subsequently rewarded by corporate office with a promotion to a larger region. The corporate office, without benefit of Jaques's insights, proceeded to appoint a new Canadian president who turned out to be capable only at stratum IV. That misaligned CEO was incapable of executing the strategy, removed many of the RO system components in place, removed the stratum IV-level VPs and replaced them with stratum III-capable VPs. The new stratum III-capable VPs failed in their stratum IV VP roles. They pulled the level of work down to the level they could handle and thus sabotaged corporate strategy.

While IQ purports to measure this dimension, IQ actually correlates very little with success in the work world. Cognitive capacity, on the other hand, looks at a person's ability to organize, extrapolate, and apply information in the making of decisions and solving of problems. It has been used successfully in many organizations to predict the success individuals might have in senior roles.

Most managers have little training in how to be a manager and fewer still are held accountable for being good managers. For an organization to get the best work from its employees, they need to be directed, supported, and held accountable by their managers. This requires three conditions. The manager must be:

1. one stratum above the employee in cognitive capacity.
2. skilled at managerial leadership practices (to be described in the next section).
3. directed, supported, and held accountable by their manager for being a good manager.

The RO Implementation Process

There are several different approaches that can be used to put RO in place in an organization. The eight-step process illustrated here is one way of getting it done.

1. Building the senior team
2. Designing the corporate strategy
3. Determining the structure needed to implement the strategy
4. Designing the working relationships between functions
5. Ensuring you have the people you need in the right roles—now and in the future
6. Managing performance and execution—ensuring your managers are skilled at managerial leadership
7. Cementing the change by strengthening the role of the MoRs
8. Building the compensation systems to pay employees fairly

In reality, each of these steps can be taken on its own, and each one will more than pay for the time and investment required. But in concert, all eight interventions build on each other.

Step One: Building the Senior Team

Dr. Jim Collins, in his book *Good to Great*, says that the first step to greatness is not a winning strategy but an effective CEO and top team. But how do you build a great top team? The two key elements are capable people and a great team process.

By capable people we mean executives with the cognitive capacity to grapple with the complexities of your market, your core capabilities, and the execution of your strategy. It's not enough to have smart people. No doubt your database analysts are very smart, but what is needed for the senior team requires a whole different level of cognitive capacity. They must be just one stratum below the CEO or they will drag down the whole team.

Building the senior team sets the foundation for re-designing and refining strategy. It also gives the CEO a much stronger executive group from which to draw counsel. Most importantly, and under-appreciated, is that it provides people to whom the CEO can delegate larger tasks, freeing the CEO to take on more.

Step Two: Designing Corporate Strategy

Having the right stratum-capable CEO and senior team in place are necessary but not sufficient conditions for success. Jaques's concepts make several additional contributions to effective strategy design.

Just as level of work complexity can be assessed, so can the level of complexity of an organization's strategy be determined and compared to that of its competitors.

The level of the strategic-planning process must be designed to produce a strategy to match or exceed competitors. For example, the required strategic-planning process for a stratum V corporation is different in many key aspects from the appropriate system for a stratum VI organization. The level of abstraction, the level of data analysis, and complexity of option development and evaluation are distinct for each different stratum.

RO concepts provide a radically improved framework for evaluating competitor strategies by assessing the level of their key functions. For example, Wal-Mart benchmarked its competitors on their IT systems support for inventory control and ordering, and then designed its paradigm-breaking system one whole stratum above its competitors, giving it unmatchable advantages in cost control and stock levels.

In another example, a major bank CEO, competing for sought-after, high-net-worth customers, sized up his competition's customer service function as designed at stratum II. He proceeded to design his own bank's customer service function at stratum III and greatly expanded market share while reducing head count. His bank's stratum III associates could relate better to the clientele and provide solutions in a two-year timeframe. Competing institutions' stratum II agents simply could not deliver the same quality.

Another contribution of the RO framework is that there will not be any vagueness about how a vision will be realized. Leaders with the right level of cognitive capacity clearly understand what specific elements they need to put in place to transform their day-to-day reality to their vision of tomorrow.

Step Three: Determining the Structure Needed to Implement the Strategy

Typically, your strategy will specify the basis on which you will compete, as in the step above. For example, "Our marketing and customer service will be the best in the industry by being designed and positioned one whole stratum above our competition."

First, your strategy determines what functions you have at the VP level. Do you need a VP of logistics? Do you need a VP sales and marketing or do sales and marketing need to be separate functions? Decisions such as these will be based on strategic considerations.

Second, your strategy will determine the stratum at which various roles must be placed. Your strategy may, for example, need a marketing function that will develop value-chain-analysis capability above that of competitors. Or the strategy may be to build a reputation for creativity within the next three years. Such strategies would require a closely linked stratum IV VP of marketing and stratum IV VP of product development.

The more you are competing on the strengths of a role and the longer the time frame of that role, the higher it must be. The more you are competing on lowering the salary cost of a role and the more you simplify the decisions made in it, the lower the stratum.

Step Four: Designing the Working Relationships Between Functions

A unique feature of requisite organization is that it coordinates the work of various functions while still giving each employee the clarity of having one and only one

LATERAL RELATIONSHIP	AUTHORITY
Advisory	Give unsolicited advice about specified topics
Service Getting	Obtain specified services. (Usually, the Service Giver has the option of specifying when they can deliver the requested service.)
Prescribing	Give orders to be followed immediately. (Authority usually given only to those in charge when health or safety are at risk.)
Monitoring	Request another employee to conform to a strategy, plan or policy. (If the other employee refuses, the monitoring employee can escalate to his or her manager.)
Coordinating	Request a group of employees to conform to a strategy, plan or policy. (If the other employee refuses, the coordinating employee can escalate.)
Auditing	Require another employee to conform to a strategy, plan or policy. (If the other employee needs to, they can escalate.)

TABLE 1.3.2: INTEGRATING FUNCTIONS

manager. This works through a unique set of six lateral relationships.

Most organizations fail their employees by not clearly defining the parameters within which they are to work with their colleagues. This leaves employees who encounter resistance to resort to manipulation, force of personality, covert actions, or tattling to get their work done. The RO framework makes it clear who can say "no" to whom and under what circumstances. It also defines the consequences for doing so. With this explicitly detailed, employees spend their time working rather than finessing authorities they need but were not given.

For example, the marketing department may depend on the customer service department's ability to find out what is happening in the field, so a customer relationship manager (CRM) may be given advisory accountability. This is the accountability to give a brand manager unsolicited advice about what is happening to her brand. The CRM's own manager holds the CRM accountable for doing this, and it is up to the brand manager to take the advice or not.

In addition, the CRM may have service getting authority over the brand manager to obtain special sales tools or point-of-sales materials; the brand manager's own manager holds her accountable for providing that service.

The brand manager may also have monitoring authority over the CRM, the authority to request that the CRM not make promises about the brand that are outside its official positioning; the CRM would be held accountable by their manager for complying with the request.

Table 1.3.2 shows all of the lateral relationships. An understanding of these lateral relationships is the fundamental tool for integrating functions. It is one of the most important and little known contributions of RO theory.

Clarifying lateral relationships is hard work, but it improves the quality, increases the speed, and reduces the friction of any work between functions.

Step Five: Ensuring You Have the People You Need in the Right Roles— Now and in the Future

Changes in structure may leave an employee in a role whose title has not changed, but which is now, for example, at stratum III instead of stratum II. When structures change, some employees will no longer be suitable for their roles.

Managers need to assess whether employees one and two strata below them are suitable for their new roles in the sense that they:
- are capable to work at the stratum of the role,
- have the skills and knowledge to do the work, and
- value the role so that they will do that work with full commitment.

After roles are filled with people capable for them, talent pool development needs to be an ongoing process. While succession planning typically is concerned only with very senior roles, talent pool development is a comprehensive program looking after the needs of the organization and its employees.

Filling roles with capable people on an ongoing basis brings a three-fold benefit:
- Effectiveness is increased, because strategic goals have been assigned to people capable of reaching them.
- Efficiency is improved, because people are doing work at the level they are paid for and because succession is planned for.
- Trust is greatly enhanced, because employees understand they have a future in the organization.

Your strategy tells you what to accomplish, your structure tells you which roles will do what to accomplish it, and talent-pool development ensures that those roles are filled by employees who are capable of doing the jobs. But employees also need ongoing management. The key to managing performance lies in 11 managerial leadership practices, all of them done in dialogue:

1. *Selection and induction*: Choosing the right candidate for a role and bringing that employee into their role, the team and the corporation to become as productive as possible as soon as possible.

2. *Context setting*: Keeping the team informed about changes in the context of their work.

3. *Team planning*: Considering as a group how to tackle major tasks.

4. *Task assignment*: Being clear with individual employees about what you want them to accomplish.

5. *Team building*: Being clear on how you want your team members to work with each other.

6. *Task adjustment*: Changing a task when conditions warrant.

7. *Monitoring*: Observing how well each employee works and what they accomplish.

8. *Coaching*: Helping each employee be a better resource for you.

9. *Appraisal*: Gauging how well each employee has worked over the past year and assigning an appropriate bonus.

10. *De-selection/dismissal*: Removing employees from roles within which they will not succeed.

11. *Continuous improvement*: Making processes take less time and fewer resources and yet yield higher quality outcomes.

These practices allow employees to give their best. They will be working on what you want them to work on, working as effectively as possible, and their abilities will be improving, all of which improves your profitability.

ACCOUNTABILITY

Built into these practices is a central principle of RO organization theory, accountability.

In task assignment, the manager makes clear what the subordinate is to work to accomplish.

In monitoring, the manager keeps track of how well employees are working and progressing towards their goals.

In coaching, the manager may bring consequences for substandard work. Employees may need to redo the work, or may need to take further training. They may also be told that they will not be given challenging work if they cannot handle it.

In effectiveness appraisal, the manager may decide not to give employees a bonus or a raise if their work has not been effective.

The ultimate accountability tool is de-selection, removing employees from their role because they simply are not doing the required work.

Managers often complain that their employees do not "feel accountable" or that their organization lacks a "culture of accountability." Accountability is not an issue of feeling nor of culture but of managers' holding employees accountable through the 11 managerial leadership practices.

Step Seven: Cementing the Change by Strengthening the Role of the Manager of Managers

The MoR plays two key roles in ensuring that the organization stays its course.

First, MoRs clarify how they want their managers to exercise leadership and then hold them accountable for doing so and not just delivering short-term results. They also monitor how well their managers are managing, and coach them to manage better.

Second, MoRs are the natural mentors of the subordinates of their direct reports in that they have a wider view than the manager of the employee's capability and the opportunities available. And it makes sense that the MoRs decide whom to promote to be their immediate subordinates.

Step Eight: Building the Compensation System

We have mentioned two ways in which organizations need to support their managers: the talent-pool development process and MoR practices. Compensation is the third required support system. Of course, employees must be paid fairly for the work they are being asked to do, with flexibility for situations in which employees with rare skills need to be overpaid to attract them. In addition, to be truly supportive of managers, the compensation system must meet the following criteria:

It must support strategy and structure and not interfere with them. Some pay systems require an individual to manage a large department in order to have a large salary. Thus, a stratum V internal consultant may be given a large department to manage to justify his or her large salary. Invariably, the individual abdicates either the internal consulting or managing the department, and strategic goals are missed.

It must support managerial authority rather than interfere with it. If someone other than the manager has authority to assign bonus, employees will work to please that individual rather than their manager. And the manager needs the authority to assign bonus according to how effectively the employee worked; otherwise, the manager has no significant means to hold the employee accountable for working effectively.

Requisite organization has templates for compensation that pay employees fairly and support strategy, structure, and good management.

ABOUT THE AUTHORS

Maurice Dutrisac is one of the founding partners and the practice leader for strategic planning and organizational design for Mastermind Solutions, Inc. a general management-consulting firm established in 1999. Maurice specializes in business strategy, retreat facilitation, organizational design, structure and change, creative problem solving, leadership development, organizational design workshops for executives, and talent pool management. He is also a member of a number of advisory boards.

Prior to his consulting career, Maurice worked for 24 years as an executive with large, complex manufacturing, service- and resource-based corporations in Canada and the United States. Maurice was awarded the BA and MBA degrees from McMaster University and is fluent in French and English. He resides in Mississauga, Ontario.

Herb Koplowitz, Ph.D., president of Terra Firma Management Consulting, works primarily as a consultant to consultants. His deep understanding of requisite organization helps human resources and organization design consultants make the best application of the approach within their organizations. He helps consultants in other fields ensure their advice is implemented; he helps their clients develop the structure, staff, and management practices required to do what the professional recommends. He has helped organizations in every sector build trust and become effective and efficient through appropriate structure, staffing, and management practices. Herb has worked with requisite organization for 15 years and has trained and lectured on it in the US, Canada, Jamaica, South Africa and India. His practice in requisite organization is informed by a 12-year professional relationship with Elliott Jaques and earlier studies in mathematics, philosophy of science, cognitive development, and general systems theory.

Ken Shepard, Ph.D., management consultant, is principal of the Canadian Centre for Leadership and Strategy and President of the Global Organization Design Society.

As a consultant, Ken specializes in coaching to senior leaders, top management team building, strategy formulation and implementation, organizational design, and installing effective accountability structures and management practices.

Ken held management positions in business, government, and not-for-profit organizations. He was program director at the Niagara Institute, a Canadian leadership center providing executive development for private sector, government and labor executives, and he designed and led national consultations on complex societal issues. He served as assistant professor of management at Pepperdine and Loyola Marymount universities, and lectured at the University of Pennsylvania and the University of Southern California.

4

Musing about the Elephant in the Parlor or "Who the Hell is Elliott Jaques?"*

Jerry B. Harvey

WHAT'S IMPORTANT

- Basic tenets of Stratified Systems Theory (SST)**

- What knowledge of SST will allow you to do.

- Why SST is effective.

- Why SST and Elliott Jaques are not better known.

- How SST affects the theory and practice of management.

- The major potential contribution of RO to society.

---

* Harvey, J. *Musings about the Elephant in the Parlor or "Who the Hell Is Elliott Jaques?"* ©Copyright 1992. Reprinted with permission of John Wiley and Sons, Inc. Article reprinted in its original form.

** Editorial note: The name of the theory prior to the use of "requisite organization."

*Despite its absence from the New York Times best-seller list, I read it (*A General Theory of Bureaucracy*) and found it to be one of the most creative, stimulating, exciting, rigorous, confrontational, intellectually demanding, and morally provocative pieces of work I had ever read in the field of management and organizational behavior. No, that's not accurate. I found it to be the most creative, stimulating, exciting, rigorous, confrontational, intellectually demanding, and morally provocative piece of work I had ever read in the field of management and organizational behavior.*

Several years ago, a respected colleague mentioned that he had come across a very different book in the field of management and organization, titled *A General Theory of Bureaucracy* (1976), by someone named Elliott Jaques.

"Who the hell is Elliott Jaques?" said I.

After providing a synopsis of the author's background that he had obtained from the book jacket, my colleague said, "Regardless of who he is, you ought to read it. He thinks in peculiar ways—very much like you. He's just a lot smarter; on a different stratum, one might say."

Acutely aware of my colleague's sarcasm but naive as to his perceptive, precise understanding and application of Jaques's concept of stratum, a major theoretical construct of his Stratified Systems Theory (SST), I went to our library and checked out the one copy of *A General Theory* that our beloved institution owned. That action itself was instructive. The book had rested—or, more accurately, slept—in the stacks for nearly three years. During that period, my colleague and I were apparently the only members of the entire university community who had seen fit to check it out. "It's certainly not one of our most sought-after books dealing with management," said our friendly librarian.

Despite its absence from the *New York Times* best-seller list, I read it and found it to be one of the most creative, stimulating, exciting, rigorous, confrontational, intellectually demanding, and morally provocative pieces of work I had ever read in the field of management and organizational behavior. No, that's not accurate. I found it to be the most creative, stimulating, exciting, rigorous, confrontational, intellectually demanding, and morally provocative piece of work I had ever read in the field of management and organizational behavior.

In light of my reaction, I began to wonder how I, who pride myself as being a semibright, relatively wellread professional in the field of organizational behavior, had not heard of Jaques's work. Despite the librarian's comment, I began to have the fearful thought that I was an anomaly; and I began to experience the pangs of separation anxiety we frequently suffer when we suddenly and inexplicably find ourselves alone in a crowd.

Fortunately, or unfortunately, depending on one's particular bias, I found that I was far from being *sui generis*. In fact, when I conducted an ongoing informal poll of academic colleagues, fellow consultants, clients, graduate students, managers, participants at corporate training seminars, human resource directors, and others who I believed would, or should, have reason to know something about Elliott Jaques and SST, I discovered that virtually none of those I interviewed had heard of him either.

Oh, I did find a couple of exceptions. One interviewee asked, "Isn't he the fellow who wrote a book about the problems involved in changing the cultures of factories (Jaques, 1951). Another said. "I think he's the psychiatrist who did an article a long time ago called 'Death and the Midlife Crisis' (Jaques, 1965). If memory serves correctly, it had something to do with all the flack that hits you during middle age. If he's the guy I have in mind that was an excellent piece of work. I have always wondered what happened to him. Since I've never seen anything else he's written, I assume he's dead."

On the whole, though, "Who the hell is Elliott Jaques?" or some variation thereof was a stock reply that echoed in the backroads of my inquiring mind. In fact, I heard the question with such monotonous frequency that I associated it with a story I had heard about an eccentric CEO of a megacorporation who housed a huge, powerful, stately elephant in the parlor of his New York penthouse. When guests visited the CEO, the elephant, in its grandiose, domineering manner, would meander to and fro about the room, brushing against them, the furniture, the walls, and the chandeliers. Nevertheless, for reasons known only to the CEO's Great Manager in the Sky, few of the visitors acknowledged its presence. In fact, when the host showed them to the door and said, "Incidentally, what did you think about the elephant in my parlor?" most replied quizzically. "What elephant?"

As you might surmise, I am impressed by the similarity between the guests' responses to the elephant and the reaction, by and large, that individuals who have an avowed interest in the theory and practice of management and organizational behavior have had to Jaques's work. That is, when confronted with the reality of a piece of seminal thinking, stately and sweeping in its design, scientifically testable, powerful in its capacity to deal with the world of which it is a part, massive in its implications for individuals and organizations of all kinds, and even more impressive when viewed in comparison with other works of pissant proportions that attempt to address some of the same issues, why do so many in the field of organizational behavior respond with "What's Stratified Systems Theory?" "Who the hell is Elliott Jaques?" or some other equivalent of "What elephant?" And that question takes on added significance when one realizes that since 1952 the elephant has produced numerous articles and eighteen books about SST starting with *The Changing Culture of a Factory* and including, most recently, his work in conjunction with Kathryn Cason, *Human Capability* (Jaques and Cason, 1994).

Consequently, in this article, I would like to muse a bit about the work of my friend and colleague Elliott Jaques, a metaphorical elephant who resides in organizational parlors throughout the world. More specifically, I would like to start by giving a summary of his theory in the context of what a moderately sophisticated knowledge of SST would potentially allow someone to accomplish. I take this approach because SST is a mega theory of organization, and I doubt that I, or anyone else for that matter, can do it justice in a simple summary. Once I have outlined what I believe to be SST's basic tenets and its potential applicability to life in organizations, I will focus on why I think a fecund work of such extraordinary creativity and importance has been virtually ignored by managers, consultants, and academicians.

As I go about my musing, please keep in mind that as I talk about Elliott Jaques personally and about his work on SST, I am speaking about them interchangeably. I say this because I agree with one of the basic assumptions of SST: that an isomorphic relationship inevitably exists between each of us individuals and the work we are capable of producing. More important, it assumes that given the particular mix of inborn capability combined with the knowledge, skills, values, and temperament we bring to a task, an isomorphic relationship exists between us and the work we do produce (Jaques and Cason, 1994).

What Knowledge of SST Potentially Allows You to Do

The following are some of what I believe to be potential contributions to the field of management and organizational behavior.

1. SST provides guidelines for building a Requisite Organization, the design of which facilitates getting work done and, at the same time, generates feelings of trust

and security among its members (Jaques, 1996). In my language, I would say that SST increases members' freedom to work by reducing the amount of energy they waste through suffering from the anaclitic depression blues.

2. SST provides you with a comprehensive, univocal language of organizational behavior. Jaques rigorously defines such terms as work, task, bureaucracy, association, manager, level, leadership, knowledge, values, and skill. Once you know the definitions, you will be able to carry on conversations about bureaucracy and other forms of organization with the same precision that physicists employ when they discuss ergs. If you don't think that the capacity to communicate in rigorous terms is a significant advance in the field of organizational behavior, ask twenty physicists to define erg. No matter what language they speak or what school they attended or what employment experiences they have had, each of them will define erg in the same way. Alternatively, ask twenty organizational development (OD) consultants, human resource development professionals, or line managers to define bureaucracy, OD, or leader. Although they generally curse bureaucracy, tout the virtues of OD, and worship good leaders, virtually no two of these people will produce identical definitions of the terms. In short, they don't know what each other is talking about. And if we don't know what we are talking about, carrying on a literate conversation about "it," whatever the "it" may be, becomes downright difficult, if not impossible.

3. If you are employed in a hierarchical organization. SST allows you to tell exactly how many levels your organization should have in order to facilitate work, reduce paranoia, increase trust, and minimize those anaclitic depression blues. For instance, SST shows you why even the largest and most complex hierarchical organizations in the world need only eight levels. If they have more than eight, they will be overmanaged: the antirequisite design of the organization, itself, will add needless financial and emotional overhead that comes from having too many people in managerial roles attempting to micro-manage people who don't need or want to be managed and won't cooperate with anyone who tries to manage them. Using SST, you need know only one piece of information—the targeted completion time (measured in days. weeks, months, or years) of the longest single task on which your organization's CEO is working (Jaques and Cason, 1994). Once you have that information, which is called the Time Span of Discretion (TSD) of a work role, you will know how many levels your organization should have in order to be "requisite." You may not want such information to be widely shared, though, because once you

and others possess it, many of the "political" factors that underlie your organization's design will be eliminated. Stated differently, it will become very difficult to justify "layering in" Fred as a vice president just because he is your brother-in-law.

4. SST allows you to ascertain, within very small limits, how much employees in any managerial accountability hierarchy will feel is a fair amount to be compensated for their work. All you have to know is the TSD of their particular work roles. The correlation between that single variable and what the person believes is fair compensation termed Felt-Fair Pay (Jaques, 1976, p. 228) is .89 to .93 (Richardson, 1971). The longer our TSD, the more money—in dollars, pesos, pounds, and so on—we believe we should receive for our work. The shorter the TSD, the less money we believe we should get. You don't even need to know what the person's work role is, how much seniority the person has, what the person's educational level is, or whether the person is in a managerial, staff, or technical role. You can calculate the Felt-Fair Pay for large groups of people very rapidly without a lot of pomp and circumstance. I wonder why organizations involved in consultation about compensation schemes apparently are unfamiliar with such a simple, straightforward approach for solving what most of them contend is a very complex problem.

5. SST allows you to measure a person's potential for serving in an infinite variety of leadership roles, including managerial leadership, parental leadership, political leadership. military leadership, and so on, by knowing the length of time—measured in days, weeks, months, or years—that the person can work into the future without knowing the outcome of his or her work. Called *capability* that potential is ultimately your capacity to cope with complexity as you work (Jaques and Cason, 1994). The greater your capability, the more complex are the problems you can solve. The less your capability, the less complex are the problems you can solve. According to Jaques, a person's basic capability is inborn and matures along a predictable trajectory, from birth to death, and that trajectory cannot be altered by education, hard work, perseverance, or training. Once you know about capability, you will also know why the styles of leaders are irrelevant to getting work done, why personality is relevant to leaders' success only if they are psychotic or deeply neurotic, why you can't train individuals to think strategically, and why leaders must have greater capability than their followers in order to lead them.

6. SST shows you how to measure the leadership potential of anyone in a particular organizational role by talking with that person about a subject in which he or

she is interested. In a startling finding, Jaques shows you how to predict, with high validity, who, at age twenty-five, will or will not have the capability to successfully carry out the role of being a competent president (or vice president, general manager, or first-line supervisor) of your organization twenty years later (Jaques and Cason, 1994). If you are interested in succession planning in your organization, such data might merit your close attention.

7. SST shows you the significant differences in organizational dynamics that are created by organizations structured as associations as opposed to those structured as accountability hierarchies. So you will know the basic difference, an association is a group of people who come together to pursue a common interest, develop some rules to govern themselves, and select one or more of their members to administer the rules on their behalf. An accountability hierarchy (generally called a bureaucracy), in contrast, is a stratified organization in which one person is accountable for the work of one or more others and enforces that accountability through the right to veto appointments, assign tasks, evaluate performance, and remove from role those individuals whose work is not satisfactory.

Once you become aware of these differences, you will know why sending people to ropes courses, sensitivity training, or team-building sessions is inherently counterproductive both for them and for their organizations, if they work in an accountability hierarchy, as do 90 percent of the people in the United States. You will also know why the practice of medicine, the generation and transmission of new ideas and knowledge, and the exploration of sacred beliefs are inevitably compromised by organizations structured as accountability hierarchies. Likewise, SST clarifies why the routine production of goods and services is most effectively carried out in organizations designed as accountability hierarchies, why it is destructive to the human psyche to try to get rid of hierarchy in any organization, and why movements designed to eliminate hierarchy are inherently absurd.

Have I overstated the potentials of SST? Probably. The only way for you to find out for sure, though, is to read one or more of the eighteen books Jaques has written.

Have I overstated the potentials of SST any more dramatically than the missionaries for such managerial panaceas as empowerment, zero-based budgeting, sensitivity training, management by objectives, total quality management, learning organizations, the Myers-Briggs Type Indicator, organizational development, managerial style, or re-engineering have overstated the potentials of their religions? Probably not. Yet virtually all professionals in the field of organizational behavior have read about, discussed, seen videos extolling, or gone to soul-saving seminars to become acquainted with one if not all of those messianic approaches to organizational resurrection. So I again raise the question, Why is SST not better known by professionals in the field, or, metaphorically speaking, Why have we for the most part ignored the elephant in our parlor?

To provide order to what otherwise could be chaos, I begin this discussion with several rationales for such ignore-ance (sic) that I have rejected and tell you why I have seen fit to do so. Then I suggest an explanation that I believe will, over time, turn out to be valid. Finally, I discuss what I believe is the major potential contribution of SST to the world of both formal and informal management and organization and perhaps to the world at large.

Rejected Explanations

Let's start with some proposed explanations I have rejected and the reasons underlying my rejections.

Jaques Doesn't Communicate His Ideas Very Well

Many individuals who have read one or more of Jaques's articles and books (particularly his earlier ones) or who have heard him speak in person about his work contend that some of their reservations regarding SST stem from the fact that Jaques is neither a poetic writer nor a charismatic speaker. Such criticism is frequently registered in concrete terms. such as, "If he wants his work to be understood, he ought to write a simple book like *The One-Minute Manager*"; or "He doesn't speak with the evangelical zeal, the melodious rhythm, and the drumbeat cadence of a Tom Peters exhorting the masses to embrace organizational excellence."

I, too, am aware that much of Jaques's writing style doesn't have quite the literary quality of a Shakespearean sonnet (although it has improved significantly as he has worked with his foremost collaborator, Kathryn Cason). I also am aware that his talks about SST don't exactly conjure up such images as those evoked by Winston Churchill speaking to the British Empire about blood, sweat, and tears. Consequently, I have nearly been seduced at times into believing that his deserved influence has suffered, if not from his own communication deficiencies, then from a shortage of competent "translators."

Ultimately, though, I have concluded that such criticism of his work is irrelevant. It's irrelevant because, if one listens carefully both to supporters and detractors of SST who offer that argument, they frequently follow it up with such statements as "I had to read his damn book five times before I thought I understood it; but each time I reread it, I understood it better," or "After Jaques concluded his talk to our group, a half-dozen of us sat in my office and discussed what he had said for three hours." Because the very people who claim that Jaques lacks communication skills frequently reread and fervently debate what he supposedly hasn't communicated, I have decided that he must communicate something fairly well. Realizing that, I have also gained a renewed appreciation of the validity of a point Jaques made during a rambling discourse to participants in a faculty seminar on the topic of leadership at The George Washington University (Jaques, 1990a). Specifically, he said that the influence of leaders stems from the fact that "they have competence [meaning "capability"] to burn and, one way or another, they communicate that competence to others." I can only wonder what might happen if Jaques were to develop Shakespearean or Churchillian communication skills. Some fairly well known people in leadership roles have been crucified for considerably less; one can only guess what might happen to an elephant.

Jaques Contends that Basic Human Capability and Consequent Leadership Potential Is Inborn and Cannot Be Changed

Apparently, we are residents of a world in which it is politically correct to assert that, with hard work and perseverance, anyone can grow up to be president, compose like Wolfgang Amadeus Mozart, sing like Luciano Pavarotti, act like Jessica Tandy, think like Albert Einstein, write like Jean-Paul Sartre, or manage like Alfred Sloan. Therefore, when Jaques says that human capability is inborn, some people complain that he violates the democratic principles that our sexist forefather Thomas Jefferson set forth in the *Declaration of Independence* when he said, "All men are created equal." Yet those same people, if asked directly if they think they could sing like Pavarotti, will admit that they don't believe they could, no matter how much they practiced and how hard they tried. "I just wasn't born with the right stuff," they will say. Furthermore, if they see a six-foot-ten-inch 265-pound young man with hands large enough to permit him to carry a basketball as though it were a

Concord grape, they readily admit that genes have provided him with the potential for playing a game called basketball in a manner that they, at five-foot-one and 103 pounds, couldn't possibly emulate. In short, although we may raise Cain about Jaques's contention that leadership capability is essentially inborn, when the crunch comes, virtually everyone admits that much of our capability to carry out a wide variety of tasks in everyday life is inborn. Consequently, I don't pay much attention to that argument when it comes to ignoring Jaques's work.

SST Can Be Understood Only by Persons in the Upper Strata of Capability

According to Jaques, your capability—your capacity to deal with complexity as you go about solving problems—can be ascertained by measuring your time-horizon— the longest time span with which you can currently cope (Jaques and Cason, 1994). The longer your time-horizon, the more complexity you can deal with, the bigger the problems you can solve, and the more people you potentially can lead. Jaques's research has shown there are certain predictable break points, which he calls strata, at which the nature of capability changes dramatically, with the higher levels reflecting more complex thought patterns and being occupied by fewer and fewer individuals. stratum I people have time-horizons of one day to three months into the future. IIs from three months to 1 year, IIIs from 1 to 2 years, IVs from 2 to 5 years, Vs from 5 to 10, VIs from 10 to 20 years, and VIIs from 20 to 50 years. The extraordinarily rare VIIIs and above, who think huge, very complex, ground-breaking thoughts, have time-horizons of 50 to 100 years or more into the future (Jaques and Cason, 1994).

Because the percentage of people occupying the higher strata is progressively smaller than the percentage in the lower ones, another plausible explanation I have heard for SST's relative anonymity is that only those with capabilities in strata V through VIII can truly understand SST. Given the low proportion of the big, visionary thinkers who occupy those strata, it will take a sizable amount of time to accumulate a critical mass of individuals who both comprehend Jaques's work and have the capability to put it into practice.

On the surface, this is a persuasive argument: and if one happens to suffer from a touch of vanity, it is particularly attractive to those whose capability is in strata V through VIII. Persuasive as the argument may be, I have concluded from my experience that neither our understanding of SST nor our acceptance or rejection of its essence is related to capability, as long as our capability is located in Jaques terms "the normal adult range" of strata I through VIII (Jaques, 1989). For example, I know a stratum VI colleague who, with temples throbbing, has vehemently rejected SST, employing abstract "arguments supported by accumulated conceptual information in which the concepts are actually related to each other" (Jaques, 1990a). My colleague contends that SST is fascistic in its underlying value system, violates Kantian moral imperatives, and is based on flawed scientific methodology. Consequently, he has concluded that SST's resulting gestalt is both scientifically and morally unacceptable as a theoretical model for conceptualizing organizational behaviour. Although I don't agree with either his premises or his conclusions, I do realize that the thought process by which he reached them is an expression of what those of us at the lower strata of Jaques's Universal Depth Structure (1976) would consider to be in the upper reach of capability. Alternatively, I have heard stratum I individuals, who live and work in the World of Concrete Language and Ideas (Jaques, 1990b) embrace SST with simple, uncomplicated assertive statements, such as "You can piss all over the guy's work if you want to, but he is right. It makes sense to me. I like what he says. It's great stuff." In short, once acquainted with the fundamentals of SST, whether by reading or through conversation with someone about the subject, everyone understands the theory, even though the specific nature of each individual's understanding undoubtedly varies as a function of the capability he or she brings to the task.

Examining that conclusion retrospectively, I don't know why I, or anyone else for that matter, should be surprised by it. Jaques, for one, has discovered that people both can and will discuss potentially complex issues such as euthanasia, abortion, or any other subject that interests them, within the limits set by their own capability (Jaques. 1990b). In fact, one can judge others' capability from the structure of thought they employ as they discuss such topics. Or, to provide a slightly different example: all of us understand the Bible, assuming we bother to read it: how we interpret its content and whether we accept or reject what we understand from reading it is an entirely different matter. Apparently, that is true for our comprehension of elephants, also. That we can discuss elephants in our own unique ways that reflect our respective levels of inborn capability doesn't provide a clue as to which of us will like or dislike having an elephant padding around in our parlors. For reasons that Jaques's theory doesn't explain, one person's elephant droppings are another's organic fertilizer.

Initially, I entertained the possibility that the spread of SST might be limited because its practical implications were unclear. To the contrary, I have discovered that if anything, the spread of SST has been restricted because its practical implications are clear.

For example, I know a human resources (HR) manager who permitted forty-eight hundred hourly employees to go on strike rather than employ SST as a conceptual guide for resolving a labor-management dispute. He did so even though he believed that the dispute clearly related to the organization's failure to provide Felt-Fair Pay and to the anti-requisite accountability relationships that existed between the organization's stratum II first-line managers and its stratum I hourly employees.

Paradoxically, the HR manager refused to use SST not because he feared it would not work but because he feared it would. According to him, SST's success would open up a Pandora's box of issues relating to the organization's basic structure, its compensation scheme, and the managerial and quasimanagerial roles played by specific organizational members. Most of all, it would call into question a lot of activities that went on in his own area of organizational accountability. In his words, "I'd rather call in a traditional organizational development consultant to do a good ol' intergroup conflict resolution design, even though I know that type of intervention won't solve the problems we have.[1] At least others around here would think we were trying to do something, and I wouldn't run the risk of being the focus of a lot of downstream flap I couldn't control if this SST stuff caught on."

Although I might question both his ethics and his business judgment for choosing a non-solution that he knew wouldn't work instead of a solution that he believed might work, I think he was essentially correct in assessing the potential ripple effect the theory might have had on him and the remainder of the organization. To him, the implications of the theory were crystal clear, and that clarity led him to reject its use. Some might say he was resistant to change. I would say he didn't want to suffer from the anaclitic depression blues that might follow the successful application of a new theoretical approach to solving his organizations problems.

In similar fashion, I have been approached by more than one director of an executive development program for which I have been scheduled to do a presentation

---

1 For a description of conflict resolution design interventions, see Walton (1987).

about SST's potential for draining the environmental swamps that produce organizational phrog farms (Harvey, 1988), with a question such as, "Talking about phrog farming is risky enough, but must you speak about SST? Couldn't you do a session on something else?" When I have asked the reason for their queries, their replies generally have been versions of, "The implications of SST to the participants are too disturbing. They will get to thinking that a lot of what goes on in their own organizations doesn't make much sense. And, more important to me, it means that a lot of the other material in the program dealing with leadership style, organization structure, compensation, conflict resolution, empowerment, the role of personality in management, career development, motivation, strategic planning, and management development won't make much sense, either. It also causes a problem for future presenters who speak on those topics, not to mention the headaches it creates for me when the participants start complaining about the contradictions between SST and most of the other material we provide."

When I ask, "Would you prefer that I present some additional material that doesn't make sense so that it would fit both the nonsensical organizational environments of the participants and the nonsensical material of the program?" they generally have said, "No, but I thought I would ask. I just don't like the implications of Jaques's work, even though his ideas are extremely interesting and, undoubtedly, represent a real advance in the field."

Nor is their attitude significantly different from that voiced by a doctoral student who took a course that I "not teach" and in which *A General Theory of Bureaucracy and Human Capability* are used as textbooks. During the course, the elephant himself occasionally wanders around and bangs against the classroom's walls as a guest professor. Several years after the doctoral student took the course, she visited my office to discuss some of her experiences.

"Do you still use Elliott Jaques's book, and does he still serve as a guest speaker from time to time?" she asked.

"The answer is 'yes' to both questions," I replied. "Why do you ask?"

"I hated the book, and when he spoke to our class, I was very upset by nearly everything he said."

"Would you mind telling me why?"

"Well, if he's correct, and I suspect that he is, then much of the material I've received in my doctoral program about how school systems should be organized and about the way in which people learn is probably irrelevant. I feel like a large part of my time as a doctoral student has been wasted..."

"Well, if you believe that, why don't you just forget about Jaques's work and 'dance with the one that brung you'?" I replied, using a Texas expression that means "stick with the concepts and theories with which you were previously familiar."

"I can't," she said. "Doing that would be like trying to sit in the corner, on command, for thirty seconds without thinking about a brown bear."

Evidently, elephants sometimes develop thick coats of fur and replace their tusks with fangs.

The Theoretical Relationships Proposed by SST Would Not Hold up in the World of Practice

A final explanation I have heard for the relatively limited spread of SST is that its basic theoretical constructs would not be validated if individuals attempted to apply them in their respective organizations. Although I have heard variations of that argument a number of times, I have never heard it offered by people who actually have experimented with SST in their organizations. In the light of such data, I see no reason to pursue that point of view further. More specifically, until someone tells me or you or Jaques or some other verifiable source that he has had an experience with an actual (rather than a hypothetical) managerial accountability hierarchy in which Time Span of Discretion is not reliably related to Felt-Fair Pay; human capability does not follow predictable developmental courses; and living. breathing human beings with stratum IV capabilities have effective work relationships, as subordinates, with stratum III superiors, I see no need to worry about the elephant's health.

Having rejected five seemingly plausible explanations for why so many people who should be familiar with—even if not necessarily in agreement with—SST are not, I turn the discussion now to what I think are the true reasons for SST's limited dissemination and the collateral question, "Who the hell is Elliott Jaques?"

SST as a New Expression from the World of Universals

In my opinion, SST is not merely a technological prescription for analyzing and constructing economically efficient associations and accountability hierarchies, although it certainly is useful for that purpose. Nor is it simply a methodological guide for enhancing organizational design or improving our understanding and practice of organizational leadership and management. Rather, using Jaques's terms, SST is an expression of encompassing "Universal" thoughts that are generated by those very rare big thinkers who come from stratum VIII and above (Jaques and Cason, 1994). These are the individuals who describe and develop universal ideas, languages, theories, values, and concepts that are required for handling whole societies, social movements, ideologies, and philosophies (Jaques, 1990b). Like all new theories generated by these people, SST requires that those of us in the field of organizational behavior either change or abandon many of our cherished, established beliefs about the nature of human organization. In addition, it requires that we either change or abandon our relationships with friends and colleagues who have supported us in holding such outdated beliefs.

In short, SST demands that we abandon not only the systems of thought but also the isomorphic networks of associates that have provided us with the emotional security we derive from maintaining those systems. Such changes, in turn, would cause many (and maybe most) of us to suffer from those anaclitic depression blues, which, as you know, is a form of depression that strikes otherwise normal individuals when the emotional support provided by other people, familiar belief systems, or organizational structures is withdrawn. As you know from Chapter Six,[2] if anaclitic depression runs its full course, it results in marasmus—a type of debilitating atrophy that can be both physical and emotional in nature; and because of that, most of us fear the anaclitic depression blues and will take whatever actions we can to avoid it.

Thus, like the alchemists, who were threatened with obsolescence by the emerging theory of chemistry, many of us associated with the field of organizational behavior probably have attempted to avoid the experience of anaclitic depression by ignoring SST and continuing to live in the thin atmosphere of false security supplied by a theoretical environment with which we are comfortably familiar.[3] As I described many years ago in an organizational sermon titled "OD as a Religious Movement" (Harvey, 1974), we are singing our own version of the traditional hymn:

---

2   Editorial note: This is a reference to Jerry B. Harvey's book, *How Come Every Time I Get Stabbed in the Back My Fingerprints Are on the Knife? : And Other Meditations on Management* within which this chapter is published.

3   Jaques is fond of describing the relationship of the current professions of management and organizational development to ground-breaking management and organization theory (of which I believe SST is an example) as similar to the relationship of alchemy to chemistry (Jaques, 1989.)

"Give me that old time religion, Give me that old time religion, Give me that old time religion, It's good enough for me."

Paradoxically, the fact that many of us have lived much of our lives in organizations that generate, rather than ameliorate, anaclitic depression doesn't help us withstand the fear of separation, abandonment, or ostracism that the threat or anaclitic depression poses for us. Experience, in many cases, is not the best teacher. At times, it may be the worst.

Fundamentally new ideas (SST being one) emanating from those who occupy the strata of Universals inevitably require us to engage in the kind of intense debate and controversy that frequently leads to strained and fractured interpersonal relationships, resulting in the anaclitic depression blues. I am convinced, therefore, that our fear of experiencing the blues has stifled the discussion, dissemination, and development of SST itself, even though it offers a potential organizational blueprint for gaining existential relief from the anaclitic depression of which we are so afraid.

Strange, isn't it? Parlor-reared elephants apparently activate whatever self-defeating proclivities we human beings inherently possess.

One is then forced to ask, "From whence comes the impetus for any fundamental change in the way of seeing or experiencing the world? Why would anyone embark on the development of a heretofore unexpressed idea, such as SST, if our inherent fear of those anaclitic blues is so great?"

Once more, SST offers a fecund hint. Perhaps individuals with capability in the Universal range are in touch with the truth and reality of the Universal ideas themselves: perhaps they receive emotional support and gain reassurance from their contact with and attachment to these ideas, ideas that have no reality and provide no security to those of us whose capability is lower. For instance "e = mc2" may have given Einstein a lot of emotional support and reassurance, but that piece of esoteric scribbling would have said absolutely nothing that provided comfort, reassurance, and security for me.

Jaques's Major Potential Contribution: A Means for Elucidating and Clarifying Ethical, Moral, and Spiritual Issues of Organization

Assuming that SST does emanate from the world of Universals, I doubt that its major contribution will stem from the practical, technological guidelines it provides for creating requisite accountability hierarchies, associations, and other forms of organization. Rather, I believe it will come from SST's capacity for providing a more sophisticated, rigorous order of concepts and language for illuminating the kind of ethical, moral, and spiritual (EMS) relationships that we human beings require both to survive and to flourish in a wide variety of organizations. It will do so, I believe, because new Universal statements—which by their nature require that we restructure interpersonal, organizational, and intellectual alliances—always demand isomorphic changes in EMS relationships within and among persons whose capabilities are found in the lower strata.

For example, SST has led me to understand that the empirical relationship that exists between Felt-Fair Pay and Time Span of Discretion is not simply the basis of a reliable technique for determining monetary compensation schedules in accountability hierarchies. Rather, it also serves as an invitation for me, and others, to consider rigorously how we express fairness and unfairness, decency and indecency, support and rejection, respect and disrespect, love and hate, kindness and cruelty, competence and incompetence, greed and altruism toward one another through the medium of compensation.

Or, by making me aware of the potential isomorphic relationship that exists between a given individual's capability and the complexity of work she is capable of carrying out, SST demands that I explore the EMS issues that arise when we create organizations in which this relationship is either facilitated or inhibited. For instance, what EMS issues stem from giving individuals work that is below or above their capability? More specifically, I am convinced that profound EMS issues are raised when we give people work at a level that bores or overwhelms them to death; and SST clearly shows us how to keep from doing that.

Or, knowing the predictable course of a given individual's development of capability over time, I am equipped with a new way of thinking about the EMS issues that are related to the education of our young, our middle-aged, and our elderly. What EMS issues are involved, for instance, when we make the rather common but false assumption that virtually all students of the same age are on the same developmental trajectory of capability? If you know SST, you will understand why grouping students on the basis of capability, not age, may facilitate their ethical, moral, and spiritual development.

Or, employing SST as a conceptual guide, and assuming that we succeed in creating an organization based on SST, I must ask whether it is ethically, morally, or spiritually legitimate for me and others to hoard our knowledge of SST and, by doing so, gain a competitive advantage over poorly designed organizations for the purpose of diminishing their relative effectiveness or destroying them.

Or, playing with the implications of SST's constructs in depth, I am led to conclude that an organization's structure can be moral or immoral in and of itself. Thus I realize that consciously constructing an organization that, by its design, impairs people's health is ultimately no different than willfully using asbestos in the construction of a brick-and-mortar building when we know that the material is likely to compromise the health of the building's inhabitants.

I suspect that knowledge of SST will likewise arouse EMS issues in you and others, the specific character of which undoubtedly will reflect your respective capabilities. In addition, I know that discussions of issues dealing with right and wrong, or good and evil, inevitably generate intense controversies, the exploration of which may result in broken relationships that lead to the anaclitic depression blues. Given the dangers involved, we may be very reticent to engage in those types of exploration. Jaques himself may have fallen victim to such reticence. For instance, in *General Theory of Bureaucracy* (1976), *Free Enterprise, Fair Employment* (1982), and *Requisite Organization* (1989), he has discussed a variety of ethical and moral implications of SST at the individual, organizational, and political levels, but he, for the most part, has refrained from exploring the deeper spiritual implications of his work.

Assuming that both he and those of us who are stimulated by his ideas overcome our fears of the anaclitic depression blues and develop the intellectual, collegial, and transcendent attachments required to explore the ethical, moral, and spiritual implications of SST, I don't think that many individuals in the organizational behavior field will be asking one another, "Who the hell is Elliott Jaques?" Rather, the next time the CEO invites us for cocktails in his spacious Manhattan penthouse, I think many of us will find ourselves earnestly puzzling over the question, "How the hell could so many of us fail to notice the pachyderm in the parlor?"

Jerry B. Harvey is Professor Emeritus of Management Science at The George Washington University. He has served as a consultant to a wide variety of industrial, educational, military, religious, and voluntary organizations. He is author of two books: *The Abilene Paradox*, and *How Come Every Time I Get Stabbed in the Back, My Fingerprints Are on the Knife?* He has written approximately 50 professional articles and is featured in several videos focusing on organizational behavior including, *The Abilene Paradox*, *The Gunsmoke Phenomenon*, and the *Asoh Defense*.

PART TWO

Enhanced CEO Performance

Enhanced CEO Performance

The significance of the CEO in the organization has never been in doubt. The daily news generally features one or more CEOs who have been hired or fired, and the new CEO is touted as the savior of the company "with full confidence of the board." No doubt there are many reasons for the coming and going of CEOs, all the way from unethical behavior to laziness. But aside from those extreme personality defects, the issue of whether the incumbent is big enough for the job is critical in judging the performance of a CEO. Before requisite concepts came along, this was largely a guessing game with the most solid measure available the old adage "the best indication of future performance is past performance." Today we realize how fragile that statement is because of the implicit assumption it makes about a CEO's future capability.

But the value of requisite concepts does not stop with selecting and judging the performance of the CEO. Companies worldwide are designing their organizations aligning strategy, structure, roles, talent pool, management practices, work processes, and compensation using the management principles of requisite organization. CEOs need enhanced tools for pattern recognition and manipulation at high levels—both in their business design and profitability models and in their management practices and systems. CEOs need to be aware of their own level of capability and maturation over time, their own tendencies to dominate and ways to moderate it, and behaviors to work respectfully and effectively across the levels of the organization. Boards need to be able to diagnose the level of the organization required to execute its strategy and to recruit the CEO with the proper capability. CEOs need to build an effective management team by appointing individuals with the level of capability required to manage the level of complexity. Perhaps most important of all, CEOs need the knowledge and skill of requisite organization to recognize non-requisite situations.

The application of requisite organization by CEOs often contributes to high-profile company success stories, but RO's role is seldom mentioned in the press. In this part, we focus on how requisite concepts relate to the CEO's role and CEO effectiveness and the documented successes achieved. Two success stories are presented, followed by a series of articles that focus on the performance of the CEO, board governance, corporate strategy and CEO communications.

Gerald A. Kraines, M.D., president and CEO of The Levinson Institute, writes about Denis Turcotte and his being named "CEO of the Year" in 2006 by *Canadian Business* magazine. Turcotte's story is one of inspiration and achievement. Kraines, who worked many years with Elliott Jaques and who wrote the book, *Accountability Leadership*, building on Jaques's concepts, has been one of Turcotte's major consultants for more than ten years in three successive senior executive roles. Here, Kraines condenses the *Canadian Business* article and describes the many aspects of RO leadership that Turcotte applied to successfully transform Algoma Steel. With the application of requisite concepts, Turcotte was able to change the culture at Algoma Steel and achieve a major turnaround in a firm that had been teetering on the brink of bankruptcy twice in the previous ten years.

Another success story, which was mentioned in the article in Part One "The Long View of Leadership," is documented in the next article by **Jos J. Wintermans** and **Paul J. Tremlett**. This is a more detailed account of Wintermans's success as the CEO of Canadian Tire Acceptance Corporation over a seven-year period. What is particularly striking about this successful implementation of requisite principles is the relatively quick improvement that Wintermans was able to make, producing some remarkable short-run results that continued for seven years. The article shows the importance of building trusting relationships within the system and how requisite concepts achieve this. Finally, the importance of having executives operating at the appropriate strata of the organization, and the problems of having too many management levels, are lessons to be learned from this success story.

Mark Van Clieaf, a consultant for many years in the area of CEO performance/accountability and corporate governance, and **Janet Langford Kelly** have used requisite theory in their analysis of CEO performance and board governance processes. The board's obligation is to determine the level of work required to execute the organization's strategy and to recruit an executive with the appropriate level of capability and compensate him or her accordingly. With the objective of having boards add maximum value to the company, they maintain that levels of work (LoW) from requisite theory should be applied to both the CEO and the board, and that boards should use LoW to specify the complexity of role of the CEO and judge the CEO's performance. Moreover, compensation levels for CEOs can be set more objectively if the complexity of the role is used as the measurement, not fictitious comparisons with other CEO roles that have much higher levels of complexity.

The unique characteristics of a small enterprise entrepreneurial CEO is the subject of **Atilio A. Penna's** article "A Method for Training CEOs of Small, Growing Entrepreneurial Organizations." Penna has consulted for many years with small entrepreneurial organizations in Argentina. He describes in his article how adding levels of work and human capability concepts to his systematic approach improves diagnosis of root causes of issues, design of his interventions, and finally the overall effectiveness of his support to entrepreneurial CEOs attempting to grow their small organizations from stratum II to stratum III. Penna also maintains that requisite concepts are more complicated in the entrepreneurial organizations since the CEO often occupies several roles simultaneously—chair of the board, CEO, and operative employee. In addition, the growth of the organization requires that the entrepreneurial CEO operate at progressively higher levels of complexity (often the limiting factor of first-generation entrepreneurs), and Penna proposes a process to assist in that development.

The importance of understanding complexity and how it relates to corporate strategy and growth is the focus of Julian Fairfield's article, "Profit by Raising a Key Function to the Next Level: Tools to Build a Work Levels Shifting Strategy". An experienced consultant with global experience in implementing requisite concepts, his position is that companies that dominate markets are those who operate at a higher level of complexity than their competitors. Similar to the approach taken in his popular book *Levels of Excellence*, Fairfield integrates other management theories—such as the McKinsey "7 S model"—with requisite concepts.

Jack Fallow, a long-time HR professional as well as CEO, was exposed to levels of work and human capability through his association with bioss. In his article, Fallow describes learning to communicate across the levels in his role as CEO, management educator, and coach to executives on leadership. He recommends a framework derived from his insight from complexity theory that uses core level-specific values as touchstones for managers to improve communications with individuals working at each level.

How Did Denis Turcotte Become Canada's CEO of the Year?

with a summary extracted from *Canadian Business* magazine

Gerald A. Kraines

WHAT'S IMPORTANT

- *Canadian Business*'s "CEO of the Year" led a masterful turnaround of Algoma Steel from bankruptcy to industry leader in a few short years.

- Denis Turcotte, a three-time CEO user of requisite organization (RO) methods, applied RO as the major management framework to design and lead the company's transformation.

- Gerald A. Kraines describes how Turcotte used his managerial leadership skills and RO concepts to overcome major challenges in:
  - redesigning the organization,
  - transforming the culture to one of accountability where people "keep their word"and"earn their keep,"and
  - transforming the organization's relationship with its unions.

Good leaders make people feel that they're at the very heart of things, not at the periphery. Everyone feels that he or she makes a difference to the success of the organization. When that happens people feel centered and that gives their work meaning.[1]

—Warren Bennis

Part 1 of this article is a summary extracted from a *Canadian Business* article about Denis Turcotte's remarkable turnaround of Algoma Steel in Sault St. Marie, Ontario. It describes his philosophy and actions and how he led an "old industry" company out of its second bankruptcy in ten years to become one of the most profitable steel companies in North America.

In Part 2 of this article, I explain Turcotte's success in terms of his understanding and exercise of personal leadership, accountability leadership, and strategic organizational leadership.

I can do this because of my experience consulting to Turcotte and the three companies he has managed over the past decade. In providing executive counsel, organization design support, and leadership training to Turcotte, his managers and employees over this period, my staff at The Levinson Institute and I have learned as much about leadership as we have taught.

Part 1: Executive Summary[2]

On a Roll

Our top CEO for 2006 took struggling Algoma and turned it into the most efficient steel producer in the world. The question is: What's next?

Denis Turcotte was in danger of losing his job—along with 1,200 of his colleagues. Barely 30 years old and fresh out of business school in 1990, Turcotte was working as a maintenance superintendent for the Spruce Falls Power and Paper Co., in Kapuskasing, Ontario. The mill's owners, Kimberly-Clark, had been trying to sell the ailing facility for months, without success. The only option left was to slash the

---

1 www.quoteworld.org/quotes/1223: Accessed March 17, 2007.

2 The original article, written by Joe Castaldo, was printed in *Canadian Business* Magazine, October 9-22 2006. Part 1 of this article is an executive summary of that Canadian Business article adapted with permission of courtesy of CB Media Limited 70, The Esplanade, 2nd floor, Toronto, Ontario M5E 1R2. To learn more about *Canadian Business*, visit the *Canadian Business* website at: http://www.canadianbusiness.com.

workforce down to 250 workers, a move that would devastate the economy of the small town that depended on the mill.

The massive restructuring had just been announced to employees at a special meeting, and Turcotte was milling around with a few co-workers. A secretary asked him, "You've got all this business training. Can't we buy this company?"

While the other employees chuckled, Turcotte returned to his office and started making phone calls. In the end, the buyout, in partnership with Quebec pulp-and-paper company Tembec, saved the jobs of 800 employees, along with Kapuskasing.

That was just the first time Turcotte proved instrumental in saving a company. The second time came as president and CEO of Algoma Steel Inc. The company, based in Sault Ste. Marie, Ont., had teetered on the edge of bankruptcy twice within 10 years, most recently in 2001.

Five years ago, more than 40 other steel companies in North America had filed for bankruptcy protection, and no one who'd been watching Algoma sink deeper into debt as steel prices plummeted could have been surprised when it followed suit. But what has been surprising has been Algoma's return to profitability.

There's no question, Turcotte, 45, has improved Algoma's standing by transform-ing it from a mismanaged hulk collapsing under its debt into a slim efficient pro-ducer—one that has rewarded shareholders with more than $500 million (CDN) in cash distributions since 2002.

He will certainly need to stay positive, since some of Algoma's biggest challenges lie ahead. But the picture is rosier than it was five years ago. Algoma had already survived one bankruptcy scare, in 1991, and it emerged on shaky ground thanks to a $60-million (CDN) bailout package from the Ontario government. In the years that followed, Algoma embarked on a program to bulk up operations and took on a mountain of debt in the process. The centerpiece of the strategy was a $440-million (CDN) state-of-the-art mill. The mill, called the Direct Strip Production Complex, was completed in 1997. The DSPC was plagued with bottlenecks. Time and money were lost on repairs, and the output was far lower than the company estimated. These issues, combined with falling steel prices and hundreds of millions of dollars in debt, forced Algoma to declare bankruptcy once again.

Into this bleak picture stepped Turcotte. Turcotte grew up in Thunder Bay, Ont., and says he comes from a "hardworking French Canadian family." After the buyout of Spruce Falls, Turcotte rose through the ranks at Tembec to become president of its paper group by the time he began interviewing with Algoma in 2002.

The similarities between steel and forestry surprised him. Both are capital intensive, commodity-based industries sensitive to market conditions. In spite of this, his inexperience in steel made some people uneasy.

Nonetheless, Turcotte's outsider status allowed him a fresh perspective. Others looked at Algoma and saw little hope of salvation; Turcotte saw opportunity. He was particularly impressed by Algoma's $1 billion (CDN) in assets as well as its production technology and capacity. A lot of the company's problems were mechanical, stemming from the failure-prone DSPC. The kinks in the DSPC were smoothed out by 2003, and it began producing at levels for which it was designed.

That was no small victory, but there remained that $300-million-plus debt, along with the troubling fact that Algoma was still a weak player in a market that was just beginning to recover. One change was to reorganize the management structure, which was ill-defined and often had workers reporting to more than one senior employee. Turcotte implemented a company-wide restructuring, simplifying the chain of command and eliminating two layers of management between the executives and the shop floor.

Regrettably, Turcotte says, there had to be layoffs. About 600 employees were let go in 2003. (A hundred or so have been hired back.) But Turcotte has also taken strides to cut costs without having to axe more jobs by enforcing a spirit of entrepreneurship on employees. Many CEOs promote that line, but few have been as successful as Turcotte. He's also the first to admit that he can't take credit for the cost savings—a whopping $180 million (CDN) since 2003. "No one guy could have done what this company has done," he says.

"You have to induce a culture where people value the input of the guys on the shop floor—who know more about running the business than anyone else," he says. That kind of change takes time, especially in a 105-year-old company like Algoma; but as management began to act on some of the ideas, employees became more confident in offering suggestions.

Given the number of cost-saving suggestions, Turcotte expected to save $100 million (CDN) within three years. Instead, it took only two. These savings and increased production from the DSPC, along with an improving steel market thanks to surging demand from China, made 2004 Algoma's most successful year ever, with $344 million (CDN) in profit. Last year wasn't bad, either: the company earned $240 million (CDN).

One of the most important things Turcotte has been able to do with Algoma's new-found wealth is pay down nearly $350 million (CDN) in debt, putting the company in a much stronger position to weather steel's ups and downs. Analysts are also impressed with his ability to handle cash. He's opted to stockpile it, spend it strategically, or return it to shareholders, instead of blowing it all on expansion.

But not everyone has been impressed with Turcotte's fiscal management. New York-based hedge fund Paulson & Co. Inc., which held a 19 percent stake in Algoma, demanded more money from the company in October of last year. So adamant was John Paulson that he pushed for a shareholder vote that could have ousted Turcotte and his colleagues from the board.

Turcotte fought back. The company had been planning a $200-million (CDN) share buyback at the end of the year, and Turcotte told Paulson that was all he was going to get. Paulson eventually acquiesced, but he reduced his stake in Algoma to 5 percent afterward.

Despite this experience, Turcotte is far from being anti-hedge fund. In fact, he's credited some hedge funds with bringing discipline to CEOs and boards. "You have to focus on short-term performance. Otherwise, there's no constructive tension. I think hedge funds bring a bit of that." As for Algoma's long-term prospects, all the company's successes lead to one thing for Turcotte: "Now we've earned the right to start thinking strategically."

The big question for Algoma now is how it will fit with the global steel giants who are leading consolidation in the industry.

Exploring joint ventures is one option. Algoma recently entered into a partnership with Germany's Schaarf Industries Co. to build a wind-tower manufacturing plant in the Sault. Such proactive strategies mark a departure from the Algoma of old, which would discount its steel just to give itself a competitive edge.

As Algoma continues to explore its role in the marketplace, a more immediate issue is a negotiation of a new contract with the United Steelworkers. Labor relations have never been easy, and with Algoma in possession of more cash than ever before, there's a possibility that both sides could get greedy. But Turcotte will approach the issue with his usual Boy Scout optimism. "The company will be reasonable, and I'm expecting the employees will be reasonable," he says. "I just gotta believe that people at Algoma today are much happier than they've been in years."

Part 2: Firsthand account of Denis Turcotte's Turnaround of Algoma Steel by Gerald A. Kraines

Introduction: What Every Leader Can Learn from Denis Turcotte's Example

The following account reveals how Denis Turcotte applied personal leadership, accountability leadership, and strategic leadership to successfully turnaround Algoma Steel.

A CEO—even one who has the raw ability, who understands business and strategy, and who understands the principles and applications of requisite organization—cannot transform a company alone. The Turcotte story emphasizes that organizational transformation requires leveraging the potential of an entire organization. And leadership is a set of actions that leverages the potential of all organizational resources.

Personal Leadership

Denis Turcotte is bright and intellectually curious. He possesses a clear moral compass, yet he is intensely competitive. He is analytical and committed to operating from first principles and logic, but he is not afraid to make far-reaching decisions based on the information at hand.

Turcotte values what they call in the UK "man management." He believes that his organization's capability depends on leveraging the potential of all his employees working effectively together. Turcotte enjoys challenging his employees, engaging them around ambitious goals, holding them to high standards, and rejoicing in their successes.

Part of Turcotte's strength is his willingness to ask questions without worrying about revealing his lack of knowledge. He has confidence in being able to figure out solutions to complex problems. When his managers would tell him things couldn't be done, he would ask them why. When they couldn't adequately back up their explanations, he challenged them to look at things differently. When they would assert that, "this is the way it has always been done," invariably he would probe until he got to the underlying principles. In this way, he *simultaneously earned their respect and forced them to think.*

Accountability Leadership

When Algoma Steel came out of its first bankruptcy in 1991, the board made a number of agreements with the union leadership in order to extract financial and other concessions to restore the company to profitability. The two most important were the unionization of all specialists and first-line managers, and the involvement of union members in nearly all managerial decisions. These decisions amounted to union veto authority over managerial business and employee-selection choices.

The effect of these concessions was decreased management authority and accountability, and a decision-making environment based on consensus that led to a culture of inaction and widespread feelings of entitlement by some, and disengagement by others. Managers who expected clarity and accountability were considered abrasive, non-team players.

Turcotte bluntly addressed the status quo when he began his tenure as president and CEO of Algoma in September 2002. "Algoma exists to deliver value to the shareholders, by serving its customers," Turcotte asserted. "The company will survive, endure, and prosper only if we deliver value that exceeds what they could get elsewhere." This was the only approach that could develop the required credibility with the capital markets and the customers. This would in turn lead to good things for employees and the community. He stated that as CEO, he was accountable for making that happen and could achieve that only by holding each of his subordinate executives and their subordinates accountable for delivering their part.

Furthermore, Turcotte made it clear that employment was a privilege, not an entitlement. All employees would be expected to "keep their word" and "earn their keep." Functioning accountably was no longer optional for anyone who wanted to continue to work at Algoma.

Turcotte was first drawn to the leadership principles of requisite organization when he attended a Levinson Institute seminar in the 1990s. At the time, he held a stratum V role as vice-president of the paper division, and general manager of Tembec's Spruce Falls Mill. The requisite leadership practices (context setting, unambiguous assignment definition, significant-incident feedback, effectiveness appraisal, coaching, etc.) not only resonated with his own experience, but they provided a framework and language for teaching and aligning the entire organization with his approach. Even prior to taking the reins of Algoma Steel, Turcotte sent the vice presidents of operations and HR to The Levinson

Institute's Strategic Organization™ seminar and had the Institute deliver Principles of Accountability Leadership training to its top 600 managers and employees.

Strategic Organizational Leadership

Turcotte saw the power of being able to proactively align his organization with strategy, using the requisite organization lenses of:

- Levels of role complexity,
- Functional alignment,
- Three-level-unit processes, and
- System stewardship.

He also realized that a software-enabled system of talent-pool assessment and development, tied to compensation, was the most reliable way to establish consistent, high standards for effectiveness.

RO Principles for Levels of Role Complexity and Three-Level Units
The level of complexity of the Algoma CEO role had devolved to stratum V over the previous decade. The board agreed that, instead, the CEO should function as a low stratum VI role, with a 12–15 year outlook. By selecting Turcotte, with stratum VII current potential, the board was able to reestablish the CEO position as a high stratum VI role after three successful years.

At the outset, when evaluating the manufacturing organization, Turcotte identified up to seven levels in a function that required only five levels. He calculated that a competitive ROI for shareholders required a total payroll consistent with 25 percent fewer employees. This was consistent with moving the average human productivity levels up from the 53 percent estimated, toward the 75 percent level defined by "top-quartile" manufacturers. He next engaged an industrial engineering group to help management evaluate process efficiency and identify where roles could be eliminated without reducing productivity. *This required eliminating two levels of supervision and reorganizing the manufacturing three-level units.*

RO Principles for Functional and Process Alignment
Algoma's previous strategy was to "sell as many tons of steel as possible," usually at the lowest price, in order to fully load its production capacity. Turcotte reasoned

that in a cyclical commodities market, this strategy was a recipe for bankruptcy. While it was important to load the fixed-cost production engine as fully as possible, he believed that a value-oriented sales approach (high prices) could be achieved with a more intelligent production loading-and-planning process. To reconcile and optimize these two needs, accountability for *production loading needed to be aligned with sales, not manufacturing.* Similarly, the accountability for *production planning needed to be aligned with steel finishing, not steel making.* This necessitated major functional and process realignment at Algoma.

To create a value-oriented sales strategy, Turcotte needed to create metallurgically unique products and services. This required *creating a new product-development capability,* which had been eliminated years earlier during the period of financial cutbacks. This necessitated implementing organizational functional and process realignment.

RO Principles for HR Systems

The most dramatic change in culture and productivity resulted from Turcotte's implementation of a rigorous process for assessing employee effectiveness and potential. Because of his long experience with our firm's talent-pool process, he understood that the systematic assessment of employee effectiveness was the best way to simultaneously 1) communicate and calibrate high standards and 2) implement meaningful accountability for people to "earn their keep." Using software supplied by The Levinson Institute,[3] Algoma Steel was able to quickly implement a comprehensive effectiveness-appraisal, gap analysis, coaching, and compensation system. Using the same system, managers were able to assess the current and future potential of Algoma's entire pool of talent. These assessments were critical in making the role-filling decisions required by the reorganization efforts.

Lessons Learned from Denis Turcotte

Denis Turcotte is an exceptional leader. He understands the value of leadership and organizational consultation. Turcotte has applied the principles and practices—first developed by Elliott Jaques and now adapted and refined by my firm—with enor-

---

3   This refers to The Levinson Institute's Sonario™ software. Please contact The Levinson Institute for further information about Sonario software.

mous success in three different companies. He was recently quoted as saying that "The Levinson Institute and its Strategic Organization™ approach were fundamental to getting the right structure, integrating our efforts, and driving home accountability. Within 36 months out of bankruptcy we drove $152 million (CDN) in annualized improvements, and over $1 billion (CDN) of equity value."

However, Turcotte's success does not stem from the intellectual prowess of his consultants. Rather, it derives from his personal leadership, accountability leadership, and strategic leadership. Not only does this story prove that one person can make a difference, but it proves that leadership itself can make a difference. Sound, moral, enlightened, and confident leaders can leverage the full potential of almost any work organization.

What then are the characteristics of strategic leaders? Here are six that I have found correlate strongly with the kinds of values practiced by Denis Turcotte.

1. *Strategic leaders value managing and leading people.* In other words, they value getting work done through others. If they are in it just for the power, prestige, or strategy, they will not create long-term value, because the sustained, effective implementation of strategy must involve every employee. Senior managers cannot lead mechanistically with carrots and sticks and expect to be successful.

2. *Strategic leaders are intellectually curious.* They are always seeking new ideas and are receptive to new ways of thinking and working. They know there is no simple formula for winning, and thus continuously strive to discern the underlying principles that will allow them to leverage every resource within their control. In particular, implementing requisite organization concepts and applications requires clear and comprehensive thinking.

3. *Strategic leaders "walk the talk."* They set context with their own subordinate managers about the bigger picture and how each of their functions must work together to support the company's overarching goals. This is how strategic leaders achieve genuine alignment and enthusiastic engagement.

4. *Strategic leaders recognize that they can never figure out all the answers by themselves.* They seek input from their people, share their thinking, and encourage debate in order to get to the best possible understanding. Then, they *push for results.* They model a balance between the need for proper reflection and a bias for action. Twenty years ago Harry Levinson, founder of The Levinson Institute, wrote

a noteworthy book entitled *Ready, Fire, Aim: Avoiding Management by Impulse.*[4] Dr. Levinson proved that strategic leaders engage their entire team in taking aim *before* they pull the trigger.

5. *Strategic leaders are comfortable with their positional and personal authority* and never shy away from holding their subordinate managers accountable for "keeping their word" and "earning their keep." They establish high standards, recognize and reward success, and confront failures to adhere to policy and/or commitments with appropriate discipline. And most importantly, they hold their subordinate managers accountable for being effective, value-adding leaders themselves.

6. *Finally, strategic leaders understand that to deliver full value, every aspect of the leadership system must be aligned with strategy: structure, processes, people, and human resource systems.* It is worth reiterating that every element of a strategic organizational system is inextricably linked to every other element.

Work organizations are powerful forces in the lives of managers and employees. The degree to which managerial leaders can create the organizational conditions in which people can succeed is the degree to which they can have a positive impact—on employees, their families, and, ultimately, on society. For you, the manager, I hope Denis Turcotte's story will act as a catalyst to help you renew your own commitment to identifying, developing, and promoting personal, accountability, and strategic leadership.

ABOUT THE AUTHOR

Gerald A. Kraines, M.D. is president and chief executive officer of The Levinson Institute, taking over from its founder, Dr. Harry Levinson, in 1991. He is also on the faculty of Harvard Medical School. Kraines's career has focused on enhancing leadership effectiveness: as an executive for healthcare organizations, as a teacher of leadership, as an executive coach, and since the 1980s, as a consultant to senior executives about leadership systems. Kraines brings a systems perspective to The Levinson Institute's research, education, and consultation. He is continuing Dr. Levinson's mission of disseminating in-depth knowledge about the psychological aspects of lead-

---

4   Levinson, H. *Ready, Fire, Aim: Avoiding Management by Impulse.* Cambridge, MA: The Levinson Institute, Inc., 1986.

ership, while integrating the work of Dr. Elliott Jaques about managerial leadership systems.

Dr. Kraines consults worldwide to companies of all sizes. He has helped to integrate and implement many successful corporate reorganizations resulting from rapid growth, acquisitions, mergers, and consolidations. Dr. Kraines is also the architect of the Institute's innovative Sonario™ Strategic Organization software system. Born in Chicago, Dr. Kraines received an undergraduate degree from Oberlin College, a medical degree from Case Western Reserve, and a psychiatric fellowship and postgraduate degree from Harvard Medical School. His critically acclaimed book, *Accountability Leadership*, was published in 2001.

Story of a New CEO's RO Application at Canadian Tire Acceptance Ltd

Jos J. Wintermans as told to and written by **Paul J. Tremlett**

WHAT'S IMPORTANT

- Requisite organization (RO) concepts are applied over a seven–year period by a CEO in a financial services subsidiary of a large Canadian retailer with 450 employees and gross revenues of $100M (CDN).

- How the CEO used RO to restructure the firm's managerial levels and to develop a new corporate strategy.

Results:

- grew 500 percent in seven years.

- year-over-year increases grew from eight percent to 22 percent.

- salary costs as a percent of revenue reduced four percent.

- became one of top 100 Companies in Canada to work for.

—Jos J. Wintermans

This is the story of successful managerial leadership, a story that began when Jos J. Wintermans,[2] as a first-time CEO, began applying requisite organization principles at Canadian Tire Acceptance Ltd (CTAL). It's a story about difficult, courageous decisions and about learning. It is also about better business results for the company, better working life for employees, about the growth of managerial leadership capability. So let the story begin—at the end—with the results.

The Outcomes

Within months of applying requisite organization principles, year-over-year increases in revenue shot from eight percent to 22 percent. In three years, the company grew from $100 million to $173 million (CDN) while lowering salary costs as a percentage of revenue by four percent.

Over the seven years while Jos was at the helm, the business quintupled in size and profitability rose with it. The company moved from an average player in the financial services industry, and one seriously at risk of slipping in 1988, to a leadership position. The new structure and effective application of requisite's accountability-based management principles enabled the top team to formulate a bold new strategy for the company and to rapidly take advantage of market conditions while executing it.

Within nine months of initiating structure and people changes, Jos began to see previously stifled managers highly energized and dealing with business issues head on, and very effectively. Eighteen months out, Jos said, "We were in full flight implementing our strategic growth programs, and it was happening!"[3] CTAL became the first non-banking organization in the world to acquire a MasterCard license. The structure change "primed the revenue engine and produced the results the CEO was accountable for."[4] Along with all this achievement and growth, the company became publicly recognized as one of the top 100 companies to work for in Canada.

---

1   Quote from Jos J. Wintermans, CEO Canadian Tire Acceptance Ltd., *Canadian Business*, May 1992.
2   The co-authors chose to write in the style of a story about Jos Winterman's experience at CTAL.
3   Quote from GO video interview with Jos J. Wintermans.
4   Comment at August 2005 GO Conference CEO panel.

What occurred that enabled such outstanding results? Why requisite organization principles as the foundation? Why not re-engineering or any of the other approaches of other companies as described in successful management books of the time?

To answer these questions, look to the new CEO. Jos was taking on the CEO role for the first time, and he knew was that he was accountable for it all, not just a function as in previous executive roles. He knew that the company, its employees, and the parent company (Canadian Tire Corporation) would suffer if he did not figure out how to be a good CEO. As such, he was looking for guidance, for a track to run on. But he also knew that whatever guide he chose, it had to be consistent with his own intellectual sense of the world of work, as well as provide answers to some past managerial frustrations. It had to be well thought out and systematic, provide order, and allow quick implementation.

Requisite organization filled the bill. Jos learned of it through a combination of an introduction to it by his boss who was mentoring him in this new role, by reading Elliott Jaques's *A General Theory of Bureaucracy*, and through consultants dedicated to helping managers successfully apply the principles.

Consultative Diagnosis

A second place to look lies in another key principle Jos firmly believes in, that one should enter a new role or organization consultatively. Jos spent his first four months or so establishing a sense of what he had inherited and what would need to change. He spent considerable one-on-one time with his direct reports, instituting a "morning coffee with the CEO" where he met with six to eight employees over coffee and muffins in his office, ultimately meeting with almost every employee. He chatted with them about what they thought of the company, how it was working, and what they wanted for the future—for the company and for employees. He also talked with customers and Canadian Tire dealers. What he learned began to align with his growing understanding of requisite principles and how they could provide some of the answers to both the deficiencies and opportunities that he found:

- The company appeared to have enormous potential, but had a senior management team Jos has described as "more interested in golf and curling than building the business." Costs were rising and the usage of the Canadian Tire credit card had fallen from 100 percent (before Visa and MasterCard) to as low as 38 percent.

- The company had talented people with great potential who clamored for increased opportunities to contribute, but who had little space to do it. Jos wanted a way to unleash this potential, but found that the organization's structure itself prevented it. Work functions had been grouped in confusing ways and the structure appeared to be "too tall," with too many layers.
- The roadblock to advancing the company was mostly at the top. Management lacked a methodology or model for managing the total organization and its key processes in a systemic way. The management ranks had "dead wood" and their approach at CTAL seemed like "a 1950's type domination organization" in style and tone.[5]

These conditions led Jos to believe that the company needed significant transformation. He understood that this change would have to start with himself. In order to fight the excuses that he would encounter along the way, the journey had to begin with building within himself the conviction, courage, and persistence which would be required to lead. He wanted to do this right and so enlisted the help of the consultants to perform an exacting diagnosis of the business and provide recommendations for change.

Structure Review

A structure review was undertaken in the spring of 1988. The results shocked Jos.

"They told us we had 11 layers of management, when we should have five," Jos said. "I hadn't anticipated that it would be that bad—but it was."[6]

In requisite organization terms, the most complex work and role in the company was the CEO, and it needed to operate at stratum V. This meant that CTAL required only three levels of managerial leadership between the CEO and frontline (stratum I) work roles. In effect there was considerable compression (or "jamming") in middle management. Accountability for key outputs was too widely dispersed, there was no ability to give people required accountability for completing entire tasks at their level, and too many managers were too close to the work of subordinate roles, such

---

5   Comment at August 2005 GO conference CEO panel.
6   Quote from Jos J. Wintermans, CEO Canadian Tire Acceptance Ltd, *Canadian Business*, May 1992.

that there was no value-adding, context-setting, work being performed. No wonder employees told Jos about being stifled and unable to bring their full potential to bear. Jos saw that reducing the levels of work in CTAL was "a clear solution to the mess, to cut through things and to clarify accountability."[7]

Matching People to the New Roles

With Jos's growing understanding of requisite organization principles, he further knew there is a correlation between complexity of work and an individual's capacity for managing it. People's capability, specifically their information processing capacity, needs to match role complexity if work outputs are to be achieved successfully. Armed with requisite-based assessment tools, Jos began the process of determining the fit to level of work (in this case stratum IV) of his current vice presidents. Rather shockingly, Jos found that four of his vice presidents were not operating at this level and likely would not do so in a time frame acceptable to him given the business challenges facing the company. Jos felt that a fifth Vice President might get to stratum IV sooner, but not without a significant amount of coaching regarding other dimensions of his managerial effectiveness.

Jos was coming to grips with just how much change was needed. Not only did the structure need to change drastically, but significant people changes were also required. "This was not the crew that was going to bring this company into the next decade."[8] As a result, CTAL removed four vice presidents from their positions, and through the organization review recommendations regarding grouping of work, eliminated two of the existing vice presidential roles. Jos would later point out that although staff reductions are not a goal of this process, they are an inevitable by-product and must be dealt with both at the beginning and along the way, where there is clear evidence roles are not needed and/or individuals are not performing to level. In CTAL's case, with the growth in the business that occurred, so came growth in the number of employees. However, the principles helped maintain salary cost as a percentage of revenue quite low by not allowing level creep.

Requisite organization principles provide significant guidance in determining how work can be grouped for increased clarity of accountability and reduced

---

7   Quote from GO video interview with Jos J. Wintermans.
8   Quote from Jos J. Wintermans, CEO Canadian Tire Acceptance Ltd, *Canadian Business*, May 1992.

coordination cost by minimizing the amount of cross-boundary activity. The principles assist in better understanding the interdependence of various kinds of work and determining where the structural integration point should occur, i.e. at what level—ideally, the lower in the managerial decision hierarchy the better. Decisions on grouping are iterative with those on level. The two principles come together neatly to clarify individual role accountability and provide people with fuller, richer, roles matched to their ability to contribute. They also help delineate the required lateral role relationships at each work level to effectively coordinate the organization's business process flow. In CTAL, the consultant study findings on grouping again confirmed Jos's intuition that too much integrating of work was occurring at the CEO and vice president levels. As a result, a new top team design was developed by merging some functions. Of most significance, according to Jos, was putting the finance and credit functions together to better deal with the inherent interdependence of funding with controls and to ensure more integrated decision making at the right stratum (IV not V) to effectively balance risk.

Communicating the Change

The announcement of this new structure, with mostly new incumbents, and the plan to continue to cascade structure and people decisions down through each function using requisite organization principles, created shock in the company. This had to be dealt with. Jos took many steps to communicate with employees to demonstrate a number of points. First, that the structure was a better representation of the CEO's accountability and that it was his accountability to the corporation and to shareholders to make the necessary changes. Second, that these were normal, business-driven changes and were not personal in terms of the people involved in job loss. Caring and supportive steps were taken to assist individuals leaving the company and dialogue was established with those remaining. Partly because Jos had done such a good job of engaging people, being enthusiastic, and demonstrating trust and openness during his entry to the company, most employees welcomed the changes. They quickly sensed that the right changes were occurring and would continue as the process unfolded.

Cascading the Change Down the Organization

The next step was for the stratum IV vice presidents, working individually and collectively with each other and Jos, to design the functional organizations. Each vice president was charged with creating his or her structures and choosing the people to staff it. Some further head count reductions occurred as a result of this cascading process, but more opportunities for integrating work occurred. The new roles that resulted were much more robust in terms of what VPs were accountable for. In the end, about one-third of the management structure was eliminated.

Individual Contributor Role

A further positive learning and structural outcome for Jos, the senior team, and several role holders was applying the principle in requisite organization that recognizes the need for individual contributor roles at the appropriate level of work (usually higher than one would expect). These roles fall into two types.

The first type is direct output support that provides managers with specialist knowledge and skills important for effective delivery of the manager's outputs. A credit and collections manager had most of what was required to be accountable for the outputs, the right information processing capability and particularly strong people management skills, but lacked the analytical skills for the work. CTAL created an individual contributor support role with this analytical capability at the next level down. It made a huge difference in performance.

The second type of individual contributor role is needed to manage significant enhancement work in the company: project roles that, by definition, are ad hoc parts of the structure. In CTAL, with the need to improve and enhance a variety of processes and systems, especially those requiring more sophisticated information technology, creating individual contributor roles in the information systems function, at higher levels of complexity than was typical in the company (i.e. stratum III), became a critical component of the new structure. Jos is adamant that the proper use of individual contributor roles provides a company with "creative, competitive advantage" because of what occurred at CTAL.

A final component of the beginning part of this story relates to values. A key aspect of requisite organization important to Jos was, and is, the fact that its underpinnings are about building a trust-enhanced company. Getting the structure right and operating with other requisite principles in place goes a long way to developing a trust-based organization. When people come to work every day knowing what they can count on from their manager, from their manager's manager, from their collateral teammates, and from critical cross-boundary colleagues, there is a huge impact on business results and on the quality of working life.

Jos, however, didn't want to rely on the structural change alone. He wanted to identify the company's desired values and bring them alive in the structure as appropriate in different functions and roles. He engaged a consultant to support the senior team in developing a set of CTAL values that would be used to run the business. The consultant then conducted 70 four-hour sessions with the CEO, another senior manager, and 15 employees at a time. These 70 sessions brought every employee into full dialogue about the meaning of the values and implications for working by these values in their function and role. For example, a credit collector could work in such a way as to actually improve the relationship between company and customer and the customer's regard for CTAL and its customer service. This helped connect people at the values level and brought out their inherent sense of the "rightness" of all that was happening in the company through this process.

Jos argues that this trust component of requisite organization is critical. Requisite defines work as the exercise of human judgment and discretion to complete assignments and create required outputs for the business. If there's no discretion involved, you automate. He found, and believes, that with good context setting by the manager and good fit, trusting that person to do the work is not only essential but, when done well, provides competitive advantage—and that occurred at CTAL. By having the right people at the right level doing the right work, Jos found that employees, including frontline workers in the company's call center, used the discretionary time and resources in their jobs in ways that helped the business and customers. He further argues that not a lot of companies understand this method and miss the payoffs it provides in terms of both results and employee satisfaction.

The Middle

As time went on, the initial glow of the beginning and the early wins faded and new challenges and opportunities arose. One of the principles of requisite, value-adding management is the need to set context for people around tasks being assigned—*why* we need to do this component of the work. A second principle is about *what* is expected. Called QQT/R, the model is clarity about quantity, quality, time deadlines, and the resources such as money, people, and decision authorities that will be provided to achieve the output.

In CTAL, Jos and the senior team implemented QQT/R presentations by the directors at stratum III. The top team had come to recognize, in a stratum V organization, that the stratum III roles are, as Jos puts it, "the glue in the organization." This is the stratum at which information is developed about trends, and at which critical hand-offs in the organization occur. It is the level that drives process change and improvement. These sessions were conducted in a three-tier setting, with levels V, IV, and III together in the same room.

At about year three in the journey, through the QQT/R presentation process and the fact that there was now a 20 to 30 percent increase in volume of work, a push arose for more people. Jos describes this as the point in the process where you get tested on your commitment to the principles and are tempted to compromise them. The answer to simply adding more people, and with it the likelihood of more levels, had to be "no." More creative solutions were required to diffuse the emotionality that had arisen around this issue. In the end, the top three-tier group determined that better measures were required to reflect role output accountabilities. Some critical process improvements were deemed needed in conjunction with it. Consultants were engaged to provide the required technical support.

Jos describes a real fit between the re-engineering work and a requisite management structure in terms of where in the hierarchy process accountabilities need to fit. The alignment of the two was so effective it encouraged him to use the combination of requisite organization and process re-engineering in subsequent CEO assignments.

Effective Managerial Leadership Practices for the MoR

In this period, changes and enhancements were made to other significant parts of the requisite management system. Emphasis was placed on the concept of three-tier management and the role of the manager-once-removed (MoR). This construct shifts the accountability for development of employees from their managers to the MoR, requiring him or her to get to know their capability, potential, and career aspirations. It also requires MoRs to assume accountability for their fair and equitable treatment: how their performance is judged, how they are progressing developmentally, how they are paid for the work they do and the contributions they make, holding on-going discussions about structural alignment and having the right people in the right roles, and succession planning. CTAL implemented regular MoR-led meetings of direct reporting managers, supported by human resources personnel, to discuss these matters.

Compensation

This MoR management process produced two key outcomes that Jos feels were particularly significant. The first outcome was the ability, over time, to align CTAL to another key component of requisite organization—felt-fair pay. A key finding of the requisite organization research is that people have an innate sense of what is fair to be paid for a combination of the level of work complexity and a demonstrated capability to carry it out effectively. They also feel it is unfair if individuals working at their level of complexity get pay corresponding to higher levels of work. The combined efforts of the management team and human resources enabled compensation adjustments to stay true to felt-fair pay principles. They were also able to implement a variable, but not automatically repeated, pay component that appropriately rewarded outstanding contributions.

People Development

The second outcome of the MoR management process was extraordinary people development. Through ensuring appropriate developmental plans for people were both in place and executed, the process delivered what Jos feels may be the biggest achievement of all—the incredible growth he saw in people. He feels this period in CTAL's history left a legacy of people "growing up" as managers. Many of them have since told him that the time together at CTAL was "the best part of their working life—period!"

Lessons Learned and Gifts to other CEOs (New or Not)

Jos believes that being a professional means being truly knowledgeable about your field of work. The professional work of a CEO is to comprehend organization and management as an integrated system. Jos found that requisite organization principles enhanced his professional knowledge. They guided him well in the CTAL journey as a "rookie" CEO and have guided other journeys since. They didn't provide all the answers, but they did enhance his ability to make good judgments.

Some thoughts on how to get the best from the principles include the following:
- Be yourself; don't be an "actor."
- Decide what you believe are true principles, then don't compromise them or let others do so.
- See the application of the principles as competitive advantage, because they can be.
- Be a sponge and be curious—seek to find out why something in the company is like it is; look for fundamental properties of the system. Requisite means "as required by the nature of it."
- Be skeptical and challenging.
- Be open to unexpected possibilities and opportunities.

Jos has held three other CEO roles in turnaround situations since his CTAL experience and has used requisite organization principles in each of those roles to good effect.

ABOUT THE AUTHORS

Paul J. Tremlett is president and a co-founder of *CORE*international Inc., a management consulting business dedicated to helping executives plan, design, and manage their organizations for outstanding performance. He has an extensive background in complex organization change management, strategic planning, organization restructuring, and management education and training. Prior to consulting he held various management roles with Imperial Oil Limited and Xerox in sales, marketing, operations, training, and organization development.

Tremlett focuses particularly on organization design and redesign. He has helped more than two dozen public and private sector organizations align their work systems to more effectively achieve strategic and operational goals. He has also provided services in management, organization, and human resources development and effectiveness. Tremlett has also designed and facilitated numerous management education, team development, consulting skills, and change management programs. Academic credentials include a BComm from the University of Alberta and an MSc in organization behavior from The American University, Washington, DC.

An experienced CEO with a record of significant value creation in challenging business environments, **Jos J. Wintermans** is president and CEO of Cygnal Technologies. Wintermans's major goal is to deliver value in turnaround situations by organizing people, assets and processes to put the business in delivery mode.

Wintermans served as president and CEO of the Sodisco-Howden Group from 2001 to 2004. He restructured the company, which subsequently became the leading distributor of Hardlines and Building Materials for Independent Merchants across Canada. He also served as president and CEO of Skyjack Inc. and Rogers CableSystems Ltd, and president, CEO, and member of the board of Canadian Tire Acceptance Ltd.

With an MBA from Queen's University of Kingston (Ontario) and a Master of Law from Leyden University, Leyden, The Netherlands, Wintermans has an honorary fellowship from Ryerson University for introducing requisite into business in Canada. He is also chair of the Junior Achievement of Canada Foundation.

The New DNA of Corporate Governance

Mark Van Clieaf and Janet Langford Kelly

WHAT'S IMPORTANT

- Too much emphasis on the compliance role of boards can jeopardize their strategic management responsibilities.

- Many companies are not achieving their potential, because the board is not properly engaged in evaluating the CEO's strategic capabilities.

- The authors use their own research and Elliott Jaques's concepts to propose a framework that describes board and CEO Levels of Work and Levels of Executive Capability to help the board in deciding the capability of the CEO needed to execute the strategic plan, in establishing CEO compensation, and in their other strategic responsibilities.

We believe that Level of Work/Level of Executive Capability can make corporate governance work much easier and clearer in providing both disciplined processes and real substance.

[1]Ultimately, governance is about wealth creation, not compliance. Here's a framework for directors to help them keep their eye on the real prize: fulfilling the strategic duty to long-term shareholders.

Enron's rapid descent into bankruptcy, followed by numerous corporate accounting scandals (WorldCom most notable among them) caused a flurry of legislative, regulatory—and ultimately commercial—activity designed to ensure against corporate chicanery. As a result, corporate governance has come to be confused with compliance activity—with directors charged with ensuring that the corporation they serve and its management are in compliance with a dizzying array of rules designed to create board independence and management accountability. The recent WorldCom and Enron settlements, in which directors agreed to pay US$31 million dollars personally to shareholders, sent further shockwaves through the corporate world. In the aftermath of these settlement agreements, many law firms issued client memos focused on ensuring that directors have fully met their compliance and oversight duties in order to merit the protection of the business judgment rule. Fully four years after the demise of Enron, compliance governance remains the focus of most governance discussions.

The problem with this emphasis on compliance governance is that compliance and oversight constitute only a portion of a director's duty to ensure that the business and affairs of a corporation are managed "by or under the direction of" the board. The ultimate goal of corporations is to continue to create wealth as a viable and growing entity for the long term; directors have a proactive responsibility to ensure that the corporation they serve has those processes and metrics in place—including strategic and financial plans—that they believe will accomplish this end. In other words, they have a strategic duty, not just a compliance duty. To fulfill his or her "strategic duty," a director must ensure that the corporation he or she serves has three key interdependent processes that, when designed effectively, integrate into a holistic organizational and leadership framework for the corporation's future and sustainability:

---

1   This article was previously published in the March 2005 issue of *Directorship*.

1. Board review/approval of three year-plus business plans and strategies and setting of appropriate metrics to evaluate longer-term management performance;

2. Succession-planning and talent-management processes; and

3. Appropriately structured pay for longer-term performance.

Given the magnitude of the work involved in ensuring such processes are in place and appropriately integrated, we estimate that boards should spend at least 60 percent of their time on their strategic duty.

Although this strategic duty is rarely discussed in corporate governance conversations, both the Delaware judiciary and long-term stockholders assume that boards have a strategic duty of longer term planning and strategic goal-setting. For example, in a 2004 speech to the Tulane Corporate Law Institute, former Delaware Chief Justice Norman Veasey reassured the audience that the business judgment rule remained available to protect the strategic review and goal-setting he assumed boards engage in:

> *Although the law of fiduciary duty recognizes the evolving expectations of the standards of directors and officers, we must keep in mind that the business judgment rule continues unabated to protect directors' decisions made in good faith, enabling them to **set strategic goals for the corporation** and to be relatively free to engage in prudent risk-taking.* (Emphasis added.)

Similarly, the Council of Institutional Investors, which represents 130 pension funds with US$3 trillion in invested assets, recently issued a policy statement on executive compensation assuming boards have engaged in long-term goal-setting and performance measurement to which executive compensation is linked:

> *The Council endorses reasonable, appropriately structured pay-for-performance programs that reward executives for **sustainable, superior performance** over the "long term," consistent with a company's investment horizon and generally **considered to be five or more years for mature companies and at least three years for other companies.** (Emphasis added.)

Unfortunately, most boards do not appear to have approved three-year-plus business plans and corresponding metrics to evaluate management performance, and then tied executive compensation to the achievement of three-year-plus goals emanating from these longer-term strategic plans (beyond a one- to two-year focus on current operations). Paul Hodgson of *The Corporate Library* recently analyzed the 2004 proxy statements of the top 2000 US companies. He concluded that 85 percent of these companies had not disclosed multi-year metrics to evaluate management performance. The 2001 proxy statements analysis by MVC Associates reached a similar conclusion: Only 11 percent of the S&P 500 had set strategic goals for management beyond three years.

Not surprisingly in the absence of such plans and goals, most corporations are not creating long-term sustainable growth and intrinsic value. A financial analysis of the top 2,100 companies in the Russell 3000 just completed by MVC Associates revealed that 56 percent of these companies have failed to return a profit greater than their cost of capital over the five years ending in 2003. This should raise a bright red flag for investors and the boards that the business model/strategy of these companies needs to be transformed.

If capitalism, and fiduciary capitalism in particular, is to live up to the expectations of the millions of people whose future financial security depends on long-term corporate growth and positive return on invested capital (ROIC), it is critical that directors and officers spend substantially more time and energy fulfilling their higher order strategic duty than on their lower order compliance and oversight duties. So how is a board to fulfill its strategic duty, its duty of sustainable governance?

Five Levels of Management Work and Capability

To fulfill its duty of sustainable governance, a board must ensure that the corporation it oversees has three integrated components:

1. A three- to five-year or longer strategic and organizational plan, with clear and measurable goals, and accountabilities (what, by when, with what resources), and decision authorities for achieving the plan that directors and management believe in (not just an aspirational plan with no clear accountabilities);

2. A leadership team capable of performing at the level of complexity required by that plan (now and in three to seven years from now); and

Measurement tools and a pay-for-performance compensation design that both enable the board to assess the execution of the plan over time and appropriately incentivize management to create long-term value while equitably sharing that value created between employees and shareholders (labor and capital).

In more than ten years of research, MVC Associates has developed a framework called Levels of Work (LOW) and Levels of Executive Capability (LOC) to help directors and officers in their governance efforts. The Five Levels of Work provides an empirically proven set of tools, processes and principles to define work complexity, accountability and decision-making authority and ensures that value is being added at each Level of Work for customers, shareholders, and global society. These levels are based on principles of complexity and how they relate to value creation, not the size of the company. This framework builds on two streams of more than 30 years of earlier management research worldwide known as requisite organization (RO) and the Viable Systems Model (VSM). We see these as building blocks for the "new DNA" of corporate governance that provides real substance to board and management processes.

The first principle is that there are five levels of CEO work and five levels of corporate governance: at any given time a corporation's strategic needs will be at one of these five levels[2]. The Level of Work (LOW) framework uses six factors to determine which of five levels of work and innovation is required by an organization to sustain itself as a viable system. Four of these factors are the level of innovation complexity; the planning horizon; the level of complexity of assets/capital managed; and the level of complexity of stakeholder groups to be managed given the number of different businesses and countries in which the enterprise may operate.[3] (See Figure 2.3.1.)

There are five corresponding levels of CEO accountability and capability. The Level of Capability (LOC) identifies the level-specific conceptual and planning skills and other competencies that match to each requisite Level of Work. Each jump in level is a discontinuous jump both in work complexity and conceptual and strategic thinking.

When a board has identified the level of work required by an enterprise, it has also identified the Organization Value Added—OVA™—that management should add at each level. This framework establishes an equitable basis for compensating the CEO role versus compensation for other CEOs, as well as internal pay equity relative to direct reports and other levels in the managerial hierarchy, based on \research.

It also reveals the shortcoming of current comparative practices, which determine suggested CEO compensation based on medians and percentiles for peer groups: CEO roles within peer groups may be operating at significantly different Levels of

---

2   The authors' CEO and corporate governance levels of work are comparable to Jaques's strata, with the CEO level 1 corresponding to stratum III and so forth so that that CEO level 5 corresponds to Jaques's stratum VII.

3   Editorial note: The author and several other authors in the book chose to use their own descriptive features for Jaques's levels of work complexity in place of Jaques's measure of time-span of the role—the length of the longest task the CEO is accountable for working on.

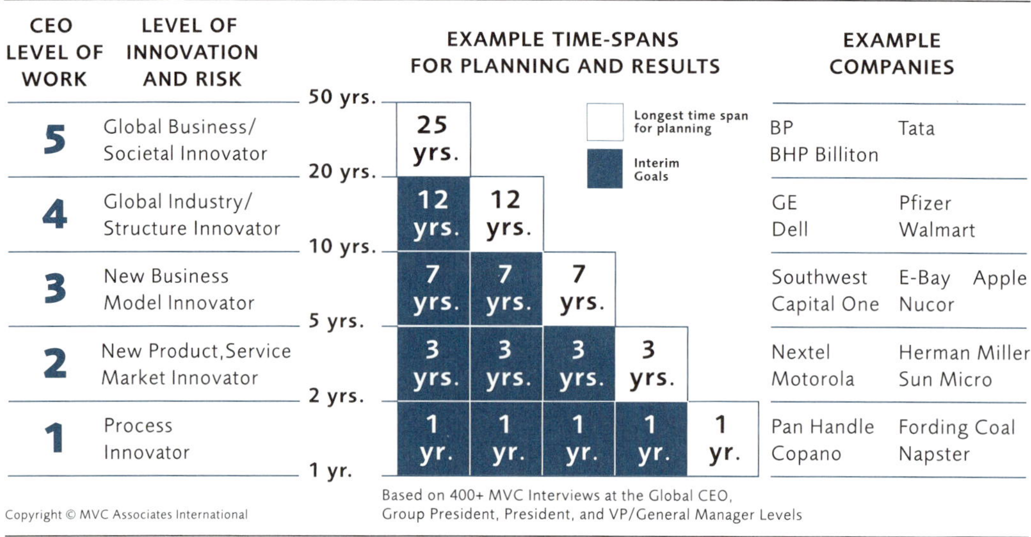

FIGURE 2.3.1 MVC ASSOCIATES INTEGRATED LEVELS OF WORK AND LEVELS OF CORPORATE GOVERNANCE FRAMEWORK

Work complexity and so traditional peer group comparisons result in overpayment of the less complex CEO roles and underpayment for more complex CEO roles.

To illustrate this, let's compare an oil and gas income trust to a global business like BP, both which are in the energy sector. An income trust (e.g., real estate or oil and gas such as Copano Energy, Panhandle Royalty, Fording Coal) focuses on maximizing quarterly dividend payouts and cash flow from the existing asset base. This enterprise, if truly an income trust, really has no strategic needs; there is no expectation for investing new capital for innovation in new products, new services, and new businesses. The focus is on operational leadership, and the decision-making authority granted by the board is for short-term core business process efficiencies to maximize return on invested capital. Given that the Level of Work is at level 1, this enterprise only requires a process innovator, level 1 CEO (Figure 2.3.1)[4]. Because the CEO role is in the operational leadership domain, it should be paid commensurate with this level of complexity, innovation and decision-making authority over assets delegated by the board.

---

4   Elliott Jaques defined eight strata of work complexity applicable to organizations. Mark Van Clieaf has worked with Jaques's work levels and defined five levels of CEO work. Van Clieaf's CEO Level 1 corresponds to Jaques's work level III and his CEO Level 5 corresponds to Jaques's Stratum VII.

Contrast this income trust with a global business/societal innovator, level 5 CEO role (e.g., BP, Unilever, P&G, Nestle, Alcan) accountable for a global entity, operating in at least three industry sectors, with 30 or more business units presidents who are accountable for investing in new products and new business models in 40 or more countries.

This corporation has dramatically more complex strategic needs and requires a CEO role accountable for, in addition to the ongoing operational needs:

- Growing profit and return on risk-adjusted capital over the next two-to-ten years from investments in new products, new services, new markets, and new businesses;
- Envisioning and making ten-year-plus investment decisions in research and development to create future industries (e.g., hydrogen energy, genomics, food from plant protein to feed the world) and manufacturing plant location decisions that will drive sustainable returns of the enterprise for shareholders;
- Defining a set of values and a purpose for business and its contribution to worldwide society today and 10-20 (or more) years into the future in enhancing peace, prosperity, and the equitable distribution of wealth globally, in so far as its business operations affect these.

A CEO role operating at this level of work complexity and long-term value creation should be compensated at a multiple of 16 to 32 times more than the CEO of the income trust if the latter CEO is paid fairly.[5]

Thus, in different corporations different levels of value can be added by the CEO role, each of which requires different levels of executive capability and merits different levels of defensible CEO compensation.

Applying Levels of Work and Levels of Capability in Fulfilling the "Strategic Duty"

Once boards step back and define the level of work required by the corporation, and thus the CEO level of accountability, the tasks of determining the strategic time frame for planning and the Level of Capability required by—and appropriate compensation for—management become much clearer and easier to accomplish. A real-life case study that we teach at the Ivey School of Business will illustrate this. The

---

5 See www.mvcinternational.com for specific articles related to research about excessive compensation, "felt fair" pay and the internal executive pay equity multiplier.

board of a US$1 billion technology company with poor financial results, responding to pressure from institutional shareholders, removed the CEO and replaced him with the best candidate from the current executive team. Within a year, the newly promoted CEO requested the board to more than triple his compensation based on the industry peer group compensation levels.

MVC Associates facilitated a discussion of independent board members using its Level of Work (LoW) framework. The independent board members agreed that the company needed a CEO role held accountable at CEO level 3—Business Model Innovator—because the enterprise required a new business model given changing technologies, aggressive new competitors, emerging new markets and the fact the company had not returned a profit greater than its cost of capital in five years. The leadership capabilities required for the CEO level 3—Business Model Innovator role included:

- Conceptualizing and implementing a new business strategy and economic model enabling the company to create a positive return on invested capital;
- Planning out three, five and seven years and setting accountable milestones for the company transformation as the industry changes with new technologies and emerging new markets; and
- Continuing to meet short-term revenue and profit growth targets while managing a change process that requires transformation of the company's structure, technologies, processes and profit drivers.

The independent directors then assessed the current CEO's Level of Capability, (we call this the Leadership Value Added—LVA™), relative to the skills/capabilities required for the newly defined CEO Level of Work. Each independent director completed a rating and assessment tool designed by MVC Associates, rating the current CEO on 12 key skill dimensions based on the agreed CEO 3 Level of Work and other strategic competencies we helped the board identify. After analyzing the rating results, it was apparent that the board believed that the current CEO was a great operator—CEO level 1-capable (LOC)—but not capable of performing effectively at the CEO level 3–Business Model Innovator level.

Finally, the board discussed the US$10 million total direct compensation level requested by the current CEO compared to the current US$1.6 million approved total compensation package. The US$10 million targeted compensation level was based on a peer group the current CEO suggested in the same industry. After analyzing the peer group companies and the level of complexity of their CEO roles (not their size,

Jaques's Work Strata	Level of Response	Level of Innovation & Investment Risk	Level of Performance Measurement	CEO Level of Work	Level of Corporate Governance
VII	Global Inter-Generational	Global Business & Global Societies	Global Sustainability & Societal Wealth *beyond 20 years*	5	Enterprise Sustainability & Contribution to Capitalism, Democracy & Peace Worldwide
VI	Global Transformational	Global Industry Structure & Citizenship	Global Integrity, Ethics, & CSR *up to 20 years*	4	Stewardship of Businesses, Reputational Risk & Public Good Globally
V	Transformational	New Business Model	Business Viability, Return on Capital & Shareholder Wealth *up to 10 years*	3	Strategic Duty & Business Model Viability & Risk
IV	Breakthrough	New Product New Service New Market	Balance Integration & Return on Capital *up to 5 years*	2	Oversight Duty & Growth/Risk Assessment Medium-Term
III	Predictive and Systematic	Process	Effectiveness of Current Operations *up to 2 years*	1	Financial Duty & Statutory Compliance
II	Diagnostic and Situational	Quality and Continuous Improvement	Efficiency *up to 1 year*		
I	Procedural	Service Excellence	Feedback *up to 30 days*		

FIGURE 2.3.2

revenue or market cap), we concluded that four of the five peer companies selected were CEO level 4—Industry Innovator roles, operating across multiple business models and multiple countries. In other words, the roles weren't truly comparable, and the more complex CEO roles merited significantly higher levels of executive compensation than either the "as is" CEO role actually being performed at the client company or the "should be" CEO role based on the strategic needs of the enterprise.

We mapped out all the diagnostic results on flip charts for the board to illustrate the interdependencies and degrees of alignment: (See Figure 2.3.2.)

- Level of Work—CEO level 3—Business Model Innovator
- Level of Executive Capability—CEO level 1—Process Innovator
- Level of Requested Pay—CEO level 4—Industry Innovator

Once this analysis was complete, the board was surprised to see the degree of misalignment:

- There was a gap of three Levels of Work between the Level of Executive Capability (LOC) of the current CEO and the Level of Work (LOW) of most of the benchmarked peer group CEO roles.
- Even more, there was a gap of two Levels of Work between the Level of Executive Capability of the current CEO and the Level of Work required by the company

Stated differently, if the board determined the CEO's appropriate compensation by the traditional approaches of benchmarking the competition, they would have agreed to pay the current CEO four to eight times more than the level of compensation merited given his personal level of leadership capability.

Mostly importantly the board not only could not justify the compensation demands, it needed a CEO role that would be held accountable at a higher Level of Work (LOW) than currently, and a new CEO capable of operating at the equivalent Level of Executive Capability (LOC). Based on this organizational and leadership analysis, the board determined that it needed a new CEO—despite the fact that the current CEO had performed admirably in doing the necessary operational work to get the corporation to its current point and had produced improved short-term financial results.

The board started a nine-month search for a new CEO, as there was no internal candidate with the requisite level of executive capability required.

Boards and CEOs also need to be careful not to allow CEO tenure to distort executive accountability. Just because a CEO may be two years away from retirement does not mean the CEO role should only be held accountable for one- to two-year operational work. Doing so risks the longer-term sustainability of the enterprise and continues to create the problem of excessive compensation for CEO accountabilities at too low a Level of Work.

In the current high-profile CEO leadership change at Hewlett-Packard (HP) with Carly Fiorina's departure, some have suggested HP needs a real operator CEO. If the HP board went through a similar process and analysis to the above case study, they might determine that this is not the case. Our preliminary analysis suggests what they really require is at least a CEO level 4—Global Industry Innovator role. This then has implications for the leadership competency profile the board should be using to assess potential candidates with a track record of performance/potential at the matching CEO 4—Level of Capability.

The Level of Work and Level of Capability framework provides the processes, diagnostics and substance to facilitate sustainable-governance decision-making and organizational design. We term this the "DNA" of strategic governance because it is the intertwined double helix of Levels of Work and Levels of Capability that makes this framework so effective. Those directors and officers wishing to discharge their strategic duty may find the logic and research outlined appealing.

We believe that Level of Work/Level of Executive Capability can make corporate governance work much easier and clearer in providing both disciplined processes and real substance. Regardless of whether these integrated principles, processes and tools we have outlined are used, however, a board that can demonstrate such organizational and leadership planning processes which were undertaken in good faith, and with appropriate external expertise as the judiciary has already outlined, will have met its fiduciary duties, regardless of the ultimate results of the chosen business strategy. A board that has not ensured that the corporation it oversees has such organizational and leadership planning processes may find itself outside the protection of Delaware's director exculpation provisions regardless of the amount of compliance governance it has pursued. As former Chief Justice Veasey wrote in the Disney case:

> *Where a director consciously ignores his or her duties to the corporation, thereby causing economic injury to the stockholders, the director's actions are either "not in good faith" or "involve intentional misconduct." Thus plaintiff's allegations support claims that fall outside the liability waiver provided under Disney's certificate of incorporation.*

ABOUT THE AUTHORS

Mark Van Clieaf is managing director of MVC Associates International, a leading consultancy in integrating CEO scorecard design, optimal management structure design, enterprise performance measurement, CEO succession planning and talent management, and executive pay for performance linked to value for shareholders and society.

With more than 25 years experience of line management in sales and marketing and consulting experience, including a number of years with Price Waterhouse, Van Clieaf's research and consulting on the Five Levels of CEO Work, Five Levels of CEO Capability, and Five Levels of Corporate Governance and the link to shareholder and societal value are recognized worldwide. Over an 18 year consulting career he has applied Levels of Work research, principles, and tools in working with clients on CEO Scorecard design, enterprise performance management, design of optimal management structures, CEO succession planning, executive search, and Pay for Performance. Widely published in publications, such as *Directorship* and *Corporate Governance Advisor*, Van Clieaf is a guest editor of the strategy issue of *Human Resource Planning.*

Janet Langford Kelly's corporate experience with levels of work and requisite organization principles, along with her expertise in corporate law, corporate governance, and the business judgment rule provides her with a unique vantage point in advising boards of directors on accountability, decision authority, and pay for performance systems design.

Janet is a member of the board of trustees, Columbia Funds; Adjunct Professor at Northwestern University School of Law; former executive vice president, corporate development, general counsel & secretary, The Kellogg Company; and former SVP, secretary and general counsel, Sara Lee Corporation. Previously, she held the positions of partner, Corporate & Securities Group, Sidley and Austin; and Associate at Wachtell, Lipton, Rosen & Katz.

 **4**

A Method for Training CEOs of Small, Growing Entrepreneurial Organizations

Atilio A. Penna, Ph.D

WHAT'S IMPORTANT

- CEOs of entrepreneurial, fast-growing organizations greatly benefit by understanding the levels of work approach to managerial leadership.

- Working with a requisite organization (RO) consultant helps an entrepreneur to apply his or her full current potential capability in growing the firm.

- RO helps to decide when growth in operations requires another managerial level be put in place, and when more formal systems should be established.

Elliott Jaques said, "Atilio, focus on the transition." Just these five words suffice to highlight a truly significant event in the latest years of my practice, words that illuminated the following ten years of my professional performance, both in consulting work and in the attempt to conceptualize the change and growth processes that entrepreneurs face and which lead them to fully effect the transition from the current level to the next.

In that sultry and rainy winter night in Buenos Aires, the heat that anticipated a difficult summer was only comparable to the intensity of the discussion in which Dr. Elliott Jaques urged me to challenge his ideas and contrast them with mine, in the framework of joint reflection on observed experiences with the entrepreneurs and their organizations.

Only the passing of time, renewed experience, and subsequent conceptualization work with my colleagues enabled me to give full value to the formidable quantum change that this encounter with Jaques triggered in my professional development.

Jaques's straightforward, vital, and generous attitude—and his encouragement to debate his ideas—surprised me and took me aback at first. But it became a phenomenal drive for fully appreciating the two long hours that our work in common lasted. The experiences, concepts, doubts, and emotions expressed by Elliott Jaques in that meeting enriched my practice for many years to come.

Used to the quiet of psychoanalytic practice, trained in economic, administrative, and sociological analysis, being an informed practitioner of the concepts and proposals of requisite organization—the presence, the voice, and the debate with Jaques were an invitation to acquire confidence and hope in my own ideas and experience.

My later work, both at work with my clients and their managers and with my colleagues in teaching, research, and consulting, were nourished in varying degrees by that dramatic turn Jaques proposed to me almost 15 years before.[2]

---

1   De Saint- Exupéry, A. *The Little Prince*. Originally published in 1943. Fort Washington, PA, Harvest Books 2000.

2   One of the products of this process was the Theory of Organizational Transition, created in 2001 and 2002 with Dr. Emeric Solymossy. Solymossy, E. and Penna, A. (2001) *Sustainable Growth for the Small Business: Theory of Organizational Transition* Second USASBE/SBIDA Joint Annual National Conference. Florida, USA. http/:www.workcomplexity.com.

In the text that follows, I will be sharing with you the present state of these practices for the assistance to growing entrepreneurs. An extended fully referenced version of this article, both in English and in Spanish, enriched with video recorded material of testimonials from Argentinean entrepreneurs, is available on the GO Society website. In addition to presenting the method, this article aims to open a debate on concepts and practices that support constructing a method for improving the assistance given to entrepreneurs to resolve the problems they confront in their roles of e-CEOs and of their SEOs (described below), which often create risky situations for small companies.

Objective

The objective of this article is to present the details and the results of a method used for assisting entrepreneurial CEOs (e-CEOs) in solving the problems they face as rapid company growth forces major changes in their work and that of their subordinates.

This method has been proven effective in:

1. facilitating the application of the entrepreneur's current potential capability to his or her performance as e-CEO,
2. solving problems created by increases in operations that require adding levels to the structure of the small entrepreneurial organization (SEO),
3. enhancing the degree of formalization of the organizational structure, and
4. contributing to the long-term sustainability of small companies, even under conditions of significant contextual crises.

The Nature of the Problem

Sustained growth of a small company increases the complexity of their operations, in both the vertical and horizontal dimensions of the organizational structure, within relatively short periods of time.

Such changes in size and complexity are a challenge for the entrepreneur, who must face problems that are new to him or her and that persist in time, and for whose solution he or she lacks the necessary experience and tools. The entrepreneur is aware that his or her knowledge, skills, and experience no longer suffice for

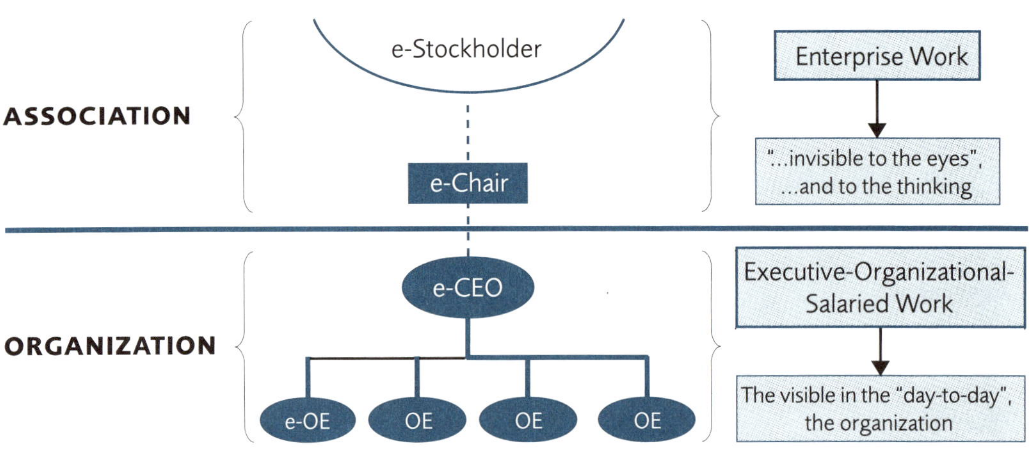

FIGURE 2.4.1: TWO TYPES OF WORK IN A SMALL ENTREPRENEURIAL ORGANIZATION

managing the business he or she has created, and which is now undergoing changes both in size and in complexity.

"I could get up to here quite well, but now I feel at the end of the rope and I do not know how to go on. I am not sure if I want to have such a large business as I have now, but on the other hand it feels to me like a sin not to take full advantage of what I have built together with my people. I do not want to shrink my business, but on the other hand I fear I may be going over my head if I continue as I am doing now." These are the words of Mr. "E," 42, married, one newborn child, founder and owner of a successful food service business in Argentina. This verbatim quotation could have come from numerous entrepreneurs who approach my consultation in the same conditions: the very success of their entrepreneurial projects led them to face challenges they are unable to solve, and less so by themselves!

Some consultants suggest that entrepreneurs take certain training courses and get advice from specialized professionals who can provide solutions for the new problems that they now confront. This approach, though valid and necessary, is in my experience insufficient. The new problems are complex and their solutions require progressive, sequential, and parallel mid- and long-term actions.

In order to obtain and stabilize the new organization required by the current volume of operations and thus achieve business sustainability, e-CEOs have to move through the present stratum of complexity in which they are operating to the next

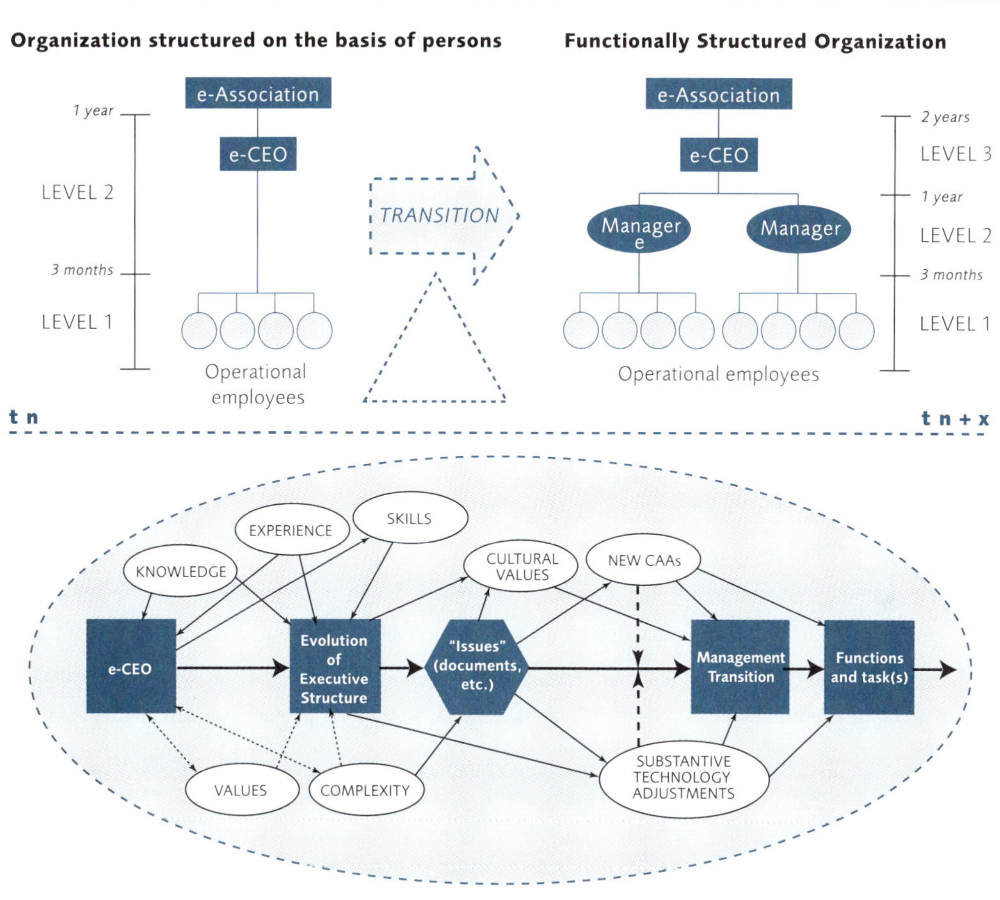

FIGURE 2.4.2 TRANSITION OF A LEVEL II ORGANIZATION TOWARDS A LEVEL III ORGANIZATION IN A SMALL ENTREPRENEURIAL ORGANIZATION, FROM AN ORGANIZATION STRUCTURED ON THE BASIS OF PERSONS TO A FUNCTIONALLY STRUCTURED ORGANIZATION

one above. This transition requires a series of parallel processes that involve not only the entrepreneur, but affect the whole organization as well.

Entrepreneurs should undertake integral training and development to obtain and build the new work skills they require. To use them properly, however, they also require the support of a process of systematic reflection on the characteristics and requirements of the new role to increase their comprehension of the distinction between executive and enterprise work.

	Factor	1990	→	2000	2001	→	2006
1	Volume of operations*	100/2	→	1100/18	1200/20	→	4000/50
2	CAC stratum of e-CEO	II	→	II	III	→	III
3	Quantity of levels in the organization	2	→	2	2	→	3
4	Quantity of managers (including e-CEO)	1	→	1	2	→	6
5	Degree of organizational formalization**	Pre-historical	→	Low	Low / Medium	→	Medium / High

(*) Expressed as total billing amount at constant prices and total of employees in the organization, assigning 100 to the 1990 total billing amount.

(**) This concept will be described in detail in point 5 G, which deals with evolution of the SEO's executive structure.

FIGURE 2.4.3: RESULTS ACHIEVED BY THIS METHOD IN AN ARGENTINE SERVICE COMPANY

It is crucial in this process to differentiate both kinds of work, as the entrepreneurs are normally engaged in both of them simultaneously and make short-term decisions that involve both, often with insufficient awareness of the future consequences in each. Figure 2.4.1 illustrates these two types of work.

Entrepreneurs who are used to action must now build new habits of reading, reflection, evaluation, and strategic analysis and discussion sessions before and while re-designing their organizations. At the same time, the transition of some existing subordinates from one stratum to another is facilitated, and also new employees are brought in to provide the required work capabilities in the strata left vacant by the vertical movement of both the CEO and some of his or her subordinates.

New methods, tools and information, communication, control, and management systems must be adapted and created to support the new roles created in the organization. Figure 2.4.2 illustrates succinctly the processes described for both dimensions: the e-CEO and the organization. Even though this was the result of joint work with Emeric Solymossy eight years after my encounter with Jaques, surely the seed of Jaques's five words was present in its conception.

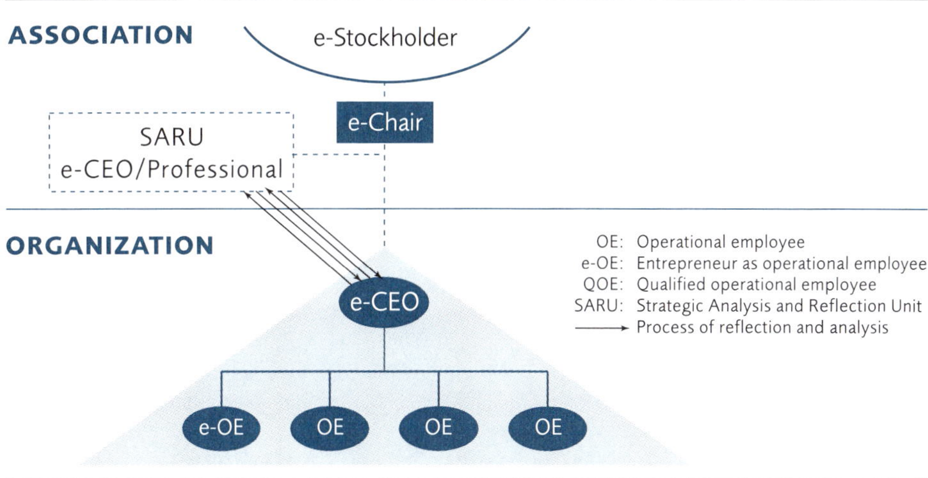

FIGURE 2.4.4: ENTREPRENEUR-CEO´S REFLECTION PROCESS

Results Obtained

The method presented facilitates the application of the CEO's capability by creating conditions for reflective and systematic practice in a simple and effective manner. It also facilitates the evolution of the executive structure (EEE) by:

1. increasing formalization,
2. increasing operational standardization,
3. adding one level to the organization,
4. developing and incorporating the current capabilities required by the new situation, and
5. facilitating the transition of an operational structure organized upon the knowledge that people possess to a functionally organized structure.

This last concept will be elaborated upon in the section that deals with the concept of the evolution of the executive structure of the small entrepreneurial organization (SEO).

Figure 2.4.3 shows results achieved by applying this method in an Argentine service company, and gives an example of the above.

Materials available on the internet, quoted in the web version of this article, provide access to testimonies from two business owners who effected the level transition mentioned in the figure above. Along with other efforts in the fields of study,

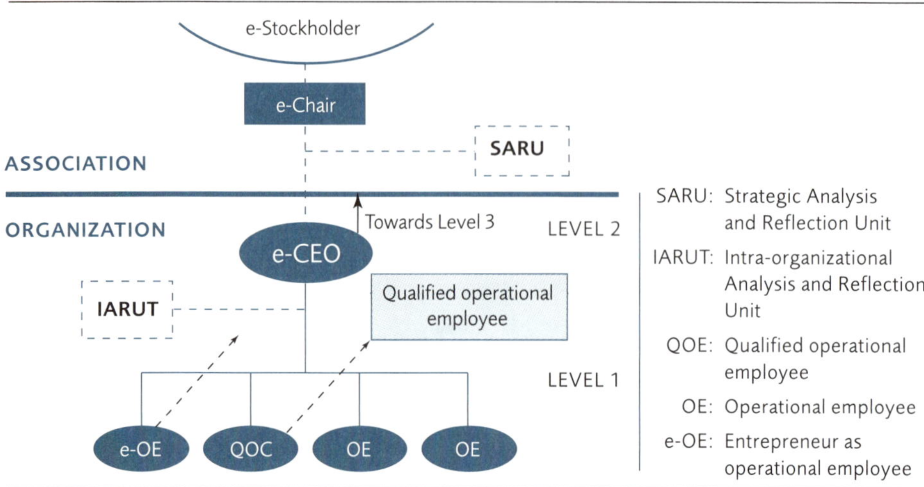

FIGURE 2.4.5: ENTERPRISE STRUCTURES AND INTRA-ORGANIZATIONAL ANALYSIS AND REFLECTION UNIT TEAMS (IARUTS)

training, and research both on the above mentioned theoretical developments and on the method presented in this paper, they contribute to surmount the confusion that comes from conceiving the SEO as a less evolved stage on the way to the final objective of becoming a large organization, without regarding the SEO as an object for study on its own, distinct and unique. While most SEOs never become large companies, many can achieve long-term sustainability through effective organizational design, right staffing, requisite remuneration and the wise use of capital, technological, and symbolic resources.

We will now turn to exploring how SEO growth distorts the designed organizational structure.

A Description of the Method for CEOs and SEOs Consultant-supported Development Process

Let us summarize the proposed method.

A) The intervention begins when the entrepreneur requests help to deal with his or her company's growing pains. The consultant begins to assist the entrepreneur by setting up a Strategic Analysis and Reflection Unit (SARU) (These are really "CEO and consultant personal development and strategy and management system planning sessions.") The SARU has two functions:

1. It facilitates the development of the entrepreneur's (e-CEO) skilled knowledge from that which served him or her well at stratum II to the skilled knowledge now required at stratum III.

2. It supports the evolution of the executive structure (EEE) from two to three levels by splitting out and raising the level of communication, information and control.

Figure 2.4.4 shows the location of the SARU we are proposing.

B) Consultant proposes an agreement on the time, space, and nature of the work to be done in common in the SARU. The responsibilities of each part are defined, as well as the content and the forms of the assistance that the consultant will provide to the e-CEO and the Small Growing Entrepreneurial Organization (SGEO). Another, more experienced consultant will in turn assist this consultant.

C) Once the agreement is made, the work on the e-CEO's problems starts, focusing on his or her own task, that of his or her subordinates and on the emotional consequences of such tasks. The consultant introduces writing and reading as working habits for the e-CEO and later for all employees in the SGEO. At the same time, the e-CEO acquires the practice of systematic reflection in the SARU. Recently, Mintzberg has highlighted the great value of reflection for the development of managerial abilities.[3]

D) The consultant and e-CEO plan agendas for their periodic strategic coaching sessions. These will include the e-CEO's leadership and organizational issues, along with both education in managerial work concepts, ways, methods, and practices inherent to strata II and III, and applying these to the current problem analysis and solution.

In the same manner, the consultant uses problem analysis to assist the e-CEO. This facilitates the inclusion of new instruments and procedures in the systems of information, control, recording, and management of the SGEO. The e-CEO can thus continue to work in stratum III—with the employees in the now restructured managerial stratum II, and operational employees in stratum I—keeping the internal processes and the outputs of the SGEO both under control and within quality standards.

---

3   Mintzberg, H. *Managers Not MBAs*, Chapter 9: The Development of Managerial Education, Berrett-Koehler Publishers, 2004.

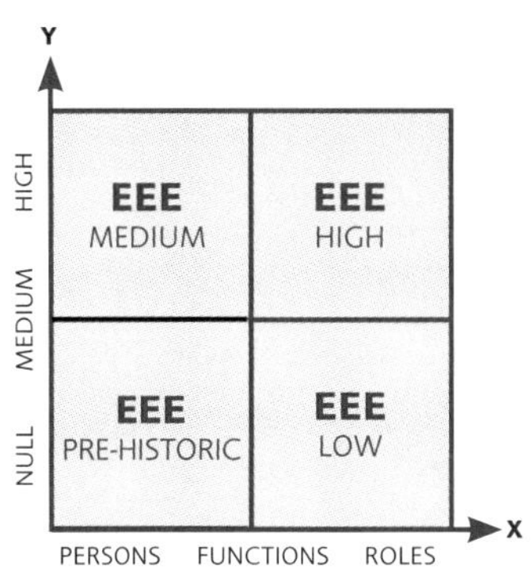

Y AXIS:

Existence and use of written records and of management tools with respect to:

1. Institutional and cultural memory
2. Stock levels
3. Financial flow
4. Economic and cost calculation
5. Calculations and forms of supply and use of human, technological and material resources
6. Activity levels b y functional area
7. Legal regulations in force in context
8 to 11: same as 1, 2 and 3 in X axis

X AXIS:

Basis for task structuring

1. Flowcharts and circuits for the structuring of functional areas and/or role specifications
2. Operational limits by person, functional area and role
3. Descriptions of tasks and operations by person, function, and/or general areas and roles

FIGURE 2.4.6: THE EXECUTIVE STRUCTURE'S DEGREE OF EVOLUTION (EEE) IN A SMALL ENTREPRENEURIAL ORGANIZATION (SEO)

E) The consultant's approach in supporting e-CEOs must necessarily be multi-disciplinary. In my practice, in addition to Jaques's levels concepts, I use concepts and methods from:[4]

- Accounting and administration tools initiated by Luca Paccioli;
- Wilfred Bion's basic assumptions groups; and
- Max Weber's types of authority.

As a result of this task, the e-CEO produces and installs in the SGEO the instruments mentioned in item D). The consultant should include, either at the request of the e-CEO or on personal initiative, other persons in strata I, II or III, whether in employment or not. This inclusion in the SGEO and/or in the SARU should be carefully managed to safeguard the proper integration of the SGEO's new capabilities into the social and work systems.

F) As the work advances and gradually materializes the objects and processes of C), D), and E), the e-CEO works in his company employing practices of direct assistance, thus integrating the new capabilities of staff in strata I and II, with the support of stratum III capabilities from outside the company, in such a way as to make possible and to effect the generation of direct delegated outputs.

The work processes described in items A) through F) require no less than two calendar years, during which the e-CEO and the consultant work face-to-face, at

---

4   Bion, W., *Experiences in Groups*, London, Tavistock Publishers. 1948. Paccioli, L. *Trattato di partita doppia*, Venice, 1494. Weber, M. *Economy and Society*, G. Roth & R. Witich, 1968.

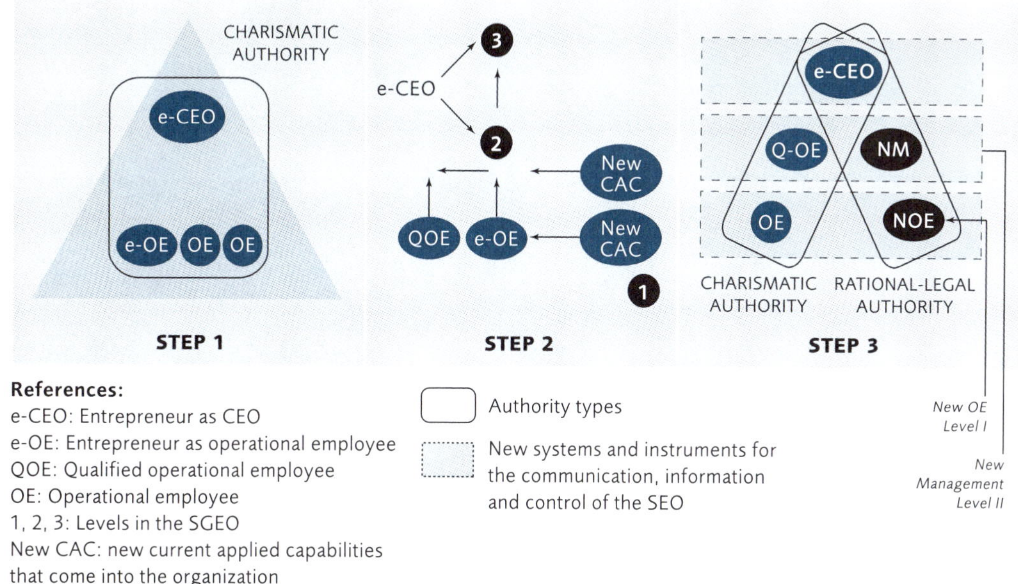

References:
e-CEO: Entrepreneur as CEO
e-OE: Entrepreneur as operational employee
QOE: Qualified operational employee
OE: Operational employee
1, 2, 3: Levels in the SGEO
New CAC: new current applied capabilities that come into the organization

FIGURE 2.4.7: DOMINATION TYPE CHANGE PROCESS (THROUGH THE INCLUSION OF NEW CACS AND WORK METHODS)

a systematic rate of one hour per week. Including other persons, as described in item E), may exceptionally require additional meetings, both in the SARU and in the SGEO. To this end, the e-CEO creates and includes other Analysis and Reflection Units in the organization (Intra-organizational Analysis and Reflection Unit Teams or IARUT) integrated, for example, by the stratum III e-CEO, the stratum II Manager and/or the consultant, as shown in Figure 2.4.5.

Consulting assistance to the e-CEO in his or her association leadership role does not usually exceed 130 hours over 25 to 28 months. During this time, the consultant supports the e-CEO to periodically reflect and evaluate the work and achievements to date. This includes not only operational and financial results for the organization, but also the e-CEO's personal progress in learning the new required knowledge and skills for his or her role and the EEE of the SGEO. Many clients, commenting on their experience with this method, report that despite 10-20 years in business they have seldom, if ever, practiced careful evaluation of each year's business results and the progress toward their goals. The absence of this culture of achievement and merit recognition plays havoc with the construction of a positive view of achievement, and

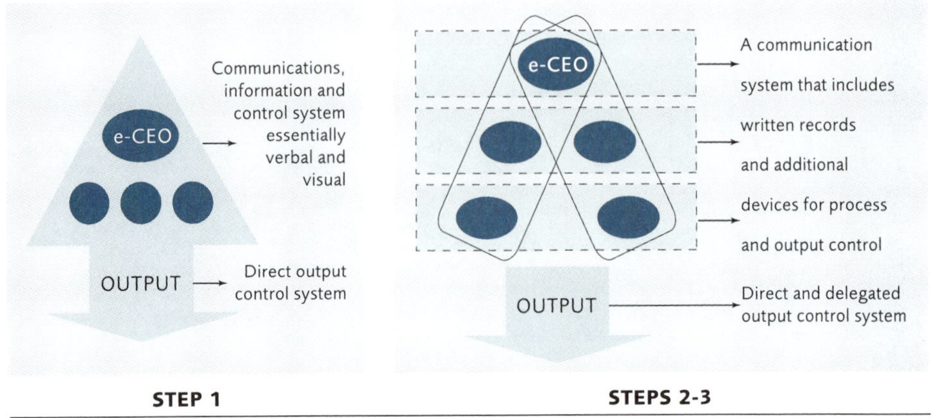

FIGURE 2.4.8: EXPANSION PROCESS OF OUTPUT TYPES AND EVOLUTION OF THE EXECUTIVE STRUCTURE

has a strong impact on the organization and its members.

Additionally, this process supports advances in the practical comprehension of the distinct nature of enterprise work (e-stockholder and e-director) and executive work (e-CEO).

G) The consultant assisting the e-CEO must understand and recognize the limits of the proposed method, which consist of achieving:

1. Transitioning the e-CEO's work from stratum II to III, attaining a new stability in applying his or her capability to the new stratum III role.

2. Evolving the executive structure (EEE) of the SGEO to the EEE High (see Figure 2.4.6[5]).

3. Restructuring the level II company into a three-level, requisitely structured organization that produces direct, assisted, and delegated outputs with a uniform degree of quality by means of controlled and economical internal processes.

In this article, I have presented the problems in this sequence to explain the method. The full application of this method, however, requires an approach that is integral, parallel, asynchronic and systematic, dealing primarily with the resolution of the problems posed by the e-CEO in the SARU.

H) Finally, the company's social system also changes towards a mixed type of au-

---

5   The statistical validation of the concept of Evolution of the Executive Structure (EEE) effected from 2002 to 2004 in 42 small companies in the Rosario area, Argentina, served to consolidate and adjust the first verifications on the importance of writing and of the crucial nature of the transition from level 2 to 3 levels in the SGEO.

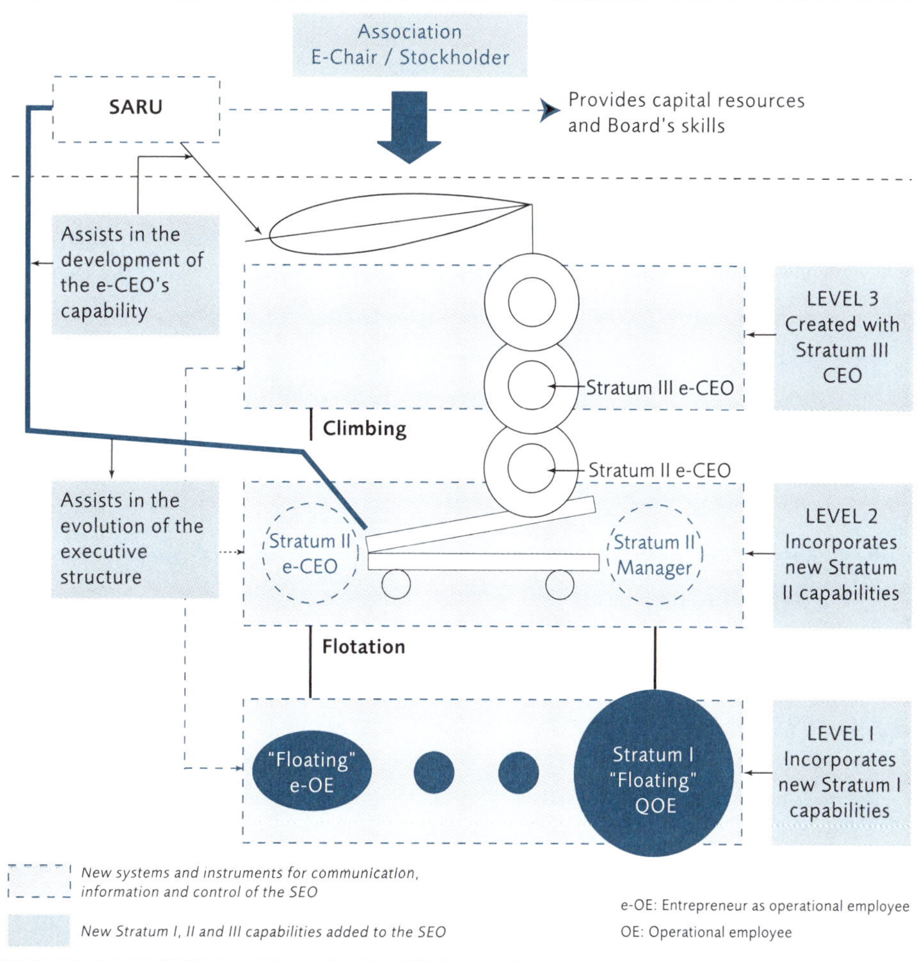

**FIGURE 2.4.9 A METHOD FOR ASSISTING THE ENTREPRENEUR-CEO
AND THE SMALL GROWING ENTREPRENEURIAL ORGANIZATION**

thority. It moves from the *charismatic* authority inherent to the level II entrepreneurial organization to one more appropriate to a level III organization, incorporating the *rational-legal* authority. The latter talent is usually recruited from the outside. (See Figures 2.4.7 and 2.4.8)

The e-CEO's transition between strata has two stages. The first or "flotation" stage occurs when the person leaves behind the operational tasks that demand a lower capability and a lower application of discretion. Here, the e-CEO "drops ballast" and rises with relative ease by using the abilities he or she recovers, applying them to more complex tasks.

During this first stage, the analyses of the use of time and values—both for the e-CEO and for the new roles of stratum II managers—are the core elements used in the SARU.

In the second or "climbing" stage, the e-CEO starts gathering new knowledge, skills and experience while still going through the uncertainties of learning-by-doing. This stage is more arduous and uncertain for the e-CEO. The instruments and tools used in it for implementing the new behaviors are created concurrently with the climbing process. This double parallel process, performed both by the e-CEO and the SGEO (EEE) and some of its members is illustrated in Figure 2.4.9.

In the second stage, the dominant need is to ensure the operation of all internal processes, and the quality and quantity of required outputs.

The emotional implications of the new tasks must be discussed in the SARU, and to complement this work with creating and operating the other Intra-organizational analysis and Reflection Unit Teams, and the essential incorporation of new capability at Strata I and II.

The method we have just presented is not a closed one; it is constantly fine-tuned and enriched. In our judgment, however, its current degree of development supports its use as a tool to help the consultant comprehend the phenomena and difficulties brought about by the growth of SGEOs, and to operate on them.

ABOUT THE AUTHOR

Atilio Penna is recognized because of his conceptual and practical contributions to the field of small and medium business in Argentina. Those contributions, which include "the Organizational Transition Theory," have been published in the US, UK, and South Africa, and are being used by professionals in Latin America.

He has a 30-year trajectory as coach of entrepreneurs, giving them support to achieve a sustainable growth for their companies. Dr. Penna focuses his work on the development of entrepreneurs' capabilities, improvement of their business structures, and building new tools and instruments that allow them to manage their organizations in a more efficient way.

This long and solid experience has added to his work as teacher and researcher making Dr Penna a well-known expert in the field of small growing business.

Profit by Raising a Key Function to the Next Level: Tools to Build a Work Levels Shifting Strategy

Julian Fairfield

One may think that a company determined to lift quality one level would focus resources on that function. Actually, the quality function can't be lifted without lifting the level of all functions that contribute significantly to quality. It requires a congruent lifting of product design, procurement, process technology and even maintenance. If these functions are not lifted, they will draw the quality function back down to the lower level. The effort will wither as soon as the quality change team disbands.

This article is the explanation of the recent thinking of a global strategy consultant and how several new ideas have changed the way that I approach creating effective business strategies. I have seen that, when possible, a work levels shifting strategy produces the greatest returns, but is also requires more creative effort and potential risk. The thinking behind a successful such strategy can be difficult, but understanding it gives you the tools to create your own, no matter what the design.

A good place to start is by seeing how the quality function has evolved over time from lower to successively higher levels of work complexity.

The Evolution of the Quality Function

When I worked on a lathe in a manufacturing plant in the UK in the 1960s, quality control was performed by *end-of-line inspection*. Every four hours a level II inspector would come around and randomly measure my output for out-of-specification conditions. For every faulty piece I produced, ten pieces were subtracted when my piecework pay was calculated.

Upon moving to the United States in 1972, I started work as a department manager in a plant that manufactured telephone cable. The approach here had developed to *quality assurance through operator inspection*.

The operator at each station was responsible for making go/no-go quality decisions and adjusting the machine accordingly. At the end of the process, the finished cables underwent final quality assurance by the QA department, led by a level III manager.

By the time I left cable manufacturing in 1979, the process had evolved to *statistical quality control*. Quality assurance had been centralized under a level IV, head-office vice-president of product quality. They had a full complement of staff, down to level II statisticians located in the plant. We still did our "go/no-go" inspections at the plant level, but the results were monitored at headquarters.

This provided the basis to both change the specifications and to develop higher levels of quality through process innovation. The objective of the quality function was still couched in terms of cost/benefit; exceptional quality was not seen as a value in its own right.

I later lived in Japan, where I was exposed to the concept of *total quality management*. There quality was the focus of level V management—even level VI. In a Japanese smelter that I studied, improving quality was the ongoing objective of every employee. Quality was viewed as a strategic variable. It continued to be valued as a method of reducing costs and improving quality for customers, but it was also valued in its own right as giving each employee meaning and an opportunity for creative activity.

Over a period of 15 years, I had witnessed the evolution of the quality function through four levels, from an end-of-line inspection to something that was part of the meaning and creativity of the people of the firm. When I learned work levels theory and reflected on my experience in light of it, I realized that one could see the same process of evolution in any function. It is the basis of progress.

The Evolutionary Path of Strategy

Strategy itself has undertaken a similar evolution, from a level III concentration on execution in a single function to a level VII focus on global markets.

Level III (1850): Functional execution, usually operations. Success was seen to be driven by the single function/holon of production. "You can paint it any color, so long as it's black."

Level IV (1900): Business unit profit. Profitability was recognized as the result of the interplay of new product development, production, sales, and finance a fully-fledged business, a holon that could sustain itself over time.

Level V (1970): Relative competitive position. Research by the Boston Consulting Group (BCG) showed that profitability was not only a function of competence within a single business. More often than not, profitability was a function of the relative competitive position of one business to all others in that industry.

Level VI (1980): Industry structure. Michael Porter demonstrated that profitability was not only a derivative of internal business capability and relative competitive position, but also of the domestic industry structure. Some industries were inherently more profitable than others. Industry profitability is a function of the relative power position not only with competitors, but also with suppliers, customers, and potential competitors.

Level VII (2000): Worldwide industry structure: The domestic industry structure model was forced to move up a level by international trade and the realization that super profitability decay curves were accelerating. It became apparent that profitability in industries with trade products was driven not by domestic dynamics, but by evolving worldwide industry and social structures.

As businesses differentiated at one level, successful strategic thinking moved up into the next higher level, integrating the lower levels. Successful strategies at the higher levels were predicated on successful execution of the strategic thinking at the lower levels.

It is this process of differentiation and integration that is explained by the theory of *holons*.

Holons and Holonic Shifting

Both in the real world of things and in the conceptual world of humans there is an upward evolving hierarchy of differentiation and integration of differences, each level of integration providing the next level of difference. This results in higher and higher levels of complexity. Everything is not only a whole in itself, but also a part of a greater whole, both a "whole" and a "part," or what Arthur Koestler called a "holon."[1]

Work levels theory is a reflection of the holonic structure of reality and consciousness. It provides insight into different levels of strategy and the organizational demands of strategic change.

The physical world shows this ordering. Starting at the bottom, we move from subatomic particles to atoms, to molecules, to complex molecules, to compounds of complex molecules, which are the stuff of planets, solar systems, galaxies, and finally to the cosmos itself.

Humans then extend this patterning of differentiation and integration into abstractions like nuclear family, extended family, tribe, nation state, unions of states, and ultimately the globe or United Nations

---

1   The idea of holons was initiated by Arthur Koestler (1967) then developed by Ken Wilber.

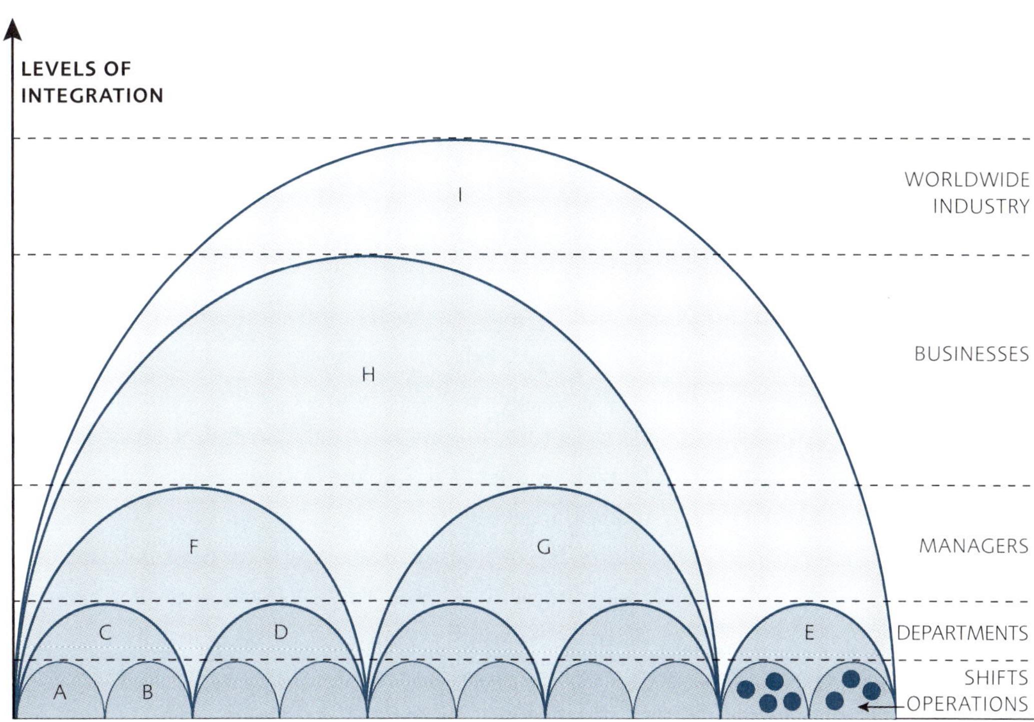

FIGURE 2.5.1 A HOLONIC SCHEMA OF BUSINESS

In the world of business we do the same thing (Figure 2.5.1). For example, an employee on the night shift is part of the assembly department, which is in turn integrated into the production function, which is integrated with additional functions (such as sales, marketing, finance, etc.) to make up a business. The business is differentiated from competitors, but integrated into a domestic industry structure, which in turn is integrated into a worldwide industry structure.

What we see in each figure is ongoing differentiation and integration:

A is different from *B* but both are integrated by *C*, which has a different emergent quality than either *A* or *B*.

C can't exist without *A* or *B*. *A* and *B* can exist without *C*, but without *C* both are somehow diminished.

A, *B*, and *C* are simultaneously in cooperation and competition with each other.

If *C* becomes an apex holon, it invites integration with *D* (which is at its level) to form the emergent *F*.

Each level contains and respects all its lower levels.

Mechanics and narrow purpose exist at the lower level. Inclusive purpose exists at the higher level.

Events at any level impact all other levels vertically and horizontally.

Business Applications of Holonic Ideas

Corporations are clearly organized in a hierarchical holonic pattern, with each level of management addressing more complexity by being both the integrator of lower holons and the responsible, purposeful owner of a holon, a zone of differentiation.

Although the argument works for any holons and their apex holon, let's take A as production, B as marketing, and C as the profit and loss business unit. Production is different than marketing, and both together create the emergent business, which is different still than either of them. The business cannot exist without production and marketing, but both are diminished without the cross-integration of the business unit manager. If this is a new business with two entrepreneurs—specialists in marketing and production, respectively—they would need a crossover general manager (GM) to maximize their performance in their specialties.

The crossover manager at each higher level is required to cross integrate more and more conflicts of purpose. Time is the currency used to integrate the conflicts between these holonic levels. The higher up the holonic structure you go, the more time it takes to reach an outcome that respects both the purpose of the apex holon and the purpose of lower holons.

Production and marketing cooperate with each other to create a profitable business. They also compete with each other for resources and approval from the business unit (and maybe, for their managers, the chance to become the new GM).

The role of the GM is to create and communicate common purpose across production and marketing. Each function will have both a functional purpose and a higher business purpose. While the business purpose will take priority, actual execution always takes place at lower levels. The GM cannot sensibly ignore or overrule either production or marketing. The GM must respect and integrate both as critical components of the business unit's success.

Lack of delivery at any level in any function—marketing or production—will dilute the realization of purpose at all other levels. Contemporary business practices like Just-in-time (JIT), efficient consumer response, *kanba*, and business process engineering all try to overcome holonic conflict and siloing by uniting holons. For example, JIT processes to remove inventory melds two holons into one.

At each discrete level, managers view the source of profitability and their purpose quite differently. Thus, they pay attention to different things; a manager's conscious attention and intention reflects the level at which he or she is operating

Insights into Applying Holonic/Work Levels Theory to Strategy

When you look at this evolution of strategic thinking and apply the holonic/work levels theory, several implications come out.

- *The strategic capability of a business is limited by the capability of its most senior manager.* For example, a CEO, appointed to a level V role, may only be capable at level IV and may make the error of being excessively production-focused with no ability to see the value of, for example, marketing (assuming that marketing has some value in this case). The business and all participants will be constrained to level IV thinking and performance.
- *Strategy is a horizon condition.* The process of differentiation is never-ending. Differentiation leads to conflict across the apex holons, which leads to integration to form the next apex holon, which leads to another differentiation. The emergence of global companies, air travel, CNN, immigration, and the Internet (i.e., increased holonic communication) will ultimately invite—and even demand—economic, environmental, philosophical, and political global solutions.
- *Each work level has different felt truths and they are hard to change.* Felt truths about the way the world is perceived to work, about how I prosper and survive, are different by holonic level and the level of skills accumulated. Our felt truths are abstractions held with survival vigor, making them resistant to change, especially in a threatening environment. These are the current personal apex holons of the manager.
- *The level IV marketing manager will know a good deal about marketing but perhaps little about production.* He or she is thus unable to integrate the needs of both. Marketing knowledge has been the basis of success and almost certainly his or her felt truths.

A levels shift in one function demands a similar level shift in all other related functions.

Level at which the function of activity is managed

VI **Chief** **Executive** **Officer**	Value proposition 10 year +	Marketing chartering driving whole company	Value balanced quality	Efficient customer response (ECR)	Virtual vertical integration	Not yet needed	Balanced scorecard ($ and humans)
V **Managing** **Director**	Industry structure 5-10 year horizon	Value Equivalency analysis	Total quality mgmt	JIT inventory	Symbiotic partnership integration	Zero failure maintenance	Shareholder value analysis
IV **General** **Manager**	Relative competition position 2-5 year horizon	Consumer segment-ation	Statistical quality control	Live statistical inventory mgmt	Strategic segregation	Reliability-based maintenance	Return on equity Return on assets
III **Department** **Manager**	Internal efficiency focus 1-2 year horizon	Mass marketing	Quality assurance	Economic order quantity	Adversarial	Preventative maintenance	Profit and loss
II **Supervisor**	Day-to-day survival 1-year horizon	Local sales	End-of-line inspection	Eyeball check	Yellow pages	Breakdown maintenance	Cashflow

CONGRUENCE   CONGRUENCE

TABLE 2.5.1 STAGES OF INDIVIDUAL FUNCTIONAL/HOLONIC DEVELOPMENT CAN BE ROUGHLY RELATED TO LEVELS OF CAPABILITY.

- *The dominant, most profitable player in a market is often operating at one level higher than its competitors in key competitive functions/holons.* In the 1970s, the American auto industry saw quality as a cost/benefit trade-off in "statistical quality control," a level IV function. Its competitors in Japan saw it as a strategic function and created TQM at level V. The rest is history, as Ford and GM have never recovered.

This shows what was stated at the start of this article: creating a strategy for improving business performance means choosing between two alternatives. The organization can either (1) become more effective at its current level or (2) shift a level upwards. Shifting levels is much more difficult, but has far more impact. Business

FUNCTION	MEASURE	GAIN DUE TO LEVEL SHIFT		
		FROM	∞	TO
Quality	• % scrap rate • Defect rates	• 12-15% • 1-2%	∞ ∞	1.8% 1:1,000,000
Purchasing	• Cost of purchase	• Cost reduction of 10-12%		
Sales	• Sales per mobile mortgage manager	• 2 per week	∞	5 per week
	• Value per mortgage	• $80,000	∞	$130,000
Maintenance	• Availability of multi-system continuous plant	• 64%	∞	85%
Admin overhead	• Total cost of administration	• Reduced by 35-40%		
Marketing	• Shares	• Three-year record of 7% value share gains based on social insight		
	• Time to market	• Time to market weeks of months		
Operations productivity	• Labour and machine productivity	• 100-200% improvement		

TABLE 2.5.2 GAINS ACTUALLY ACHIEVED BY LEVELS SHIFTING

thinkers have long known how to improve performance by increasing effectiveness at the current level, but it is only through the lens of levels and holonic evolution that we can see what shifting levels requires.

There is considerable overlap between work levels theory and the ideas of holons. Strategic attention changes as you move up to higher levels. Higher levels of strategy (the answer to the question, "What drives sustainable profitability?") demand an increasing ability to integrate more and more competing functions across continually expanding time and space.

Functional evolution, understood as holonic evolution where the new apex holon integrates the lower ones, can be viewed through a work levels perspective. Using the 7 S Model[2] exposes the organizational changes required as one moves through work levels, and why there are considerable gains to be achieved through shifting of work levels.

Table 2.5.1 shows what different levels look like across different functions/holons. At this higher level of abstraction, you can see how each apex holon integrates the differentiation of the next lower one, and all other holonic levels below.

---

2   See Pascale, Richard T. and Athos, Anthony G. *The Art of Japanese Management.* New York: Penguin Books, 1981. Peters, T. and Waterman, R. *In Search of Excellence.* New York City: Harper & Row, 1982. Waterman, R. Jr., Peters, T., and Phillips, J.R. "Structure Is Not Organisation." *Business Horizons*, 23(3): 14-26. 1980.

DESCRIPTOR	STRATEGY	STRUCTURE: • Leader of function • Lowest paid in function	SKILLS REQUIRED	SYSTEMS	OUTCOMES: "THE PRIZE"
Level V: **Total quality** **management** **(TQM)**	• Seek competitive advantage through quality and its through-effect on other processes	• Operations Directors (QA responsibility) $250k p.a. • Quality management officer $70k p.a.	• High level, broad based competencies in customer value offering • Forefront of continuous improvement techniques • Product/production skills less important	• Cross-functional and thorough level integration of quality function • Individuals within teams working to 2 sigma • Integration of customer into the process both for design and feedback • Failure the absolute exception. No scrap, no repair • International Standards Organization (ISO) accrediting and governing international industry standards	• Failure rates in units per million • Increased speed to market locally and globally • Quality a strategic tool
Level IV: **Statistical** **quality control** **(SQC)**	• Reduction of complete process costs	• General Manager (Quality) $175k p.a. • Quality assurance officer $70k p.a.	• Broad business comprehension • Competent quality assurance and control skills • Strong numeric and diagnostic skills	• The quality function still largely separate from other functions • Massive measuring and monitoring systems in place, trend analysis, talk to customers • Quality circle processes starting • Some failure accepted and repair function still in place • National associations co-ordinating industry standards	• Failure rates measured in parts of a percent • SQC used as a cost/ profit trade-off
Level III: **In process** **inspection**	• Reduction of production costs • Incorporates pre and post production	• Quality control manager $100k p.a. • Inspectors $35k p.a.	• Competent statistical and analysis skills • Beginnings of specialized quality control technical skills • Writing of design specifications • Troubleshooting	• In process and end of line go, no go inspection • Repair very much a part of operations • Scrap rates measured in percentage points • Hardly ever see a customer • Industry discussion groups • Standards set but at a low level	• Failure rates in percentage terms • QA a cost to be lowered • QA as good as competitors
Level II : **End of the line** **inspection** **and customer** **return**	• Reduction of returns	• Production supervisor $70k p.a. • Operators $35k p.a.	• Production/product expertise • Go, no go measurement	• End of line inspection • Customer lives with lots of defects • Repair a large function pre and post sales • End of line, go no go specs on key utilities	• High failure rates but customer often wears it • Focus on repair

TABLE 2.5.E: 7 S MODEL FOR QUALITY BY WORK LEVEL

Why Lifting an Organization up a Level is Difficult

Over my career I have been able to witness the impact of work levels shifting. Table 2.5.2 highlights some of the real gains that I have seen either as a consultant or as a line manager. This has more than convinced me as to the power of work levels shifting and also the difficulty achieving it. Shifting an organization is extremely difficult because it requires both personal self-awareness and congruency within levels as necessary, if not sufficient, conditions.

When I first encountered the work levels theory, I recognized intuitively that as any business function evolved, it demanded a different organizational design. This led me to use McKinsey's 7 S Model as an organizational template to describe the changes as one moves up levels.

Taking the levels/holon model together with the 7 S model, one can develop a picture of how organizational design shifts as you move through work levels. Table 2.5.3 is a highly abstract example of the holonic evolution of the quality function using the 7 S Model. This process can be taken down to a low level within the organization.

Managers' capacity to lift themselves up one level is critical. Shifting a level requires a higher cognitive capability, a new set of felt truths and skills: this is why apex managers are often replaced when a business shifts upward.

One may think that a company determined to lift quality one level would focus resources on that function. Actually, the quality function can't be lifted without lifting the level of all functions that contribute significantly to quality. It requires a congruent lifting of product design, procurement, process technology, and even maintenance. If these functions are not lifted, they will draw the quality function back down to the lower level. The effort will wither as soon as the quality change team disbands. (See Table 2.5.4.)[3]

This is another example of the holistic holonic theory in practice and leads to two general rules.

An organization's overall level is determined by the lowest level of any of its key functions for success.

Less obviously, if a level shift has not been achieved (i.e., breaking new ground), it must initially be led at one level above the final level.

---

3   Editorial Note: See Glenn W. Mehltretter, Jr.'s and Michelle Malay Carter's article in this book..

	Typical Level III Function		Typical Level IV Function		Issues
IV			General Manager	x 1	Can old III become IV?
III	Manager	x 1	Managers	x 4	Where do I get four IIIs?
II	Supers	x 6	Associates	x 20	Where do I get 20 IIs (usually okay 1/3 1/3 1/3 rule)?
I	Operators	x 36			Need to lay off a number of people
	Total = 43		Total = 25		Net reduction of 18 people = 41%

TABLE 2.5.4 LEVEL SHIFT DIFFICULTIES

Another example will illustrate this:

As a young plant superintendent, I was part of a new plant startup that was to operate non-union, to double productivity, to halve the scrap rate, and to improve all quality parameters significantly. In retrospect, our existing unionized plants were level III operations, while the new plant was designed to operate at level IV.

Without the benefit of work levels theory but with strong intuition, senior management appointed a level V plant manager who then hired a team of level IV direct reports. Within 18 months, each objective had been exceeded. Within 30 months, virtually all of the team had been promoted and moved on. The plant had stabilized at level IV and there was not enough level IV work to keep them engaged. Structurally the site had moved from a level V organization to a level IV. The shift has significant benefits, but the difficulty of achieving it is real. Each level develops its own issues:

At level IV: Can an existing manager fill this role, or do you have to go externally, with all this entails, especially in relation to the attitude of the current level III manager?

At level III: Where do I suddenly get four level IIIs? Will this include my existing three? Often one or two level IIIs are waiting underutilized in the wings, but one can rarely fill all these roles internally.

At level II: Similarly as level III. Although there are larger numbers at this level, this is more easily addressed because within the level I roles, there are often significant numbers of people capable of doing higher level work.

At level I: The level I roles have largely been eliminated, creating a significant issue with redundancies. Personnel reduction at level I is the source of cost reduction and must be realized.

In my experience, it is easier to achieve the level shift by initially overstaffing a greenfield site than to lift an existing organization.

Conclusion

I've shown how in my work life I've experienced the quality function going from end-of-line inspections (level II) to TQM (level V) and how business strategy itself evolved in a similar way. With the idea of holons added to work levels theory, we see how the differentiated functions/holons at one level can only be integrated by a new, emergent holon at the next level. The emergent holon is always one level greater and provides what can seem to be a miraculous value—not merely summing the parts—but providing a transformation of them.

Let's end by integrating these ideas into praxis, showing they have affected not just how I think, but how I do strategy with my clients. Starting a new strategy, I always go the Porter Five Forces Model[4] and populate it in *holonic* form. It can have as many as 30 or 40 *holons* of potential interest:

- Competitors with several key functions for success
- Suppliers
- Market segments

Afterwards, I gather data, including interviewing for opinions around the client, competitors, and the industry to determine where the power is and who is getting the surplus. Is it: Suppliers? Competitors? Consumers? This must be reviewed for each market segment.

From this data-rich position, I decide whether the best deliverable approach is an improvement strategy—creating incremental improvements in performance at the firm's current level—or a work levels shift strategy—shifting the power balance in one or more functions/holons in favor of the client. This may mean giving up more power to the consumer and is always a climbing up of the holonic structure, the miraculous processes of the new emergent level that integrates the differentiated holons below it.

---

4   For more about this model, see Porter, M.E. "How Competitive Forces Shape Strategy," *Harvard Business Review,* March/April 1979. Porter, M.E. *Competitive Strategy: Techniques for Analyzing Industries and Competitors.* Canada, United Kingdom, New Jersey: Free Press, 1980.

Shifting a level is the best way to get high returns on change, but such a strategy is very difficult to implement. The existing structures, values, and personnel all come into play. By acknowledging the felt truths and bringing them into self-awareness, one gets the opportunity to establish new felt truths by integrating and creating the new emergent apex holon.

Last, I always suggest getting creative, climbing the holonic ladder wherever appropriate!

ABOUT THE AUTHOR

Julian Fairfield's first career experiences were in manufacturing where he ended up as plant manager. From there, he moved to work for McKinsey where he specialized in strategy and organization. As part of the organizational work, he led for two years the seminal reorganization of CRA (40,000 employees) that utilized and expanded on the "levels of work" concept. This work was the basis for a book, *Levels of Excellence*, which explains levels and their relationship to systems. Julian is currently working on another book on the nature of human evolution in terms of how consciousness interfaces with our biology to produce culture(s). This has led to the interesting insight that global warming may be the most wonderful opportunity the human race has ever had. It challenges us individually and institutionally to think and act within the context of global culture or face the consequences.

6

On Being Heard:
Insights from Complexity Theory and Values as Touchstones for Effective Executive Communication Across the Levels

Jack Fallow

WHAT'S IMPORTANT

- A work-levels-based approach that executives may use to construct their communications to employees that will promote trust.

- How to use complexity theory and an understanding of attractors to enhance communication between organizational levels.

- Examples of different communication strategies based upon attractor values.

Most CEOs are not seeking to be poets. But they do want to be heard. To be heard, as opposed to merely being listened to, a leader must have something to say which is worth hearing—a stimulus that evokes a response, something that is attractive. Shaping communications so that they are attractive for the different audiences at each organizational level is a central challenge for managerial leaders.

There are many studies about leadership but few about followers. A notable exception was the development study led by Wilfred Brown, managing director of the Glacier Metal Company. Brown was especially interested in the representation of followers. He explored how industrial organizations could develop clear "constitutions" that would enable workers and managers to feel involved and engaged. As part of his quest, Brown started working with the Tavistock Institute and, in particular with Elliott Jaques. As part of this work, effective communication was central.

In the current management literature, leadership is often used to describe behaviors to elicit willing compliance and is often described separately from the manager's role. Brown and Jaques combined the concepts and used the term *managerial leadership*. They also identified specific communication practices, such as setting context, building an effective team, frequent dialogue with direct subordinates on key issues, and holding meetings with managers and subordinates from three levels of the hierarchy.

Brown advocated holding effective meetings[2] at which all staff are involved, while Jaques advocated asking employees questions relevant to their work at each level. I am not aware of suggestions of any behavior or language tips to compose one's conversation when attempting to speak at a given level of complexity.

In 1996 I became particularly interested in some of the difficulties of communication across levels. My interest arose when I founded a company owned entirely by

---

1   Malle, L. Quote from movie, *My Dinner with Andre.* 1981.
2   In his desire for clarity, this technique was called *contraction..*

the workers. GasForce Ltd. was an employee buy-out from the old company, British Gas. Before GasForce started, I had a series of conversations with technicians in the works canteen.[3] They exhibited extraordinary clarity about the commercial opportunity that their employer was missing. The readiness of the market, the breadth of skills available, and the size of the opportunity[4] were clearer inside the truck and tool bag than in the boardroom.

When the workers (as shareholders) can vote you out of office in 21 days, communication becomes vitally interesting. It became apparent that any lack of integrity in leadership values, behavior and communication would be clear to the frontline and deeply unattractive. By integrity, I don't simply mean the normal honesty that most citizens would exert. Rather, it is the sense of things being properly integrated, hanging together well with the joins or discontinuities in the systems being properly understood. Integrity matters at the frontline. It is valued.

There are three key thoughts that underpin all of the following ideas:

1. Purposeful organizations are examples of dynamic living systems and consequently are naturally hierarchical.

2. Followers have choice over the extent to which they commit themselves and unless their leader offers something attractive, they will withhold discretionary energy.[5]

3. Being a leader is not a choice made by an aspiring leader. In free societies, followers decide whether someone is a leader; either they follow or they don't. However, it is possible to consciously engage in behaviors that are designed to increase the likelihood that a potential follower will offer their discretionary energy.[6]

Winning the Discretionary Energy of Followers

Jaques made it clear: employee audiences can be categorized in a number of ways. People who are comfortable looking less far ahead expect their bosses to be com-

---

3   The company cafeteria in North American terminology.

4   In six years, GasForce added 1530 percent shareholder value.

5   Discretionary energy signifies that which is not required directly from the routine contract. It is the extra commitment that any employee/follower can withhold or offer depending on the attractiveness of circumstances. In the context of a leadership discussion, the offering of discretionary energy may be considered to be a signal that the leader is making a connection with the potential follower.

6   Editorial note: Jaques's model proposes that a requisite organization hold all managers accountable for requisite managerial practices designed to elicit and support employees working with full commitment. And within this full engagement work culture, managers hold all employees accountable for working with full commitment.

fortable looking farther ahead. How far ahead? This was the key question and Jaques established the set of time-span norms. Ralph Rowbottom and David Billis added muscle to this skeleton with their elaboration of the theory in their article "Stratification of Work and Organizational Design."[7] Gillian Stamp, Jaques's successor as director of BIOSS, worked with physicist D. John Isaac[8] to develop the Matrix of Working Relationships. Their work, together with those of many others like Warren Kinston and Walter Mahler in his consulting work at GE, can help us to understand the nature and meaning of work at each level, widening our understanding beyond issues of time-span. Indeed, there are many other ways of looking at the patterns of stratification or discontinuity.[9]

Given that so few executives have been exposed to the richness of these models, the reader might wonder why add yet another way of thinking about levels of complexity. The stimulus has been ideas that come out of complexity sciences. In 1997, I noted that there were parallels between the attractor patterns[10] that I was reading about in complexity science and the geometric modeling of discontinuities led by D. John Isaac.[11] This encouraged me to take the thinking about levels of abstraction in a different direction. This is not to minimize the significance of the other approaches. Rather, it is to offer an alternative framework based on the attractor patterns that are described in *complexity theory*.[12] While I am not an expert on attractor patterns or complexity theory, I have examined them enough to believe that there is some benefit in using these analogies as a way of thinking about the levels. By adopting this approach; I hope to offer a different view of the levels.

---

7   *Human Relations*, 30 (1) 53-76, 1977.

8   D. John Isaac met Elliott Jaques in 1961 at Acton Technical College, where Wilfred Brown was the chair of the college council.

9   For example see works by Clare Graves, Jean Piaget, and Lawrence Kohlberg.

10   Attractors: Some dynamical systems are chaotic everywhere, but in many cases chaotic behavior is found only in a subset of phase space. The cases of most interest arise when the chaotic behavior takes place on an attractor, since then a large set of initial conditions will lead to orbits that converge to this chaotic region. An easy way to visualize a chaotic attractor is to start with a point in the basin of attraction of the attractor, and then simply plot its subsequent orbit. Because of the topological transitivity condition, this is likely to produce a picture of the entire final attractor. For instance, in a system describing a pendulum, the phase space might be two-dimensional, consisting of information about position and velocity. One might plot the position of a pendulum against its velocity. A pendulum at rest will be plotted as a point, and one in periodic motion will be plotted as a simple closed curve. When such a plot forms a closed curve, the curve is called an orbit. Our pendulum has an infinite number of such orbits, forming a pencil of nested ellipses about the origin.

11   Jaques, E. Gibson R. O., and Isaac, D.J., *Levels of Abstraction in Logic and Human Action*, Heineman, London (1978)

12   A theory of non-equilibrium nonlinear systems related to Chaos Theory. Complexity theory is part of the theory of computation dealing with the resources required during computation to solve a given problem. The most common resources are time (how many steps does it take to solve a problem) and space (how much memory does it take to solve a problem).

Level	Attractive Leadership Forms of Managerial Leadership	Key Value that followers seem to seek
6	Transcultural	Tolerance
5	Transformational	Integrity
4	Transitional	Progress
3	Transactional	Excellence
2	Transmissional	Consistency
1	Formational	Accuracy

TABLE 2.6.1: THE LEVELS OF ATTRACTIVE LEADERSHIP

While "levels of work" can be measured by time span,[13] they are well understood to relate to how we model complexity, i.e., how we let others know what we are thinking about, what we value, what we are worried about and what we do and do not want to see happen. In other words, what is attractive and what is unattractive to us?

In this context I am using the notion of values expected by followers of their leaders—values that I anticipate will be necessary for followers if they are willingly to offer their discretionary energy. This hypothesis arose from considering the attractor patterns as models of cognitive processes. I then compared these conclusions with my observations and experience. Since the ideas came from attractor patterns, I have adopted the name "Attractive Leadership" for these ideas.

The particular names for the managerial leadership levels and the key values are derived from complexity sciences. In the complexity world, commentators describe four different types of attractors: 1) point, 2) limit-cycle, 3) Torus, and 4) strange attractors.[14] Each of these has a kind of pattern that shows the way that a mathematician would understand the flow of activity in a process. I am not such a mathematician! However, I am intrigued by the analogy that the attractors offer for the ways that Elliott Jaques set out his four-level quintave model. The complexity attractor models apply to all dynamic living systems so they should also apply to organizations. The significance of this is so that we can consider the values that followers may

---

13   By Dr. Uri Merry, website for Learning Organizations, 1998: "Distinctions between levels: It has been accepted that different levels of complexity have different rates of change, higher levels change slower, organizations change slower than teams. Higher levels have different time cycles than lower ones, and different size and dispersion over space. What we are adding here is that as we move from the level of cell, through organ, through biological system to organization, - we might be moving to processes with little subsystem autonomy to processes that demand a higher level of subsystem autonomy."

14   While most of the motion types give rise to very simple attractors, such as points and circle-like curves called limit cycles, chaotic motion gives rise to what are known as strange attractors, attractors that can have great detail and complexity.

be attracted enough to that they offer their discretionary energy to the leader.

Level One: Formational Leadership

Level one workers seem to be attracted to **accuracy**. *(Figure 2.6.1)*

Level one workers seem to be attracted to, or value, accuracy; something clear that does not squander their energy. A worker waiting for advice regarding his or her activity responds to instruction. Either the instruction is accurate or it is not. If not, they know that they will waste energy and effort. In my experience, workers are delighted to make friends with anyone keen to make them happy, but their highest appreciation is for bosses who give them accurate instructions. I call this giver of instructions, or level one leader, the *formational leader*. I use this term in the sense that level one leaders set the routinely accepted standards for most activities. They issue routine tasks and set the standards of acceptable behavior within the team. *Formation* is the French word for training and it is from bosses at this level that most workers get their apprenticeship.

In complexity theory, this type of system is described by the term *point attractor*. An example would be a device connected to a fixed-point thermostat; as soon as it moves beyond the required temperature it starts to move back in the other direction. It is attracted to the point. This self-regulation is effective so long as you have set the target for the thermostat correctly!

Level Two: The Transmissional Leader

At level two, people are attracted to **consistency**. *(Figure 2.6.2)*

Effectively, level two leaders transmit messages about their expectations of consistent performance; what constitutes the acceptable limits of performance and behavior and how they are changing. I call this boss the *transmissional leader*. A key part of the level two leadership role is to transmit the key messages that the organization (or the profession) has about the way of operating and of not operating.

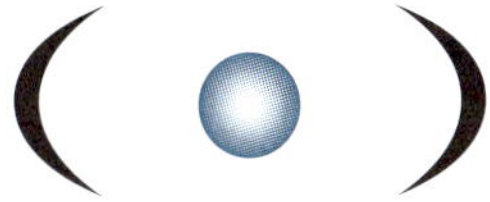

FIGURE 2.6.2: THE LEVEL TWO LIMIT-CYCLE SETS BOUNDARY CONDITIONS FOR LEVEL ONE TASKS.

In chaos theory,[15] this is mirrored by the limit-cycle. In a limit-cycle, the data and activities can flow both ways between two limits of the cycle. An example would be how professional human resources staff will guide managers on how to conduct an interview by establishing limits on what might be asked. Similarly, a level two accountant, in transmitting the standards of the organization, will question the rights (i.e., limit the freedoms) of a senior manager to record figures outside the routine standards. Thus, they establish consistent and trustworthy records.

Level Three: The Transactional Leader

*At the third level, people are attracted to **excellence**. (Figure 2.6.3)*

At the third level, people are attracted to, or value, a focus on excellence: I call this level of managerial leadership the *transactional leader*. In the transactional role, the key emphasis is on excellence and effectiveness. Does the system do what it says it can? Can the system work any better? The level three managerial leader is trying to make all the limit-cycles join together elegantly, so that everyone's energy losses (what economists call the transactional losses) are minimized and best practice is established. This may produce pressure on those who are managing in the level two limit-cycle environments as each of their processes is constantly refined to ensure that the overall effectiveness of the whole level three system is maximized.

In the third attractor, the *Torus*, the data, or patterns of data and activities don't just switch between two limits; there are many limits. We gather together a number of *limit-cycles*, and attempt to assemble them to form a three-dimensional ring, with data able to move in all directions: back and forth, up and down, round one way and

---

15   A name given to recent wide-ranging attempts to uncover the statistical regularity hidden in processes that otherwise appear random. Systems described as chaotic are extremely susceptible to changes in initial conditions. As a result, small uncertainties in measurement are magnified over time, making chaotic systems predictable in principle but unpredictable in practice.

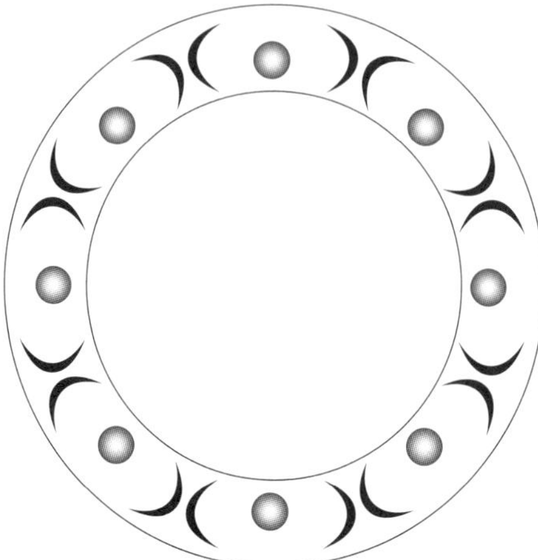

then round the other. The Torus is potentially very messy, with endless opportunities for each of the limit-cycles to mess up the whole system.

Level Four: The Transitional leader

At the fourth level, people are attracted to **progress**. *(Figure 2.6.4)*

Once we have established routine level three transactional systems, the next challenge is to manage the future. What happens when the activities in the Torus no longer fit what the customer will want in the future? What happens when the technologies are becoming redundant? Now, the *transitional leader* is required.

Imagine a Torus[16] that represents the domain of the transactional leader working in today's organization. Alongside it, bring to mind another to represent the future responsibility of a transactional leader working within the same organization in five years' time. It is the challenge of the transitional leader to guide these two chaotic and complex systems towards each other, somehow facilitating a docking together of the imagined future and the present, so that a peculiar fig-

---

16   Torus is the Latin word for "ring." To imagine this as an elegant ring would be to oversimplify what is involved, but it serves to illustrate the purpose.

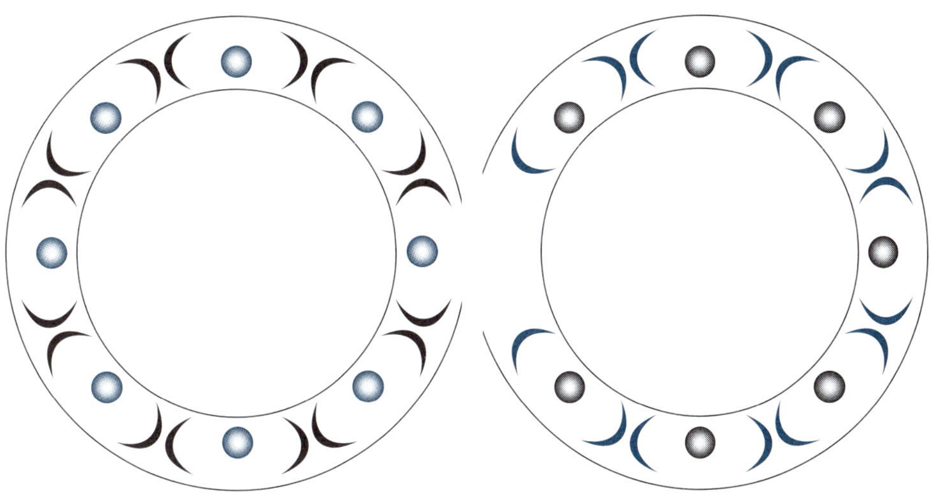

ure-eight is created.

This new system is observed in chaos as the strange attractor. For many people, this is the attractor pattern that they will recognize: it is the one that looks a little like a butterfly. In the strange attractor, there is a zone of chaos, right in the center. However, on one side there is the currently perceived certainty; on the other is the uncertain future with all its possibilities. The work of level four transitional leaders is to navigate between the current certainty and the best of the preferred futures, working in the area that has become known as "the edge of chaos."

Level Five: The Transformational leader

*At the fifth level, people are attracted to **integrity**. (Figure 2.6.5)*
Here there is the notion of weaving together all of the level four strange attractors, integrating all that has gone before in the previous levels. However, there is a problem: the physical world does not have a fifth attractor. In fact, just like the work of Elliott Jaques, it finds that recursions and quintaves must be the way ahead.

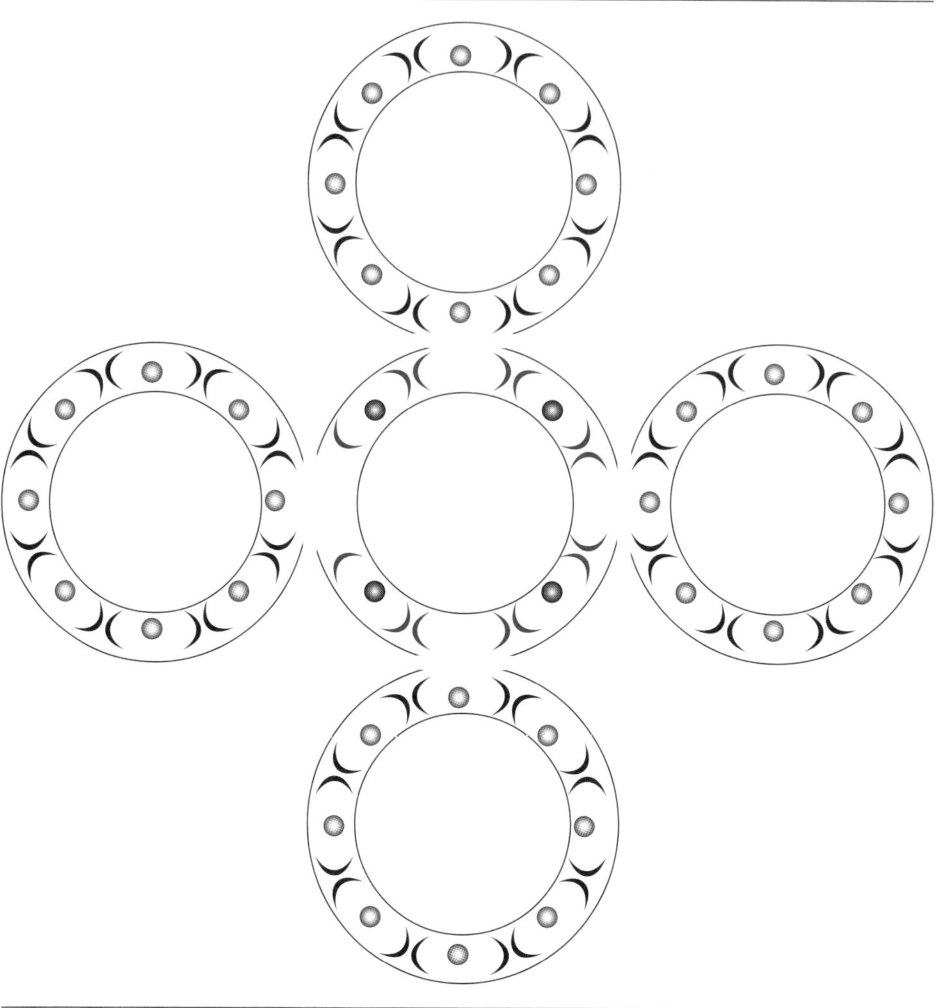

Therefore, we must look for a quintave of the formational level, the first level. Thus, it is the *transformational leader* role that applies at the fifth level. Do I mean transformational leader like all the other leadership theories? Not really, but there is neither time nor space to discuss all that here.

At the first level, the key issue was to be clear in answering, "What is the point of

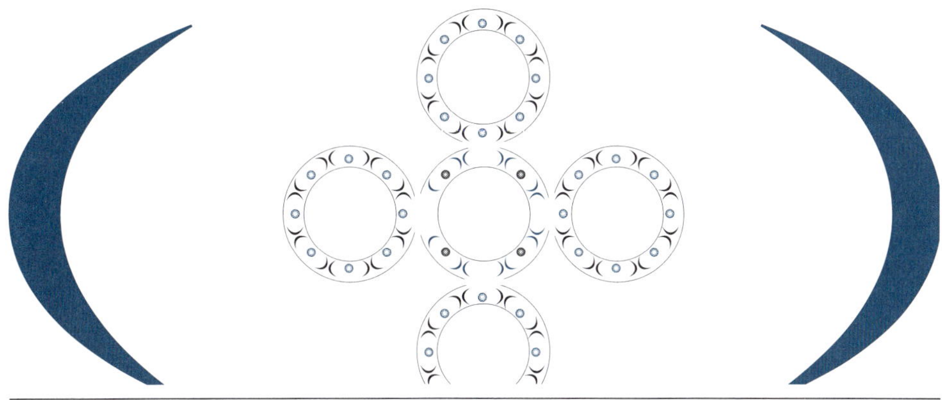

FIGURE 2.6.6: THE TRANSCULTURAL LEADER SHAPES THE ORGANIZATIONAL LIMITS AROUND THE RANGE OF BEHAVIORS THAT ARE ACCEPTABLE WITHIN THE VARIOUS ORGANIZATIONS IN THE INTERNATIONAL GROUP.

this task?" At the transformational level, the most important question is, "What is the point of this organization?"

Level Six: The Transcultural Leader

*At the sixth level, people are attracted to **tolerance**. (Figure 2.6.6)*

At the sixth level, people value tolerance. The CEO is acting internationally[17] and has to demonstrate a quintave of the level two limit-cycle attractor. This time it is to establish limits in the cycle that are partially determined internally by the organization's values system and partly by the distinctive cultures in which the organization's activities are hosted. An example might be an energy company that has an internal values system that was developed in its home country. The board decides to move into a new geography with partners drawn from the government in a new country. Now it has to balance its own values with those of the new country. They are unlikely to be the same. One end of the balance cycle of values will be the "home" set; the other will be the novel values of the new host country. If the new value set fits comfortably with the original value set, then there is no problem. But what if the new host country's values challenge some of the original values?

---

17 I am making no distinction between international, multi-domestic, trans-national, and global organizations, which have different needs for senior levels of capability.

At level two, the values were set by clarity in the local market place; now they must be set by clarity in the organization's value place—as a citizen in a very crowded world. In this world, it is the tolerance of diversity in cultural norms that determines what is acceptable. Not just how to behave at dinner, but how to establish the acceptable central and local degrees of freedom and trust to allow appropriate decision making.

So What in Practice?

Now let us return to the original issue, "on being heard." If we as CEOs desire to be heard rather than just to be speakers, the attractive values that are suggested above might assist in that process. There are two ways in which they might help. One is to ensure that we include relevant commentary that will be attractive to the listener. The other is to assist us in forming questions that show that we have some knowledge of the specific world that the listener occupies. In the following suggestions, I have assumed that the people are all in some kind of flow-state,[18] by which I mean that they are working in their comfort level.

For example, talking to a transactional manager (focused on excellence at the third level), the CEO (focused on integrity from the transformational level, stratum V) might ask about the current transactional system, what problems are being experienced with suppliers, customers, does the manager have a wish list for new kit, systems etc. The CEO might then go on to talk about the new changes that are coming up from company developments and ask how the systems will need to change. "So what will the next year or two look like from your perspective? Are there any aspects of what we are planning that you need to talk to your boss about?" In this conversation, the CEO is signaling his or her understanding of what the transactional world looks like and seeking information that will help with his or her own need for transformational integrity.

Then the CEO talks to the transmissional (level two) manager. It is possible that the difference in levels of complexity will make the CEO difficult to understand. To be heard, a CEO in this situation will focus on the value that matters to the second level transmissional challenge: How to lead with consistency? "How are you finding it to get staff with the right level of skills? What are we having difficulty controlling? What do

---

18   Many people are not employed in their optimal level and their responses to questions aimed at their employed level might help reveal mismatches.

you find is giving you the most problems? Are there any new customer messages coming through?…You might be interested in some new stuff that we are looking at…it is all about helping customers/suppliers/logisticians/employees get a better view of the company. What do you think about these ideas? What new problems would they give you and your people? Is there anything else that we might be missing?"

The CEO conversation changes in a different way when speaking with a frontline worker. The level five transformational leader is the quintave of the first level formational leader. In my experience, there is a profound relationship between levels one and five. Often, the established level one worker is the first to see/hear the discontinuities arising from any lack of integrity at the transformational level. They experience the gaps in integrity as a problem between what they are supposed to do and what they can deliver. Frequently this sounds like criticism of their bosses, especially the transmissional and transactional leaders, who are trying to cope with the discontinuities in boardroom thinking. However, this first level is a rich source of information and has enabled leaders to make dramatic transformations of organizations as they gain insight into the changes that will rebuild the organization.

The model can help us to direct conversations that take place with a specific level, but what about those times when a CEO needs to talk to all employees with one message? Again there is the need to think about the audience. If proposed changes will impact disproportionately on one of the levels, then the message must be targeted to make the best of the potential engagement. In my experience, the key communication challenge is to identify which of the internal audiences must offer their discretionary energy before the proposal can succeed. Is it at the third level, those who lead transactions, or those who transmit the values and standards, or those whose accuracy is foundational?

In conclusion, I have offered a way of thinking about how managerial leadership might construct conversations that are *attractive*. To be heard at his or her best, each leader has a variety of ways of presenting both messages and questions. Awareness of the varying needs of followers for level specific values, accuracy, consistency, excellence, progress and integrity, and tolerance, can be helpful. I have found this way of using attractive leadership helpful. I hope you will too.

Jack Fallow's career started in British Steel. Active in the trade union, he became an industrial relations officer. In his trade union role, he discovered the Elliott Jaques's perspective.

At British Gas, he was a director in human resources, service engineering, and operations. As a member of the international strategy team, he originated the concept of a company charter to integrate governance, strategy, values, and behavior. From BG, he was seconded to the UK government's Home Office.

In 1996, he founded GasForce Ltd, an employee-owned business. Jack led the £1.4m (UK) buy-out from British Gas. In 2002, the workers shared £21.7m when the company was sold.

Jack has been a director in other business sectors, including manufacturing, packaging, and electronic media. He is a co-founder of The Centre for Organisation Effectiveness Ltd.

He was a council member at Brunel University and a trustee of BIOSS. In 1992, Brunel University awarded him an honorary degree. As a failed rock drummer, he is proud to be a director of the National Youth Jazz Orchestra of the UK. His interests include the complexity sciences and their impact on strategy and leadership and on the 21st century implications of the 1215 Magna Carta.

Major Applications of the Levels of Work Approach

Major Applications of the Levels of Work Approach

One of the major strengths of requisite organization concepts is its applicability to all types of organizations—profit, non-profit, NGOs, and government. This is because it deals with the fundamental constructs of organization—i.e., the nature of work, role design and role relationships, and human capability—constructs which underlie the effectiveness of all types of organizations. To provide a sense of the robustness of requisite concepts, in this part we present articles describing a variety of organizations that implemented requisite concepts and the results achieved.

The first example of a total organizational design is related by **Elliott Jaques** and details the implementation of requisite concepts at Commonwealth Industries, a major aluminum rolling company that produced sheet aluminum and specialized aluminum products. Although Jaques notes that one cannot attribute the turnaround in the company's fortunes solely to the implementation of requisite organization concepts, it is clear that it contributed substantially to it. The data provided on the turnaround, including changes in union-management relations, are spectacular.

Business unit senior executives are always challenged in negotiating for corporate resource allocation. One business unit president sought to maximize productivity and profitability by using requisite principles and practices. **Nancy Lee**, a senior management consultant, mentored by Elliott Jaques, and with several successful full-scale requisite organization project implementations to her credit, tells the story of how a business unit president used RO to help grow a company from a 3 percent domestic market share for their product to a 35 percent share of the world market. Especially interesting about this project are Nancy Lee's design of extensive management orientation, education, and development to support the work, and the careful design and alignment of new systems, including compensation, to support employees in 24 countries around the world.

How do you take a struggling appliance manufacturer and turn it into a national leader by increasing sales by 33 percent in just two years? **Maurice Dutrisac**, who was vice president of administration with Inglis when Whirlpool Corporation bought the company, worked with Elliott Jaques and **Stephen D. Clement** to implement requisite organization on a company-wide basis to meet the performance expectations of the new owner. Their article is an excellent description of the challenges and opportunities executives face when implementing requisite concepts. Their experiences cover the gamut, from eliminating management levels, to ensuring that managers are capable of handing the complexity of their roles.

Although this book is assembled primarily for the private sector executive, it is important to note that the initial 35 years of work to develop these concepts included extensive applied clinical consulting with governmental, not-for-profit, religious, and charitable organizations as well as private sector businesses. The careful developmental work demonstrated that the concepts were valid for managerial employment hierarchies in all sectors.

The first of these non-profit applications articles is by **T. Owen Jacobs** and **Stephen D. Clement** and describes the extraordinary resource commitment, length, and scale of a project in a stratum VII organization (the US Army) starting at the top with the Office of the Joint Chiefs of Staff. The well-designed research program largely validated major Stratified Systems Theory concepts and their adoption led to substantial improvement in senior leader development. The article also describes the use of levels of work and human capability concepts in the redesign of elements of a major branch of the US Army.

The second non-profit application relates to a recent case of a major requisite-based organizational redesign in a high-profile, global, not-for-profit humanitarian agency to demonstrate the universal applicability of these beneficial concepts. **George Weber,** one of the co-authors and Secretary General and CEO of the International Federation of Red Cross and Red Crescent Societies between 1992 and 2000 sponsored the project, and **Dwight Mihalicz**, also a co-author and project director, tell the successful redesign story.

Elliott Jaques advised us that his concepts were appropriate for managerial employment hierarchies and cautioned against their use in associations or other forms of membership organizations except in those parts of the organization that had employed managers and employee subordinates. Nevertheless, the application of requisite concepts still has useful applications, as is explained by **John Morgan** in the final article in this part, "Requisite Organization Goes to Church." Morgan used Jaques's and Cason's concepts on human capability in his doctoral dissertation to evaluate the cognitive capability of several historical religious figures. Now in his role as senior pastor of Pinion Hills Community Church, a mega-church in New Mexico, he describes how he used RO concepts in church governance and administration to increase the effectiveness of the Church.

 **1**

Report of a Major Requisite Organization Project at Commonwealth Industries

Elliott Jaques

WHAT'S IMPORTANT

- One of the few case studies Elliott Jaques ever wrote about his clinical support of major organization redesign projects.

- A Global company using RO sponsors in a full RO implementation together with Statistical Process Control in a newly acquired US subsidiary.

- The company also used RO to assess proposed acquisitions for fit and ease of integration into parent company.

- Management levels were reduced from eight to four.

- Substantial gains were achieved in productive effectiveness, competitiveness, sales, customer satisfaction and mutual trust.

- Examples of how to sequence an organization design project.

This is not intended as a description of some kind of utopia, but merely as an example of the great social power of the CEO. It is quite possible for any CEO in any company to maintain a principle-based set of managerial structures and managerial leadership processes that really do provide enhanced productive effectiveness and a high-morale, mutual-trust organization that is actually good for employees personally, inevitably good for their families, and eventually good for society.

—Elliott Jaques[1]

It is not my intention to claim that certain gains in effectiveness can be traced to a direct one-to-one result of certain specific changes in organization along the lines that I have been describing. Changes in the effectiveness of any given organization are always and inevitably the result of multiple other changes occurring both simultaneously and interactively. Nevertheless, it will also be clear that the organizational developments made a significant contribution to the changes achieved, and indeed made possible smoother transitions than in the past. I will illustrate the kinds of progress that would be reasonable to expect with full scale implementation of the requisite organization structures and processes based upon the concepts and principles that I have been outlining.

For the purpose in hand, then, I have decided to give a reasonably full account of highlights of development in one company. I have chosen this particular example, because there has been a consistent development over a period of nearly 20 years with the same leadership, including a Board and ownership committed to a requisite organization, and this development with this same leadership is still actively continuing. In this last regard, the project is different from most others. One of my difficulties has been that major developments accompanied by significant results, even over periods of years, are suddenly terminated by changes in top management in which the new leaders find that the requisite developments run counter to their assumptions or traditions, or as I believe, run counter to their misconceptions.

The results are in terms of substantial gains in productive effectiveness, in competitive sales, and customer satisfaction, and of substantial gains in mutual trust, good feelings, high engagement and identification with the company and its man-

---

1   This article was originally published in 2002 as Chapter 17, "Some Results in One Company", in the book *Social Power and the CEO: Leadership and Trust in a Sustainable Free Enterprise System* by Elliott Jaques. It is reprinted here in its original form by permission of Quorum Books Westport, Connecticut, London.

agement of employees within the company. I shall add some specific examples of various types of result from some other organizations.

The Company: 1985-1992

The company in question, Commonwealth Industries, Inc., is an aluminum rolling company producing sheet aluminum and specialized aluminum products for a wide range of industrial uses. At the beginning of the project in 1987, it had head-quarter offices and one plant in the mid-west United States. It employed some 1,350 people and it was producing about 25 million pounds of rolled aluminum per month.

In 1985 the Company was purchased by CRA, an Australian mining company, whose Board intended to use it both as an outlet for its own produced aluminum and as part of a plan for expansion into North America. The new parent company had been engaged since 1979 in a substantial organization development, in which I had been involved. This development led to the establishment of systematic con-cepts and principles for organizational structuring, managerial accountability and leadership, and human resourcing and talent pool development. It contributed to many of the new ideas that I have described in these pages.

The new Australian owners found that its new subsidiary was in considerable trouble. Substantial capital had been put into production process improvements, but had not paid off. Quality and delivery standards were inferior to three-quarters of the nation's aluminum producers, and recovery rates were low. In addition, a se-rious strike threat was brewing over industrial relations difficulties that had been building up over the previous two to three years.

By the end of 1987 the CEO was retiring. In order to try to overcome the prob-lems, the Australian owners decided to appoint one of their most experienced man-agers as the new CEO. He was a metallurgist who had become expert in the par-ent company's systematic approach to organization and managerial leadership. The terms of reference given to the new CEO were to turn the company around if it were not to be sold. He decided upon a three pronged thrust:

1. A requisite organizational development.
2. Introduction of statistical process control and continuous improvement at all levels.

3. Analysis and improvement of all major systems, including information, finance, and marketing and sales.

PHASE ONE: CREATING A REQUISITE ORGANIZATION

In line with the parent company's established practice, the new CEO took as his phase one a full-scale reorganization driven by a special internal project team of six, plus a team leader immediately subordinate to himself and trained in requisite organization, with a six-month completion target. That target was achieved, with the following results:

- The company had four managerial layers instead of eight.
- Every managerial role, including the shop floor first-line managers, carried full managerial accountability not only for the work of subordinates, but for exercising full-scale managerial leadership, as defined.
- The beginnings were made of a change from results-based performance appraisal to personal effectiveness appraisal.
- Evaluation of potential capability (time-horizon) and talent pool analysis began to work down from the top layers, and eventually reached the shop and office floor.
- Two-way manager-subordinate meetings were introduced at all levels, and offices for such meetings were built down on the shop floor.
- A clear separation was developed between mainstream business functions and specialist staff functions.
- Cross-functional accountability and authority was established.
- There was also a move towards, but not yet full implementation of, equitable payment.

PHASE TWO: INTRODUCING SPC

Following the establishment of an effective managerial leadership organization, statistical process control was introduced. An outside specialist consultant was brought in. This consultant, as is common, wanted to set up quality circles at each level to initiate changes. But he was instructed to work from level to level directly down through the new managerial hierarchy.

As a result of this process, all managers (and many operators) had sufficient preliminary training to be held accountable not only for the permanent sustainment of continuous improvement priorities and projects, but also for ensuring that quantitative procedures were used in ferreting out problem causes and priorities.

PHASE THREE: BROAD SYSTEM IMPROVEMENT

The ongoing development was then filled out with the methods improvement work in sales and marketing, and in finance and information.

Some Other Significant Changes

While the above developments in managerial organization and managerial leadership were going on, two other significant events occurred.

The first of these events was the appointment of a new factory general manager, Mark Kaminski,[2] as an immediate subordinate of the CEO. This manager took like a duck takes to water to the requisite concepts, principles and practice, and gave an enormous push to their rapid and effective implementation throughout the production shops. Mark Kaminski was promoted to become the company CEO in 1990, as the CEO from Australia was taken back home for a promotion in the parent company. Kaminski later arranged for the financing of the purchase of the company from its Australian parent. It became a free-standing American public company with its own shareholders and Board of Directors. Kaminski stayed with the company in its new situation, and remains its CEO today.

The second of these crucial events was that the strike that had been brewing occurred in 1989. It was a very militant 11-week strike, with the full panoply of baseball bat smashing of car windshields of managerial and office staffs who remained at work and kept some production under way. In terms of appreciating later constructive developments on trust, morale, and productive collaboration, it is important to understand the low level to which morale and trust had plunged.

The morale and industrial relations situation is perhaps best described by the response on the shop floor to the news that the new Australian parent company was replacing the retiring CEO with a CEO from Australia. The response was for the local trade union leaders to buy a life-sized stuffed toy kangaroo, and to hang it by its neck from one of the telephone poles at the door of the local union house used as an office just outside the front gate of the plant. This attitude was reflected in the way in which union supporters would turn their backs on managers as they walked through the shop. The kangaroo remained in its hanged position for well over a year after the strike.

---

2   Editorial note: Mark Kaminski was CEO when this article was written in 2002.

Some Results of Developments to 1992

Recall: new Australian CEO, and new general manager, 1987; introduction of improved managerial system, 1988; strike, 1989; new American CEO, 1990; improved systems, 1990-1991. By 1992 the following results had been achieved.

In summary, there were dramatic improvements in productivity and in customer relationships. For example, a 35 percent increase in output was being regularly produced with 20 percent fewer people. The company moved to the top third in the nation in quality and delivery and continued rapidly to rise, and customer satisfaction continued to grow. Internal recovery had risen by 7 percent to world class, customer rejects had fallen by 50 percent, and total inventories had been reduced by over 50 percent.

It will be obvious that these substantial improvements were not produced by organizational and managerial developments alone, but they were certainly facilitated by the new managerial developments. And indeed, it is the unequivocal conclusion of the CEO and executive staff that these results could not have been achieved without the improved managerial system. This conclusion is supported by the following developments that occurred during this same period.

A major influence was the effect that the new managerial arrangements and leadership practices had upon shop floor relationships and attitudes. There was widespread shop floor involvement in improvement work through first-line managerial leadership. First-line managers began to meet regularly in full team meetings with their operators in two-way discussion of issues, just as any executive manager would be expected to meet with his or her subordinates. Operators were actively involved as members of first-line managerial, and unit managerial, improvement project teams. A state-of-the-art learning center was built, in which operators could be periodically involved in updating work process specifications, and upgrading their own skilled knowledge.

Against this background of total managerial change, the long years of embattled trade union relationships culminating in the 11-week strike had been totally transformed into an extraordinarily positive collaboration from the union, directly as a response to the new organization and positive managerial leadership of the operators. The turning-the-back hostile behavior changed to a reassuringly friendly reception of managers from all levels, and an extraordinary willingness and desire to discuss useful ideas on how the work could be improved. Quite an extraordinary change had taken place, and it is an indication of how mutual trust can be created out of trustworthy systems, for the employees remained the same.

Systems drive behavior. A further indication of shop floor change was that shop floor grievances had fallen from 315 still being processed at any time in 1990 to a mere three in 1991.

Change Continues to 2001

The company, without outside specialist assistance, has continued to grow and develop in customer satisfaction, productivity, profitability, and growth in size. By 2000 the position had become as follows.

The company has acquired other companies, and has grown to $1.2 billion in sales, 10 operating locations, and approximately 2,000 people. All new acquisitions have been reorganized in line with the company's managerial and organizational policies and practices. They are recognized as world class.

In addition to its full implementation and use over the years in the parent company, the application of requisite organization has been useful in two other ways. The first way is in due diligence evaluation of a possible acquisition. Here a rough and ready diagnostic evaluation of the extant managerial structure, talent pool, and managerial practices gives a useful idea of how readily a potential acquisition could be fitted into the company organization, and where the difficulties likely would arise. The planning that becomes possible smoothes the way to a much quicker adjustment.

The second way is by the immediate implementation of requisite organization within a new acquisition. In a most notable example in Commonwealth, one such development contributed (did not cause, but contributed) to an increase in output of over 100 percent within the first two years.

Turning now to the impact on the employees of the implementation of requisite managerial structures and processes, there have been many examples of major changes for the better. One such example is that trade union relations have improved beyond recognition and a further change has taken place. They had been a "me-too" company, that is to say, a small company which followed and automatically accepted the conditions negotiated every three years by the two major firms and the national trade union. Their local union took the initiative in instituting their own

	1996	1997	2000
Production (tons)	110,780	132,828	168,268
Recovery %	71%	75.51%	80.20%
Cost per lb.	$0.21	$0.19	$0.19
Promise Performance	55%	71.41%	92.10%
Customer Claims	1.0%	0.50%	.2%

TABLE 3.1.1: IMPROVED RESULTS IN PURCHASED FACTORY

negotiations and conditions, 3 to 6 months in advance of the national negotiations. That change is a major sign of growth in mutual trust, which is the most significant criterion of a healthy and constructive atmosphere that breeds a sense of well-being and security in employees.

The same atmosphere and outlook pervades at all levels. During recent years a number of mid- to high-level people who left to accept greater opportunities offered by other employers have sought to return. They report that they found the standard conditions that exist in other "good" companies to be really unacceptable. There is highly-effective cross-functional collaboration as a result of the clarity of accountability and authority bolstered by the general sense of well-being and opportunity for self-actualization that suffuses the company.

This is not intended as a description of some kind of utopia, but merely as an example of the great social power of the CEO. It is quite possible for any CEO in any company to maintain a principle-based set of managerial structures and managerial leadership processes that really do provide enhanced productive effectiveness and a high-morale mutual-t rust organization that is actually good for employees personally, inevitably good for their families, and eventually good for society.

To take the most recent example, a new plant was purchased in 1997. Table 3.1.1 shows the results of a rapid application of requisite organization practices. Within the first year, production had increased by 20 percent with a 10 percent decrease in total expense. Revenues had improved by a significant 4 percent. And promise performance had increased by over 15 percent. At the end of four years, production had increased by 50 percent with no further increases in total expense, recovery had increased to world class by another 5 percent, and promise performance had shot up to a record 92 percent. A sharp increase in customer satisfaction was shown in a reduction of customer claims from 1 percent to 0.2 percent. Did the organizational developments explain all these results? The answer is no. But did the organizational developments contribute significantly to the achievement of these results? The answer is yes.

ABOUT THE AUTHOR

Elliott Jaques, pioneer in the theory of human development, is considered one of the 20th century's leading psychologists. Dr. Jaques, whose contributions were multidisciplinary, is well-known for identifying what he called the *mid-life crisis* and for the breakthrough idea that the capability of human beings to perform complex tasks is predictable and evolves over time. He made fundamental contributions to society's understanding of the meaning of work, to the evaluation and development of the worker, and to a method for objectively measuring the complexity of work roles. And, he was the first to develop a numeric, provable method for testing and measuring human behavior, which has subsequently been used to analyze the work of military generals and to assess leaders in politics and business. Dr. Jaques is the author of more than 20 books, including *A General Theory of Bureaucracy, Human Capability* (with wife Kathryn Cason), *Requisite Organization*, and *The Life and Behavior of Living Organisms*. His noteworthy awards include the Joint Staff Certificate of Appreciation, presented by General Colin Powell, for "outstanding contributions in the field of military leadership theory and instruction …"

Designing the Novus Management System: Aligning Requisite Systems Across 24 Countries

Nancy R. Lee

WHAT'S IMPORTANT

- A new CEO of a Japanese-owned, US business unit with $250 million in revenues used RO to grow the business.

- A comprehensive organization design and implementation process included:
  - systems to create effective managerial leadership behaviors.
  - a new management system with aligned policies including compensation for employees located in 24 countries and operating in 83 countries.
  - unusual attention to interpersonal effectiveness.

- Benefits included:
  - growth from 3 percent of domestic market to 35 percent of of a rapidly growing world market,
  - productivity (sales per full-time employee grew from $1.5 to 2.5 million), and
  - employee satisfaction.

When Dr. Elliott Jaques recommended me to Dr. W. Joseph Privott, president of Novus International, Inc., it was the beginning of an almost ideal requisite project. Just a year earlier, in 1991, Mitsui & Co. Ltd. and Nippon Soda, Ltd. acquired the Feed Ingredients Business from Monsanto Company. The company was given the name Novus at that time. Novus is the Latin word for "new beginning."

Dr. Privott had joined the Monsanto group in the early 1980s to develop and execute the marketing plan for methionine, after the company built the world's largest methionine plant and began to grow market share. But by 1990, Monsanto had decided to concentrate its efforts on crop chemicals and to divest its feed ingredients business that had methionine as its major product, leading to the acquisition by Mitsui & Co. and Nippon Soda. The new owners asked Dr. Privott, who was then running this business, to become president of the new company, and gave him the freedom to establish the philosophy and practices that he felt were most appropriate. The company—with a mission to "help meet the growing worldwide demand for high quality, affordable food"—had 160 employees and gross sales around US$250 million dollars.

From the start, Privott wanted to find ways of creating a work environment that would both result in a successful business and treat employees in a socially responsible way, providing a great place to work. As part of that effort, Privott attended a week-long seminar at The Levinson Institute, where Jaques presented.

"One of the things that appealed to me initially about Jaques's ideas," Privott said, "is that it gave us tools to make clearer judgments about individuals. We all make those judgments, but with requisite concepts and language we had a sophisticated mental model of what we were doing, which gave us more confidence in our assessments."

The logic and internal consistency of Jaques's requisite organization (RO) model also interested Privott, because he perceived Jaques's approach to management as a science rather than an ad hoc art. Privott, who was a Ph.D. scientist, thought this foundation would appeal to the other scientists as well who made up the bulk of Novus' senior managerial ranks.

When Privott asked Jaques to recommend someone to come to St. Louis to help Novus implement the system, Jaques suggested me, since I had been working with his ideas for a number of years. Privott then asked me for a commitment of two weeks per month until the implementation of requisite concepts was well underway. "During the project there were several events that were particularly significant in our ability to use and embed requisite concepts," Privott recalled. "One was the opportunity to discuss emerging issues directly with Jaques. He made himself available to Nancy and me by telephone and visited us in St. Louis on several occasions."

A New Beginning Using Requisite Principles and Practices

Early steps in the introduction of requisite organization at Novus included:
1. Educating the senior management team of nine individuals;
2. Analyzing the extant or currently existing organization; and
3. Getting preliminary judgments of the complexity of information processing (CIP) of each person in the top three levels.

Educating Senior Management

Privott decided to introduce the senior management team to RO concepts as part of their regular weekly management meetings. Each meeting was extended to allow Privott and me to make a one-hour presentation on a particular aspect of RO followed by a question-and-answer period. We intended both to educate these managers and to gain their agreement on the reasonableness and usefulness of these concepts. I also prepared a brief written paper on each key concept for use in these meetings.

At a critical time early in the project, Novus was fortunate to have Sir Roderick Carnegie visit a senior management meeting. Carnegie had worked for more than a decade with Elliott Jaques in the formation of many RO concepts. He made a presentation on his experience with requisite ideas as CEO of CRA, an Australian mining company. During the question and answer period that followed, senior management explored their doubts about RO procedures, which Carnegie helped address from his years using requisite organization. Carnegie's visit brought a great deal of credibility to the requisite organization approach and encouraged senior management to spend the time and energy necessary to put their new learning to work.

Analyzing the Extant Organization

I undertook a review of the organization as it then existed, looking at roles, reporting relationships, the work being done, and the time span of key tasks in major roles. First, I interviewed Dr. Privott about the work he expected of each of the management team's units. Next, I interviewed each member of the management team about his or her understanding of the results expected from the units. I explored how work was assigned and how functions were divided among subordinate roles.

At the same time, I sought data on some of the longest tasks for which the managers believed they were accountable, as well as information on the longer tasks they delegated to subordinate roles.

Occasionally the views of Privott and a given manager were not fully aligned. When this was this case, I worked to achieve full clarity and agreement.

This information yielded a picture of a stratum VI organization with very few roles at stratum I. The president's role had a time span of more than 15 years and the senior vice president roles had time spans of typically 7 or 8 years.

Initial Judgments of Employees' Complexity of Information Processing (CIP)

Privott provided initial judgments of the CIP of each of his subordinates and subordinates-once-removed. Senior management team members also judged the CIP of their subordinates and subordinates-once-removed. This gave a picture of the capability of the employees from stratum VI through to stratum III.

Privott felt Jaques's approach to judging complexity of information processing clarified the issue of capability and separated it from values, knowledge, and temperament. He also felt that requisite organization provided concepts, a vocabulary, and tools to consider these quite different issues and to talk about them.

Privott's judgments of his immediate subordinates and subordinates-once-removed were recorded over a number of years. The changes in judgments of individuals paralleled the expected maturation of CIP as reflected in Dr. Jaques's Potential Progress Data Chart.

Addressing Issues of Temperament

As the power of requisite practices became evident, Privott turned his attention to issues of temperament. He wanted to assist individuals and groups to behave more effectively at work through a method of understanding and discussing behavioral issues. He also sought a way to take temperament into consideration in staffing decisions.

I recommended Ken Wright, a specialist in this area, who also has a deep understanding of requisite organization. Wright used the Human Synergistics instrument as an information-gathering tool and catalyst, both for individual discussions and to enhance understanding of interpersonal issues within groups and teams. Work in this area began along with the ongoing implementation of requisite practices, helping key employees to see themselves and how their behavior at work affected others.

"One of my key employees told me that he couldn't stop himself from having his first thoughts about ideas be negative ones," Privott said, "but he could control what he did with those thoughts. He said that once he realized the impact of this behavior on others, he learned to stop himself from making cynical, put-down remarks that cut off creative discussions."

Examining Cross-Functional Working Relationships

Another area that was addressed early in the project was that of the interface between units. Privott held an off-site meeting to review areas where Novus could increase effectiveness by improving clarity in the accountability and authority between roles that reported to different managers. We used the RO descriptions of cross-functional working relationships to address some of these issues and to specify what the roles involved needed to do. Privott knew that the lack of clarity in these relationships between roles in different areas caused many interpersonal problems. Describing the accountabilities and authorities assigned to each role reduced those problems.

Developing the Novus Management System

Sabrena Hamilton, the director of human resources, and I developed a document to state key accountabilities fully and clearly. It was appropriately named the Key Accountabilities Document (KAD). We coordinated the KAD with a Personal

Effectiveness Appraisal (PEA) document that we designed at the same time to be used at the informal mid-year and formal annual appraisals. Hamilton and I also reviewed all Novus policy documents to modify any aspects of policies and procedures that were non-requisite.

We then developed a manual for all Novus managers that described the integrated process of identifying and communicating employees' key accountabilities. This process included providing feedback and coaching when tasks were completed, and judging the overall personal effectiveness of each employee. The manual also included eight other RO managerial leadership practices.

All of the new processes and procedures were named the Novus Management System (NMS) and were described in one comprehensive document.

Key Accountabilities Document

We designed the Key Accountabilities Document to include key tasks, general responsibilities, team assignments, and critical cross-functional accountability and authority. We included a general statement that managers would also be judged on their full use of the requisite managerial leadership practices.

Privott found that an important contribution made by requisite concepts was that accountabilities should identify the manager's intended time to task completion. This might well be shorter or longer than the annual appraisal cycle. When it was necessary to judge tasks lasting more than a year for the annual Personal Effectiveness Appraisal (PEA) review, managers designated a milestone in the progress of that task or reviewed progress on the task to date as part of the appraisal. If the task were shorter than a year the manager gave feedback to the employee when the assignment was completed.

Privott found that these RO concepts continued to provide value as the company grew. "The concepts embodied in capability and level of work of a role," he said, "were especially helpful in understanding situations where individuals, who had been capable of their roles, seemed no longer effective as the organization and the work grew in complexity. This problem is common in successful and growing organizations and is a very difficult one to deal with. Understanding its causes is a giant step toward deciding how to resolve the problem while valuing the worth and dignity of the individual involved."

Educating Employees about the Novus Management System

With the KAD and PEA processes and forms and the Novus Management System manual ready for use, members of the senior management team set up an educational session for all of their subordinates. I assisted in these programs that were held not only in St. Louis, but around the world as part of regional meetings. This education was completed for all employees over a period of about three months.

Other Requisite Practices

As the second year of requisite implementation began with the task assignment and appraisal processes in place and the initial education completed, attention turned to other requisite practices, such as selection and orientation. Hamilton and I wrote a manual to aid managers throughout the world in applying requisite principles in interviewing and selecting employees. We also designed an orientation program for new employees.

Level of Work and Organization Structure

Privott and his team had reviewed issues of organization structure and the level of work of each role during the first year of the implementation, using the level of work principles from the educational process. Some changes had been made where, for example, a role incumbent did not possess the level of CIP required for the role's work. However, it was not until this point that a decision could be made in determining how Novus would use the level of work concepts.

All senior staff worked together to calibrate the Novus roles across the organization, using a combination of time-span measurement and executive judgment. Over time, the staff was gradually deployed requisitely, based on the judgment of CIP and the other aspects of suitability for role—skilled knowledge and commitment to the work.

"There is a tendency to want to quantify performance," Privott said, "but one needs to make a judgment about whether each person was operating at full capability under the prevailing circumstances. This can't be measured: it has to be judged.

"Jaques's concepts gave us a frame of reference for making and reviewing these judgments of employees' effectiveness under prevailing circumstances."

Compensation

With Novus organized requisitely in terms of roles and people in them, we started to consider using requisite principles for the compensation system. Only when an organization is requisitely structured and staffed and requisite managerial leadership practices are in place is it possible to implement requisite compensation.

Hamilton, the director of human resources, had many years of compensation experience in a global company. She asked several compensation consulting organizations to assist her in using requisite compensation, but none of them could integrate requisite concepts into their existing methodologies.

"So, I had a number of conversations with senior managers and Nancy on this topic," she said, "and then shut myself in a room for two days to fully understand the implication of using 'X' and pay differential based on level of work of a role as the basis of total compensation. I made some initial calculations as to what this would look like in some of the many countries around the world where we have employees.

"It became apparent that since we had uniformly defined complexity of roles worldwide, we could benchmark pay at each level and then adjust as needed to the realities of various labor markets. We separated pay increases from structure movements. Our calculations included all aspects of compensation, such as benefits, which tend to vary widely between countries plus the annual and the long-term incentive plans.

While Novus may never have a purely requisite compensation system because of its incentive pay for all employees, Novus has been successful in applying most of the principles.

Hamilton also found an interesting side-benefit to implementing RO concepts in the Novus compensation practices. "We found that once you understand and apply the basics of requisite compensation," she said, "you don't need compensation specialists to keep the system going."

Talent Pool Development

Early in year two of the implementation, Thad Simons, corporate counsel and head of human resources and new business development, worked with Hamilton and me to set up a requisite talent pool process. The senior management team met several times a year to review all roles that would need to be filled in the next several years and the employees who were judged to have complexity of information processing (CIP) required to fill those roles.

In these meetings, they shared the judgment made by the manager and manager-once-removed (MoR) of each employee's CIP, as well as information on education, experience, skilled knowledge, and what the employee valued in the work environment.

We developed a form that captured this information about the employees under consideration:

- Whether or not they were judged to currently have the CIP needed for the role or when they might be expected to have matured into it;
- Whether or not they valued the work of the role, and what steps should be taken to explore that further;
- Whether or not they had the necessary skilled knowledge, and what steps to take to develop it.

All employees who were judged capable of working in middle-management roles (stratum III) or higher were reviewed and added to the talent pool on a continuing basis.

The senior management team commented on how constructive this approach was compared to earlier experiences that largely focused on issues of personality.

"The talent pool process we developed using requisite concepts helped us to think about the organization we needed in the future in terms of roles and the level of work that would be involved," Privott said. "We had a common language to do an assessment of our current talent pool and to analyze our current staff members in terms of their complexity of information processing, their commitment to the work of the role, and their knowledge, skill, and experience. We then had a sound basis to provide development plans for specific individuals that we wanted to prepare for future roles."

Embedding the Novus Management System

Also starting in the second year, Privott instituted an annual review of the full Novus Management System (NMS) at the annual meeting of employees in St. Louis. He conducted this review personally, sending a clear message of the importance of requisite practices and procedures that made up the NMS and ensuring that all employees were familiar with them. Privott also participated in all new employee orientation sessions, giving the segment on the NMS, which demonstrated his commitment to it. He also used each issue of the Novus newsletter to address some aspect of the NMS. He ended these articles and the educational sessions by asking employees "to hold him accountable for following the system" and saying that he would "hold them accountable for doing so as well."

Thoughts about the Novus Project

Joe Privott retired from Novus in 1999, and subsequently became a consultant to corporate presidents, helping them understand and implement requisite organization. He has thought a great deal about the experience of bringing these concepts into Novus.

"As one involved in Novus from its inception, I had a passion to drive the company forward successfully," he said. "Using requisite principles gave me additional courage and confidence to develop my vision for the company and implement it."

Privott believes that by implementing RO in conjunction with a focus on temperament "excellent business results were achieved (in both growth and profitability) compared to competitors and a healthy, constructive place to work was established."

"What started," he said, "as a small unit in Monsanto that had 3 percent share of the domestic market for its product grew to have 35 percent share of a world market that was itself growing at 6 percent to 10 percent annually. Using requisite principles contributed substantially to our success over the years and enabled me to deal openly, fairly and honestly with my employees."

Reflecting on Elliott Jaques, Privott was succinct: "He is sorely missed."

Novus in the 21st Century

With Thad Simons succeeding Dr. Privott as president of Novus, the corporate vision has evolved, and it is now to "help feed the world affordable, wholesome food" and Novus's goal is to "build a self-renewing multi-product company."

Requisite practices and procedures, embodied in the Novus Management System continue in place and are well embedded in the culture. Attention to setting clear goals and enhancing individual effectiveness has improved efficiency at Novus from about US$1.5 million in sales per full-time employee to more than US$2.5 million. The clarity, logic, and consistency of requisite organization principles provides a substantial foundation for guiding and integrating the work of Novus employees who are located in 24 countries and operating in 83 countries. With sales approaching US$500 million and continuing a strong growth rate of more than 10 percent per annum, Novus is an outstanding example of a successful global organization that has implemented requisite principles and practices.

ABOUT THE AUTHOR

Nancy R. Lee is president of Requisite Organization Associates Inc., a firm that helps organizations understand and utilize effective structure, staffing, and managerial practices. She has extensive experience as a corporate manager and consultant to senior management in the areas of organization design, human resource development, succession planning, executive coaching, management education, marketing, and information technology.

Lee has taught management development throughout the US, the UK, and Australia, including at Simmons College in Boston and Banking School at the University of Washington. She has been a speaker at major conventions, such as the American Institute of Banking, the American Bar Association, and the American Management Association. Clients with whom she has worked include: Citibank, Chase, IBM, IATA, Hoffmann La Roche, Kellogg's, MetLife, Norsk Hydro, Ontario Hydro, the Royal Bank of Canada, and the US Treasury. Lee was employed by General Electric, Macy's New York, and Wedgwood. She was graduated with honors from Cornell University and attended the Graduate School of Management at Boston University.

Doubleday and Ballantine Books published her book on management development entitled *Targeting the Top*. She has also written *The Practice of Managerial Leadership*, based on requisite principles and practices, which is available from www.xlibris.com.

The Inglis Story:
How It Became the Number One Appliance Company in Canada

Maurice Dutrisac and Stephen D. Clement

WHAT'S IMPORTANT

- At start: A No.2 Canadian major appliance manufacturer and distributor with declining sales of $450 million (CDN), was purchased by Whirlpool and told to reduce costs by $60 million (CDN).

- Implementation: Full RO implementation with major restructuring and key re-staffing.

- Results: Increased sales 33 percent in one year in a flat, recessionary market to become No. 1 in Canadian market for first time in industry history.

- Using a requisite approach made it easier for a new CEO to transition into the job.

Mike Thieneman and Maurice Dutrisac first heard Elliott Jaques's theory of requisite organization in early 1991 at Whirlpool's first global management conference in Montreux, Switzerland. They looked at each other and said, "What do we have to lose?" They were President and CEO and the VP administration, respectively, for Inglis, the No. 2 home appliance company in Canada, and the company's future no longer looked so bright.

Some of Inglis' turmoil came from the normal changes of acquisition. Whirlpool had become sole owner of Inglis in early 1990, when they purchased the remaining shares of the company. David Whitwam, chairman and CEO of Whirlpool, and Dave Marohn, the North American president, insisted on several changes, including a $60 million (CDN) reduction in selling, general, and administrative costs and a marked rise in the efficiency of corporate staff.

They also wanted Inglis to become the No. 1 appliance company in Canada, a position that Camco/GE had held since 1977, when it was formed by the merger of the white goods divisions of Westinghouse, Canadian General Electric, and GSW. In 1991, Camco had $150 million (CDN) higher sales revenues than No. 2 Inglis and seemed to have the momentum to take sales away. Inglis faced a daunting task to become No.1 in a flat, recessionary Canadian market. They would have to steal market share from their competitors, especially Camco.

Bad Market, Hard Times

Serious problems loomed before the buyout. By 1989, Inglis had sales of $500 million (CDN) and owned or manufactured an array of Canadian white goods brands including supplying home laundry products to Sears Canada, owner of the Kenmore brand, one of the most popular white goods brands in North America. But sales fell in 1990 and the company's profit left with them. Canada was mired in a recession that drove the major appliances market 20 percent lower between 1988 and 1991. What was left of the market was moving from independent dealers, where Inglis had been traditionally strong, to power retailers that Inglis had a hard time penetrating.

Even worse, Inglis' outdated production system and corresponding poor quality threatened to destroy the business. Sears threatened to pull the contract for Inglis' private label manufacturing of the Kenmore brand, which made up almost a third of sales, if Inglis didn't reduce the current six-week lead time to be closer to Camco's five days.

These problems did not create the best environment for increasing sales 30 percent!

Inglis was aware of these problems and had been making some progress to improve its situation. The company was able to stop the slide in revenue, and it instituted new quality and empowerment programs. The new management at Inglis knew that the entitlement culture had to be replaced with stronger work values and trust. Six-day "boot camps" were implemented for all salaried employees and union leaders. So far, however, management's efforts had stopped the decline without leading to new growth. It was searching for a missing piece of the management puzzle that they could not seem to find.

That is, until the Whirlpool conference in Montreux where some of the top consultants, leadership gurus, and vision experts were brought in to give half-day workshops to the assembled executives. One of these gurus was Elliott Jaques, who had been working on Whirlpool's talent pool evaluation system. Jaques stirred more interest than any of the other speakers, provoking heated debate and strong disagreements among the Whirlpool executives. Most of the Whirlpool American team members didn't like what they were hearing, especially when Jaques told them that Whirlpool's non-requisite organization was causing many inefficiencies and constraining growth. However, the more that Thieneman and Dutrisac thought about Jaques's ideas, the more they were interested.

"If you put in place what I am telling you," said Jaques, "your organization will flower by 20 percent to 40 percent productivity and growth."

Requisite Comes to Inglis

Figuring that they had nothing to lose, given the seemingly impossible task that Whirlpool had handed them, Thieneman and Dutrisac asked Jaques to come to Inglis' corporate office in Mississauga, Ontario later that spring to do a two-day workshop for the top 20 executives. Jaques brought along Dr. Stephen Clement, a retired US Army officer who had been working with him on Whirlpool's talent pool system.

As Dutrisac remembers it, the meeting was far from boring. "Elliott proceeded to insult or browbeat most of the 20 Inglis managers in the boardroom," he said.

Jaques's ideas flew in the face of everything that the Inglis executives had learned in management school. They would have to do business very differently. The cost of the change would be great. Would it be worth it?

Dutrisac himself wasn't entirely on board with Jaques's ideas. He had studied Jaques's ideas about Felt-Fair Pay, but Jaques's science of organizing a business worried him. "It's hard to change your belief system," he said. "When you're faced with this new stuff, it's hard to learn, and it's depressing because it defies your earlier belief systems. When you do learn it, you say, 'Why didn't I know this in my previous executive postings?"

The Change Process

Despite their reservations, Inglis' management team members decided to go forward with a restructuring of their organization and roles. Dutrisac would head the project, with the Inglis management committee acting as the steering committee. Jaques recommended using Dr. Clement as the external consultant. Clement had co-authored *Executive Leadership* with Jaques following the groundbreaking work both had been involved with at CRA, an Australian mining company. He was one of the few consultants in North America during the early 1990s who not only understood Elliott's complex ideas, but who also had experience in implementing them.

"I don't think we could have pulled it off with anyone other than Steve Clement at that time," Dutrisac said.

Dutrisac assembled a Requisite Project Team of six highly regarded managers. Each of these managers would continue their regular duties while working on the restructuring process. In a move that surely sent a shudder through the entitlement culture, the team took over the former executive dining room as the "Requisite War Room." Employees got the message: management was serious about this project and was willing to start the restructuring process with its own entitlements.

In June 1991, the team began its work. For the next six months they conducted hundreds of interviews to help them understand how the work at Inglis really got done. The team also studied the functions at the corporate office, discovering gaps and compressions that prevented Inglis from being able to compete with Camco and Frigidaire.

On the people side, the Inglis senior executive team was forced to demote, fire, or retire early a number of the Inglis managers following a three-day meeting of the senior executive team to assess and calibrate the cognitive ability of all the managers. Some of the lower-level managers were promoted when it was determined that they were working below their cognitive ability. Maurice Dutrisac then used a professional recruiting firm to hire 25 high-potential individuals that had the cognitive ability to work at the complexity required to make headway towards overtaking Camco. Many of the individuals recruited performed at a higher level than their predecessors within four to six months of their appointment, even though many had not previously worked in an appliance company.

At Inglis, corporate functions had grown into silos that were insulated from each other. Hand-offs tended to be blind and incomplete, a factor that had led to the recent failure of the introduction of Inglis' newest product, the P2000 refrigerator. To get at proper accountabilities and responsibilities within and between the functions, Dutrisac and his project team had each function go offsite to work it out.

"We would go into a hotel and each function would work out the accountabilities and authorities within each role and function," Dutrisac said. "Then, all of the functions would meet in a larger room and determine if these accountabilities fit with their understanding." Finally, the functional teams determined how the accountabilities worked laterally between the functions. The same review process was used to evaluate the manufacturing plants.

"Within the team," Dutrisac said, "they would ask for each of their many accountabilities within their roles, 'Is this prescribing? Is this monitoring? Or is this advisory?'" The functions had heated discussions over who was really responsible or accountable at various points.

Each team would determine how it worked together within its own function. It would then tackle how it saw the accountabilities and responsibilities of its interfaces with the other functions. The process included a review and assessment of all managers at Inglis. "We had a true manager-once-removed process," said Dutrisac, reviewing not only the person's direct supervisor, but also the supervisor's boss.

The company's existing culture meant that many people were under or over-employed. The restructuring that the team would ultimately recommend meant that many people would have to move out of their current roles.

A New Structure for Sales

The sales function provides a good example of the extent of the restructuring process. The Requisite Project Team determined that the existing organizational structure, when seen through the lens of requisite organization, had several problems.

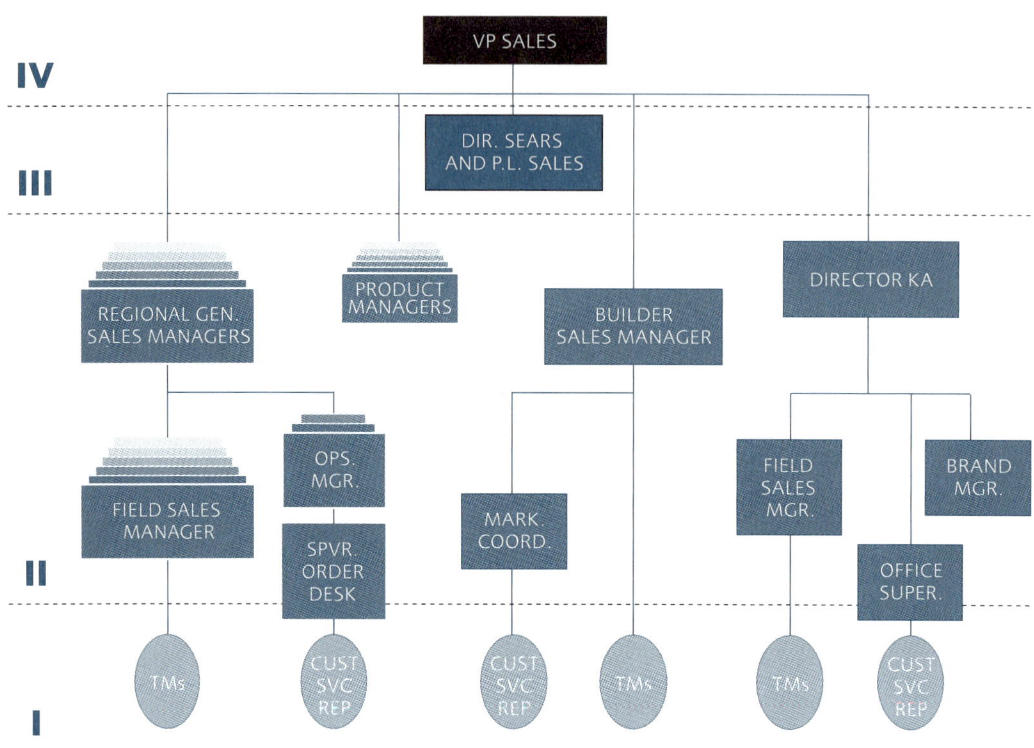

FIGURE 3.3.1: SALES ORGANIZATION BEFORE THE CHANGE

(See Figure 3.3.1.) People were not reporting to a role or person one real level above them. There were several jam-ups at level II, where managers worked at the same level as their subordinates and therefore did not add value. The VP had direct reports that were working two levels below him.

This inefficient structure caused the VP of sales, Jacques Lebeuf, to work at level III, meaning his more complex tasks at level IV, including growing sales, were not being done. Even though he was a very experienced appliance manager, Inglis had started looking for a replacement because he seemed mired in the weeds.

The team reviewed how work got done in the function and evaluated the sales personnel, including Lebeuf. The VP assessed at a strong level IV. Lebeuf who was a strong charismatic leader was not the problem: the way the work was organized forced the sales function to be inefficient. Jaques had been right: the organizational structure had defeated the best efforts of qualified and motivated personnel.

The new structure would ensure that each role worked requisitely. (See Figure 3.3.2.) In many ways, the sales function was brand new. Existing positions were eliminated and new positions were created. Eight new director level positions (level III) were created to support the VP sales. Support services were consolidated in the corporate office, with a new sales training role. The ten order desks were centralized into one.

Since sales was closest to the customer, all company functions that were customer-oriented would move into sales. Merchandising moved from marketing, because it needed to be embedded in customer details, such as next week's spiff or point-of-purchase material. The credit manager role was moved from finance, also to be closer to customers.

Several new positions were created to fit the strategy and direction of the company. A director of financial analysis was created to analyze client accounts to ensure that sales people met the margins targets, rather than just volume targets. The director of key accounts was created to focus on the more demanding and complex power retailers to gain quick penetration in a channel that Inglis did not service well. Also, the manager of builder sales position was elevated to a director-level position in order to better compete in this channel.

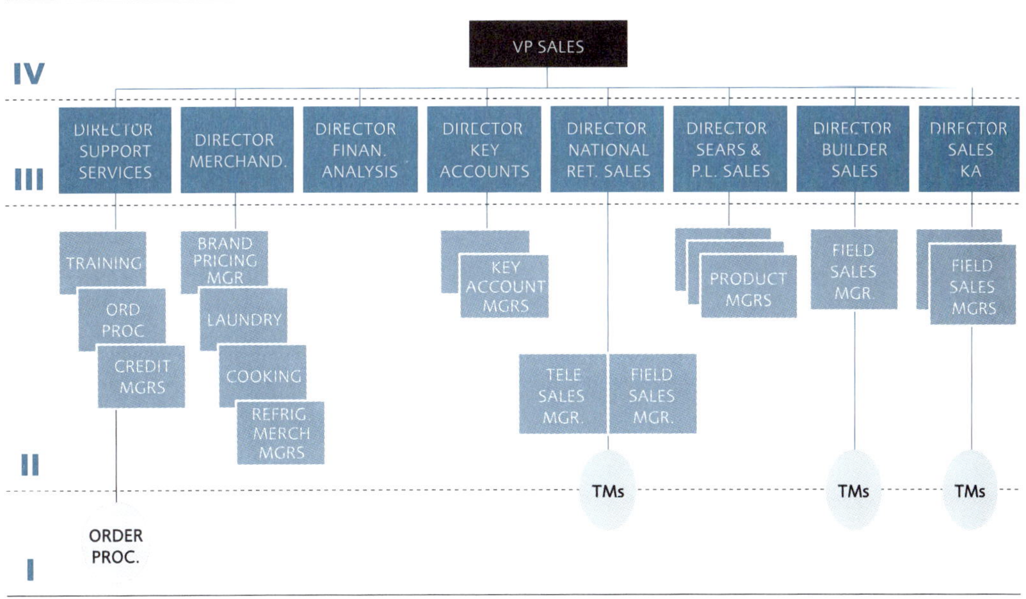

FIGURE 3.3.2: SALES ORGANIZATION AFTER THE CHANGE

The Requisite Project Team also reengineered how sales serviced the 2,500 dealers who distributed Inglis and Admiral appliances, creating a telesales function to replace many of the outside territory managers. With the central order desk and telesales team, Inglis could provide better service to their clients, and at a lower cost. It was not simply adding personnel.

"In actuality by merging the Inglis, Admiral, and Whirlpool brand sales forces," Lebeuf said, "by eliminating the administrative work, such as order desks, being done in the sales regions and by eliminating some of the territory managers and replacing them with telesales representatives, the net result was a 20 percent savings in the sales function cost to service our clients. In the end, it was this strong sales team with clear accountabilities and authorities buttressed by centralized support functions to free them to sell that went out and started stealing profitable market share from our three key competitors."

"Once the sales function had the right structure, the right people, and the right accountabilities," Lebeuf added, "it was like magic and sales took off. I was also able to start working on my longer term tasks and stay out of the weeds."

Other Functions

The Requisite Project Team at Inglis led this same type of analysis in all of the other corporate functions, as well as in the manufacturing plants.

In the marketing function, the level III director of marketing role was elevated to a level IV VP marketing. A level III director of product development position was also created to give direction and integrate the work of the product managers. In turn, these level II product managers were given clear accountabilities, authorities, and resources to work with the sales, market research and product engineering functions to develop and design kitchen and laundry appliances that would surpass the expectations of Canadians. For example, the cook top that the cooking product manager and a strong cooking engineering design team produced is still rated as the best cook top in Canada. A new level III position of director market research was also created so that Inglis could understand what Canadian consumers wanted for home appliances for years to come.

Another example is the parts and service function comprised of 39 service branches across Canada. When the Requisite Project Team studied how the service branches served the Canadian market, it was able to determine that only 26 service branches were required, if the branches provided their service technicians with the resources and clear accountabilities and authorities to deal with customer service calls. With fewer service branches covering wider regions of Canada this meant that the service technicians did not have to return to their branches daily, and parts for repairs could be shipped to their homes. Another major change was to centralize the parts ordering and dispatching functions into the Inglis Mississauga head office. These dispatching and parts ordering roles had been replicated in each of the 39 service branches at a great cost to Inglis. For example, the centralized dispatching system required just four dispatchers, and it accepted customer calls over a longer day. The resulting cost savings in administration expenses for the parts and service function was greater than 30 percent.

Painful Lessons

The Requisite Project Team presented its recommendations to the Inglis management committee in Oct 1991, and the company began implementation the next month. In early 1992, after restructuring the corporate offices, the remaining three manufacturing plants were restructured using requisite organization principles.

The process wasn't without pain. Employees were used to the old entitlement environment and found it hard to adjust to the team's recommendations. "Some employees retired early, some found positions elsewhere during our review," said Dutrisac, "and some we had to let go."

Inglis also continued to have shuffles at the top. Fran Scricco, a former GE executive who had run GE's TV and air conditioning businesses, became CEO in early 1992 when Whirlpool appointed Thieneman president of its compressor business in Torino, Italy. Thieneman himself had replaced Bud Wampach, who had joined Inglis in 1988 after a long career at Whirlpool, where he had been responsible for all manufacturing. Wampach retired soon after Whirlpool acquired Inglis.

"There is no doubt that having three successive CEOs during this tremendous growth phase caused some angst amongst the managers," said Lebeuf, "as each CEO had his own distinct style. However, the fact that each of these CEO's had very high cognitive ability and strong leadership skills compensated for these rapid changeovers."

Throughout the process, there were difficult lessons to be learned. In retrospect, Dutrisac admits that it would have been better to have team members assigned full-time to the requisite change project. This would have reduced the strain and stress on their personal lives. As it was, they worked six to seven days a week, 10 to 16 hours a day, so that they could complete their regular duties along with the project work.

Although the hours continued to be long, the team kept working. "There was a lot of adrenaline," Dutrisac said, "because I started to see that this was going to work and as project manager, I had the responsibility of ensuring that it would work. I had a lot of sleepless nights, because I felt that this was so important to the future of all Inglis employees."

The process also took too long. "When I do this for my clients now, as a consultant, I do it faster," said Dutrisac. "But the process was quick once we gave them the recommendations."

Dutrisac also says he would have listened to external consultant Stephen Clement about designing and implementing the 11 key leadership practices training modules for requisite to have full impact. Inglis trained staff on performing assessments (including the manager-once-removed process), performance management, and some on setting the context and tasks assignments. However, the 11 key managerial leadership practices were not inculcated into the Inglis culture. If Dutrisac could do it again, he would spend more resources to fully train managers on the managerial practices of selection and induction, context setting, team planning, tasks assignment, team building, tasks adjustment, monitoring, coaching, appraisal, continuous improvement, de-selection/dismissal, and manager-once-removed assessment.

The Results

The pain paid off. By the end of 1992, in a recessionary, flat market, Inglis had become the largest appliance company in Canada, supplanting Camco/GE's long term market-leadership. Sales in 1992 exceeded 1991 sales by 33 percent to $600 million (CDN).

Quality and process improvements also shone through. Made-to-order manufacturing that used to take six weeks now took less than a week. Quality issues like the P2000 refrigerator were now caught in design, and issues on the plant floor often could be resolved there. Inglis had penetrated the power retailer channel and were taking market share from Camco and Frigidaire. Inglis' 2,500-dealer network was getting unprecedented service due to the new ordering systems and centralized telesales and order desk. Employee morale went up with the winning team. Inglis became an exporter of talent, and many of the high-potential employees that Inglis had developed were transferred to other Whirlpool business units.

The success continued. The 1997 Whirlpool annual report celebrated Inglis as having unprecedented record sales and profits. To this day Inglis (now called Whirlpool Canada) is still the No. 1 major appliance company in Canada.

Fran Scricco maintains that he was able to "hit the deck running" when he arrived at Inglis because it already had the right structure, the right people, and the right accountabilities and authorities to drive the strategy to become No. 1 in Canada. "Actually, I didn't fully realize what had been accomplished at Inglis by Maurice Dutrisac and his Requisite Project Team until I became the CEO of another company," he said. "It made my job at Inglis so much easier."

Thieneman and Dutrisac may have thought that Elliott Jaques was showboating when he said that his ideas increase productivity and growth 20 to 40 percent. After the implementation, they couldn't believe that it had actually happened.

They are now firm believers in requisite organization. When asked how much of Inglis' success could be attributed to this one set of ideas, Dutrisac is clear: "Without requisite organization it wouldn't have happened."

Clement summarizes why more companies do not take advantage of these organization design concepts. "Unfortunately, it is a lot of work to implement a requisite organization and the results are not instantaneous. CEOs want quick quarter by quarter fixes because their tenure as CEOs is becoming shorter and shorter. It is ironic that they don't use this system of management to ensure not only their long-term survival, but also the success of their companies."

Maurice Dutrisac sums it up with the following: "You can have the best strategy in the world, but without the proper structure and the people in the right levels, you will not achieve all you can."

ABOUT THE AUTHORS

Maurice Dutrisac is one of the founding partners and the practice leader for strategic planning and organizational design for Mastermind Solutions Inc. a general management consulting firm established in 1999. Dutrisac specializes in business strategy, retreat facilitation, organizational design, structure and change, creative problem solving, leadership development, organizational design workshops for executives, and talent pool management. He is also a member of a number of advisory boards.

Prior to his consulting career, he worked for 24 years as an executive with large, complex manufacturing, service- and resource-based corporations in Canada and the United States. Dutisac was awarded the BA and MBA degrees from McMaster University and is fluent in French and English. He resides in Mississauga, Ontario.

Dr. Stephen D. Clement is founder and president of Organizational Design, Inc. (ODI), a Texas-based consulting firm. He has been involved in the application of requisite organizational design principles and concepts for more than 20 years. Steve worked closely with Dr. Elliott Jaques and Sir Roderick Carnegie in a ten-year year collaborative effort at CRA (a major Australian mining company) where many of the principles were first refined and tested in an operational environment. He is currently involved in applying RO-related concepts in several long-term industrial and government studies. He is the co-author of *Executive Leadership: A Practical Guide to Managing Complexity* with Dr. Jaques.

 **4**

Contributions of Stratified Systems Theory to Military Leader Development and Organization Redesign in the US Army

T. Owen Jacobs and Stephen D. Clement

WHAT'S IMPORTANT

- Validated time spans in the top four levels and the extraordinary importance of cognitive power to deal with the increasing complexity of the work at senior levels.

- Catalyzed a major shift in leader development theory and practice from leader-centric to systems, including organizational processes and structure.

- Catalyzed policy documenting the responsibility that strategic military leaders have for shaping organizational culture, climate, and operational processes.

- Emphasized development processes for high-potential individuals.

- Provided the conceptual framework for redesigning major parts of the US Army.

...Dr. Jaques brought a rich understanding of the interplay between organizational structures and processes and the capabilities leaders at various levels required. Perhaps of even greater importance, he underscored the moral imperative that organizations provide opportunity for members to engage the full extent of their capabilities in the work they do. He thus was in the forefront of those who challenged the bureaucratic traditions of the Industrial Age form then prevalent.

This article reports a program of research and application employing Stratified Systems Theory (SST) in the US Army. In Part 1, T. Owen Jacobs describes research intended to validate the applicability of SST principles in a military organization. In Part 2, Stephen D. Clement describes significant further efforts, mostly his own work, in which these principles were applied to the transformative redesign of elements of a major branch of the US Army.

Part 1: The Impact of SST on Military Leader Development Theory and Practice

The collaboration between Dr. Elliott Jaques and scientists at the US Army Research Institute for the Behavioral and Social Sciences extended from 1979 to 1994, and had significant impact on military leader development theory and practice. To appreciate this impact, one must understand that, in the 1970s, military leader development was still viewed by most from a leader-centric perspective. Relatively little attention was paid to organizational processes and structure. Leader development thus was concerned with what needed to be "done to" leaders to make them more effective. US military leadership doctrine reflected this perspective strongly. In the U.S. and elsewhere, the scientific study of organizations as living entities had achieved substantial maturity, but an understanding of the interface between individual leadership and organizational behavior had not yet seen the light of day in military doctrine. More pointedly, there was little codified understanding of the responsibility that strategic military leaders have for shaping organizational culture, climate, and operational processes, so as to achieve organizational excellence. Clearly, many "great" military leaders did understand these responsibilities. However, the doctrine on which leader development practices were based at that time just did not address these organizational factors.

In addition, officer personnel management, analogous to management development in the private sector, was based on industrial-age concepts of questionable appropriateness for the evolving information-age, global society. While weeding out the less capable, these practices also discouraged many young officers of high potential, leading to early termination of their military service and rendering the military organization itself less capable of truly transformative thought.

It was into this context that Dr. Jaques brought a rich understanding of the interplay between organizational structures and processes and the capabilities leaders at various levels required. Perhaps of even greater importance, he underscored the moral imperative that organizations provide opportunity for members to engage the full extent of their capabilities in the work they do. He thus was in the forefront of those who challenged the bureaucratic traditions of the Industrial Age form then prevalent.

Initial Application: The Office of the Joint Chiefs of Staff

The initial application of SST was at the highest level of the US military establishment, the Office of the Joint Chiefs of Staff (OJCS). The OJCS was essentially a consensus body. In its organization and functions, it resembled the topmost levels, the strategic apex, of a super-scale private-sector corporation. The opportunity to work at this level was quite important, because it allowed a test of the theory. If SST principles hold up at this level, the way would be clear for a much larger effort, particularly within the US Army.

The first effort was quite successful. Jaques interviewed three-star, two-star, and one-star generals in OJCS, and was able to get descriptions of the work done by the four-star generals. Officer ranks compared with private sector civilians as shown in Table 3.4.1.

As Table 3.4.1 shows, the observed time spans were quite close to expectations, based on earlier findings in large-scale private sector companies. Of even greater importance, the observed time spans had practical significance with regard to the work involved in these positions. There were two broad timeframes. One, six to eight years, corresponded to the annual "hard" budget (PPBES) Department of Defense (DoD) request for Congressional funding. It provides specific funding over the following two-year period, and projections of funding for a subsequent five-year period.

Officer Rank	Theoretical Time Span	Observed Time Span	Comparable Civilian Managerial Roles
FOUR-STAR	20-50 years	20-25 years	Large-scale corporate chairman and CEOs
THREE-STAR	10-20 years	12-15 years	Corporate VPs and EVPs
TWO-STAR	5-10 years	6-8 years	Subsidiary CEOs
ONE-STAR	2-5 years	3-4 years	General management

TABLE 3.4.1: THEORETICAL AND OBSERVED TIME SPANS (OJCS)

The second, 12-15 years, corresponded to a concepts development cycle. The concepts document was policy guidance for funding research and development programs and incremental investments in capital-intensive systems. For SST, the separation of these two broad timeframes had extraordinary meaning. It corresponds to the point at which the use of analytic methods commonly used in mid-level management generate uncertainties so large that the predictions cease to have great utility. In essence, analytic tools were used at the two-star level as in running a business. At the three-star level, creative vision and imagination were used to project new business directions.

However, Jaques did not actually find the expected 20-plus year forward view in the OJCS, probably because the 20-plus year outlooks existed in separate services. He concluded that "... inter-services collaboration probably could be fully effective only in the context of 20-25 year programs which could be focused and directed from OJCS level."[1] In this conclusion, he was remarkably prescient. The Defense Reorganization Act of 1987 required the chairman to begin reviewing major systems acquisitions, the 20-plus year major decisions, proposed by the separate services. In 2000, the Chairman published the first joint vision, effectively requiring synergy among the services.

Whether Jaques's insights and recommendations led to these developments cannot be said. It is enough to know that SST principles generated conclusions about needed organizational change that eventually came to pass. SST principles were clearly applicable to more organizations than just the private sector.

---

1   Jacobs, T. "Military Applications of Stratified Systems Theory." *Festschrift for Elliott Jaques*. Arlington, VA: Cason-Hall, 1992. P. 258

The OJCS work led to the study of strategic leadership in the Army. Improved understanding of strategic roles was needed to prepare officers for the huge step up from mid-level roles. Officers attending Joint/Senior Service Colleges (J/SSC) are at the last point at which education can materially influence their subsequent development. Students will have spent 17-20 years in the "production" level, an extremely long period of socialization by an overabundance of rules, procedures, precedents, and other constraints on dealing with complexity. The one-year sojourn in J/SSC institutions is designed to help graduates develop thinking and problem-solving skills more suited to the strategic arena. That is a relatively short time to become capable of dealing with multi-linear, abstract, and ill-structured strategic issues. Thus, deeper understanding of how to manage this transformation was of great importance.

A General Officer Coordinating Council (SLCC) was formed to oversee a broad set of initiatives to improve the Army's commissioned officer development process. Under the aegis of the SLCC, a team was formed to do fundamental research on general officer roles, guided by SST. The team consisted of Dr. Elliott Jaques under contract from Brunel University, T. Owen Jacobs and Carlos Rigby from the Army Research Institute, and Stephen Clement from the US Army. This work was to develop fundamental understanding of general officer roles and responsibilities in a framework that would guide development of "growth" paths. The team interviewed 115 general officers, distributed across all ranks. Important findings emerged from this work, both for SST and for military leader development.

The mental frames of reference, what the generals thought about and how they did it, strongly supported SST predictions. Four-star generals were concerned about national and international politics, economics, and social structures, the role of the military in society. They were less concerned about "internal" matters. Officers who were two-star and lower were more concerned about "running" their elements or organizations. Table 3.4.2 shows these shifts. The three- and four-star transition from internal to external is shown by decrease in concern about systems understanding, and increases in concern about Joint and combined relationships, and external perspective.

Time perspective differences were evident from both the interviews and specific time-span responses. Planning/envisioning responses showed a strong trend, as did time-span measures shown in Table 3.4.3. Time spans did, in fact, seem to increase

COMPETENCY AREA	BG Level IV	MG Level V	LTG Level VI	GEN Level VII
Systems Understanding	60	90	42	38
Joint and Combined Relationships	25	45	54	73
External Perspective	40	60	61	88
Planning/Envisioning	25	40	64	88
Dealing with Uncertainty/Risk taking	19	29	54	54
Consensus Building	65	80	88	88

(Percent of those interviewed responding)

TABLE 3.4.2: COMPETENCY AREA MENTIONED IN INTERVIEW

with level in accord with SST. However, the increases were not always as expected. We concluded that (a) some officers were over-promoted, (b) some jobs were inappropriately assigned by rank, and (c) task complexity might need to be estimated by some other means than time span. (Jaques's initial formulation related time span to felt responsibility and this may be a more appropriate linkage.) Time span for task completion may be more strongly correlated with resources flow, e.g., how much can be spent on a project in each unit of time. Thus, capital-intensive tasks might depend more on the availability of capital than on the conceptual capacity of those charged with executing them.

Jaques had postulated that top-level executives would operate in a "collegium" sort of way, and our data supported his expectation. Especially at the four-star level, persuasion and consensus-building were felt essential. We concluded that the four-star generals operated very much as a collegium.

YEARS	BG IV	MG V	LTG VI	GEN VII
0-4	10	27	5	0
5-9	9	12	7	2
10	2	6	5	2
11-14	2	1	6	0
15-20	3	0	6	0
20+	1	1	5	4

TABLE 3.4.3: TIME SPANS IN YEARS FROM INTERVIEWS

Finally, these interviews led us to question the SST proposition about the discrete nature of levels of human ability. Our thoughts on this will be shown later, in our conclusions.

What We Have Learned About Executive Leadership

If there is a single, "most important" theme in SST, it is that "cognitive power" is extraordinarily important. Our generals commented often about the complexity and uncertainty at the strategic level (Table 3.4.2). The critical tasks at higher organizational levels are simply more demanding than those at lower levels. Mastering them requires a threshold of capability to comprehend complexity, and that threshold level increases by level. This has extraordinarily important implications for succession planning and leader development.

Succession Planning

No modern organization can hope for competitive advantage unless it can identify young leaders with high potential and bring them forward as they mature. An assessment process pioneered by Gillian Stamp at Brunel University enables early identification of high potential. This foundation work has been used successfully in a component of the Special Operations Command to identify officers with high potential and is a part of the assessment process at one of the J/SSC institutions described below.

Development

Early identification of high potential is not enough in itself. Potential must be developed. The procedure Stamp pioneered suggests at least three key developmental dimensions.

    1. Concept Formation. One part of the assessment is a concept formation task. People differ in how they approach the task. Some strategies are more effective than others. Rapid trial and error is much less effective than stopping to think more holistically about the task. This is a self-awareness dimension that appears critical to successful performance at the highest organizational levels.

    2. Curiosity and Openness to New Experience. A second key part of the assessment is a measure of attraction to complexity and innovation. Most of our high-capacity general officers were interested in a broader range of topics beyond the military. They spent a lot of time "exploring" and their enhanced awareness frequently aided the performance of primary tasks.

3. *Reflective Awareness.* This is fundamental to learning from experience. The top-level generals were more reflective than the others. The Center for Creative Leadership at Greensboro, NC, found much the same thing in their study of executives. The developmental implication is that organizations should "grow" managers and leaders by encouraging reflective analysis of experience.

What We Have Learned About SST

- *Requisite Organization.* Our work does not challenge the SST postulate of approximately seven organizational levels when the complexity of the work requires it.
- *Time Span.* Time span may not always be a reliable method for estimating role complexity. The original time spans came from capital-intensive industry, which was subject to the flow rate of capital resources. They seem to apply reasonably to the US military in peace, because the military is hugely capital-intensive. However, Jaques himself noted that "time compression" occurs in combat, though complexity remains high. If time span, the time an incumbent is given to accomplish his or her longest task, can vary while complexity remains the same, it may not be unequivocal as an estimate of role complexity. Jaques's first formulation of time span was that it related to felt responsibility.[2] This may be a better formulation.
- *Levels of Human Capability.* We concluded that while large-scale organizations may well have seven discrete levels, there may not be that many levels of human capability. We found three significant "paired" levels. Levels II and III have similar complexities, both concerned with essentially "hands-on" operations. Capable incumbents at level II could learn to perform level III roles over time, though not necessarily level IV roles. Levels IV and V were similar in this regard, as were VI and VII. We concluded that these pairs encompass three broadly differing levels of complexity and required cognitive skills. Not surprisingly, these three "pairs"

---

2   Editorial note: There are a few roles, most notably in the fighting part of the military in combat, comprising only short, complex tasks. These roles tend to burn out their incumbents and time span does not measure their complexity accurately.

look a lot like the classical differentiation of levels in large, multidivisional organizations in the private sector. We consequently concluded that succession planning and management development (leadership development in the military) should be viewed from a "three frames of reference" perspective.[3]

- *Cognitive Power.* We also concluded that there were corresponding cognitive processes that are requisite for building these frames of reference: concrete representation and action; abstract representation and analysis; and abstract representation and synthesis. Where any given person finally "plateaus out" is determined by that person's use of these processes, moderated by that person's fluid intelligence. This is a highly simplistic statement, addressing a much more complex underpinning of cognitive theory that is beyond the scope of this paper. However, this perspective is remarkably facilitative in early identification and development of high-potential individuals.

How It Helped

Our research strongly confirmed the applicability of SST principles for leader development in the military services. We have made what we believe to be three important applications.

1. Strategic Leadership Doctrine. The research led directly to publication of a Department of Army pamphlet detailing the complex responsibilities we found at the topmost levels and the skills and abilities a general officer must have to be effective at these levels. Current doctrine now reflects awareness of organizational processes as a context for leadership and the essentiality of systems thinking in complex problem-solving.

2. Joint/Senior Service School Curricula. At the US Army War College (USAWC) and at the Industrial College of the Armed Forces (ICAF), our research results influenced both the nature of the topics covered by the leadership departments and the methodologies used to teach them. In both cases, a course in creative and critical thinking was developed for officers who were firmly embedded in rule sets and procedures, as opposed to open-ended problem-solving. At both institutions, the focus was explicitly on "how to think" not "what to think."

---

3   Editorial note: These conditions have not been found in other organizations but are worth monitoring.

3. Assessment. At both institutions, a battery of assessment instruments was offered to students. While including broad evaluation of other personality dimensions, the strong focus was on conceptual skills and openness to new experience. The assessment process was intended both to increase self-awareness and to enable development plans aimed at strengthening the critical skills and abilities that would be needed for the future.

Conclusion

Stratified Systems Theory has contributed strongly to our understanding of the roles of strategic military leaders and to improvement in military leader development. It is an extraordinarily useful lens for understanding not only requisite organization, but also for understanding assessment and development processes to ensure a stream of "growing" leaders and managers who will regularly be prepared to assume heightened responsibilities as they are thrust upon them.

We see this as quite important. The pace of change is faster now than it was even two decades ago. Information technology not only enables the more rapid development of new technology, but also the faster employment of that technology. We see the next century as one filled with probably greater challenges than any previous century in recorded history. It is fortunate that tools such as SST may help meet those challenges.

Part 2: Application of Stratified Systems Concepts in the US Army

The true test of the lasting impact of any theory on organizational performance is whether or not it gets institutionalized in the culture of an organization. As described previously, SST concepts have made their way into Army doctrine and the Army School system. Students passing through that system have internalized many of these concepts. As a result, a number of significant organizational applications have occurred.

For example, in the early 1990s the newly selected Army Surgeon General elected to reorganize the Army Medical Department based on concepts taken directly from SST. The Surgeon General had learned of these concepts as a Brigadier General while associated with the Training and Doctrine Command (the Army School Command).

As a result of an extensive three-year study effort, the Army Medical Department reorganized itself into ten separate business-unit-sized organizational elements. These organizations encompassed separate product categories and different delivery systems. Each consisted of five organizational layers consistent with SST concepts. More important, however, was the clear differentiation between corporate work (strategic) and operational work (business unit). Significant improvements in operational effectiveness (approximately 30 percent) occurred as a result of this restructuring effort. The soundness of this effort is evidenced by the fact that this structure remains in the Army Medical Department to this day.

Several additional applications of SST concepts have emerged more recently. In 2005, the new Secretary of the Army embarked on a massive business transformation initiative. All facets of the Army's non-war fighting structure and supporting work processes and systems were scrutinized. Currently underway is one of the largest known applications of systematic organizational analysis and redesign and lean Six Sigma process reengineering. The organizational analysis effort is applying a number of basic organizational design principles whose origins can be traced back to the work of Dr. Jaques. The application of these principles to several Army organizations to date has led to increases in productive effectiveness on the order of 30 percent.

What is perhaps more significant, however, are the potential savings to be generated when organizational analysis efforts are paired with lean Six Sigma concepts.

Business Transformation Principles

1. Focus on the customer.
2. Concentrate on the core business.
3. Organize around the work.
4. Differentiate between strategic level staff work and operational work. The present will always drive out the future.
5. Establish the correct number of organizational levels.
6. Align functions at the correct organizational level.
7. Establish clear accountabilities and authorities. Delegate decision making authority to the proper organizational level.
8. Define the nature of required working relationships.
9. Develop and implement a change management strategy.

SST concepts have also been applied recently to managing the Army's senior executive talent pool. In the past, senior civilian leaders were generally left in place while all of the general officers were routinely reassigned as part of their ongoing development program. As part of the business transformation initiative, the Army is now developing its senior civilians much as it does its general officers. A talent pool "war room" has been established to facilitate the process of managing the career development of civilians. Implicit in the management process is an on-going assessment of the underlying complexity of the work assigned to all civilian roles. Currently under review are all aspects of the existing potential assessment process.

Finally, the Army is in the process of currently overhauling its entire education and training system. A recently completed study has recommended a number of changes to the existing school system. Many of these recommendations can be traced back to the earlier work of Dr. Jaques and his colleagues at the Army Research Institute.

What is clear from the efforts currently underway in the Army is that introducing change in a large organization is both difficult and time consuming. Most large organizations tend to resist rapid change. Yet, when concepts and theory are sound and thoroughly understood by operators in the organization, change will occur. In the case of SST concepts, that change is well underway.

Suggested Further Reading

Publications from the research program are available from the Defense Technical Information Center. A good integration of the overall program and its findings within the broader literature can be found in Stephen J. Zaccaro's book, *Executive Leadership: A Conceptual and Empirical Analysis of Success*—published 2001 by the American Psychological Association.

ABOUT THE AUTHORS

Stephen D. Clement is founder and president of Organizational Design, Inc. (ODI), a Texas-based consulting firm. He has been involved in the application of requisite organizational design principles and concepts for more than 20 years. Clement worked closely with Dr. Elliott Jaques and Sir Roderick Carnegie in a ten-year year collaborative effort at CRA (a major Australian mining company) where many of the principles were first refined and tested in an operational environment. He is currently involved in applying RO-related concepts in several long-term industrial and government studies. He is the co-author of *Executive Leadership: A Practical Guide to Managing Complexity* with Dr. Jaques.

T. Owen Jacobs is co-founder and partner of Executive Development Associates, LLC. From 1997 to 2005, he held the Leo Cherne Distinguished Visiting Professor of Behavioral Science Chair at the Industrial College of the Armed Forces, National Defense University. He taught strategic leadership, and created the College's Executive Assessment and Development Program. Previously, at the US Army Research Institute, he collaborated with Jaques to identify strategic performance requirements and strategic leader developmental processes.

He authored *Leadership and Exchange in Formal Organizations* and *Strategic Leadership: The Competitive Edge*. He was leadership section editor and contributor (with Dr. Jaques) of *Handbook of Military Psychology*. In 2000, he received the John C. Flanagan Lifetime Achievement Award from the American Psychological Association Division of Military Psychology.

Redesigning a Global Organization to Deal with Increasing Complexity: The International Federation of Red Cross and Red Crescent Societies

George Weber and Dwight Mihalicz

WHAT'S IMPORTANT

- A CEO describes the implementation of a stratum VI organization in a global system with 5,000 employees, 16 regional offices, 185 national societies with $24 billion (CDN) in annual expeditures

- The CEO used RO to enhance the organization's fast reponse capability in disaster situations, the increasing complexity of its international operations, and the leadership capability of local areas.

We were trying to deal with crisis situations around the world, the consequences of armed conflicts and disasters, and, at the same time change the organization in very fundamental ways, while dealing with a multinational culture operating in four official languages.

—George Weber, Former Secretary General and CEO[1]

The key drivers in the private sector, employee satisfaction, client satisfaction, and improved organizational effectiveness, are the same in the public and the not-for-profit sector. In the private sector, one can measure the bottom line in terms of increased profit, or return on investment. In the not-for-profit and public sectors, one looks at how effectively and efficiently the donor or tax payer dollars are being used.

In this article, we will present how organization design principles can be applied in a not-for-profit organization, and in particular one that is truly a global organization, an agency recognized around the world simply as the Red Cross.

Context

Despite the high profile enjoyed by the Red Cross,[2] its failure to execute a strong organization design was threatening its ability to deliver on its key mandate, helping the most vulnerable people of the world. I was appointed Secretary General and Chief Executive Officer of the International Federation of Red Cross and Red Crescent Societies (International Federation) in 1992.[3] Based in Geneva, Switzerland, the International Federation is a global body that directs, coordinates, and links the activities of 185 (at press time) National Red Cross and Red Crescent Societies.

Today, as then, the International Federation is the largest international humanitarian organization in the world. It comprises a total of 97 million members and volunteers and 298,000 paid staff members that in turn provide service to 233 million people on an annual basis. With some $24 billion (CDN) in annual expenditures, the International Federation operates directly and indirectly in nearly every country of the world.

---

1   George Weber is Former Secretary General and CEO, Dwight Mihalicz is Former Project Director: This article represents the views of the authors and does not reflect the official position of the International Federation of Red Cross and Red Crescent Societies.

2   For simplicity's sake we use the popular term "Red Cross" to refer to Red Cross and Red Crescent in all of its international and national components.

3   Although this is a co-authored article, as a matter of style we have used the first person of the CEO.

The purpose of the organization is to improve the situation of the most vulnerable people through the coordination of disaster relief and providing them with the capacity to cope. It operates in some of the toughest conditions around the world.

Beyond the need to have an organization that can move swiftly in its relief operations, the International Federation also has the responsibility for the development of National Red Cross and Red Crescent Societies. Through support and development, the intent is for National Societies to be self-sufficient in terms of domestic programs, to be able to deal with disasters of a local nature, and to have the capacity to be the first wave of response for cataclysmic disaster.

The International Federation also represents the collective interests of its member national societies in their dealings with other inter-governmental bodies and international organizations, such as the UN, and acts as a permanent body liaison amongst the National Societies. The International Federation is governed by a General Assembly that meets every two years. It is made up of the entire member national societies and observers (UN and other international organizations), some 800 people in the body, to which the Secretary General is held to account for the activities and operations of the International Federation.

When I took over as Secretary General in 1992, I inherited a Secretariat headquarters in Geneva, Switzerland, with 12 regional offices. The International Federation was assisting about 15 million people around the world, through its relief operations, and had 149 member national societies. During my mandate, from 1993 to 2000, the regional offices grew by about 30 percent. In addition, there were 50+ country offices around the world, a number that rose or fell on almost a monthly basis, dependent upon various major relief operations in any country around the world. I had some 5,000+ Secretariat employees of 92 different nationalities working around the world.

The organization was faced with increasing demand. The sheer number of people who had been displaced by natural calamities and political upheavals was escalating. The International Federation also had to turn its mind to the complexities of dealing with different types and increasing numbers of security issues. And as national societies were created and developed new capacities, they wanted different types of assistance to further evolve their capacity. For instance, the newly created National Societies had competent leaders in place who wanted their people trained instead of bringing in foreign delegates to do the work. While this increased overall capability, it also increased the complexity of a disaster operation. There were also requests for the International Federation to provide more timely services and different types of services to the National Societies as they increased in strength.

On top of everything else, the call for more accountability and transparency was getting louder. As much of the funding was raised from governments, the Secretariat had to be accountable for reporting in their formats and to meet their standards. And having dealings with 30 different governments, each with its own systems, meant that the International Federation had to do customized reporting.

Despite these new and pressing needs, staffing at the Geneva headquarters wasn't keeping pace. The Geneva staff complement remained relatively constant during my term, while the delegation and locally hired staff fluctuated depending on the number and size of disaster relief operations under way.

In summary, this period of time was marked by increasing complexities, increasing demand, higher standards of accountability, and a budgetary requirement to meet these needs with the same or only slightly higher resources.

Need for an Organization Assessment Review

Prior to my arrival, there had been a one-year period without a Secretary General and the organization had drifted somewhat. The role had 16 direct reports, at different levels, and functional alignment was not ideal. And as a new CEO, I needed to travel six to seven months a year in order to energize the organization on realizing its potential, to get the national societies and donors to cooperate with the Secretariat, and to deal with the governments.

The Secretariat had greater volumes of information requiring specialization, and the environment was increasingly competitive, because more humanitarian organizations were developing international programming.

There was a desire to maximize effectiveness within available resources. There was money for direct assistance and operations, but not a lot more money to deal with core infrastructure. There was a need to expand services, enhance competencies, and to handle a larger and more difficult workload, but with nearly similar resources.

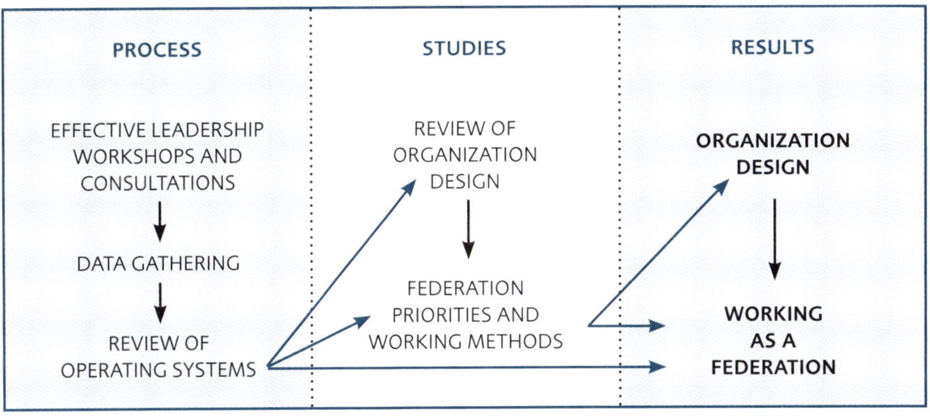

FIGURE 3.5.1: INTERNATIONAL FEDERATION CHANGE MAP

Method

Figure 3.5.1 shows a map of the method used.

Column 1 shows the three streams of work I launched early in my tenure. This work was carried out in my first year to create a climate ready for change. One of my first steps was to put in place workshops and training for managers to help them be more effective in their roles, and to establish ongoing development for the high potential employees.

In parallel, I launched significant data-gathering processes, workshops, SWOT (strength/weakness/opportunity/threat) analysis exercises, and we consulted with national societies. In early 1994, I set up a project team under the leadership of Dwight Mihalicz (article co-author) to review the operating systems based on all the feedback. This resulted in sets of recommendations for improvement in 12 major areas.

The results of these three streams of work became input, as shown in Figure 3.5.1, to the next steps in the change process, labeled as studies. Column 2 shows this work.

For the review of the organization design, we engaged Capelle Associates for its specialized expertise in organization design assessment and implementation. The Capelle Associates approach, based in large part on Elliott Jaques's Requisite Organization concepts, included a complete assessment of the organization design. The internal project team supported the process. Capelle Associates did the following:

- Conducted a literature review to identify best practices;
- Reviewed strategic or other internal documents;
- Interviewed every manager, both in Geneva and the field, to collect time span information and gather information on their roles and those of their direct reports; and
- Conducted a task analysis in terms of how did people do their work to help us understand how to better align work to roles.

The time span information was used to help understand the current number of levels in the organization, and to identify the gaps and compression between managers and their direct reports.

This resulted in a comprehensive report on the organization design changes required for a properly stratified organization and the recommendations for change.

In a parallel stream, an internal task force worked on International Federation Secretariat priorities and working methods. Even though there was a strategic plan that had been approved by governance, the organization was not aligned in terms of execution. This group also provided a series of recommendations.

We set up five task forces to help implement the recommendations. This led to a new organizational design, and a new working concept of "Working as a Federation." Fundamental to the change vision was a desire to do less with internal Secretariat resources and engage, borrow, and use more National Society capacity to do some of the work, so that the Secretariat could better cope with its mandate.

Findings

Although there were dozens of recommendations coming out of the various streams of work, the findings can be summarized in four areas.

1. The first and most significant finding is that there wasn't enough management depth to deal with the global complexities facing the organization. The Secretariat needed greater management depth, both in terms of capability and in terms of specialization. The organization design of the Secretariat was not appropriate to handle the complexities and challenges facing it. A key recommendation was to add another layer of management, to change the International Federation from a stratum V to a stratum VI organization

2. Second, systems and procedures needed improvement, both in Geneva and worldwide, together with improvements to the linkages between Geneva and the field.

3. Third, the Secretariat needed a better balance between relief functions and development functions. It is easier to raise money for relief operations than it is to get money for developing institutional capacity. However, by developing local institutional capacity, there is a better ability to cope with local disaster situations, when one only has to send in one or two foreign workers to assist a local capacity, as opposed to a whole team. In cases of larger disasters, the increased capacity means that the first wave of the relief operation in the hours after the disaster can be handled locally, while the resources of the International Federation are being marshaled.

4. Finally, the planning system needed refinement.

Results

Capelle Associates recommended that the Secretariat restructure as a stratum VI organization to deal with the complexity that it faced as a global organization. The plan included placing the Secretary General role at VI, with four subordinate stratum V roles, thereby reducing the Secretary General's span of control from 16 to 9 direct reports. The Constitution, i.e., the Statutes of the Federation required that the executive council (i.e., the board) approve the general outline of the Secretariat. An overview of the new organization design, including the addition of the two new Under Secretary General roles was presented and approved for implementation.

The reorganization created two core units of the Secretariat. The first was Disaster Response and Operations Coordination (DROC), accountable for both disaster response and operations coordination. The second was National Society Cooperation and Development (NSCD), accountable for relations with national societies and for spearheading the concept of "Working as a Federation." The two other approved Under Secretary General roles (Finance and Administration and Communications and Policy Coordination) are not included in this figure.

There were two aspects to the increased complexity. One was in terms of addressing the organization's ability to move swiftly in employing its relief operations. Yet, it was also clear that if the organization were to grow, it had to ensure that people put more emphasis on the longer term. This included the development of capacities

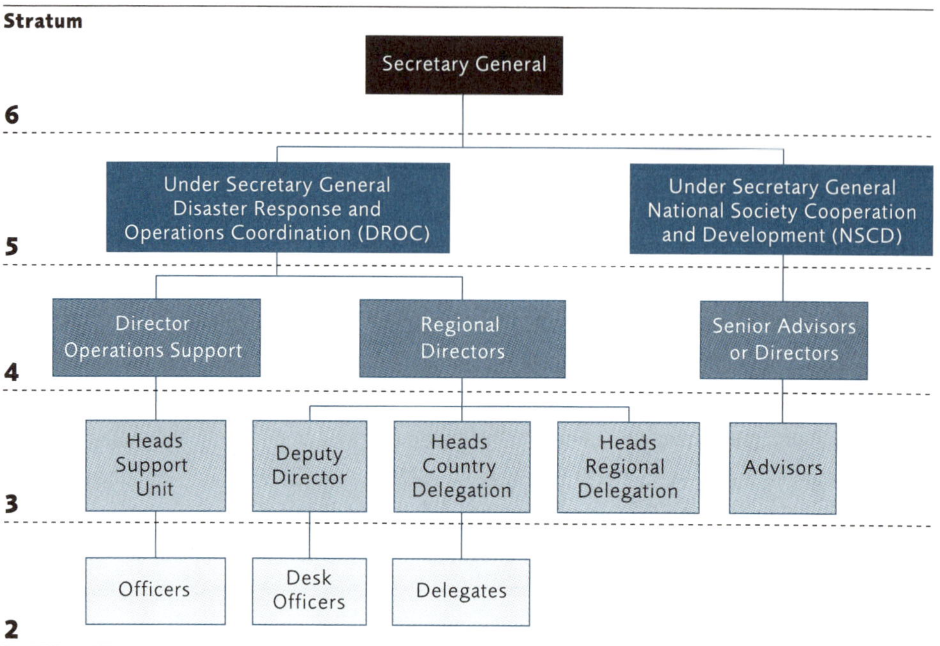

FIGURE 3.5.2: ORGANIZATION DESIGN OF INTERNATIONAL FEDERATION CORE AREAS

locally within the institutional capacity and building the relationships that would be necessary with donors.

It was important to have a better balance between the short-term orientation, which as a disaster response organization was the operating culture of the host, and the need for longer-term strategies and activities for the development of the International Federation.

We also created deputy director positions in larger regional departments. We created five regional departments, with a regional director and some desk officers similar to the situation in a foreign ministry. They were accountable for the delegations and the national societies in their region. This made it possible to clarify the accountabilities between the field and Geneva. The heads of regional and country delegations were to be the direct reports to the directors of the regional departments. In some cases, the heads of regional and country delegations did not know who, in fact, they were reporting to, at many times, because the Desk Officer was the main contact. That situation was resolved and the compression in this area was removed.

The three roles of deputy director, head of country delegation, and head of regional delegation were direct reports of the stratum IV regional director role. This greatly clarified the accountabilities of the field-based roles, who could be confused about the relationship between their role, the desk officer in Geneva, the functional specialist in Geneva and the functional specialist in the region. The deputy director and the two head roles were given clear managerial accountability, and the regional director was made accountable for the integration and setting the context for the cross-functional relations.

A process was then put in place to clarify cross-functional accountabilities and authorities. Many of the delegates, as part of the regional or country delegations, were specialist delegates. This required a relationship back to the specialist departments in Geneva. So, at times, they were taking instructions from and listening more to the Geneva specialist people rather than their country delegation manager. The clarification of managerial accountability and authority as well as cross-functional accountability and the authority system resulted in a clearer direction and better understanding of relationships, as opposed to everybody doing their own thing.

We also put in place a new business planning and review process. Each manager was accountable for developing a business plan. The process started with the Secretary General and his operational plan for the Secretariat (which was linked to the Federation's strategic plan), and cascaded down through the organization so that each plan was a subset of that person's manager's plan. This clarified the key accountabilities of each person, which would help to achieve the strategic plan of the organization. It also reinforced the managerial and cross-functional accountabilities and authorities.

Change Process

There were three parallel processes used in order to implement the change:
1. Implementation of the new organization design;
2. Establishment of International Federation priorities and working processes; and
3. Improvements to operating systems.

It was unusual to do this work in a parallel way. Traditionally, the priorities work is completed before the organization design work is started, because of the implications for strategy. However, this turned out to be one of the real strengths of the project. By setting up close communications between the two project teams, and planned iterations between them, both pieces of work had even better results than might be expected in the more traditional approach. It was also possible to move ahead more quickly. This was achieved by setting up a strong internal project team led by co-author Dwight Mihalicz, project team director. Mihalicz and his team provided support to each of the processes to assure the necessary iterations were carried out, and then supported the managers accountable for the implementation of the changes.

There was extensive communication. Bulletins were issued on nearly a weekly basis. These were supplemented with e-mails and staff meetings, both in departments and total group meetings. There was continuous communication over an 18-month to 2-year period.

Through the extensive use of task forces, project director Mihalicz was accountable for keeping the project on track. Implementation was then the accountability of line management with support from the project team. The complete implementation process took two years. The Executive Management Group continued to monitor and handle implementation once the internal project team had finished its work.

Lessons Learned

In terms of lessons learned, it was important that the Secretariat had external consulting support to bring necessary expertise, objective judgment, and analysis to the undertaking. This was especially important for the transfer of knowledge and skills in organizational design and taking work out of the system through process mapping and task analysis. While obtaining methodology from outside was important, it was also important that the internal project team and the external support worked very closely together.

In an international organization, fundamental change to an operating culture is difficult. It takes at least five to eight years to change an operating culture. A multinational culture can be more difficult to change, because people from all over the world with different levels of understanding of management systems are trying to work together for change.

It was important to constantly re-energize the process. This was challenging, as it was important to maintain operations at the same time. As a consequence, change of this nature, in an organization of this type, takes much longer than would normally be the case,

Employees attracted to an organization such as the International Federation tend to have a value set oriented towards assisting people and making a lasting change in the world. When that is a person's orientation, it is hard to get them to focus on process improvements. Communication and initiatives need to be persistent and compelling to help people see the big picture and to help them understand that investment of energy now can enhance effectiveness later. Helping employees understand the benefit of this trade-off was essential to success.

One of the key elements was getting the accountabilities right with respect to Geneva and the field. This was important for the managerial accountabilities and authorities, which were established in the restructuring. What was even more important, and more difficult, was getting the cross-functional accountabilities and authorities right. This was an ongoing process that needed continuous reinforcement.

Another lesson learned was the importance of moving quickly to fill key positions. There was a delay in filling one key position, which caused some issues with some of the key checks and balances within the Geneva Secretariat.

The change process was without question a success. In 1992, the International Federation had been handling some $410 million (CDN) annually in appeals. This money would be used, for example, to assist a country's population to cope after a natural disaster, or to help it reinforce its infrastructure to deal with the effects of an armed conflict situation, such as refugee movement or internally displaced persons. By early 2000, appeals had grown by 54 percent, to $631 million (CDN) in relief operations, but the number of beneficiaries assisted had doubled. And there were an additional 27 national Red Cross / Red Crescent Societies, about an 18 percent increase.

Summary

- The International Federation was able to help more people. The number of beneficiaries doubled while quality of service also improved.
- The donors supporting the International Federation increased their financial donations and provided more people and materials to achieve International Federation objectives.

- National Societies were able to do more work. This is critical, because it's the local people, at the community level, responding in the first hours of a disaster that make the biggest difference. The capacity of the national societies to handle a threshold of numbers of people affected by various situations increased by at least 50 percent. Because of this increased sustainability, the International Federation was able to increase the overall range and scope of its activities.
- Internal staff surveys showed that employees were positive about what had happened in terms of this change process, the reorganization, and new organization design.

After two years, we brought Capelle Associates back to Geneva to assess the progress we had made against the changes recommended. Significant progress had been made, including the following:

- Change had occurred.
- There was the beginning of an attitude shift that change is necessary.
- There had been good staff involvement in the change process.
- There had been good communication to staff about the change process (updates and other communication forms).
- There was a clearer Secretariat direction, including "Working as a Federation."
- A new organization structure had been implemented.
- There was greater clarity about accountability lines ("who reports to whom").

The review also helped us reinvigorate the change process, by helping us understand where we needed to increase our efforts in order to institutionalize the changes.

The bottom line is that the Secretariat was able to meet all of the expectations placed upon it under very trying circumstances. These results were only possible because an aggressive change plan was developed, implemented, and reinforced over a period of time. Obtaining external expertise and transferring it internally was essential. As a result, the International Federation was able to do more with its scarce resources. Not only was it able to make a greater difference in people's lives, the employee's felt better about themselves and their work. In total the International Federation improved at carrying out its fundamental mandate, to improve the situation of the most vulnerable people in the world.

Dwight Mihalicz was the internal project director for the assessment and implementation process described in this chapter. He currently consults for, and is senior vice president of Capelle Associates Inc. He has held senior management positions in national and international organizations, where he has been involved in the leadership and strategic planning for large-scale, complex projects, such as global redesign and start-up operations. He has extensive experience in project and change management processes with large organizations.

Mihalicz completed his MBA at the University of Ottawa and is a certified management consultant (CMC). He is the author of several publications, and director of the board of UNICEF Canada, where he has held several volunteer positions including chairperson of the board.

George Weber is Secretary General Emeritus of the International Federation of Red Cross and Red Crescent Societies (one of the largest humanitarian organizations in the world), a distinction he received following seven years as its chief executive officer. Prior to that, he was the Secretary General and CEO of the Canadian Red Cross Society.

Weber is currently CEO of the Canadian Dental Association, a professional membership organization and chairs one of the five major international committees of the FDI World Dental Federation.

In addition to his current responsibilities, he continues to serve on several boards. He attended McGill University in Montreal, Canada, and the Graduate School of Business Administration at Harvard University in Boston, Mass. and is trilingual, speaking English, French, and Spanish.

6
Requisite Organization Goes to Church

John Morgan, Ph.D.

WHAT'S IMPORTANT

- A New Mexico mega-church used RO concepts to grow from a weekly attendance of 800 to more than 1,500.

- While most churches operate stratum at II or III, Piñon Hills Community Church is a stratum V organization with a board capable at stratum IV or above and managers capable at each level to handle operations.

- Executive pastors at stratum IV are accountable for major ministries and groups of remote campuses.

- The Church runs its own community leadership training center that provides talented leaders to support its continued growth.

Pastoral mega-churches are surely the most important social phenomenon in American society in the past thirty years. This to my mind, is the greatest, the most important, the most momentous event, and the turning point not just in churches, but perhaps in the human spirit altogether.

—Peter Drucker[1]

I am the pastor of one of the large and growing evangelical churches that make up what Peter Drucker described to *Forbes Magazine* as the mega-church phenomenon. It was in this type of church that I learned and applied requisite organization ideas that led to great growth and much better management.

Congregations in the mega-church phenomenon differ from mainline congregations. These large, growing Evangelical congregations are churches with large Sunday attendance, non-traditional worship and led by the head pastor. Like many other such churches, we are not legally affiliated with any denomination or other church, although we cooperate with many other evangelical churches in various ministries. And unlike mainline hierarchical denominations, the final authority in our church rests with the congregation. They can vote to remove the board or the senior pastor, and indeed hired me 12 years ago after I interviewed for this position. They recommended me to the congregation, who approved my hire by a 90 percent vote, more than the two-thirds vote required by our constitution. As chief executive, I am the head of our employment system, so no other hires or dismissals are brought to the congregation for their vote.

The nature of this kind of church requires good management and leadership. I often describe our kind of church as "entrepreneurial," because our mindset is to take the risks necessary to seize opportunities to accomplish our mission, which is to add people to the faith. So our management and leadership more closely resemble that of a growing business than that of a mainline traditional church. Churches in the mainline denominations tend to focus more on maintaining their traditions and leading by consensus. The result has been much less growth and also lower demands on their management and leadership.

That is why the pastors of large, growing evangelical churches tend to focus on "leadership." They study leadership and seek to apply it. Some of the best leader-

---

1   "Management's New Paradigms" *Forbes Magazine*, October 5, 1998

ship training in America is delivered by flagship, growing, American churches like Willow Creek Community Church in suburban Chicago and Saddleback Church in Lake Forest, California. But unfortunately, they do not differentiate between the leadership necessary to run the staff organization, leadership to lead the association of the congregation's people, and spiritual leadership.

I believe managerial leadership of the staff hierarchy and leading the congregation's people overlap. You can't do one without the other, yet I see them with some distinction. Part of that is from my theological background. I believe God gives some the spiritual gift of leading the congregation and some the spiritual gift of managing the employment hierarchy per se.

Leading the congregation, in my mind, is the ability to get people to follow you in a direction to solve problems. The more people you can get to solve more complex problems, the greater is your leadership capability. In my mind, managing the staff means staying on top of many people, tasks, and situations to guide them in a cooperative direction. Another kind of leadership is spiritual leadership. I believe that is being an example of how to follow God by faith and effectively communicating the faith to others.

How I Came to Requisite Organization

My introduction to requisite organization came at a providential time several years ago. Our church and staff were growing, but we had hit a bad cycle of conflict and turnover. At the same time I was working on my Ph.D. in organizational leadership. My primary interest for my research and dissertation was the phenomenon of the levels of leadership capability that exist in any given population. I had almost completed my coursework that included a review of every major leadership theory, and none of them adequately explained this phenomenon.

Then my dissertation chairperson recommended that I complete my final class credits in an independent study on requisite organization. I could not believe my eyes. As I researched it further and read Elliott Jaques's works, I knew I had discovered the holy grail of leadership that answered the questions I was asking.

So I did my doctoral dissertation on the phenomenon of leadership levels using Jaques and Cason's ideas on human capability.[2] My method was to analyze the lead-

2   Jaques, E. and Cason, K. *Human Capability. A Study of Human Potential and Its Application.* Green Cove, Florida: Cason Hall & Company Publishers, 1994.

ership levels of three high-level, historic Christian leaders—Jesus, Martin Luther King, Jr., and Pope John Paul II—through the construct of complexity of information processing. The result provided a sound explanation for the complexity of these three leaders' important ideas and communications and the correlating historic impact that they had.[3]

A Theology of Human Capability and Organization

As a leader of my organization and congregation, I got a new perspective on how to develop an organization to accomplish a mission. I came away with a working theory of leadership and management that is a smooth integration and theology of human capability and organization that is consistent with the teachings of Jesus and the Bible.

A "theology" of any topic is a philosophy of belief about that topic that includes all truth that God has given us. I follow a classic line of philosophy that goes from the Apostle Paul, to St. Augustine, to St. Thomas Aquinas, to John Calvin, to Pope John Paul II that "all truth is God's truth." We believe that God gives us truth through revelation, truth from the Bible, and reason, our intellectual ability to find truth that is testable, logical, and consistent. So, my theology of human capability and organization is based on the revelation of the Bible and the reason of requisite organization and other sources of leadership and management wisdom.

Putting the Right People into the Right Roles
Doing the Right Things

I came away with the understanding that successful organizations place the right people in the right roles doing the right things in alignment with the mission of the organization. Organizations in general are bad at doing this, but churches tend to be worse because, in the name of helping people, they let some people work in roles for which they may be incapable. The result is often ineffectiveness. I decided to lead our church away from this mentality when we were growing past 800 people in our weekend worship attendance, a crucial time in our history.

---

3   Morgan, J. "An Analysis of the Leadership Levels of Jesus, Martin Luther King, Jr., and Pope John Paul II through Elliott Jaques' Construct of Complexity of Information Processing." (Doctoral dissertation, Regent University.) UMI/Digital Dissertations. 2005.

First, it meant I had to let my second-in-command staff member go. He had showed himself ineffectual in selecting the right people for staff positions and incompetent to give them adequate management and leadership. He had brought several bad hires on in a row and had managed them so poorly that when they left our staff, it caused major shock waves to go throughout our congregation. I had to de-select him, because I had to bear the responsibility for his unacceptable output.

Second, it meant I had to train our staff and key non-staff leaders in the principles of requisite organization, so that we could begin aligning ourselves properly. We were a stratum III organization where I personally managed all ministry staff and treated them all as organizational equals in defining the mission and strategy of our organization. We imploded in cycles of conflict with many lobbying for their various agendas. Our board was made up of strata II and III people who could not think beyond short-term operational issues and who participated in every employee management decision.

Since I had been assessed at stratum V as part of my doctoral work, we established clear levels of employment that began with me at stratum V, then cascaded down to volunteers and staff who function at strata I and II. We established the four major responsibilities of all managers which are the following:

1. Select the right people.
2. Assign them the right work.
3. Give them the right feedback.
4. De-select those who won't do the right work.

We focus our hiring practices now on the following four criteria for all candidates. Of all of our management challenges, clearly assessing candidates for these criteria is the greatest.

1. Does their work capability fit the role?
2. Do they have the knowledge and skills needed for this role?
3. Do they have the desire needed to fulfill this role?
4. Do they have enough character to fulfill this role?

One of the key improvements that requisite organization has made in our staff is how we hire and dismiss. In the past, all of these decisions were made by the senior pastor with the counsel of the board. As the congregation and our employment system grew to be several layers, these decisions were transferred to the managers and managers-once-removed. I do bring hires and dismissals of my immediate subordinates to our board for their counsel, but hires and dismissals below that level are handled by the managers of our employment system.

This has allowed our board to stay out of operational issues, unless there is a legal issue. For example, recently our stratum III student ministries director received the resignation of one of his stratum II subordinates after a series of management meetings with him to correct problems. The director conferred on his management and possible corrective actions with our stratum IV executive pastor. When the resignation came, the executive pastor informed me, and we in turn gave it as an information item to our board. This issue was handled properly at the right level. A search for a new hire will be handled by them also.

My own work changed, and illustrates how I view managerial, congregational, and spiritual leadership. I manage my direct relationships with my subordinates and, as their manager-once-removed, give career direction to staff two levels down. I lead our whole staff by continually casting vision and strategy to them, holding a monthly all-staff vision and strategy session that is followed by a social lunch. I lead our board by setting the tone of vision and strategy with them, and including them in the process of defining our exact directions and methods. I lead our whole congregation by communicating the faith to them in weekly preaching and casting vision and strategy to them in semi-annual messages about the church as an organization. I personally deliver the operational ministry work of personal pastoral care to a number of our people who are in crisis. Most of that is delivered by our staff, but I have my share of these duties too.

The third major thing we did was to train our board of directors in requisite organization. Now, when new candidates are being nominated and selected for our board, one of the criteria for selection is that they must be capable of doing at least stratum IV work. While this is unusual in mainline congregations whose boards are often at stratum II or III, our church attracts highly capable people from across the region. Our board members are busy people in demanding roles outside the church who believe that the mission of our organization is a vital part of their lives.

Many people wonder how we can attract such capable people to be committed to such a large task. We attract them through a monthly, half-day leadership training program for executives. This draws in the leaders in our church and community. Our current board also recruits candidates who have demonstrated spiritual commitment as well as leadership capabilities in their lives and work. Last, having a senior pastor at stratum V is most important, because leadership cascades. Ultimately, stratum IV people are attracted by strata V and VI leaders.

This has helped our board become productive at working on vision and strategy, instead of becoming bogged down in operational issues that our staff and their volunteer teams should be solving. This has been not only a major improvement for our church, but it also has a real benefit for me as the leader of our organization.

We also changed how we work with our members as volunteers. This problem is inherent to churches, but not a part of a business's normal operations.

We will occasionally have stratum II programs led by volunteers, but they answer to a stratum III staff person. When a program grows to stratum III complexity, we bring it under paid staff supervision if it is going to stay under our church, thus keeping mission alignment within our organization.

Regardless of the working level of a volunteer, we try not to have employees answer to volunteer managers. We found that it simply does not work well.

We also found that volunteers can stay motivated for a time volunteering at levels below their capabilities. However, the longer people volunteer in our system, the more they seem motivated to serve in areas that tap more of their capacities, which has made identifying and engaging high-capacity people in ministry one of the key challenges of our church.

It has been said that a business makes money at strata I and II. In a church, we do ministry at strata I and II through our community groups, making this our most important ministry. We found that one needs to be capable at high stratum I or II to do well in leading a community group. Thus, the entry point for our most important and most needed volunteer position is accessible by most adults.

Finally, we created a leadership training organization that trains people in requisite organization principles of management and leadership. As described above, this half-day training venue for people in business, non-profit organizations, and churches has also served as a place to train existing congregational leaders and recruit new ones into it.

Requisite Enabled Growth

It is clear to me that implementing RO concepts has enabled us to grow into a dynamic congregation that manages our employment structure and volunteers in a way that both produces growth and creates a environment for spiritual growth. In fact, we measure the spiritual growth of our congregation by the following criteria:

- Professions of faith and baptisms of new converts
- Number of community groups and percent of our congregation who are involved in these groups, which are home-based and lay-led spiritual support, growth, and ministry units
- Number of community and cross-cultural service/ministry projects
- Overall retention of membership and growth
- Overall engagement of our people in volunteerism
- Overall unity and spirit of vision and outreach by our congregation
- Quality and quantities in our key ministry departments, e.g., children's, youth, and community groups; worship and arts; women's and men's ministries

Within the last year, it became clear to me that our biggest organizational need was for staff members who could function at stratum IV, just below me. My new second-in-command could function at that level, but our organization was becoming so broad that I felt we needed three there. So we hired two more people who work at stratum IV, which we call our "executive pastor" level. This change has paved the way for major improvements in our existing ministries and created new ministries that serve entirely new groups of people.

We now have about 30 staff members. As previously mentioned, I function at stratum V as the senior pastor. My executive pastor, ministry development pastor, and community life pastor function at stratum IV. Under them, stratum III managers manage our major ministry departments, such as our children's and youth ministries. We have some strata I and II employees who work under these managers. Most of our board function at stratum IV or higher.

Success

We have grown from 800 in weekend attendance to just fewer than 1,500, and our income from supporters has grown faster than our attendance. We are entering a building program to relocate to a new 60-acre campus that will allow state-of-the-art ministry and outreach. Within the last year, our congregation has completed more than 50 community service projects. We have started our first satellite video-venue church campus 150 miles away in Rio Rancho, the fastest growing city in New

Mexico, and we are expecting the campus to break 200 in attendance by the end of its first year. One of the three executive-level pastors who work under me manages the campus pastor of that congregation. We are in a fast-paced growth and development mode, which is only possible because we are learning to place the right people in the right roles doing the right work in alignment with our mission.

Exciting Future

The future is exciting to me because I sense that I will be transitioning in my own capabilities from stratum V to stratum VI in the next few years. This means my vision, thinking, and work capability will allow me to be the top executive and spiritual leader of multiple organizations. I will lead multiple church campuses, each one with its own campus pastor, as well as the expansion of our community foundation that does non-profit community work, the expansion of our leadership training program, and the expansion of my own message through writing and speaking.

A big part of my message is that whether you are in business, non-profit leadership, or religious ministry, the best way to get the most people doing the best things is by organizing according to requisite organization principles.

Biblical Affirmation of Requisite Concepts

Let me make one more note about something I referred to earlier. Requisite organization is built on the core concept of the varying levels of human capability to do work. What Elliott Jaques discovered by research is also affirmed theologically in the Bible. In the Old Testament in Exodus 15, Moses' father-in-law, Jethro, consulted him on his organizational problem of leading Israel: everyone came to Moses for judgment on civil disputes. There was a long line of people waiting to see him every day, and it was wearing him and the people out. Jethro consulted Moses to set up a system in which people who were capable at different levels of work would be responsible for leading various groups of people and Moses would be the apex leader. These people were chosen according to their capabilities.

Also in Jesus' parable of the talents, he told the story of a wealthy person who gave three people different amounts of money to manage in his absence. The amount that was entrusted to them was based on his estimate of their capability. Many Christian theologians have understood this story to be about the abilities that God gives us and our responsibilities with them.

Finally, the Apostle Paul was the major biblical writer in the New Testament to present the idea of "gifts" that God gives people for His service. These gifts are God-given capabilities to do work in the service of God and His church. They range from having an aptitude for sympathy and mercy to being able to make and give money to leadership and administration. The bottom line in Christian teaching is for each person to serve according to the capabilities God has given him or her. So, the Bible affirms that the various levels of human capability are God-ordered.

As a pastor and a leader I see an objective, carefully defined, researched and validated process for effective organizational design. I also see how RO helps individuals be all that God intended them to be.

ABOUT THE AUTHOR

The Rev. Dr. John Morgan is the lead pastor of Piñon Hills Community Church in Farmington and Rio Rancho, New Mexico. He is the founder of the Piñon Hills Community Foundation and the founder of a leadership training organization called The John Morgan Company. He holds a master's degree in divinity and a Ph. D. in organizational leadership. He is the co-author of *How to Discover Your Personal Life Mission* (2007, Xulon Press) and the author of *Horsepower: How Leadership Works* (2007, Xulon Press).

Morgan and his wife Greg Lanee have five children. His favorite avocation is salt water fishing and he is the co-leader of a ministry of male-initiation that leads men in a weeklong spiritual transformation that takes place at fishing resorts in Mexico and Costa Rica.

Partial Applications of the Levels of Work Approach

Partial Applications of the Levels of Work Approach

The implementation of requisite organization throughout an organization can appear to be a formidable task. When executives first encounter the theory, one of the first questions they ask is, "can this be done on a small scale?" Sometimes a project is too big in scope and it may be wise to do a pilot project, or single out a division or department to begin the implementation. The next question is, "where do I start?" These and many other questions are the subject of this part dealing with partial or special applications of RO.

We begin this part with an article based upon one of Elliott Jaques's most notable applications of requisite organization. After writing *General Theory of Bureaucracy*, Elliott Jaques worked with Sir Roderick Carnegie in a ten-year effort to improve the managerial effectiveness, productivity, and business results at CRA, an Australian mining company with 25,000 employees. **Catherine G. Burke**, **Ian Macdonald**, and **Karl Stewart** played important roles in that effort and in their article, "Structure is not enough: Systems are the Drivers of Organizational Behavior and Culture," they describe their learning and insight over the length of the project. They recommend that designing roles at the right level and staffing them with the right people is only the first step of a complete implementation. They evolved an approach that pays early attention to values and organizational culture and designs new systems to shape desired behaviors and culture

The levels of work literature often describes implementing requisite organization as a major systematic change in structure and complementary management system components planned and led by the top. **Sheila Deane**, an Australian consultant who works worldwide, describes the personal experience and reported feelings and insights of a level IV general manager who champions an RO-based pilot project in her own functional area. Deane tells the story of this general manager's path in learning how to implement RO concepts into her divisional team, and the results that were achieved on her "90-day plan." An unexpected benefit of the project was that a Six Sigma project that had been ineffective for two years came dramatically alive once the work was set at the right level with the appropriate accountabilities and authorities in place.

One of the strengths of the requisite organization concepts is their ability to make "competing theories" more effective. Consider, for example, the popularity of the team approach that was proposed as an alternative to hierarchical arrangements. Many of the forays into "team management" failed because of problems with authority and accountability, so another fad passed away. Used properly, however, teams can be a very effective management tool. **Charlotte M. Bygrave**, a strategic human resource management consultant, tells the story of how Roche Canada implemented requisite concepts to design product launch teams and develops the more general conclusion that teams cannot function well in an organization that is not properly structured. Roche Canada built an RO-based management system and was able to product extraordinary results in improved cross-functional team projects.

Organizations require many types of cross-functional teams that operate within project management structures. Often these teams are staffed by highly specialized and technically trained individuals who may not have been trained in managerial accountabilities or managing people. **Richard B. D. Brown**, an experienced human resource executive, describes the management muddle he commonly has encountered in project management and specialist team settings, and recommends application of principles as a dependable path toward appropriate managerial behaviors and increased project successes. Interestingly, he notes, the sorting out of the complex role relationships were first detailed over forty years ago by Wilfred Brown and Elliott Jaques in their development of the "co-manager" concept. Brown details how he sorted out these complex relationships in one project management situation.

Many of us can identify with the "black hole" label for information technology, i.e., the continual and escalating costs of IT, often times with no discernable benefit. With IT an increasingly critical part of an organization's competitive strategy, it is important to manage the function to generate maximum effectiveness. **Piet Calitz**, managing director of BIOSS International, proposes that using the work levels approach to managing IT can generate improvements in its effectiveness. Too often, he maintains, organizations do not understand the complexity of the IT change process. Changes in technology often impact the culture of an organization, and the IT manager must possess a level of capability that allows him/her to manage the cultural change.

Paul McDowell, a senior IT executive with years of experience in a variety of major corporations, shows how a lack of appreciation for levels of work and levels of complexity can cause serious long-term consequences for the IT function in an organization. His article "CIO: **C**hief **I**nformation **O**fficer or **C**areer **I**s **O**ver?" he makes a conceptual presentation, and then details a real-life experience that affected the strategic success of an organization.

Elliott Jaques wrote that non-requisite organizations were often paranoiagenic in that role structures and practices created conditions that stress employees unnecessarily. The resulting personal and emotional problems often result in great cost to both the individual and organization. Jaques claimed that requisitely designed organizations were trust-inducing, and, under requisite conditions, that serious personality dysfunctions were rare. Jaques advocated fixing the organization first with the expectation that most "personality issues" would vanish, and only then dealing with the few remaining individual issues. **George Reilly**, a psychologist and employee assistance program counselor who is also a requisite organization consultant, writes about his experience in therapy with troubled individuals, and illustrates how the understanding of their problems, including the context of their work setting, and design of their treatment, can be improved by using requisite concepts

Structure Is Not Enough:
Systems Are the Drivers
of Organizational Behavior
and Culture

Catherine G. Burke, Ian Macdonald, Karl Stewart

WHAT'S IMPORTANT

Conzinc Rio Tinto of Australia (CRA), a 25,000-employee Australian mining and refining company, worked more than ten years to improve its competitiveness through the implementation of RO.

After early systems design failures due to poor setting of managerial accountabilities and authorities, the authors describe improving their principles and practices to design and implement a successful transformation of a CRA business unit, New Zealand Aluminium Smelter, with large improvements in productivity, profitability, and worker satisfaction.

A key principle is that the design of systems, including their foundational values, the values that employees perceive imbedded in them, and the design of system controls and audit, is a high-level task requiring a minimum of stratum IV capability.

To be a good leader you must understand your own mythologies and the mythologies of your workforce.

After writing *A General Theory of Bureaucracy*, Elliott Jaques worked with Sir Roderick Carnegie in a ten-year effort as Sir Roderick worked to improve managerial effectiveness, productivity, and business results at CRA, an Australian mining company with 25,000 employees. It was with CRA that Jaques worked with people from CRA to develop the details of his then more theoretical Stratified Systems Theory (SST) ideas. The outcome was published by Jaques in his book, *Requisite Organization*.[1]

Karl Stewart and Ian Macdonald played important roles in the transformation of CRA. Catherine Burke worked in a parallel project in the US, and all three worked together on the development of the theory based on their respective experiences. In their article, they describe their learning and insight over the length of the project. They recommend that designing roles at the right level and staffing them with the right people is only the first step of a complete implementation; of itself it is not sufficient. They evolved an approach that places the design of new systems at stratum IV or above, pays early attention to human values and organizational culture, and designs new systems to shape desired behaviors and culture.

CRA's 14-year experiment (1978-1992) in applying Elliott Jaques's theories of management is often cited as one of the key implementations of requisite organization. (See sidebar for a chronology of the work.) This article describes two situations—one at CRA's Hamersley Iron unit in 1985 and one at their NZAS unit in 1991—in which the authors participated and that illustrate how hard-learned early lessons led to great success later.

It was in these years that we learned something important: systems and mythologies are powerful tools for the CEO to change the organization's behavior and culture. The design of systems, controls, and audit, and the values the systems demonstrate, as understood by employees, is a high-level task requiring minimum stratum IV capability. Trying to implement a requisite organization without taking these into account will lead to failure, as we learned at CRA's Hamersley Iron business unit where we first met.

---

1   For a more detailed description of the CRA work by Sir Roderick Carnegie, then CEO of the group, see "Jaques and the Early Years in Australia," *International Journal of Applied Psychoanalytic Studies*, 2(4): 332–344 (2005).

Mid-1970s: Sir Roderick Carnegie, CEO of CRA, sets goals to improve company international competitiveness, and to move from 14th to top 5 in the world by 2000 by bringing in the world's best management practices and "winning the hearts and minds of employees."

1978: Carnegie retains Elliott Jaques as advisor. This was a first try and then there was a gap when Elliott was brought back in 1981/82.He decides to implement internally rather than depend on consultants and to lead the project himself at stratum VII. He also assigns stratum VI corporate executives and appoints stratum V organization development heads. Commits five percent of payroll to the project.

1979-81: Organization development projects were implemented at Woodlawn Mine, Broken Hill, and then Sulphide Corporation.

1983: Hamersley's management culture rejects first efforts to install requisite concepts in the CRA's iron ore division.

1978-83: Karl Stewart works as general manager at Weipa mine site making many major changes independent of Carnegie and Jaques work in CRA.

1984-86: Karl Stewart appointed stratum V group consultant. Jack Brady, stratum VI group executive. Carnegie asks Stewart to develop corporate systems theory to improve both organization development (OD) and organizational work processes. Stewart assigned to lead the OD team at Hamersley. Stewart and Macdonald brothers, Ian and Roderick, develop values theory as part of OD theory development. Productivity begins to improve after the 1985 restructure.

1985: NOT-TO-GO pilot project—success and ultimate failure with powerful learning.

1986: New Zealand Aluminium Smelter (NZAS) was restructured.

1987: Karl Stewart appointed stratum V managing director of CRA's Smelting business unit including NZAS.

1988-90: Period of dissonance at NZAS as management improves significantly and old myths fail as predictors of outcomes.

continued on page 244

1990: David Brewer appointed general manager of NZAS and pace of system change increased.

1991: Employment Contracts Act passed in New Zealand legislating that an employee or a group of employees could retain the union as their agent, appoint a representative agent other than the union, or could represent themselves to negotiate their contract of employment.

1991: NZAS General manager and managers effectively removed overtime. Managing director offered staff employment contracts to all employees.

1991 and ongoing: Major benefits achieved.

Stewart had been assigned to lead an OD team to develop systems theory to improve OD and organizational systems and work processes in the unit. Burke and Macdonald were consulting with the OD teams, developing an implementation of Jaques's theories into an integrating working system of management. Our work together is a good place to start, because the lessons we learned there about systems and mythologies led us to successes later, first and particularly at the NZAS unit.

(For a fuller handling of the complexities of workplace mythologies and value analysis, and the stories we discuss, see our articles on the GO Society website.)[2]

A Failed Systems Design: What Went Wrong

The rail system at CRA's Hamersley Iron unit was one of the world's largest in ton-kilometers-per-day, and the rail operations and maintenance group had been the first part of Hamersley to go through the restructuring based on Jaques's ideas. The NOT-TO-GO system involved the maintenance of the rail stock, necessary to prevent expensive derailments. Created with the input of both groups, the new system increased work performance and cross-group communication. The crew superintendents of both the maintenance and the examiners said, "It has succeeded beyond our wildest expectations."

---

2 "The NOT-TO-GO Card," "Systems: The Drivers of Organizational Behavior and Culture," and "Structure Is Not Enough." And in *Systems Leadership: Creating the Positive Organization*, Gower Publishing, 2006.

It ultimately failed. Eight months after the implementation the new system had collapsed completely, except for a redesign of certain forms.

A careful review revealed a number of critical problems in project design and execution including:

- Project ownership had been assigned to the implementation team, rather than to the Rail general manager, where it properly belonged.
- A related problem was that the purpose of the system-improvement project was unclear with various parties holding different views.
- Adequate controls were missing and managers at various levels were allowed to change the new system without outside consultation or approval.
- We had not paid attention to how workplace mythologies, the stories and beliefs that different groups told each other (and discussed below), kept the existing system strong and in place. (The full theory had not been developed at this stage.)

We thought of the project system analysis as being primarily about the work itself. Instead, we came to realize that it was also very much about the associated systems, symbols, and behaviors and the core values that they demonstrate. These insights started us down a road that led to the great success later at CRA's NZAS unit, so it's worth looking at them in depth.

"Systems Drive Behavior"

A CEO has essentially three means of influencing the behavior of the people in the organization: behavior, systems, and symbols. His or her own behavior, while a powerful and important tool, is not always visible to the vast majority of employees, so it is potentially less influential than the CEO's use of systems and symbols.

Systems, the business methods and processes in use, are the major driver of the organization's behavior and culture. Systems are to organizations what habitual behaviors are to individuals. Both can be observed and both are interpreted as visible manifestations of who and what are valued positively or negatively by the leadership.

Systems are powerful because they operate all the time, even when leaders are not available, and they can form the culture. Like habits, they require such a specific repertoire of behaviors that operators become accustomed to and act in accordance with them over time. Systems, like habits, can be either good or bad, and even

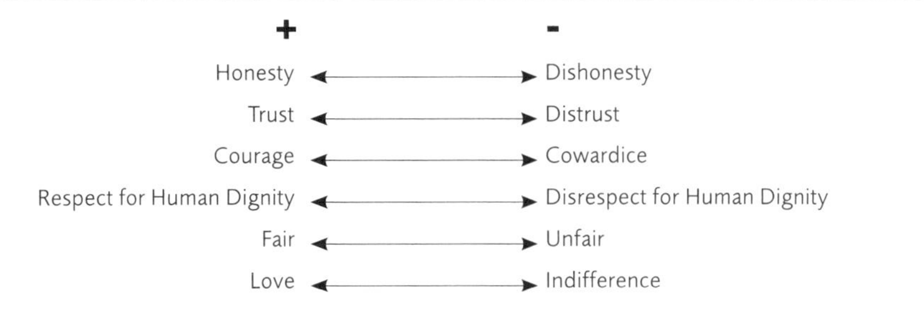

FIGURE 4.1.1: UNIVERSAL CORE VALUES

good systems can become outdated and counter-productive. As one of the authors (Stewart) said at the time, "Systems drive behavior."

Core Values

We believe, and have tested our belief in practice, that core values are the underlying principle that allow human beings to bind one to another. Working with the Hamersley Iron organizational development (OD) teams and Roderick Macdonald, we identified a set of six shared core values necessary for the continuing existence of human social groups. Behavior interpreted at the positive end of the scale strengthens the social group while behavior interpreted at the negative end weakens it, eventually destroying it.[3] (See Figure 4.1.1.)

Most of members' behaviors must be assessed to be at the positive end for others in the group to accept and rely upon them. Without positive, reliable behavior, social groups fail.

The basic propositions are the following:

For a group to maintain a productive relationship, members' behavior must exemplify the positive end of the scales of the core values.

If a group member demonstrates behavior judged by the others to be at the negative end, the person will eventually be excluded.

If several people exhibit behaviors that are similar but judged by the rest of the group to be at the negative end, the group will break into factions or separate groups.

---

3   Macdonald, Ian, Macdonald, Roderick, and Stewart, Karl. "Leadership: A New Direction" *British Army Review*, 93, December, 1989

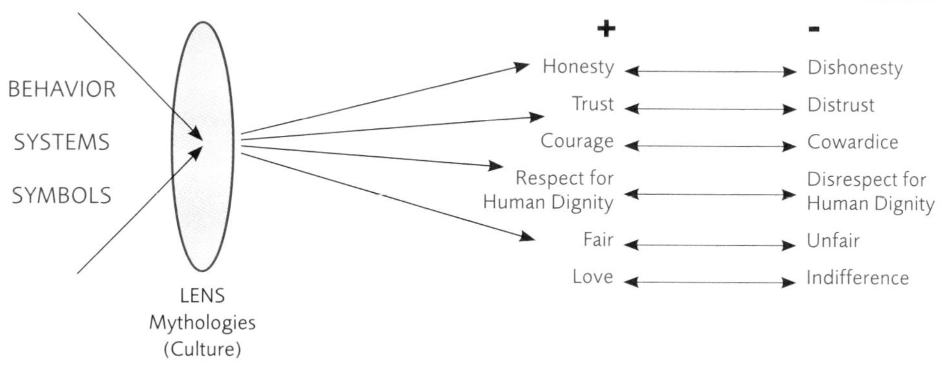

FIGURE 4.1.2: THE MYTHOLOGICAL LENS

Mythologies and Culture

A *mythology* is the assumption or belief that allows us to assign value to behavior and classify it as positive or negative on the scales of shared values. Throughout history myths have been stories that contain within them a fundamental truth. They define heroic and cowardly behavior, the meaning of human dignity, behavior that demonstrates love and caring for others.[4] They allow us to assign values to behaviours and to position them on a positive/negative scale. A behavior may demonstrate several values, each placed on a scale from positive to negative.

Because the myth gives meaning to events in the world, which provides predictability and safety, the myth is always true to the myth-holder, even though others may see it as bad or false. The mythology acts as a lens through which behaviors, systems and symbols are interpreted and arrayed on the scales of shared values.

Though core values may be the same, people from different cultures will often have quite different interpretations of the same behavior, system, or symbol. People of the same culture will have similar interpretations. This is because a culture is a common set of mythologies, and we interpret behavior through our mythologies.

Although *culture* is defined in many ways by anthropologists and others, we define it here as a group of people who share mythologies. That is those who judge specific behavior similarly on the values continua. (See Figure 4.1.2.]

---

4   Campbell, Joseph, *Hero With a Thousand Faces.* Commemorative ed. Princeton, N.J: Princeton University Press, 2004.

Railway workplace mythology was a major reason for the collapse of the Hamersley Iron NOT-TO-GO system redesign project. Previously, neither the examiners nor the maintainers received any recognition from their respective leaders for the work they did. The new system corrected this problem, and the system itself provided information that improved examiner and maintainer productivity and satisfaction and their inter-group relationships. These new behaviors directly conflicted with the old behaviors and myths underlying the former work culture. As we soon learned, the management of both groups depended upon these myths to maintain what they perceived to be their leadership authority. The new behaviors openly challenged this authority, often through information provided by the new system. And this led the threatened managers to alter the new system without consultation to re-establish the old predictable behaviors.

Another lesson that "systems drive behavior."

Systems Analysis and Design

To be a good leader you should understand your own mythologies, but you must understand the mythologies of your workforce. When you implement a system you must know whether it will be perceived as fair or unfair, honest or dishonest, as respecting human dignity or showing disrespect.

A good leader designs systems so the organization's good people, who are in the majority, see the new system at the positive ends of the values scale. Those who would cheat the system or use it to hurt their fellows should place it at the negative ends, because you are showing them they can no longer get away with poor behavior.

Good managerial leaders also design systems with a clear statement of authority, control, and audit. *Authority* says what an individual may do, and within what limits, carrying with it the accountability for exercising proper judgment. *Control* verifies that the system is being used, including a judgment of the quality of judgment used by the person given the authority. *Audit* checks that the controls are in place and being used, and that the system is achieving its purpose and functioning effectively as intended. Part of the failure with the NOT-TO-GO project came because the system design team had not yet recognized the critical importance of control and audit as system elements, but carried them out on an *ad hoc* basis.

The pilot project showed that the system design team had more work to do to understand the complexity of system design.[5] With more experience, later efforts worked. Carnegie presented a chart that shows the productivity gains at Hamersley beginning in 1985, after the first year of OD.[6] These insights and methods were carefully documented and built into a CRA approach to be used in systems design in subsequent years across the 25 or so CRA business units and they would find their first full demonstration at the NZAS unit.

Changes in Systems and Management Behavior

In 1989, CRA's NZAS was the second largest of seven smelters around the world that shares the same technology, but ranked second, third, or fourth on most measures of smelter performance. The cost of electricity to the smelter had risen substantially in recent years and additional increases were being threatened. This was placing significant cost pressure on the smelter as electricity made up almost 30 percent of its cost base.

David Brewer, who had led the requisite-based restructuring at the unit three years earlier, was now the departmental manager (stratum III) and Stewart was the new stratum V managing director of the smelting division business unit consisting of three smelters. They believed that they could improve NZAS both in performance and as a place to work by using their hard-learned lessons to change the symbols and leadership behaviors, thus changing the workplace.

With the general manager in a role at stratum IV, they started by reinforcing existing systems that had been allowed to drift. Training and education in these systems was followed by new enforcement. Managers also took strong action to improve safety. These were significant changes in manager behaviors that in turn began to generate dissonance such that the traditional workplace mythologies did not predict any more.

5　For a more complete discussion, see our book, *Systems Leadership: Creating the Positive Organization*, Gower Publishing, 2006.

6　Carnegie, Roderick. "Jaques and the Early Years in Australia," *International Journal of Applied Psychoanalytic Studies*, 2(4): 332–344 (2005)

Workforce Myths, 1987-90

The dominant myths of the staff[7] in 1987 centered primarily on love and fairness (the pay issue) and courage: "the company will not support us when we discipline someone;" "they will not take a stand against the union;" "they will not get rid of bad managers."

The dominant myths of the workers who were union members included a justifiable perception of "bad management behaviors" over the years, and union leadership found it useful to reinforce these mythologies. Reinforcing the old mythologies allowed union leaders to claim their ability to protect workers from poor management behavior, behavior interpreted as validating the myths. As a result of the changes instituted by Stewart from 1988, union leader efforts to maintain these old mythologies became less and less credible.

The entire workforce, non-union ("staff"), and union ("award"), during 1988–90 experienced profound dissonance. Management's changes in behavior, systems and symbols meant the old myths were no longer reliable models.

The change process at NZAS was not an attack on unions, union leaders, or the freedom of unions to function in a society. The change process was an open competition for the leadership of the workforce between the union's leaders and management, with management acting based on its understanding of systems leadership theory.[8]

More Systems Changes

Overtime was a significant cost burden for the smelter. The collective agreement often required paying overtime as double or triple time. Each successive management initiative to reduce overtime lost effectiveness as things reverted to "normal." A concerted effort in 1989 had reduced overtime from 45 percent to 20 percent of hours paid, but it was creeping up again.

The new general manager designed and introduced a system change that left the authority to assign overtime with the frontline supervisor, but required a written

---

7   Staff refers to non-union employees working under individual contracts.

8   The whole theory is covered our book, *Systems Leadership: Creating Positive Organizations*. London: Gower Publishing, 2006.

justification be sent directly to the general manager afterwards. The general manager reviewed the justification and sent it back to the supervisor with comments. The outcome was the effective removal of overtime at NZAS by September 1991. It was, however, not a system that could have maintained this outcome over time.

Staff Working Conditions Accepted

The managing director recommended that all award (non-staff) employees be offered staff employment, which the general manager and managers supported. The managing director required that they undertake workforce reduction at the same time. This began with an offer of voluntary redundancy, and with the clearly stated intent of forced redundancy, if the voluntary program did not reduce total employee numbers from 1500 to around 1100.

Letters signed by the general manager were sent to award employees at their homes explaining the proposal. The letter invited those interested to make a time for an interview with their manager-once-removed (stratum III department head), where a typical staff contract would be available for them to examine and take home. Another letter to all employees, again signed by the general manager, explained the intention to reduce total employee numbers.

All of the managers at stratum III went through detailed briefings and practiced interviews with each other to guarantee the coverage of issues and the consistency of response. In these meetings, managers explained the mechanics of staff employment, including that staff were required to perform any tasks assigned to them, providing they were competent to perform them safely.

When they decided to offer staff employment, the managing director had required that the general manager and his managers identify and analyze all the systems, symbols, and behaviors critical to the offer, acceptance, and maintenance of an all-staff workforce. This was done over an intense two-day workshop led by one of the authors (Ian Macdonald) who, as a consultant to Comalco Smelting, had suggested the idea to the managing director.

At a mass meeting called by the union leadership, which drew 850 of 1250 award employees, unanimous resolutions were passed rejecting the staff offer and appointing the union as the agent of employees. These same employees then returned to work and made appointments to discuss the offer with managers.

The salary incentive to join the staff ranks averaged about three percent. The other conditions of staff employment were superior, except that no overtime was paid. The great majority of staff worked additional time when it was required.

Employees were advised that they had the choice of (a) remaining an employee on the existing conditions; (b) accepting a redundancy package, the entire quantity of which was available to them; or (c) signing a staff contract of employment. Each employee was advised to think carefully about the decision and to discuss it with his or her family.

Prior to the interviews, managers-once-removed had identified employees they judged would have difficulty making the transition to staff. This assessment was given to the employee. Each employee was also advised that the decision whether or not to retain union membership was his or her own business. Each was told that the staff employment relationship did not allow for third-party intervention, except under exceptional circumstances.

Ninety-eight percent of the workforce who did not choose a redundancy package signed staff contracts. The redundancy option gave a dignified exit path to those who knew their performance would be unacceptable under staff conditions or whose philosophical position about unions did not allow them to join the staff of an organization seen to be "getting rid of" the union. The organization wanted many of these employees to leave anyway.

Discussion of the Process

Crucial to the move was the work done by managers at stratum III in their interviews. From their position as manager-once-removed, they could put the proposal into context, fully explaining the wider issues and answering questions with authority. The symbolic impact of their 16-hour days and interviews on night shift was not lost on the workforce. "This must be really important! Managers are here day and night!"

The work done in the intense two-day planning workshop to identify symbols, systems, myths, and behaviors and to plan the response was invaluable. The smelter management group had identified all the critical issues and was not thrown off course through the turmoil of the change. No CEO can know all the myths of his or her workforce nor recognize the impact of all the systems, behaviors, and symbols that drive them. Bringing in a range of staff to assist in this analysis is an essential part of a successful major change process.

Results

While improvements in cost and performance had been predicted, the size and speed of this change was not.[9] After all, this was not a smelter in trouble!

Overall cost of production fell by more than 20 percent. Overtime paid and employee numbers changed directly as a result of new systems. Qualitative changes, such as current efficiency, off-specification metal, and high-purity metal, were the result of all employees paying attention and taking more care of the detail of their work, and of having the freedom to do so. As one new staff member said later, "I don't have to leave my brains at the gate any more."

While some initially perceived the changes as primarily to achieve cost reduction, the resulting increasing in revenue from improved quality far outweighed any cost savings. Revenues from additional tonnage of high-purity metal, which sold at a substantial premium, exceeded savings in labor cost from the 310 employee reduction in workforce.

Through changes of their own behavior, the systems and symbols of the organization, management had helped to create a new set of mythologies: that they could be trusted; they would do what they said; they had the courage to remove people who were not carrying their fair share of the load, including supervisors and managers; and that they treated their people with dignity and provided a safe workplace.

Caveat

This was not easy. Be warned, old mythologies do not die; they are only over-laid with new mythologies. One slip during the change process and the old mythologies will be stirred up like silt in a river. They will rise to the top, stronger than ever because, "Fool me once…"

Over time as the new mythologies become more deeply embedded, slips are seen as just that, mistakes. If, however, new leaders change the systems without under-

---

9   For run charts graphically illustrating the difference these changes made, see pages 249-256 in *Systems Leadership: Creating the Positive Organization,* by the authors of this chapter. Published by Gower Publishing, 2006.

standing the value interpretations embedded in them, or change their behavior in ways that appear dishonest, untrustworthy, unfair, or disrespecting of the dignity of their employees, the old myths will return, behavior will change for the worse, and one can expect support for union protection.

Conclusions

These two stories illustrate the earlier points: systems and a knowledge of mythologies are powerful tools a CEO has available to change behavior and the culture of the organization. They determine whether the CEO is perceived as a good or bad leader irrespective of what he or she thinks.

The key element is to recognize the design of systems, the design of controls and audit, and consideration of the values demonstrated by the system is a high-level task requiring minimum stratum IV capability. Corporate systems need to be designed at stratum V or higher. This is one of the primary tasks of corporate leadership roles. The CEO who recognizes the importance of systems and makes sure that they are designed to demonstrate value statements he or she wishes to promulgate in the organization, will also make sure they are not tampered with without his or her approval.

ABOUT THE AUTHORS

Catherine G. Burke, Ph.D., is Associate Professor at the University of Southern California, School of Policy, Planning and Development. Catherine's research focuses on organization and systems design, management theory, and leadership, using Stratified Systems Theory and Systems Leadership Theory. She has been a consultant to a number of public, private, and non-profit organizations. She has also served on a corporate board of directors.

Ian Macdonald, Ph.D. is managing partner of MAC Associates, Ltd. He was a Research Fellow at BIOSS working with Elliott Jaques, Gillian Stamp, and others on a wide range of civil service, mental health, and other projects. He has been a consultant to numerous public, private, non-profit organizations, churches, and communities in England, Australia, the US, Canada, Russia, and the Middle East.

Karl Stewart is a mining engineer. He was the group consultant to CRA, Ltd. where he led the development of implementation and system theories to allow managers to bring about positive organizational change. He later successfully applied this work as managing director of Comalco Smelting. Prior to these activities, he was the site manager at Weipa Bauxite mine and vice president of human resources of Comalco, Ltd.

A Gift for Managers

Sheila Deane

WHAT'S IMPORTANT

- Shows how a newly appointed level IV general manager led a pilot organization development project for a stratum V-led utility; successfully implemented a requisite organization-based framework to deliver impressive business outcomes; and solved some long-term problems with the full commitment of her direct report team.

- Presents a proven framework of integrated RO constructs, principles, and practices dealing with business and organizational leadership, managerial leadership, and relationship management.

- Identifies critical business and execution issues, e.g. clarification of organizational purpose, structure, role clarification, cross-organizational working, six sigma team effectiveness, major business systems project.

In summarizing this leadership development work I want to pass on a message from my own manager (Jenny Bailey). Jenny has offered this to us as a "gift" for managers. It has become a way of thinking for her and for me and has changed the way we work in our leadership team. I am now passing this gift on to you so that as leaders we can continue this work in our own teams. In carrying this legacy forward I hope you will feel its value personally as well as the collective power of its principles.

—Tarnya McKenzie, Yarra Valley Water's Call Centre Manager, introducing her subordinate managers to the company's new requisite organization (RO) based Leadership Framework[1]

I had the good fortune of providing consulting support to Jenny Bailey, general manager of Yarra Valley Water for customer operations, in pilot testing my firm's RO-based leadership framework for the company. This article is the story of how Jenny learned the RO-based concepts and then applied them successfully in her own function and in the redesign of several of the company's key cross-functional work processes. I've tried to relate some of Jenny's feelings, thoughts, insights, and learning as we worked together over the eight month period.

The key players in this story are the following:
- Yarra Valley Water (YVW), a Melbourne (Australia)-based retail water utility (See Figure 4.2.1)
- PeopleFit Australasia (PFA), a consulting company specializing in requisite organization-based organization and leadership development
- Tony Kelly, YVW's managing director (MD)
- Jenny Bailey, YVW's general manager (GM), customer operations
- Tarnya McKenzie, YVW's Customer Call Centre Manager (Customer Operations)
- Andrew Edney, YVW's manager, connections

PeopleFit Australasia has developed a framework-based approach to installing requisite organization quickly, practically, and effectively. The following are some key features of the approach:
- There is a customized leadership framework of constructs, principles and practices primarily based on the work of Elliott Jaques and Wilfred Brown.
- Line managers induct their subordinates into the framework and set clear expectations and accountabilities for its application in the workplace.

---

1   Jaques, E, *Requisite Organization*, Arlington, Cason Hall & Co, 1998

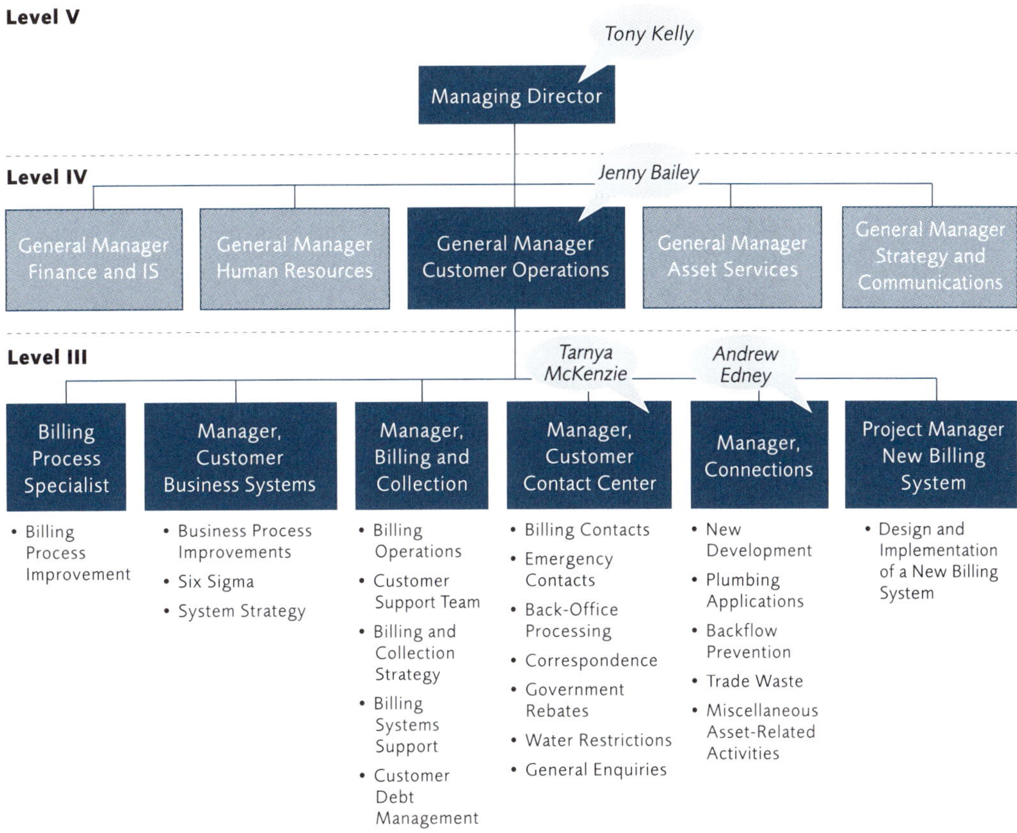

FIGURE 4.2.1

- Business direction, objectives, key success issues, and performance measures are linked directly to application of the framework.
- The framework-based initiatives are monitored by organization/leadership evaluation.
- Specific implementation plans are developed between managers and teams to transfer concepts to real workplace improvement.

Following an overview presentation and demonstration of the framework-based approach, Tony Kelly, YVW's managing director, initiated a pilot organization and leadership improvement project in YVW's customer operations group in March 2006. He intended to demonstrate successful implementation in a key operational group and to thus create a "pull through" effect in the organization. The leader of that pilot project was the newly appointed general manager of customer operations, Jenny Bailey.

With a BE degree, a post-graduate environmental science qualification, and an MBA qualification, Jenny is capable, practical, and action-oriented. She reports her experience of this RO-based project has been a significant contributor to her effectiveness as a leader. Specifically she indicates that it has been a life-changing shift, which strongly connects with her values about people at work and about how people should be treated in order for them to give their best. In using RO-based principles, Jenny also reports step change improvement trends in her group since the pilot started and a growing confidence in her and her team's capability to do real continuous improvement and to tackle more complex problems.

Introducing the RO Principles

Jenny told me that her introduction to requisite organization principles and practices was just in time. As a newly appointed leader of this function, she needed to very quickly work out what her true work was and how she could best add value to her team. Equally important, she needed to work out what she should not be doing.

Jenny says that she quickly came to see that improving organizational performance must start with a focus on the organizational conditions within which employees are being asked to work. She was immediately comfortable with the RO principles of trust, fairness, and the clarity around the work of the manager, and she believed that the RO-based framework provided those conditions. She read widely to understand the body of theory and explored her thoughts with the author. With her background in science, she had little tolerance for the management fads that come and go. She became intensely interested in the carefully defined terms and measures that link the various components of RO's comprehensive and systematic approach and the research in the development and validation of the theory that underpins the practice.

Key Issues

Jenny used the elements of the RO framework to help her examine her business. Her first task was to talk to each of her direct report managers to understand their work and their key issues and concerns. The emerging issues were the following:

BUSINESS PURPOSE

- A lack of clarity and shared understanding of the purpose of the group and the definition of customer satisfaction

STRUCTURE

- A lack of clarity in the team about the type of work that needed to be done at each level of complexity
- Some mismatches of person-to-role and the predictable tension and conflict between manager and direct report
- A six sigma team set up to service the whole organization, but with a reporting line to the GM customer operations, resulting in misaligned accountabilities and authorities
- The process of initiating projects and tasks and drawing on resources within the group and across the company without the right levels of authority resulted in a plethora of misaligned work engaging willing and committed individuals who were already suffering overload
- How to manage and set up an $18 million (AU) IT billing project with significant implications for the business

SYSTEMS AND PROCESSES

- A concern about the effectiveness of cross-division and cross-company processes, especially relating to accountabilities and authority for ownership of steps in the processes
- The continuing discussion about the difficult and complex "nuts" that had been around for years and hadn't or couldn't be cracked
- A focus on short-term work, i.e. operational work, driving out future focused work, or improving work
- A concern about getting the right measures for business improvement

APPLICATION OF CONSISTENT MANAGERIAL LEADERSHIP PRINCIPLES

- How to assign and manage tasks to keep control of the many strands of work without interfering or dipping down into the work of the team
- How to build mutual trust and accountability into the people systems, so that every person knows what is expected of them and what they can expect of others in delivering their promises

The 90-Day Plan

Jenny developed a draft 90-day plan to initiate work on the key issues, and then engaged her team of managers in an extended work meeting to refine the plan. "I am fortunate to have inherited a committed and capable team. This framework helped me to work with my team to plan what we needed to do. I could see a way to get things done."

The first big "AHA!" for her managers occurred during the first team workshop, when they engaged the purpose of the customer operations group and specifically in getting clarity around the issue of what's the work we do, and how do we do it? This resulted in the following:

- A shift from assuming sole accountability for everything relating to the customer, to accountability to provide a critical link between customers and those elsewhere in YVW who are accountable for delivering services to customers
- Initiating work to clarify the continuous processes and their role relationships with all relevant parties in the business
- Working more closely within operations to get agreements on respective accountabilities and authorities and to set up appropriate cross-functional feedback channels

Jenny and her team clarified their understanding of YVW's value chain. They discovered that a number of processes ran across the group and YVW without clear accountability, which resulted in broken processes and process workarounds that couldn't maximize productivity. Jenny could see this as allowing unproductive and unreliable systems.

Jenny restructured her group to focus on key work processes in an effort to institute efficiency and effectiveness in the value chain. Using a structured teamwork process, she received valuable input from her team about the issues and the work needed to make the change. As a result of this early teamwork, she brought her managers along the journey of discovery so that each of them understood what needed to change and why. Where structural adjustments could be seen as threatening and painful, their need was now obvious, because they were linked to effective work flow and appropriate work complexity. She achieved full commitment of the team to accepting clearer purpose, role accountability, and matching authority.

The manager of the connections team, a direct report manager to Jenny, described a significant improvement in his ability to improve the output of his team through the framework-based examination of the key processes of connecting water to a new customer. There are two elements to connecting a customer: one is the physical connection for which his team was accountable, and the other is the management of data for ongoing metering services, for which another manager was accountable. The examination of the end-to-end process indicated an obvious benefit to draw both functions together under one manager. As a result the metering team was disbanded.

The manager of the connections team described his success:

I now have accountability and authority to manage the end-to-end process. This has enabled me to identify and quickly resolve problems by looking at systems, processes, and individual capabilities. Aligning the structure to the natural way we work, the team can "see" the whole process and are now more confident that decisions can be made to deal with the workarounds that previously existed. When they bring issues to the table, they have more influence over the system and decisions can be made quickly. This "whole-of-process" picture and their improved level of influence has changed their mindset.

With clear ideas about the structure, Jenny checked her thinking by preparing "thumbnail" or summary descriptions of each role and task type of her direct reports. She was able to check complexity of work and alignment of work to the value chain. She reinforced these expectations in symbolic "commissioning letters" to each of her reports, making explicit the need for delivery of outcomes against measures as well as collaboration and effective leadership. This enabled the shift from drive-to-achieve incentive bonuses to a more holistic and systemic approach to the work.

Jenny also realized that a piece of her technical work, the development of methods and processes for the group, should be assigned to a technical specialist. She established a full-time level III staff role that reported directly to her and that provided specialist support to her and her managers in the identification and improvement of the billing process. She appointed a Six Sigma specialist from a dedicated Six Sigma implementation team to this role. As a result, she had the competencies in place to strengthen the focus on targeted improvement work and to provide a specialist resource to all of her managers so that they could better deliver on their improvement targets. She believed a key to the success of this role was to engage her managers in aligning this new role with their roles in the team. She worked with the author to design a framework-based process to align the specialist role with the core operational work.

The team developed the following important insights:

- They had incorrectly assumed a common picture of the complete billing process and respective accountabilities, resulting in conflict of accountability and rework.
- Previous assumption of specialists' accountabilities to implement improvement processes in other managers' areas resulted in diffusion of true managerial authority and a lack of accountability for delivery of the process in their own area.
- Role clarity enabled the general manager to reduce time resolving accountability based conflicts and to increase time focusing on value-adding integration of the work as the cross-over manager.

Teamwork and Task Assignment

There was never any question that employees in Yarra Valley Water enjoy working in the business and that they work diligently. The big questions were: is this the right work to be doing now, and are the right people doing the work?

As she began to understand the RO framework, Jenny saw opportunities to improve the way projects were initiated and tasks assigned. The problems were the following:

- Too often a person would be given a task or self-assign desired work without critical evaluation of how it would fit with the company's strategy and business plan.
- Accountable managers were not engaged in the identification of tasks requiring input from their function or use of their resources. This resulted in the generation of unauthorized work across the business, with people regularly being tapped on the shoulder to do the work. The result? A large amount of work was being done without a clear link to the business priorities, without appropriate managerial approval, and without reference to systems that ensure good governance, such as clear budgeting, coordinative planning, and effective authority.

When Jenny first came across the task-assignment model and the team-working process, she wondered what she could learn. Hadn't her MBA given her all the management tools she needed to do her work? It hadn't. The framework gave her the following specific tools:

- Identify the true task, its complexity and appropriate resources
- Identify issues impacting success and desired outcomes with the full input and commitment of her team
- Authorize the work at the right level with the right accountabilities and authori-

ties: this enabled her to better utilize the capability of her team

- Initiate appropriate cross-organization manager involvement and authorization of work where that work is required as part of her function's tasks

Imagine the incremental improvement in productivity when the right resources are assigned to the right work without pleading, coercing, or manipulating. And if the work shouldn't be done, getting the right input to identify this and addressing it up front, rather than letting the "black-widow" projects drag on miserably.

All team members realized the value of sharing in this process, not only to get a clearer context for their work, but also to develop a deeper understanding of the whole task and how it was to be achieved. This enabled them to mobilize their own capability and creativity to contribute to better outcomes. Suddenly, those difficult nuts were being cracked open.

There were a number of significant successes. For example, YVW has a service promise to repair water leaks within 24 hours of a customer call. On some occasions the nature of the problem requires an extension to this time. In these circumstances, the call center had struggled for years to get an effective outcome from the maintenance teams. This was mainly because the process had not been clearly articulated, and specific accountabilities for the various steps of the process had not been clarified or agreed upon. The result was that maintenance would do what they thought was their role, to fix the water leak. Without a shared understanding of the whole process and an understanding of the call center's role to communicate to the customer, the outcome was that communication between operations and call center did not occur in a timely way and the customer was left out of the process.

The manager of the call center used the framework models to give her the confidence to approach the manager accountable for maintenance. She facilitated a team-working session between the functions for the identification of issues and mapping of the process. With all parties in the room contributing to the issues, a clear picture of the process and who was accountable for what emerged. The managers could then confirm process and accountabilities and it enabled YVW to consistently and reliably deliver to the customers as promised. It also provided a method for those directly impacted by the problem to share their experiences and thoughts and commit to the agreed resolution.

The call center manager was delighted with the outcome. "Using the RO principles and the teamwork process was a way of unveiling the problems and revealing the issues and accountabilities in a natural way," she said. "No one needed to have anything forced on them." Her experience reinforced a key principle of requisite organization: most conflicts in organizations arise from unclear accountabilities and inadequate authority to carry out those accountabilities, not from some sort of dysfunction within the individual. The tools enable leaders of teams to take constructive and purposeful action to address the problems objectively while focusing on the business outcome.

The manager of connections loves the clarity around task assignment and the involvement of his team in the work: "My team wants more of the team-working and task-assigning tool. They are excited about attending a task assignment workshop, because they value a process that enables their contribution and they experience accountable decision-making and resolution of long-term problems."

Performance

Understanding the framework-based model of individual capability assessment helped Jenny and her managers to select better for roles and to diagnose apparent performance issues. She and her team were astounded at the implications for their team outputs when faced with the realization that the manager is accountable for the output of the team member. They were humbled by the degree to which the team member's personal effectiveness is impacted not only by his or her own capability, but also by organizational factors such as efficacy of cross-functional role relationships, role accountabilities, key performance indicators, as well as his or her manager's effectiveness.

"Over the past six months," the connections manager commented, "my team's performance has improved from achieving 66 percent turnaround of applications for water and sewerage connection in four days to 84 percent turnaround." He has done this through application of a number of interrelated practices including teamwork, system and process improvement, and talent pool management to correctly match the right people to the right roles. He used performance diagnostic tools to identify an individual who had not been performing to expectations, who was in fact working in a role that did not fit her current capability. She was subsequently transferred to a role that better matched her capability and this resulted in a promotion. Decisions such as these were previously unheard of. The manager believes these tools have given managers diagnostic capacity to identify "what's the work and the fit for the work" and more confidence in making judgments about their people's capability.

How Did Jenny Do This?

- Jenny committed to study the original texts to ensure she had a good understanding of the theory.
- In recognizing that this was not a process, but a whole system of management which would have deep implications for her business area, she obtained her managing director's support for full discretion to implement the practices in her own area.
- She used a consultant for one-to-one coaching to guide her application of the framework to her workplace issues and to assist her managers to cascade this to their teams.
- She developed a 90-day implementation plan with her subordinate managers to ensure their input and commitment.
- Jenny used the models consistently and rigorously in her team and presented them to her peers when the work impacted other areas. She practiced the team-working process for all complex and cross-team tasks
- Jenny focused on changing work behaviors by concentrating on the processes of work, including the accountabilities and authorities and the personal needs of each person in executing his or her own work.

Results

Jenny has an impressive record of achievement and feedback from her manager, her direct reports, and through a well-known 360-degree feedback tool on leadership effectiveness. After eight months in the role she has just received her result, which places her in the top five percent of the Australia-wide sample of managers for the achievement element of the assessment. This is consistent with her demonstrated ability to deliver on her business objectives in a short time frame. She is well on the way to achieving all of her identified key tasks and she has established a team committed to working together to achieve demanding targets. She has observed growing confidence of her managers to exercise their leadership roles appropriately. In fact, her pride in her team of direct reports and the capability they are building in their own teams is palpable. She feels in control, and she is now confident in successfully delivering the organization's most significant enterprise resource planning (billing) project.

The call center manager's reflection on this work is compelling. She has been able to use the framework to create the right conditions for work and thus to resolve one of the workplace's constant dilemmas: how to deliver to the demands of the business and how to meet employees' legitimate psychological needs for work.

"The effect of this framework has been quite profound for me," she said. "I have always enjoyed having the privilege as a manager to help people achieve their best work and to develop them to move on to do even better things. I have always tried to be a good manager, but the requisite organization framework has provided the missing link for me—the clear link to the business. It has provided me with the complete picture of work and our reason for being. Now I truly feel I am on the pathway to become a great manager."

The manager of connections is confident that the integrated set of principles and practices will deliver continued positive results. "In the past," he said, "Connections was the area that collected pieces of work that didn't seem to fit anywhere else. Now I am very clear about what I am and am not accountable for, and I can concentrate on what I must do. I feel much more effective in my role."

ABOUT THE AUTHOR

Sheila Deane is a director of PeopleFit Australasia, a consulting company specializing in requisite organization-based organization and leadership development.

Deane is a former HR professional and line manager. She has more than 20 years experience in the practical application of RO principles and practices, much of this developed while working with CRA Ltd, the pioneer of RO-based organization reform in Australia. She has made a substantial contribution to developing practical, business-focused, and trust-based methods and tools aimed at making RO-based development more accessible and immediately useful to practicing line managers.

Deane is a skilled presenter and facilitator and is much sought after to assist executive teams in their organization development initiatives. She has worked successfully in a range of cultural settings in Southern Africa, North America, SE Asia, and Australia.

Teams Can't Be Better Structured Than Your Organization: How Roche Canada Created High Performing Cross-Functional Product Launch Teams

Charlotte M. Bygrave

WHAT'S IMPORTANT

This article shows that high-performing teams can only be established in a well-structured organization.

Enabling high-performing teams requires:

- Clear accountabilities and authorities of team leaders and members;

- Clearly defined role relationships between teams and the rest of the organization;

- Selection criteria and processes for team leaders and members;

- Processes for delegation of authorities; and

- Guidelines for applying human resource management policies in areas of personal effectiveness appraisals, rewards and recognition, training and development, and other types of team support.

Celebrations were held and rewards and recognition granted. Dr. Jaques's principles were turning out to be useful and practical 'stuff'.

This article examines how Roche Canada, the Canadian affiliate of F. Hoffmann La Roche Ltd., solved what appeared to be the intractable problems of getting the best results from product launch teams. The senior management applied the requisite organization principles to create teams that produced results far greater than those that would have been achieved by one functional silo "throwing a project over the wall to the next," or with highly capable and committed teams facing barricades to performance.

The requisite organization principles placed Roche Canada on the path to creating high-performing teams, reducing time-to-market, and saving millions of dollars. The requisite organization approach is a total management system. Roche Canada adapted it to the existing culture and business, and entitled it the Roche Management System. This system enabled the creation of the conditions under which all employees could be more successful and managers could, in a fair manner, be held accountable for the results of their staff.

While this article focuses on the establishment of product launch teams, Roche Canada implemented the entire requisite system. This full-scale implementation is described in an article on the GO Society website.

Background

The pharmaceutical industry has long been one of the world's most complex industries. This complexity began accelerating in the early 1990s at a spectacular rate and as a result the critical issues, such as patent expirations, price pressures, drug development challenges, and regulatory and political pressures, grew in intensity.

F. Hoffmann-La Roche, Ltd, a leading global, research-oriented healthcare company, headquartered in Basel, Switzerland, responded to these issues with mergers and acquisitions, improved manufacturing processes, licensing-in of new drugs, and strategic alliances. "Roche" articulated new directions, which included managers acting as coaches and mentors, the elimination of "turfs" and organization silos, and the building of a stronger goal-and-process orientation throughout the company.

The president and CEO of Roche Canada, the Canadian operating center, and his management team searched for ways to maintain and achieve more success in this unprecedented business environment. Roche Canada generated approximately $500 million (CDN) in sales annually, or three percent of the company's worldwide profitability. It was a mid-size operation that served a sophisticated and demanding medical market and ranked with the company's larger affiliates as a member of its "international business board."

The Canadian team wanted to be well prepared to achieve the anticipated benefits of a recent and major acquisition (Syntex Inc.) and effectively positioned to regain its place as one of the top three pharmaceutical companies in Canada within ten years. The strategies to achieve these ends were in place and it had good people. What the team needed was an optimal organization structure, and the best managerial leadership practices to enable talented people to deliver the results.

The team had been introduced to Dr. Elliott Jaques's approach to organization design and management, requisite organization, and in 1995 asked him to help build the capabilities of the organization. The ideas presented in the book *Requisite Organization* were consistent with Roche's values and presented what the team considered a practical approach to achieve the company's vision, mission, and strategic objectives.

The president and CEO, Vic Ackermann, asked me to take on the role of project manager and work with Dr. Jaques and Nancy Lee, president of Requisite Organization Associates, to develop a plan to achieve the benefits to be gained by making Roche Canada a requisite organization.

Working Across the Functions

Before describing how we solved the issues of the product launch teams, it's best to describe how we first established the context of better working relationships across functions.

Dr. Jaques, Nancy, and I held workshops with function managers to identify the cross-functional working relationships that were hindering the quality and speed of cross-functional work. This work involved two or more people not in a manager-direct report working relationship who needed to work together to each get their own work done. Neither was to be accountable for the other's outputs, but each was to be accountable to his or her own manager. These situations often lack clarity.

We assisted the accountable managers in learning how to define clear cross-functional accountabilities and authorities, establish dispute resolution mechanisms, and set the context for dispute resolution. They learned that they needed approval of the accountabilities and authorities from their *cross-over point managers*, the first manager whom two people, who do not have the same immediate manager, have in common and the first manager accountable for integrating the work of these two people, departments, or functions.

For example, producing marketing brochures generated a great deal of confusion between the functions involved in getting this work done. The work slowed down when several vice presidents, each accountable for some aspect of producing marketing materials, could not agree on which one of them had the authority to make a final decision.

The president clarified the accountability and authority that he wanted these vice presidents to have in the development of marketing materials. He gave the vice president of regulatory affairs, the group accountable for securing government approval to market drugs, the authority to monitor and audit all materials for scientific and medical accuracy, including the final decision about the scientific and medical contents of all marketing materials. The vice president of clinical research had the accountability and authority to provide input/advice to regulatory affairs. The vice president of marketing retained the accountability and authority for the final production of medically and scientifically accurate marketing materials. With these clarifications, the marketing, regulatory affairs, and clinical research functions could work more efficiently together.

The greater clarity of accountabilities and authorities between roles and functions also lessened organizational silo-ing and the lack of collaborative efforts thought to be due primarily to negative "politics" and "personality conflicts." It replaced the vague or ill-defined integration mechanisms often used by organizations, such as "matrix organizations," "dotted-line relationships," "liaison task forces," "sponsors and champions," and committees. It allowed people to get on with their work in a more effective way, reducing conflict and inefficiencies and releasing employee energy, initiative, and creativity.

The HR team and I found ourselves busy helping managers prepare new role descriptions to clarify and communicate cross-functional accountabilities and authorities that would facilitate more collaborative work among individuals and functions.

Establishing High-Performance Product Development and Launch Teams

Before starting this initial organizational design work, the president had already established six or seven cross-functional product launch teams. He had previous experience working with these types of teams and knew their value to the timely launch of new products. He had assigned accountability and authority for the teams to the executive committee. The teams were accountable for analyzing the medical, scientific, and financial potential of new drugs in the Canadian market, recommending to the executive committee the inclusion of new drugs in the Canadian portfolio, and developing and implementing product launch plans for the approved drugs.

We were quite excited about these teams and very pleased with their performance. They were "leaping high hurdles" and "running obstacle courses" to achieve outstanding results. It should have been obvious to us that they could not sustain this pace for long. Soon, dissatisfaction was brewing within the teams. The director of new product development (assigned the role of coach to the teams) came to me to discuss their concerns. We decided to bring in an external consultant to help review team processes and identify issues. The teams identified the following issues and presented them to the executive committee:

- They were quite pleased to be team leaders; however, several members of the committee were assigning tasks to them. This extra workload, along with their product launch team work and the regular work assigned to them by their functional or "home-base" managers, put the team members into overload. Soon, it would be impossible for them to continue performing well. Our analysis indicated that they had too many priorities and too many bosses to please. Could the executive committee help them resolve this problem?
- The home-base managers still expected their direct reports to fully meet all of their work standards, whether or not they were also assigned to one of these special teams. Who would decide the work priorities? Who would help the team members mend the deteriorating work relationship with their real or regular managers?
- Team members had concerns with performance appraisals and compensation for the two jobs they were performing. What effect should their team work have on their annual overall performance appraisal and compensation awards? Who

would appraise their "team work" and decide on rewards and recognition?

- The teams did not know how to respond to questions from their peers regarding how one got chosen to be on a team, and especially appointed team leader. Employees knew that the selection criteria were not written down and concluded that the decisions were political.

There were other conflicts to be dealt with, too:

- Escalating interpersonal work issues: Once the team leaders had exhausted their best influencing and persuasive skills, who would resolve problems within the teams or between the teams and other functions and departments?
- What accountability and authority did team leaders and members have?
- How were the team leaders and coach to solve problems, such as members not attending important team meetings or a member performing below standards?
- Who could initiate the removal of a member from the team (when removal was warranted)?
- How should the teams and functional departments interact?
- Were the home-base department managers in any way accountable for the teams' success and performance?

The executive committee members were shocked. They had no idea of the extent of the teams' problems. Of course at this point without the concepts, theories, and language of the requisite principles, we were not able to correctly diagnose the root causes of the teams' problems and identify appropriate solutions. Our solutions were not comprehensive, integrated, or coherent. They included the following:

- Giving the teams more "down time" or a break from their work. This, however, would not solve problems long term, since the workload issues and other frustrations would remain.
- Controlling the flow of work to the teams through a single identified committee member was a good start, but would not fully resolve their complaints either. The conflicts between the teams and functions would remain.
- Requiring home-base managers to support their department staff placed on the launch teams.
- Providing team leaders with training, particularly in leadership skills and problem solving.

Analysis

When Dr. Jaques and Nancy Lee arrived, we presented the teams' issues to them. We eventually formed a small senior management task force, with Dr. Jaques as the external consultant and me as the internal advisor to review the issues.

How to structure and manage six or seven critical teams (the number growing due to several new products in the pipeline) was an organizational design problem that brought a furrowed brow even to Dr. Jaques's face. While we learned from him and Nancy Lee that we could apply the organization design principles to select, establish, and manage project or coordinative teams, he eventually realized that product launch teams at Roche presented a special case.

He realized that each product launch required two very different types of teams. Project teams were needed to analyze and recommend a product's inclusion in the portfolio. If the executive committee approved the recommendation, then a coordinative team was needed to plan and execute the market introduction of the new product.

Although the two teams might have many of the same staff, their accountabilities, authorities, and role relationship to the rest of the organization were very different. Clarity about the types of teams Roche needed and how to build and connect them to the organization was the foundation needed to solve the teams' issues and sustain their motivation and performance.

Resolution

The Roche launch process was now logical, coherent, and transparent. We developed the accountabilities and authorities of team leaders and members for both project and coordinative teams. The project team leader would have managerial authority with respect to the team members. The leaders were accountable for the outputs of the team, and therefore were given the authority to veto the appointment of someone to the team (based, of course, on sound evidence), define and assign tasks to the team, judge the performance of team members, and determine special awards, within company policy.

Project teams had all the resources needed to get their work done. The procedure to request the completion of work by someone not on the team was well defined. If the teams needed someone outside the team to complete a special piece of work, the team leader made a request through the normal managerial process to the appropriate function/department manager. Other than this special request, the work of the project team did not commit others outside of the team to do anything.

The project team morphed into a coordinative team perhaps with the same or new members. Member changes were task- and resource-driven. The accountabilities and authorities of the coordinative team leaders and members were very different from those of the project teams. The coordinative team coordinated the timing and resourcing of several departments and/or functions needed to achieve the stated objectives of the new product launch.

Unlike their counterparts on project teams, these team leaders did not have managerial authority but coordinative authority with respect to the members on the team. That is, they had the authority to call members together, make suggestions about how the work should be approached, and help overcome problems or setbacks.

Members of the coordinative teams were representatives of their departments or functions. The department (home-base) manager retained accountability for the performance or outputs of his or her people on the team and granted special awards or recognition within policy. This made the team members' working relationships much like that of any cross-functional working relationship between individuals reporting to different managers. Of course, both project and coordinative team leaders worked under the authority of an accountable executive manager.

Given the number of such teams and their importance to the organization's success, we communicated to all employees the nature of the two different teams and how they were attached to the structure of the organization. Clear criteria and processes for selecting team leaders and members were documented and made available to all employees.

The authorities of team leaders and teams were documented and we developed processes for the delegation of key accountabilities and authorities. We decided, for example, that the president was ultimately accountable for the teams, but obviously it was not appropriate that he manage these teams directly. While he retained accountability for the teams, he delegated his authority to a manager. The manager could, in turn, delegate accountabilities and authorities to the coach for the teams, for example, helping a coordinative team leader and home-base manager resolve a team member performance issue.

We developed guidelines for applying human resource management policies, personal effectiveness appraisals, rewards and recognition, training and development, and other types of team support. It was recognized that fair rewards and recognition were important aspects of establishing and sustaining effective teams. Team leaders and members received bonuses and other softer forms of recognition (special awards dinners, plaques, etc.). Dr. Jaques warns against the disadvantages of predictive criteria-based bonuses for which the bonus criteria are expected to drive or determine the individual's initiative and efforts. However, bonuses and bonus amounts decided after determining how well the individual worked toward achieving the expected results is most appropriate.

We reviewed, revised, and documented guidelines for establishing and maintaining the teams. The new team design and infrastructure reduced team frustration, increased morale, and enabled the teams to get on with their work, including reducing launch times. Multiple bosses were eliminated, workloads were reasonable, intra- and inter-team collaboration and cooperation increased, and teams completed work faster and with higher quality.

Celebrations were held and rewards and recognition granted. Dr. Jaques's principles were turning out to be useful and practical "stuff."

Requisite Rewards and Recognition

Before concluding, it would be useful to briefly touch on how we implemented requisite rewards and recognition, as it is relevant to our work in the product launch teams.

We took an approach to rewards and recognition that was far "outside the box." The usual bonus systems were rendered ineffective due to the complexity of Roche's work and the unpredictable and unanticipated obstacles employees face in the progress toward their goals. This unpredictability was especially inherent in the complex work of the higher level roles.

Traditional performance management systems are based on predictive criteria. They make no allowance for actual performance conditions that vary significantly from the predicted conditions, rewarding employees for achieving a certain level of results or outcomes, which is usually quantitative. This directs employees to focus on achieving the numbers that could require behaviors that are inconsistent with doing the right thing. Also, one employee might get a lower bonus even though he or she accomplished higher quality work under more difficult circumstances, but with lower quantitative results than another with less complex work under less difficult circumstances.

At Roche Canada, the bonus programs sometimes caused poor morale, precipitated employee behaviors outside of acceptable standards, and created poor relationships between management and employees. Employees would often ask, "What does the bonus reward me for? Doesn't the company expect my full commitment and best performance for my base pay?" These difficult questions and the dissatisfaction of employees and their managers with bonus results led us to examine our assumptions about bonuses.

Each of the three Roche Canada business divisions had the authority, however, to decide what they felt was best for their business, whether to retain or eliminate bonus pay schemes. They decided to roll incentive pay into base salary. Two divisions retained incentives as a small part of total compensation for sales and marketing staff.

Special awards, reviewed by the manager and human resources to ensure consistency, could still be granted to any employee for exceptional performance. However, these cases were determined after the fact at the end of the performance period.

The human resources department worked hard reviewing the impact of this change on salary-driven benefits programs and particularly on the defined benefit pension plan. It was a change affordable for the company.

The entire compensation program was reviewed to ensure pay ranges were linked to organization levels and levels of complexity of work. Clearly defining roles' accountabilities and the alignment of work complexity with organizational levels reduced employees' concerns about equity and fairness in performance assessment and increased managers' consistency and reliability in judging performance. Managers were able to make more accurate judgments and to recommend fair merit increases.

We replaced the five performance appraisal categories, which ranged from "outstanding" to "unacceptable," with six performance categories which enabled more accurate judgments of an individual's performance against the requirements of the role. The new categories asked the manager to judge where in the range of the role an individual was performing. For instance, were they at the top or bottom half of the role, and within these halves at which of three levels (high, medium, low) were they?

The manager-once-removed (the manager's boss) reviewed the performance ratings and recommended merit increases prepared by his or her managers to ensure each was applying a standard, fair, and accurate rating process to all employees.

Performance appraisals and merit increases, two highly emotionally charged issues, could now be handled more efficiently and effectively.

Employees understood that the changes meant the "performance bar" had not been lowered; it had been raised. They agreed this exchange was fair.

Conclusions

From our experience, the key lessons for organization and management in the pharmaceutical industry include the following:

1. High-performing teams can only be established in a well-structured organization: An optimal organization structure provides the conditions under which good people can perform their best.

2. Clear cross-functional accountabilities and authorities: Clear cross-functional accountabilities and authorities (rather than the vague and confusing definitions of "dotted line or lateral relationships" and "matrix organizations") are essential to reduce organization silos and "turfs," and to create effective working relationships between functions that increase the flow and quality of work across the organization. The increasingly intense levels of interaction required between functions, corporate offices, and country-level affiliates, and across the supply chain, demands clear specification of accountabilities and authorities. Unclear accountabilities and authorities lead to extreme inefficiencies and acrimonious working relationships.

3. Effective managerial leadership practices: Capability or raw cognitive power is a necessary, but not sufficient, condition for effective managerial leadership. Clearly defined managerial leadership accountabilities, authorities, and practices are essential for good organization governance and performance.

4. High-performing teams: Well-established project and coordinative teams can accomplish the intense collaborative work required within and between the major functions of pharmaceutical organizations. To enable high-performing teams to function well requires the following:

- Clear accountabilities and authorities of team leaders and members for both project and coordinative teams;

- Clearly defined role relationships between teams and the rest of the organization;
- Selection criteria and processes for team leaders and members;
- Processes for delegation of authorities; and
- Guidelines for applying human resource management policies in areas of personal effectiveness appraisals, rewards and recognition, training and development, and other types of team support.

With good organization and management as one of its key initiatives, the pharmaceutical industry would be better positioned to regain credibility with customers, suppliers, and other key stakeholders. This would be an additional strategic resource to generate a robust future for an industry that creates critically important health-care solutions.

ABOUT THE AUTHOR

Charlotte M. Bygrave is the principal of Bygrave & Associates. Her firm specializes in working with clients to create optimal organization structures, facilitate strategic change, and implement a broad range of human resource management systems.

Prior to consulting, Bygrave was a human resource executive with a record of achievement in multinational firms such as American Express Co., Xerox Canada Inc., The Bank of Nova Scotia, and Hoffmann-LaRoche Ltd. She has also been a member of the boards of directors of the Wellesley Central Hospital and the Sherbourne Health Centre.

As vice president human resources at Hoffmann La Roche Ltd, Bygrave worked extensively with senior management and Dr. Elliott Jaques to implement a reorientation of the organization's structure, staffing, and managerial leadership practices. This work led her into the field of consulting. She has consulted in a wide range of industries and organizations including health-care, pharmaceuticals, financial services, manufacturing, and high technology.

She has presented with Dr. Jaques to organizations such as the Academy of Management and the Ontario Society for Training and Development on the topic of organization design. She has also worked with Dr. Jaques, as one of two co-authors of an article on strategic planning for *The International Journal of Organizational Analysis.* She holds a Bachelor of Science degree from the Pennsylvania State University.

Effective Management of Specialists in Cross-Functional Teams

Richard B. D. Brown

WHAT'S IMPORTANT

- The common cross-functional, and even cross-organizational team-management muddle often includes project managers who direct the technical work of team members, but often do not see themselves as line managers, and line managers who do not see themselves as having any responsibility for their staff who are seconded to projects.

- Use of RO in project management can prevent poor staffing, poor assignments of tasks, contractual difficulties, poor morale and low retention, and project failures.

- The author's recommendation is to establish minimum managerial accountabilities and authorities, and then articulate clearly defined cross-functional accountabilities and authorities.

The assumption was made, and stated in contract, that new staff were fully competent in order to meet risk and liability requirements. To admit otherwise might have caused future problems.

The Cross-functional Team Management Muddle

Elliott Jaques and Wilfred Brown, in their Glacier project writings, paid extensive attention to the most effective ways to manage specialists. They went to considerable lengths to detail the responsibilities and roles of those involved. Brown, in his book *Organization*, includes an extensive description of how to structure the organization so as to deploy specialists effectively.

However what Jaques and Brown described was within the context of large manufacturing organizations. Specialists in most of these situations were employees of the same organization that used their services. Managers of these specialists and the line managers who utilized them ultimately reported to the same boss. What they did not address in any detailed way was the management of projects and the utilization of specialists within them.

This is a pity, for the deployment of large numbers, perhaps hundreds of specialists in project teams is a matter of great managerial complexity.

However, the processes Jaques and Brown developed and described in this area, and in particular their description of the roles of co-managers, are, I believe, applicable to projects whatever their size. Their application and the rigor they demand in detailing role accountabilities and authorities are likely to give many benefits and lead to improved project success. This article is devoted to an explanation of how and why this should be so.

Wide-spread Problems in Cross-functional Teams of Specialists

Let me start by describing the situation I found in several large projects. I will then describe briefly what Brown and Jaques said about co-managers and show how this might be applied to project management.

As a contract HR manager, I have had the opportunity to hold resourcing and recruitment roles in some very large construction/infrastructure projects (i.e., in excess of US$100 million). I was asked to recruit scarce resources to fill a number of different types of vacancies in the project teams. This task brought me face-to-face with the complexity of their structures, because to recruit you need (a) to know the recruiting manager trying to fill the vacancy, and (b) from them, identify and analyze the details of the role together with its selection criteria. Getting this knowledge often was quite difficult.

Generally, major projects are organized into a typical pattern. There is a project director, charged with overall responsibility of the project, who, if the client organization commissioning the project has run projects before, might be one of their employees. Alternatively, he or she (mostly he) may be a member of a contracted specialist project management organization or, often for smaller projects, a senior employee of the major contractor carrying out the project. Typically reporting to the project director will be a number of project managers who are either responsible for a major area of the project, a major phase of the project, or both.

- *Specification*: determining exactly what was wanted
- *Design*: producing the designs to meet specifications
- *Implementation*: completing the work to the designs and specifications

(Note that each phase may require different specialist skills.)

Within each of these areas, sub-project teams may be responsible for some specialist aspect of each phase. Members of each of these teams will be drawn from a variety of sources with different types of employment contracts, such as the following:

- Employees of the client organization
- Employees of a sub-contractor
- Individual sub-contractors directly contracted with the client organization
- Individual sub-contractors directly contracted with sub-contractors.

In the biggest project in which I was involved, there were as many as four levels of sub-contractors, not including the labor contractors who actually did the final work.

Their responsibilities were defined in legal contracts, precise in law, but often imprecise in detailing the managerial and specialist accountabilities and authorities. These contracts were ostensibly designed to clarify the work for which each person would be held accountable, but it was not until the project progressed that anybody could specify exactly what an individual would be expected to contribute. This could make it very difficult to determine fault for a project failure. As financial penalties were attached to some faults, there would be much heated discussion, and perhaps displays of personal rancor, in the process of determining individual accountability for failure. As can be imagined, this did not help the development of the collateral relationships requisite for project success.

If this were not complex enough, some employees of the client organization held several roles in different parts of the project, answering to different project managers, which created issues of how their time was allocated between them. It was often a bone of contention, particularly when their work lay on the critical path.

I went into this situation with some fairly broad instructions to recruit employees for the client organization, either to increase the size of the team or to replace contractors. Cost considerations drove the latter and not the overall resource requirements of the client organization. Little or no reference was made to the head of the specialist function in the client organization concerning this switch of resources. It was thus no surprise that he had little interest in who and what was being done in that specialist area, except when it impinged on his area of interest, as when he feared that his staff would be poached from "normal" duties to the project.

The project director laid down the recruitment process. He approved the filling of vacancies in the project organization based on his view of how the project was proceeding in that particular area. The project manager of the area affected would know what positions he could fill without any further reference to the project director. A complex paper-based approval process had to be completed before recruiting could begin, including the design of a job description. Unfortunately, these descriptions were almost exclusively confined to the technical/specialist aspects of the job, and rarely mentioned any responsibility concerned with the management of people.

At the time I joined there were some 170 vacancies, many critical to project progress. I was continually requested to find staff to fill critical positions in the teams. Recruiting managers were often not employees of the client, but nevertheless were accountable for selecting and appointing new employees for the client. On some occasions a new employee would be taken on without meeting a single employee of the client organization that she or he was joining. Induction and training of the new employee was cursory, for although the recruiting managers saw this as important, many felt that they could not justify the time spent, nor did they see themselves as responsible for an activity that was not part of their contract. The assumption was made, and stated in contract, that new staff were fully competent in order to meet risk and liability requirements. To admit otherwise might have caused future problems.

Reflections on a Better Way

During my six months on the team I filled some 65 vacancies, but the net number of vacancies increased due to staff turnover. At the time, it was difficult to stand back and consider the ways that matters were organized. In hindsight, I have considered how Brown and Jaques's ideas about deploying specialists might be applied in this type of situation, and I have tried to see if their ideas could make the whole process more effective. I offer these ideas as a contribution to the management of projects and not as the definitive answers. A Ph.D. student could carve his or her name into this subject with profit.

The first question to ask is, "Who is accountable for project success?" From the external viewpoint of the client, there can be little doubt that the project director/ manager is going to be held accountable. But many of those project directors/managers will refuse to accept fully such accountability for sound reasons.

Brown and Jaques have always argued that if you are going to hold managers accountable for the performance of subordinates, they have to be given certain minimal levels of authority. These include the authority to:

- Veto appointments to their direct command
- Set tasks
- Assess performance
- Establish pay differentials among direct subordinate groups
- De-select individuals who do not perform adequately

In many organizations, it is unusual to find line managers with such power. After 30 years of work I have found very few, so it is hardly surprising to find that project managers rarely possess the requisite authority in any of these areas. Under these conditions, it is hardly surprising that project managers are not willing to accept full accountability for project success. They do what they can, but in the event of failure will claim a host of mitigating factors to explain why they did not bring the project to completion on time and to budget.

Establishing Authorities

The first area that anybody establishing project teams under a project manager should consider is giving these authorities to the project manager/director and to subordinate project managers at all levels. It is necessary at the same time to ensure that there is an effective appeals procedure, so that any individual who feels that a manager has treated him or her unfairly can appeal the action. However, the exercise of such power is far from easy even where these authorities are granted. So, let me describe how I believe they could be deployed in even the most complex of projects.

Appointments

In making appointments to the team, some of the roles will be fully understood by the project manager. Thus, he or she will be able to assess whether the candidates put forward to join the team are acceptable. This will apply particularly to subordinate project managers. There will be other roles of whose specialization he or she may know very little, and therefore will not be in a position to make proper assessments of the technical competence of the people in them. In addition, he or she will find some difficulty in assessing if that person is working effectively, particularly if he or she is a member of another organization.

How is this problem to be resolved? The solution lies in establishing co-manager roles and responsibilities. Let me describe them by going back to that manufacturing world familiar to Brown and Jaques.

Line managers need to have access to specialists on a range of subjects in order that they can meet their targets. For example, a large production operation may need to have a dedicated specialist for financial support and advice. The line manager has convinced her manager (the production director) of this need with a detailed specification of what she wants and why. The production director has discussions with his boss (the CEO) and the finance director, and they have agreed to dedicate a financial advisor/specialist to the team.

With a rough idea of her needs in mind, the line manager approaches the finance director and discusses the details of the work that she wants carried out. However, since the line manager is likely to have little means of assessing whether any given financial advisor might be competent to provide the financial services she requires, she relies on the finance director to provide her with a competent specialist. She says in effect "Because I am unable to effectively assess whether any person put forward for this role is a competent financial specialist, I look to you first to provide me with such a competent resource and, second, to review the technical/ professional aspect of that person's performance to assure me that it is satisfactory."

The finance director (as specialist co-manager) identifies a suitable person. This might be an existing staff member or this may require external recruitment. The line manager and the finance director both interview the person so selected. As co-managers, they will be held jointly responsible for the performance of this new resource and must therefore satisfy themselves that the candidate can do the work required and understand the new assignment. Because the finance advisor may well need some knowledge and understanding of the department he or she will serve, there would be a mutual agreement about any development and training required.

Task Briefing

Together as co-managers, the finance director and the line manager would brief the newly appointed finance advisor on what was required of him or her as he or she worked as part of that line manager's command, and would tell him or her that he or she should discuss ongoing task assignments with the line manager. He or she will be told that for all day-to-day task setting and work he or she must consider himself to be part of the line manager's command.

Performance Assessment

The co-managers will carry this out jointly, because it is quite possible that while the line manager may feel that the finance advisor had worked well, the finance director may feel that the services delivered had been below the standards required by professional standards and the company's finance policies. If true, the finance director co-manager would then propose remedial actions, including any training and development that might be needed. On the other hand, if the line manager believes that the finance advisor was not providing the correct service, he would call upon the finance director to act. Fresh targets will be given to the finance advisor, with perhaps some training and development.

Pay Reviews

Both co-managers will carry out pay reviews. However, the line manager's views will be the more significant, for it is the internal differentials between members of her team that are the most important.

Changing Assignment

If there is a need to change the agreed assignment by either co-manager, for example, if the line manager wants the finance advisor to do more or less work, or the finance director wants to use the finance person to work for other line managers as well, they must seek mutual agreement. If this fails, they will have to turn to their mutual boss for resolution. Hopefully, it is clear both who the co-managers are and what their individual responsibilities are.

De-selection

In the event that the finance advisor fails to perform to a satisfactory standard after suitable actions, it is the responsibility of the finance director to remove him or her from the line manager's command and find a suitable replacement. Note that the line manager can only request that the finance director remove the finance advisor, deselecting him from the line manager's command. The line manager does not fire the finance advisor from the company.

This is a very short version of a complex process involving both the line manager and the finance director as co-managers. I cannot see any insuperable reasons why such a process should not be adopted for projects.

If the project team is drawn from the same organization, just substitute "project manager" for "line manager" in the above descriptions. If drawn from different organizations, both organizations employing the respective co-managers must adopt this approach. It may require attention to the contracts, but incorporating the clearly defined relationship and roles of co-managers should materially enhance the operation of the contract.

If there is no appropriate co-manager within the client organization, then it will be necessary to hire the services of another service provider to carry out this role. In practice, this will usually be a senior member of the contracting/service-providing organization.

The Basis of These Recommendations

Let us now see what was stated in the *Glacier Policy* handbook of 1965 (more than 40 years ago!).[1]

Attachment of Specialists

Managerial authority and accountability with regard to attached specialists shall be shared between the operational co-manager and the specialist co-manager in the following manner:

1. The two co-managers shall be jointly accountable for the selection of the attached specialist and for his merit assessment.

2. Only the operational manager shall assign operational responsibilities to attached specialists and he shall be accountable for:
    a. informing the specialist co-manager of any major changes he introduces in the operational use of the attached specialist
    b. the type of responsibility he assigns
    c. the discipline of the attached specialist in the discharge of these responsibilities

3. The specialist co-manager shall set the terms of reference governing the techniques which an attached specialist uses in the discharge of his responsibilities and he shall be accountable for:
    a. informing the operational co-manager of any major changes which he makes in the technical terms of reference which he sets
    b. ensuring that his specialist subordinates are technically equipped to carry out the requirements of the roles which they occupy
    c. the technical discipline of specialist subordinates

To translate this for construction and similar projects, first substitute "project manager" for the operational line manager/co-manager. The role of the specialist co-manager needs further definition.

If the specialist is an employee of, or contracted to, the specialist organization/department charged with providing that specialist resource, then the specialist co-

---

1   Brown, W. *Exploration in Management*. London: Penguin Books, 1965.

manager will be a senior manager of that organization/department, as for the financial advisor I described before.

However, if no one within the client or contracted organization has the competence to carry out the role of the specialist co-manager, life becomes more difficult. Where the work is relatively minor in terms of impact and cost, it may be possible to dispense with that role by taking careful references of that person's work.

If the role is major, it will be worthwhile to hire another specialist or specialist organization to carry out the role. As a consultant, I know how easy it would be to rip-off a client because they have no means of judging at the start whether the work you propose to carry out is (a) necessary and (b) good value. Although it adds to costs, I believe that hiring specialist co-managers saves money in the long term.

Let us look at the definition of *attachment* and see how it might operate in practice.

The two co-managers shall be jointly accountable for the selection of the attached specialist and for his merit assessment.

The specialist co-manager will have the responsibility of finding the resources and then putting them forward. This will relieve the project manager of the difficult task of finding these resources and ensure that the attached specialist knows very clearly who his manager is in the long term. This is important because at the end of the project the project manager may well disappear leaving the attached specialist wondering who is looking after his interests. Small wonder therefore that as a project completion gets close, key specialists start leaving the project for alternative employment.

Only the operational manager shall assign operational responsibilities to attached specialists and he shall be accountable for:

- Informing the specialist co-manager of any major changes he introduces in the operational use of the attached specialist
- The type of responsibility he assigns
- The discipline of the attached specialist in the discharge of these responsibilities

This already will occur in projects where contractors are used because the project manager will need the approval of the contractor for any change in the terms of reference of the contract that he wishes to make. If the specialist co-manager is a senior employee, this action should ensure that the attached specialist is not drawn into fresh areas of work that have not been mutually agreed.

This also makes clear that it is the project manager who sets work for the specialist. I have found that specialists can find themselves in difficult situations when both the project manager and his "boss" issue conflicting commands. Who does he respond to? The clarity that the above provides can be very helpful in avoiding this dilemma.

Clarity about discipline is also helpful. Managers are often curiously reluctant to discipline staff and will opt out of it if given the chance. On the other hand, I have found furious project managers who feel they cannot discipline team members because they do not feel they have the authority to do so.

The specialist co-manager shall set the terms of reference governing the techniques which an attached specialist uses in the discharge of his or her responsibilities and shall be accountable for:

- Informing the operational co-manager of any major changes which he or she makes in the technical terms of reference which he or she sets
- Ensuring that his or her specialist subordinates are technically equipped to carry out the requirements of the roles which they occupy
- The technical discipline of specialist subordinates

This is immediately applicable and should cause no problems whatsoever. However, its application will provide substantial benefits because it requires that the specialist co-manager define the terms of reference. Often specialists will join project teams with only the vaguest idea of what they are expected to do. Having their accountabilities and authorities set down helps all parties and adds substantially to project effectiveness.

I hope that I have drawn attention in this article to the benefits of applying systematic thinking to the management of people on projects. It is a curious phenomenon that whereas in these projects much attention is given to the definition of the technical and physical processes required, but scant attention is given to the equally complex issue of the management of people.

Richard B. D. Brown has been working in the field of human resources for more than 30 years. With a degree in production engineering he started with Kodak, then BOC where he moved into HR/personnel and then Sperry Univac (now Unisys). He worked for them in the UK, then the US, and then Italy before joining Ambrosetti, an Italian consulting organization. Upon returning to the UK, he went independent as an HR consultant.

He has had almost a lifetime of interest in organizational design and operation, and his involvement in some major projects and their inefficiencies in the management of team members have sparked this article.

 **5**

Achieving the Information Technology Promise Using Work Levels as the Framework

Piet L. Calitz

WHAT'S IMPORTANT

- A CEO who uses the work levels approach in designing and implementing strategic Information Technology projects can win a competitive advantage.

- In tight executive markets, companies often make costly compromises by staffing key IT manager positions with individuals who may have the scarce technical knowledge but who are not capable of working at the right managerial level.

- Making the effort to staff and resource these projects at the appropriate senior level and to establish the appropriate accountabilities and authorities can go a long way toward aligning work and meeting expectations.

The CEO is left with an abundance of options, choices and dilemmas, yet he or she cannot ignore what has become an integral part of longer-term strategy. Longer-term investment in IT is no longer a choice; however, how to go about it is.

Introduction: The Promise, The Investment, The Risk

Information technology (IT) provides a microcosm of the challenges facing CEOs. First, there is the promise of the potential of what could be achieved by effectively harnessing the power of IT for increased productivity and corporate performance.

Examples include reduced transaction costs, immediately up-to-date information and instant communication, exceptional marketing and advertising reach, and of course, reduced dependence on human reliability.

Second, organizations strategically cannot afford to fall behind their competitors. The shadow side of the relentless advances in technology and IT is high expenditure and investment in IT infrastructure, and in hiring the new skills required or retraining existing staff. In addition, there are the ever-present threats of obsolescence, redundancy, and disruptive technologies.

CEOs also have to face various conceptual and implementation difficulties to make the investment in IT work in their organizations. This is exacerbated by continuous developments and changes in the innovation-driven nature of the IT industry. One consequence is a confusing array of alternatives: an alphabet soup of acronyms, techno-speak, and a feeling that any investment in IT is a bottomless pit without conclusion or measurable return.

This article will consider the use of work levels as a framework for CEOs and leaders to make sense of the IT investment required, as well as to address the implementation of IT or to remedy previously unsuccessful implementations.

Using work levels as a framework assists in understanding the daily realities of decision-making in organizational life, i.e. the different needs and solutions at various levels in the organization. Thus work levels can provide a baseline to preview the potential investment required, view the actual implementation, and review whether the return on the IT investment was realized. In addition, the various perspectives of stakeholders within the organization can be included to facilitate the associated change management.

It should be noted that the approach used in this article is to provide an overview perspective of the use of IT in organizations as opposed to focusing on the IT

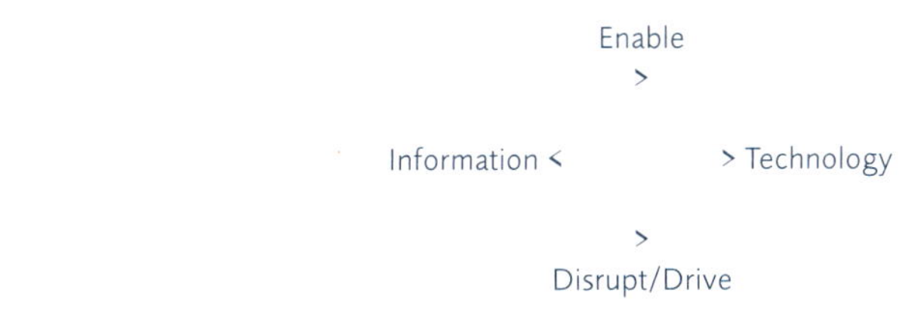

FIGURE 4.5.1

function itself. The assumption is that the IT function should facilitate, as opposed to drive, the use of IT in an organization. IT has become as integral a part of every leader's accountability as financial or people management.

Different Needs and Different Solutions: The Work Levels Approach As Framework

Seeing IT in Context

The precise definition of IT has become problematic. First, it is often difficult to distinguish between the "information" as opposed to the "technology" side. As technology develops, the established and currently understood means or platforms for transmitting, sharing, or accessing information are becoming less relevant and more dependent on the imagination of the manufacturer or investor. (In fact, there is probably a good argument for broadening IT to include communications technologies as well and hence to refer to ICT.)

Second, while IT interventions could lead to anticipated benefits, the interventions will also impact, sometimes severely, the way people conduct their duties and the organizational culture.

For example, the so-called enterprise systems (such as SAP and Oracle) that offer business function integration will often have best practices built in; as a result the enterprise system will drive or enforce work routines, flows, and standards.

Figure 4.5.1 shows the summarization of these dilemmas.

Hence what is often of benefit to one part of the business may be a disadvantage to another part, and the resultant lack of commitment to or cooperation with "someone else's" problems is often less a case of resistance to change, but rather the consequence of being forced to change established work behavior and practices.

This goes beyond the normal conflict between production (or revenue generating) and supportive (non-revenue generating) functions or disciplines in organizations. It can also be seen clearly in the conflict between the needs of corporate/group management and those of operational management.

The introduction of a major IT intervention, by its very nature, is likely to disrupt the normal and traditional, generally accepted work conventions. The more complex the scope of the IT intervention, the more disruptive and necessary other interventions (such as change management) will be.

What is also crucial to note is that by enabling, IT could also disrupt the normal flows of accountability and organizational structures. Hence the understanding of what is required from IT may paradoxically necessitate re-conceptualizing IT in terms of the actual organization, as opposed to comprehending the IT itself.

In addition to these internal IT dilemmas the executive leadership also needs to consider the following related contextual aspects:

- *The use of IT by competitors, especially by global competitors.*
- *Disruptive technologies.* This refers to new developments in technology that make current standards inadequate, and in some cases obsolete. In the worst cases, the disruptive technologies replace the existing technology/standards at a reduced cost, or lower barriers to entry into a market/industry, thus negating the advantage that the previous investment in technology provided.
- *The state of supportive technology in general/IT industry.* The potential or promise of what IT could do often reflects an ideal world, and sometimes a world a number of years away. However, in other cases new technology may provide solutions and options at lower cost not previously imagined.

The intelligence on global competitors may not be readily available, and in the case of potential disruptive technologies nearly impossible to obtain. Global competitiveness, be it commercial or technological innovation, is a reality and an integral part of business life. Potential developments in IT, therefore, should be anticipated or at least factored in as part of the longer-term strategic positioning of the organization.

As a result, the CEO is left with an abundance of options, choices, and dilemmas, yet he or she cannot ignore what has become an integral part of longer-term strategy. Longer-term investment in IT is no longer a choice; however, how to go about it is.

The various users of IT within organizations have different interests from those who lead the development of IT, deriving not only from dissimilar functional needs and applications, but also from diverse perspectives/organizational levels. (See Table 4.5.1 for further illustration.) To assist in understanding these needs, we can broadly divide the organizational IT needs into the following two categories:[1] *Operational/transactional.* This category refers to the use of IT for those activities conducted on a daily basis by staff, customers, and suppliers, normally with follow-on activities such as tracking, authorization/s, and the general flow of work in and between departments/functions. Reports related to these activities are also included in this category.

1. Strategic/business intelligence. This information is used to obtain an overall or integrative view of the total business. This category is more of a "portfolio" than transactional nature. Such intelligence can be provided as indicators in a graphic display or "dashboard" format. IT can also be used to provide such intelligence in "real-time" or up-to-the-minute updates for corporate performance management, External information about the industry, competitors, geopolitical developments, and global trends may be linked to the business intelligence, but would normally be provided in separate reports or updates about trends/developments.

For organizations the size of a business unit or smaller, the transactional information may be sufficient, with some additional tweaking, to provide the business intelligence. For larger organizations with multiple business units or even businesses, this may not be the case and an additional interface may be required.

The additional interface is the so-called *data warehouse*, a depository to extract data from various transactional (or business unit/business) sources, and to translate/load such data into the required format for the business intelligence system. Designing and implementing the additional interface requires a shift in focus to those who will be affected (and how), as opposed to the needs of those for whom the system is being designed.

Furthermore, it should be recognized that those affected may need different and specific IT solutions to address their own work. Understanding of the different needs and solutions required at the various organizational levels can be enhanced by using a work levels approach.

---

1   The author wishes to acknowledge Vera Massyn for her conceptual suggestions.

CATEGORY	ELEMENTS AND FUNCTIONALITIES	EXAMPLES
Business Intelligence	Integrative and overall information, supported by functionalities such as performance indicators (dashboard), real-time, drill-down abilities	Consolidated profits and losses, capital investment, return on financial and human capital, reserves, environmental impact, market shares, economic value added, exposure, return to shareholders
Operational/ Transactional	Reports/budgets and variances Authorities and workflow Activities and tracking	Logistics, accounting, e-commerce, suppliers' portals, employees' self-service centers, call centers, off-shoring, customer relationship management (CRM), manufacturing execution systems (MES), advanced planning and scheduling (APS), payrolls

TABLE 4.5.1: EXAMPLES OF INFORMATION REQUIREMENTS FOR CORPORATE PERFORMANCE MANAGEMENT BASED ON IT INFRASTRUCTURE

Using the Work Levels to Develop a Framework for Understanding IT

As illustrated in Table 4.5.2,[2] by combining work levels and the categories above, the reciprocal interaction between IT and the organization can be better understood and mapped, and thereby increase the chances of successful implementation.

Armed with an understanding of the overall organizational IT design, and with work levels as a framework, we can consider the practicalities related to the implementation of IT with the perspective of the investment required, and the possible returns on such investment.

Perspectives and Choices: Realizing the Investment

By using work levels, all of the different perspectives can be accommodated and integrated into an overall framework for implementation and for clarifying the decisions and trade-offs that may be necessary.

---

2   The overall complexity of organizations may differ hence the references to organizations are for demonstrative purposes only. Each organization should be viewed in terms of its own characteristics as to its respective overall complexity or "level" as an organization.

Note that level V work, where it forms part of a more complex group or global organization, will form a translation level and hence the need for "data warehousing."

CATEGORIES AND ELEMENTS		WORK LEVELS	EXAMPLES OF ACCOUNTABILITIES
Business Intelligence	Integrative and overall information	VI and VII	Corporate performance management for global organization or group*
		V	Corporate performance management of organization/strategic business unit or similar*
Operational/ Transactional	Reports/budgets and variances	IV	Integration of the various disciplines for overall business performance Review and correction with regard to business strategy Change management
	Workflow	III	Discipline specific and embedded service/operational delivery Continuous improvement/best practices development
	Authorities	II	Service delivery to internal/external clients Managing deviations from expected standards
	Activities and tracking	I	Processing/input Internal/external client interaction Direct control in terms of waste

TABLE 4.5.2: COMBINED CATEGORIES AND WORK LEVELS WITH EXAMPLES OF ACCOUNTABILITIES

Notes on Implementation Using Work Levels

Before organizations embark on a major IT intervention, the following strategic business drivers behind such an intervention need to be clear:

What is the overriding or primary purpose the organization wants to achieve, inclusive of whether it is trying to address a strategic or an operational/transactional need?

How best to achieve this purpose; does the organization want to anticipate and lead by being the first (or among the first) to invest in and implement the IT? Or should it respond once the nature of the basis for competing/disruptive technology/competitors has become more clear or a reality?

With the purpose to be achieved and its strategic implications clear, the type of returns desired and the investment necessary can be charted by work level, the stakeholders affected, and the related change management required. (*Change management* is pragmatically viewed as the various activities that need to be managed in order to ensure collaboration/participation/buy-in, and also for preparing and providing skills training for those affected by the IT intervention.)

The following seven steps are recommended in following work levels as a framework for implementation:

1. Clarify and design the specifications for the IT implementation in terms of its primary purpose and the most senior end-users/recipients of the future IT system. If the primary purpose of the IT intervention is for the transactional category, this is still appropriate.

2. With the primary purpose/information requirements established, the other users involved/affected can be approached to clarify their requirements and information needs. This needs to happen level by level and as a cascading process.

3. As the cascading continues, the requirements/information needs by work levels should be validated, aligned, and clarified or corrected. The design information obtained in this way can now be transformed into a prototype design with dedicated outputs by work level.

4. Conduct a stocktaking exercise in terms of the developed prototype to determine the impact of previous investments in IT, i.e. to determine whether what is already available inside the organization can be amended, added to, or completely replaced. Simultaneous scanning of available options in the market should be conducted for comparing and modeling with regard to the purchase and ongoing costs/additional developments required as well as any other criteria highlighted by the prototype.

5. Once the financial modeling has been completed, the purchasing vs. development decision can be made. The prototype now needs to be linked to the various workflows per level, and the assessment needs to be made in terms of the new skills/change management required. New skills could be those necessary for existing staff or the need to recruit the appropriate skills.

The benefits/returns of outsourcing IT and the extent of such outsourcing should also be modeled.

Change management should also be done in a work levels fashion and depending on the original needs identified. Refinements could be introduced here, e.g. the clustering of staff according to their interdependency from an IT perspective in addition to the work level.

6. Staffing can be enhanced by matching individuals' capability with the commensurate work level challenges. This is a core principle of using a work levels approach. When individual capability is matched to the work complexity or chal-

lenge, such individuals experience "flow," a concept adapted from work by Mihaly Csikszentmihalyi.[3] Flow has various benefits to the organization and the individual (see below).

7. Follow up and review at suitable periods to check and confirm whether the primary purpose and objectives set per each work level have been met, whether corrective action is required, as well as to quantify the actual investment returns.

Some Benefits of Using Work Levels for Implementation

Difficulties with implementation of major IT interventions may be due to purely technical aspects, but are more often related to the support (or lack thereof) from senior management, resistance to the new changes, lack of skills/understanding with regard to using the new technology, as well as general project management challenges.

When using the work levels framework, the normal principles of large-scale organization change and/or project management still apply. The major benefits, however, are that certain of the problem areas will be avoided or lessened. These include the following:

- Re-conceptualizing IT in terms of the organization, as opposed to understanding the organization in terms of the IT to be used. Although IT may drive/enable business practices, this should not replace accountability and judgment in the organization, especially in instances where IT/parts of IT may be outsourced.
- Obtaining commitment/support from the organizational sponsors at the appropriate levels up front. This is especially relevant when a large financial investment is required, and to ensure that the investment is for the overall business and along with its strategy.
- Designing the IT intervention from the top down, and therefore moving from the more complex requirements to the less complex requirements, reinforces focus and emphasizes outputs. If outputs subsequently do not relate to the outputs at the more complex levels, then the discrepancies can be investigated and corrected. The net result is the prevention of investment in elegant but inappropriate solutions.

---

3   Csikszentmihalyi, M. *Beyond Boredom and Anxiety: Experiencing Flow in Work and Play.* San Francisco: Jossey-Bass, 1975, 2000.

- Increasing the appropriate involvement of stakeholders. By following a level-by-level analysis of stakeholders, a more comprehensive perspective can be used for the design and implementation.
- Staffing work levels appropriately. By matching the individuals to the right work levels, an important precondition is met for effective and productive work, as well as for individual well-being (flow). Although additional skills training may be necessary and other factors, such as motivation and interest, may still be needed, it provides important information for appointment decisions.
- Providing a conceptual map of what should be addressed, anticipated, and provided for at each level during implementation. This allows the implementation program to be audited and corrected prior to commencing the implementation itself, as well as having points of reference during the implementation.
- Guiding the post-implementation review to ensure that all the objectives (i.e. at all levels aimed at) are included.

Conclusion

IT, in its various guises, is a critical component of organizational competitiveness. Due to its innovative and intensive nature, and the limitless possibilities for delivery of services, cost reduction, and market expansion, IT is likely to play an ever increasingly important role in future.

Convergence, or the trend that content and functionality can be provided independent of the platform (e.g. using mobile phones for watching television or doing banking), will lead to even more innovation. More will be possible and current standards and practices will be under pressure.

Accordingly, fitting judgment at the appropriate level of work will also rise in importance, and may be the true "edge" in competitive IT. Organizations must recognize that complex IT decisions at the strategic level not only must be guided by individuals operating at the appropriate work level, but that IT should be an integral part of strategy/business. No doubt many IT projects have not produced expected results and millions of IT dollars have been wasted because organizations have not recognized this fundamental principle of leadership.

Pieter L. Calitz is managing director of bioss International Limited (bioss). In his global role, he is extending the footprint of bioss across divergent host cultures and markets. He has a master's degree in organizational psychology, and has done extensive consulting in organizations in private and public sectors in Southern Africa. Calitz is especially interested in leadership development in uncertainty and in turbulent times. In addition, he is the author of the meta-competencies matrix, an integrated and unique levels framework for enhancing leadership.

CIO: Chief Information Officer or Career Is Over?

Paul McDowell

WHAT'S IMPORTANT

- Information technology (IT) often fails at the strategic level because organizations do not understand how levels of work and complexity affect the design and implementation of IT systems.

- Why sending IT functions off-shore can make the situation worse.

- Technical proficiency with IT systems is often mistaken for capability to manage complex managerial problems.

- The strategic value of an organization's IT system will depend upon the level of capability of the most senior IT executive.

All of our approaches to IT have failed to acknowledge the associated complexity of working with systems, the capability of people who do the work and the people who manage those people, the roles needed to address this complexity and the mandates the roles should have. In addition, the technical convolution of systems was confused with the complexity, which has caused us to place people who know a particular technology well into positions of powerful influence that they should not have. In fact, this mistaken expertise in any technology is really more a system instruction mastery than a true ability to solve problems.

How to do information technology (IT) right? It is something that plagues firms every year as they become more dependent on information systems. The answer lies in requisite organization (RO) design principles being properly applied. This is my story of what I have experienced directly and how to leverage the RO principles of levels of work to make IT work.

Reflecting Back

In the late 1990s, I experienced my first week as VP and CIO. I have made it to the top of my field in an organization after 15 years of continual hard work. From starting as a junior Cobol programmer in a cubicle at my first company to finally becoming head of IT reporting to the president at another. It feels good behind my antique century old desk in the corner office, high above the city. Now the work begins: I will do what all the CIOs I have encountered in my career have not done: be strategic and deliver business. The company has staked its future on its newly launched revenue generating website. My phone rings; it is my director of infrastructure: "Hi Jane," I answer.

"The site is down. She left the building crying!" Jane is frantic.

"Who?" I ask puzzled.

"The data admin, fixing the database, she erased it all instead!"

"Use the back-up," I say wondering why a VP has to be involved.

"She erased the back-up too. We lost everything! When she realized what she had done, she ran out of the building crying!"

About now, my brilliance as a strategic thinker wanting business results seemed immaterial. Paying customers across the country were without service. The gem in the crown of our future had fallen out leaving a gaping hole. My clients and customers scream if there is an outage of a few minutes, we could be down for days, weeks! The antique desk and executive trappings were suddenly meaningless. I wished I was a Cobol developer in a cubicle again.

The Legacy Burden

CIOs the world over have similar stories: a backlog of work, failing systems, legacy burdens, not enough money in the budget, late projects, failed projects, and failing mission critical systems. Their teams are losing morale and are seen as expensive. Legacy systems are costly to maintain, yet we are highly dependent on them. The finger pointing between the business users and IT is common. Business users are unclear and fluid in their requirements; IT is inflexible for changing business user needs and demands too much detail before doing work. Who is right? Why is this so common? What can be done? What did I do? The issue at bottom is the true complexity of IT and the capability of people needed to address it. These need to be truly understood and approached with the RO design principles. RO is used in many industries, but, how do we make it work in IT?

General Problems of IT: Failed Solutions

From the beginning, IT staff have been seen as too expensive and in need of replacement with a cheaper alternative. By the early 1970s a language to simplify working on IT systems came to the fore: Cobol (Common Business Oriented Language). It had instructions that were very much like English. In fact, the cover of a leading journal pronounced the death of programmers as business people would be writing Cobol programs themselves.

This never happened because the complexity of understanding the computer system and translating a Cobol program proved too much for anyone but a programmer! Despite the simplicity of the language, one still had to instruct the system exactly how and where to obtain the data, change them, and output them. From the 1970s to today, new techniques and tools to make programming easier and more reliable continued to emerge: structured methods (organize the work!); third and fourth generation languages; databases (make the language simpler so programmers aren't needed); Computer Automated Software Engineering (CASE); code generators (get the computer to write the system for you); packages (buy instead of build); entity relationship data, object oriented, client server (get rid of the mainframes and their high priests!); even outsourcing (get someone else to do it instead!). Each of these was an attempt to streamline work and eliminate the need for IT staff.

Every attempt to stamp out the irascible creatures failed. Why? *The complexity never went away*. All of our approaches to IT have failed to acknowledge the associated complexity of working with systems, the capability of people who do the work and the people who manage those people, the roles needed to address this complexity and the mandates the roles should have. In addition, the technical convolution of systems was confused with the complexity, which has caused us to place people who know a particular technology well into positions of powerful influence that they should not have. In fact, this mistaken expertise in any technology is more a system instruction mastery than a true ability to solve problems.

"Offshoring" is the latest trend (if we can't beat them, at least let's keep them on the other side of the planet!). Offshoring is a form of outsourcing that leverages the fact that people in India (or wherever) are highly educated and intelligent, yet grossly underpaid by our standards. No doubt given that these people are intelligent and in demand, their rates will go up as more offshore firms compete for limited talent.

To address this serious and generic problem with IT, the complexity of building IT systems must first be addressed, and there is no simple solution to make it go away. Second, the people staffed at almost all levels of IT organizations are not enabled to or capable of addressing this complexity. This causes the expensive delays and failed projects. In turn, this frustrates the business clients and IT management. Tools, techniques, and the approaches mentioned have been tried, but the complexity itself must be addressed head-on. New tools and arrangements are generally applied to incumbent IT staff who usually lack the capability to solve the problem or appreciate the techniques. Hence the failures.

IT is a new field and it is hard to distinguish what is truly complex from what is not. RO design practitioners fall prey to interviewing incumbents, and therefore shape the new design around them without any ability to know what is complex. With incumbents generally populating the field for the wrong reasons, this leads to issues even when RO design principles are attempted.

IT is barely 50 years old. Engineering, architecture, accounting, law, and medicine are all centuries old with many lessons learned already and much rigor applied to their professions. I have a dictionary from 1947 that defines "computer" as "a person who calculates." It is no wonder that we are plagued with the same misgivings of the other professions in their early years: unclear standards of professional accreditation; no professional governing boards (which the other fields have); no common set of terms, diagnoses, and prescriptions. Only through malpractice and disaster did the other professions strengthen their mandates and criteria to qualify. IT has not yet done so, although the costly disasters are occurring: Y2K, financial systems failures, and the spread of computer viri, to name but a few.

But today to be an IT professional, one merely has to declare it. How do we know who is truly capable? People get rewarded for producing fast results, but do those systems have sustainable quality or require rework over the years? Others are rewarded for being heroes and fixing systems late at night as they fail, but why are the systems these people touch regularly failing? Others are hailed for being the only ones who know exactly how a given system works and are depended upon to be the only ones to touch them. Yet knowledge of convoluted hard coded instructions and aberrant system behavior is mistaken for expertise in systems. Ironically, the things these people are hailed for would not exist if the root causes were addressed.

While there is talk of algorithms, data structures, and object classes, few practitioners deeply understand and use these concepts. IT systems allow apparent results to be had faster each year. The pressure is on from businesses to deliver faster. But what is being delivered is not necessarily addressing the complexity.

The essence of the problem can be simply expressed: computers do exactly what they are told. They process instructions unambiguously. In all other fields, people can interpret the ambiguity of a request into a result. An example would be ordering food in a restaurant: requesting your steak done medium rare is a highly ambiguous statement that the waiter and chef must interpret in order to make a series of judgment decisions.

A computer following such a request would need to have inputs and settings for exact temperatures, durations, chemical constituents, and colorations. It sounds ludicrous that machinery would be built to establish taste and experience of the food. Yet humans do this quite well when they are experienced and trained in gastronomy. In organizations using IT, the human side of business must understand customers better; otherwise, the statement "launch a new product" is a highly ambiguous statement that must be translated into *exact* terms that will be executed on IT systems.

These instructions will be carried out powerfully, quickly with high volume, but above all, the computers will follow them *mindlessly*. Because, yes it's true, computers are dumb machines that do exactly what they are told.

People running businesses arc constantly using their human judgment to make decisions and take action. Translating from the world of ambiguous drivers to the unambiguous world of computer instructions is incredibly complex. Yet this task is often delegated to the most junior developers who can code or create a system that seems to *behave* properly, but may not be constructed in a way that is truly needed. It is like using Excel spreadsheets with people who have little understanding of arithmetic. The numbers may add up, and we can believe the computer will not make a mistake, but if the constructs are made by people who do not understand what they are building, then it is a dangerous game. Developers, for the most part when given a task, begin by copying an existing system that does something similar and then alter it until it behaves as desired.

Many unintended side effects can be introduced. Note the difference between truly designing something and altering an existing thing to behave the same way. The first builds the coded instructions from the ground up, and if done right does not introduce unintended effects. The second, though faster, can be fraught with errors. As this is the most common approach, the cost of maintenance and "bug repair" in production then increases. For despite what your annual reports say, despite what your CEO says, your accounting department, marketing, et al, regardless of what they claim, the business rules are bits and bytes of unambiguously processed instructions on your computers. And ensuring that those are the right instructions unique to your corporate safety and competitiveness should be the role of IT.

Levels: Pitfalls of How Not to Do IT

Levels of work (or complexity) are difficult to put into action, even when you understand them. Following is a story from personal experience. (I have changed the names to protect the innocent, the guilty, and me!) One of the most brilliant leaders I have encountered understood the importance of levels, complexity, and accountability. Joe, CEO of our firm, had a vision that was ahead of its time. He saw that for a simple retail credit card organization in the early 1990s, we could position ourselves, not just to process customer data faster, but to leverage information from the transactions to transform the company and turn us from being a simple credit firm to being a matchmaker between consumers and sellers around the world.

This was a vision of a worldwide web e-commerce with capabilities like eBay, Google, and Amazon at a time when these concepts were likely not even considered by their founders. He not only had the vision, he had a route to the vision, which speaks even more of his brilliance. Central to that would be an information systems capability built on the most powerful foundations of modern thinking of the time: relational databases. Joe delegated this to the CIO, Drew. Drew in turn delegated this to the director of information resource management, Brian. Brian gave it to his database manager, Mike. Mike gave it to his star database administrator Lydia. Lydia employed an outside consultant who had attended conferences on learning the latest about relational technology. At the time, we were mainframe-based and the grand repository of data would be on the DB2 platform. Lydia and her consultant locked themselves away into a lab with terminals and stacks of DB2 manuals. They were diligent for months: in the lab daily from morning until evening, staring intently at the screens, typing madly, and taking disciplined breaks. I was impressed with their work ethic. What were they building? DB2 knowledge clearly was a career maker at that time and to be at the kernel of it was an enviable position. As a fellow developer, I was envious of Lydia, her access to the latest knowledge and the opportunity to build the foundation for the future of our firm, the basis of the new world Joe envisioned for us. Alas I was tasked with implementing a system to aid developers with system changes. One key aspect was a help package I wanted to buy, which would enable the 100 or so developers to master the new system quickly with on-line manuals (instead of seeking out the dog-eared sole copy that floated around the main floor). Management was never open to new purchases of the day, but DB2 always carried a cachet about it.

Lydia told me that she was concerned the developers would not embrace the new DB2 technology readily. I needed to get my system going too, though it was not nearly as crucial as her work. The package I ordered had the entire set of DB2 manuals included! With Lydia on my side, and therefore Mike and hence Drew (because Drew did anything Mike wanted and Brian was irrelevant!), I was anxious to see this package installed. So I fearfully knocked on the lab door to interrupt their furious typing. Lydia let me in. I described the package to her: she could meet her goals with all of the DB2 manuals. She told me she could not endorse such a package: it would undo everything she and the consultant had been working on all these months. How? She gestured to the stacks of DB2 manuals, all open to different pages and then to their respective computer screens. The screens showed the text of the manuals. They had been typing the manuals into the system for months. All this lab work was literally transcription and typing! I was aghast. Not only would my project not be endorsed by a key supporter, but I had found out that the underpinnings of the future of the company were being handled by two stenographers! How was Joe's dream going to become reality? Did Mike, Brian, and Drew know? Did Joe know?

The fact was that Lydia herself did not know and she thought her work was perfectly right. Now I had to tread carefully, for while I had not gained support, if I were not careful I would gain an adversary and the added burden of whom to tell! As I left, Lydia and her paid-by-the-hour consultant went back to typing furiously. DB2 never came to fruition as intended.

They thought it was perhaps too slow a system and invested in new storage and retrieval technologies. Those attempts took too long to perfect, and Joe left the organization. His successor, a frustrated client of IT, had most of the function outsourced. The vision never became a reality. As right and as advanced a thinker as Joe was, it was the lack of connection from his clear thinking, goals, and planning to the women typing manuals furiously into their terminals in the lab. He entrusted Drew with too much. Joe was probably operating at level VI, Drew maybe at level III, Brian and Mike certainly at level I or level II, and Lydia was a level I clerk.

The delegation of the vision happened the wrong way with the wrong people. Ultimately, despite my love and admiration for Joe, it is he I must indict for not sniffing out Drew's inability to manage IT. The gap was between Joe and Drew. And in levels terminology, that makes it Joe's accountability. The tragedy is, despite it still being a great firm, it would have been ahead of Amazon and eBay today. That was 15 years ago. Joe, Drew, Brian, Mike, and I have left the company, but Lydia is still there in IT, probably typing something important.

Levels and Accountability. How to Do IT

The principles are straightforward: level the work by complexity, ensure accountability with clarity, staff according to capability. Unfortunately, even seasoned practitioners in the RO design field are not familiar enough with IT to do this right. In using RO principles, one must start at the top of the organization and determine the critical nature of IT to the firm. How much of the core business depends on it? In this day and age, IT is seen as vital to the company as the CFO role. The importance to the business must first be agreed upon. The complexity is then addressed. It must not be dependent on the technology implementation, but on the strategic importance of IT for the organization. For a level V standard business, IT is usually a level IV function. Each of the roles in subsequent levels can address IT aspects of internal systems, customer systems, and enabling technologies.

There are many ways to organize these functions. As long as one is consistent and considers the business strategy, this is not too hard to get right. What is vital is creating the layers to match the complexity. This means the CIO at level IV should be willing to have designers and system architects reporting to them at level III. It also means that the ability of people at those levels must be rigorously assessed and managed. The management layers are crucial, but so too is acknowledging that the complexity of some roles, like systems architects and designers, can be at level III or even higher yet not have any direct staff reports. Depending on the role of IT required for a firm and the level of the firm, the CIO could be at level V with direct staff reports at level IV. Truly understanding how to design the roles for these functions at these levels is where the work is. It can only be done by someone with a deep understanding of IT and the RO principles.

How did I do it? I was fortunate enough to experience RO principles directly in Joe's years before I became CIO elsewhere. I had familiarity with RO and direct experience in IT. My first step was to build a new organization and staff it right, so this would not happen again (after, of course, paying the database vendor a fortune to recover the lost back ups!). The cost of the error and the liability our systems incurred gave me license with the CEO to pursue the path. It takes effort, but I built a case showing how much work was on the books, how much effort and thus cost was being spent on maintaining failing systems, and the failure for IT to align to strategic goals.

One of the first issues was defining the work. This was done by looking at what our systems were supposed to do: engineering applications that process information on specific technologies. There are three roles right there. Add to them architecture, the essential understanding of the configuration and limits of the systems, and we had our answer. The database that failed during my early days as CIO had smaller failures occurring virtually every day. The manager overseeing the system was actually a former journalist who got the role through hard work and hardwiring of her solutions. She was seen as an indispensable professional. I replaced her role with a database architecture manager and hired an experienced professional with a doctorate in systems from MIT (a controversial move to be sure, as she was liked and seen as vital while he was expensive and seen as an outsider). But not long after hiring him, he built an organization of properly leveled and capable professionals. In a month, the database problems waned. Eventually to weekly, then monthly, and finally none at all!

In six months we went from chronic failures to none. But he did more than that; soon after the fires disappeared, the database system emerged as a *solution* to other problems. This was the beauty of his and the team's abilities. Most importantly it was the beauty of the approach being applied properly. We did not end there. For applications, I created the role of director, application engineering, and the same effects were felt for our ability to deliver and manage the systems that yielded results for the business. Staffing was again a problem, but finding the right person for the role with the right capabilities brought success.

This effort must come from the CIO and must be endorsed by the CEO. I have achieved success by demonstrating the value and costs associated with the current approach and the revised approach. I am also unrelenting in defining the roles at the right levels and staffing them properly. It takes, discipline, understanding, over-communication (cultural impacts can be huge), and time. But it can be done, creating a powerful organization, fulfilling the needs of the business and the people who work so hard to achieve this. IT can deliver.

ABOUT THE AUTHOR

Paul McDowell has more than 25 years experience within the information systems and human resources fields. His credentials include leadership roles and experience in IT architectures, data warehousing, large systems integration, software engineering, and program delivery. He has held positions in virtually every IT role, from systems programmer to VP and chief information officer. He has applied the work levels approach to redesigning several executive-level organizations at Canadian top 500 firms. The industries in which McDowell has specific experience include financial services, publishing, logistics, pharmaceutical, and human resources.

He lectures in colleges and in professional circles on enterprise architectures, systems integration and technology, managerial leadership, and organization design. He was graduated from the University of Toronto with studies in mathematics and astrophysics; he was graduated from Ryerson Polytechnic in computing systems technology; and he earned the Certified Computing Professional designation in software engineering and IT management from the Institute for Certification of Computing Professionals.

McDowell is an avid filmmaker, currently producing a documentary on levels of work. He works for BearingPoint Inc, an international management and technology consulting firm where, as managing director, he heads the financial services technology practice for Canada.

Case Studies in Organizational Design as a Major Determinant of Employee Health and Well-Being

George Reilly

WHAT'S IMPORTANT

- An employee assistance program psychologist validates the strong contribution of Jaques's concepts to work-related counseling by relating three case studies.

- Non-requisite organizational situations can either create so-called personality disorders, or make existing psychological problems worse.

- Contrary to the traditional "fix-the-person approach,"the solution described here is to use requisite concepts to fix the organization before prematurely deciding to fix the person.

A Blending of Principles

As a psychologist working in a small industrial town, I've had the privilege of delving deeply into people's lives. For many it meant struggling with the vicissitudes of working life, while trying to sort out all sorts of personal problems, from major depressions to mild concerns about career paths.

And as a consultant, I have had the good fortune of discovering the works of Elliott Jaques and his colleagues which are amply described in this book. The notion that we all, each and every one of us, have an optimum level of functioning, that at our best we thrive on solving problems that have a certain level of complexity to them, has provided an ever-ready touchstone in my basic grasp of people's needs.

Regardless of the context, family, community, school, work, having the basic notions of requisite organization available has given me a solid, trustworthy place at which to begin my work with people. As an example, a long-term counseling process with a client I'll call "Julie", comes to mind.

Recovering from Abuse

Julie first connected with me some 20 years ago. She was a marijuana-addicted, 30-year-old single mother, working as a care aid in a senior care facility. Julie struggled for several years with continuing counseling. She gradually found the courage to commit herself to Narcotics Anonymous, and take the huge and unusual step of voluntarily giving up her son to foster care through social services. Both of these decisions involved massive admissions of failure, and the facing of immense shame. Lost in drug addiction from her early teen years, she used self-medication to blot out her

---

1   Quoted from *Explorations in Management*, a training film of the Glacier Institute of Management, London, England, 1970.

painful childhood. She abused her son, who had been born of an abusive, short-lived relationship with an out-of-control alcoholic. Finding herself the perpetrator of an all-too familiar pattern, Julie had become the abuser.

My initial sense of Julie was that beneath the confusing cloud of marijuana and almost catatonic shyness, she possessed a cognitive capacity much higher than that called for by a care aid level of employment work. In terms of requisite theory, she was working a stratum I job, but showed signs of stratum II current potential capacity, and of being at mode IV maturational curve.

One indication of her stratum II functioning was taking the initiative to approach and persuade social services to take her son into foster care while she sought help. She diagnosed the problem and came up with a solution to it. This is a characteristic of stratum II thinking, which distinguished it from the stratum I mindset, which is to carry out directions as prescribed.

Once "clean and sober," her son safely with a capable foster-family, Julie set out to upgrade her less-than-high-school education. This took the form of adult education at the local community college, then a social service worker diploma program, which she gobbled up with scarcely a notice save for her slow and painful emergence from her pervasive blanket of shyness.

With her feet on somewhat solid ground, Julie enrolled in a university distance education social work degree program. She has never looked back. With the support of her employer, Julie eventually became a senior social worker in her community's senior healthcare facilities; a solid stratum III position with potential to go on to higher levels in her profession.

My work with Julie has been primarily of a personal counseling variety. We have spent many hours sorting out her painful childhood past; what I call "healing the historical self." But in recent years, our work has shifted to a vocational coaching mode. And here is where requisite organization concepts have come more and more into play. Seeing Julie as a mode IV has allowed me to take a supportive stance with her as she struggles to retain an education, to engage the local social service employment sector, and to work her way past the prejudices of those people who saw her as a low-level worker, until she had proven herself and developed a solid reputation as a highly competent social worker.

As I mentioned, Julie now holds a key position in the senior care services sector. This is a solid stratum III position. She is implicitly in a productive working relationship with her stratum III administrative manager, actually managing her manager in many respects. As well, she continually expresses stratum IV thinking when she discusses her administration issues with me these days.

I suspect that in our current sessions I am providing Julie with a broader context, at least a full level or more capability above her own, within which she can continue to ground her thoughts, concerns, intuitions, and ways of handling the various demands being made on her in her work. I am likely providing a higher level of management support, what she is lacking in her actual employment situation. Because of this, she is able to continue to blossom as she deals with each problem that arises changing crises into manageable issues.

I suspect this is what happens in mentoring programs that are popular with organizations these days. These programs involve a person who is capable of functioning at two strata above the capacity of the person being mentored, providing a sounding board. Such a mentor could be called a "manager-once-removed" in the requisite model. Since this crucial role is seldom available in today's confused, non-requisite organizations, companies are busy outsourcing this function to people who are contracted as "coaches" and "mentors." Julie may be finding it through me.

A note in passing: Julie's son was in foster care for just a couple of years. She got him back once she was sure she had control over her abusive impulses. She successfully mothered him through his adolescence and into a responsible adulthood. She has also crafted a successful, long-term, non-abusive intimate relationship with a partner who too is recovering from a dysfunctional childhood and is busy learning to allow his potential cognitive capacities to flourish in the world of work.

The Chaos of Consensus

Many modern workplaces are hotbeds of consensus-induced chaos held together by human competencies in spite of themselves. How have we been caught up in the confusion of unmanageable, unstructured, role-less organizations? The ideas of the "flat organization" and "team accountability" have led to *guilt of management.* In other words, how dare anyone "manage" anyone else? After all, such a view implies that one person "is better than another," and we can't have that in this age of democracy and participation. If one does have to "manage" other people, it has to be done in a sufficiently tactful way that does not offend the other's sensibilities. It must be carried out using the utmost in supportive psychology and positive thinking. Team building and empowerment training have been two of the "flavors" that have been indoctrinated into people's how-to-behave-at-work psyches.

This has left what I tend to see as an epidemic of workplace desperation placated by placebos of stress-relief training, counseling referrals, psychiatric medications, and well intentioned attempts to "alter the organizational culture."

A Mushing of Modalities

Again and again, I have had people seek out my services to help them adapt to the modern workplace, This usually happens at the initiative of a manager who is following company policies to refer "problem people" to some form of mental health professional. One illustration that comes to my mind is that of a bright, young engineer I'll call Frank.

Frank contacted me one day with a desperate tone of worry that he was in danger of losing his mind. He had been working for five years as a development engineer in an industrial setting and quite successfully, he thought. Recently he had run into a barrage of criticism from his immediate manager and from several plant operations managers with whom he was to be providing trouble-shooting and problem-solving services. The word was that Frank was no longer a "team player," that he was haughty and not listening to the needs of the plant people, as if he was superior to them in some way.

Frank was flabbergasted. He couldn't understand what they were getting at. He was having trouble sleeping. He was getting short-tempered with his wife and young child, and he was barely able to hold back from angry confrontations with the plant managers at work. His manager suggested that he was falling apart and maybe depressed. It was suggested that he seek out professional help. So here he was, sheepishly talking to me in hope of allaying a "mental breakdown."

My first impression of Frank was that of a congenial, caring person who lacked the slightly abrasive touch that many bright young engineers in industry can carry as they get their feet wet in the "real world," as the plant people like to call it. As I listened to his conscientious attempts to relate his family history and conform in a "good patient" manner to how educated people in our psychologically sophisticated modern world expect the counselor-client relationship to go, I suspected that Frank was not in my office out of the present eruption of some long-standing personality problem. Rather, he presented an appropriately confused reaction to a current situation that didn't make sense that was "anti-requisite" in the perspective presented by requisite organization.

Sure enough, when we explored his work situation in some detail, the inappropriate forcing of Frank's participation in weekly "team sessions," in which process operators, plant foreman, plant superintendent, and Frank, were all expected to participate as equals, came to the fore. Requisite principles that this well meaning exercise was violating, in my mind, were that individuals of four different strata of work complexity were being artificially expected to function as one. Here we had people whose capabilities to handle complexity varied from short-term, hands-on, up-to-three month's variety of stratum I; all the way across the foreman's stratum II, practical problem-solving type; to the superintendent's one- to two-year stratum III overview of the plant's needs (technology changes, financial requirements, manpower projections, integration with other plants in the overall operations, etc.); to the development engineer (i.e. Frank's) stratum IV work to produce innovative ways of processing materials in the plant that would change how things were done across the board, and could make the company a bundle through increased efficiencies. Whew! No wonder Frank was finding the weekly team meetings confusing!

Once we had a lay of the land, and Frank had perused Jaques and Clement's book *Executive Leadership*,[2] his "depression symptoms" disappeared. This dramatic change in his state of well-being was clear evidence to me that his emotional problems were not any kind of reflection of a personality disorder that might be impeding his ability to function on the job. This is the sort of thing that Jaques referred to as −T, or "negative temperament," in his earlier books. It is a real enough phenomena, and needs to be recognized as such when it does occur. It is stimulated and artificially provoked in situations such as that Frank in which found himself. This is the down side of the inappropriate, overly enthusiastic, application of psycho-social principles, such as team functioning and empowerment in the work world.

Soon, Frank was able to take part in the weekly meetings without trying to get the others present to understand his truly developmental ideas, which involved abstract, cutting-edge metallurgical principles. He stopped belittling himself for lacking a deep interest in the day-to-day issues that preoccupied the operators. Within a

---

2   Jaques, E. and Clement, S. *Executive Leadership.* Boston: Blackwell Publishers, 1994.

few months, the weekly meetings died a natural death, and Frank was on assignment to collaborate with a university-based consultant on the metallurgical initiatives he had conceived.

When Temperament IS a Problem

The problems of negative-temperaments, or what I think of as the various neurotic styles that characterize many people that populate our workplaces, are real enough on their own and they interact with the non-requisiteness of organization—whatever that might be. As an illustration of a seemingly innocent, all-too familiar situation that on the surface is doing just fine, but underneath is a cauldron of confusion and distress, this is the story of a client I'll call Elaine.

Elaine was a middle manager in a familiar community service institution funded provincially and municipally through grants and governed by a board of directors drawn from the local community. Our society is rife with these sorts of organizations, sometimes acting as disguised extensions of the civil service, but serving a useful function for social cohesion—if not for actual financial, or organizational, efficiency. The covert malaise of misplaced consensus is rampant in such not-for-profit, socially responsive workplaces. And Elaine was being both victimized and nearly traumatized by it in her high-profile, valuable-to-the-community position. Her childhood issues were being triggered—big time.

The sources of Elaine's triggering came from both above and below in the implicit, hidden accountability hierarchy. I say implicit, because, again, in keeping with the workplace political correctness of the day, everyone is supposed to be having all the information and be consensually involved in decision making of all sorts. And Elaine's job was to make it all happen: to involve everybody, to keep them happy, and to exemplify the "search for excellence" in her service institution. Above her was the board: a dozen well-meaning citizens chosen for their success in their occupations, who were representatives of the variety of interests in the community. Below her was the staff, half a dozen women who had worked in this setting for much longer than Elaine, who was, by comparison, a veritable newcomer. Elaine was well educated, experienced in much bigger centers, and likely overqualified for the job when she first took it. She took the job because getting out of the frenzied pace of a big city seemed like a good thing to do.

In addition, the unionized workplace had developed a "power-to-the-people" set of attitudes that proved to be a source of frustration, exacerbating the "consensus culture," which called for invisible management.

Elaine did her best, and she was very successful. My estimate of her potential work capacity was at stratum V heading towards VI. The role she was employed to do was at stratum III. In requisite terms, this is a recipe for extreme frustration in and of itself. Elaine had kept herself going by actually spending as little mental energy on her managerial tasks as she could get away with, and by involving herself in a variety of community and professional commitments where she could make use of her capabilities. At the workplace, her higher-than-called for capability allowed her, as I saw it, to subsume all of the varied confusions perpetuated by the board and near constant battle with the union—over minor matters that were continually cropping up. These matters ranged from dress codes to clerical procedures to staffing timetables and so on. Then there were big-ticket items, such as province-driven restructuring and geographical regionalization. Again, everybody was supposed to have a say in everything, much the way that Japanese management was portrayed in the Theory Z depiction some years ago. This left Elaine expected and expecting herself, to facilitate it all together.

When Elaine first came to me, she was at her wit's end. She felt her life spinning out of control, both at work and in her personal life. Elaine's childhood had not been straightforward. In fact, she had survived a very confusing family situation with some quite bizarre distortions. This may have been fodder for a fascinating novel, but it had been quite a challenge to survive. Her native intelligence, which in requisite theory is what is considered one's "mode," or long-term potential mental capacity, seems to me to have been her saving grace in allowing her to meet the childhood challenge and basically parenting her parents as well as several younger siblings. And now, she had recreated the family scene by finding herself in this particular kind of workplace. Here were all the elements: bickering, small-minded, often emotionally abusive parents, in the guise of the board; the cast of siblings, in the form of the staff, demanding attention and protection from the nasty parents;, and all of them distracting Elaine away from developing her creativity and involving herself in things that were of appropriate interest for her.

There were other things going on in Elaine's life as well. These could also be seen as self-destructive recreations of aspects of her childhood, but her workplace was certainly providing a major stage for her troubling re-enactments. With Elaine, I did a lot of training in how to see the triggers in present adult life, i.e., events that cue automatic emotional reactions, also "over-reactions." The principle is that either over-reaction or under-reaction to the unpleasant events of adult life are likely clues to some unresolved aspect of childhood, which is surfacing in a person's consciousness. These are really opportunities to "work," in the sense of resolving personal issues that may well be keeping a person stuck in unproductive, unconsciously driven, childhood patterns. It is here that growth-oriented counseling or psychotherapy has its place. And where requisite principles can be very useful in providing a perspective that clarifies just how the workplace mirrors the family and vice-versa.

Parenting Principles Mirrored in Management

We may not be able to readily see the levels of living in family life anymore than we can readily see them at work. In both cases, the variety of activities seems to obfuscate the complexities, and seeing the different levels of complexities is even harder. Yet, once Elaine understood how her intense, albeit privately experienced, anxieties and self-deprecating confusions were triggered memories of childhood situations and events, she started to see the pattern of parents and siblings at home mirrored by the dysfunctional pattern of her board and staff at work. It was then that I introduced her to requisite principles, and loaned her Jaques and Clements' book as an introduction to the authority/accountability pattern that actually needs to exist at work or, by extrapolation, at home.

Things changed dramatically for Elaine from that point. We now had a common model, and language, to very quickly put the confusions at work into perspective. The board members were not being hard-nosed, mean-spirited, union-haters. They were people thinking into the two- to four-year and sometimes five- to ten-year vistas. They were continually frustrated by what they thought was willful obstruction by the staff. The staff members were not stick-in-the-mud, change-resistant, spoiled brats who wouldn't go along with change just because it wasn't their idea. They were stratum I and II people crying out for clarity and concrete direction to do their day-to-day service jobs, without having to think ahead to how changes in policy and strategies might affect them five or more years in the future.

With the requisite perspective in mind, Elaine was able to very quickly and effectively institute several procedural changes that cleared up long-standing, bitter back-biting among the staff, and between the staff members and the board. Without provoking thc union, she managed to restructure a couple of key roles and role-relationships, allowing for some much needed management procedures to happen without threatening the political correctness of how people thought they had to talk about their workplace interactions. By analyzing combination of triggers of one staff person and one board person who had been "thorns in her side" for a long time, and then by seeing how they functioned according to their current potential capacities, Elaine "miraculously" found both no longer to be problems for her.

Now that her workplace is bereft of much of its "drama," Elaine is entertaining thoughts of moving back to the demands of greater work complexity to be offered in the city. Her new-found self-confidence, grounded in both skills at processing previously debilitating personal issues and with the model of how workplaces actually function regardless of whatever feel-good rhetoric may be au courant, has produced a year of comfortable accomplishment that has left Elaine shaking her head in amazement.

The Future IS Friendly

The combining of such emotional healing and conceptual modeling principles as can be found in seeing the requisite principles as "required by the nature of human nature," offers the basis for a very satisfying counseling/consulting practice. I look forward to such principles becoming increasingly integrated into our society, as initiatives such as requisite gain momentum. From my perspective, this can be accomplished one person at a time as our culture matures to appreciate the validity of individual experience as the criterion of understanding, and we learn to discriminate between what are empty-calories of management-speak and what is the real thing of involvement in the world as a growing expression of one's own human potential. The workplace has the potential to be more than just the laboratory with which Jaques and others have discovered, tested and formulated the levels of work and human capability principles, but also the playing field where more of us can discover, test, and fulfill our humanness.

George Reilly discovered requisite organization in 1978, while working in-house as an industrial psychologist and organization development consultant. It profoundly changed his understanding and approach to working with groups and individuals. This led to his leaving the employment confines of the mining and smelting company he was working for, in order to test and apply requisite principles in the wider arena of psychological services in a rural-industrial region. Work with school children, social services, expert witness in the courts, EAP services to a wide gamut of organizations, manpower planning consulting with large companies, and both individual and group psychotherapy work with all ages, provided just such a rich context of practical testing and application. While now sampling semi-retirement, Reilly is available for consulting from a requisite organization perspective, in organization design and human resource matters.

Fitting the Right Person to the Right Role

Fitting the Right Person to the Right Role

If anyone needs justification for the scientific-based approach to talent pool management, we need only to recall the tongue-in-cheek book *The Peter Principle* (1969) in which Laurence J. Peter proposed that individuals keep getting promoted until they reach their level of incompetence. This haphazard approach to executive development was, according to Peter, bound to result in an organization staffed almost totally by incompetents. But once we accept the fact the level of work (responsibility) can be measured, and that an individual's capability for managing successively more complex levels of work can be measured and projected into the future, our prospects for effectively managing the pool of human talent available increase dramatically. Just as Jaques observed many years ago that a mandatory retirement age of 65 arbitrarily amputates a wealth of human capability from the workforce, today the potential for developing national as well as internal organizational policies that will increase the utilization of human resources is larger than ever.

While all businesses are interested in the right person in the right role, larger stratum VI and VII systems tend to have the best developed formal processes—General Electric is famous for it. In addition to managing the firm's talent pool effectively, an executive also needs to be interested in his or her own journey and talent pools he has been in before and will potentially join in the future. In this part we present three articles that bear relevance to the nature and importance of talent pool management, as well as system to implement a talent pool management system on a world-wide basis within a single firm.

One of the responsibilities of an HR function is to identify individuals with high potential capability and subsequently provide the proper development environment to achieve the high potential. In "From Potential to Performance," **Judith Hobrough** and **Peter Taylor** of bioss Europe have articulated what needs to be done to provide individuals with the skills, knowledge and experiences they need to reach their maximum capability. They also point out that capability is only part of the puzzle in developing human talent, and approaches that do not recognize the other parts of the puzzle will be less effective.

Andrew Olivier's article "Individual Capability and Our Working Journey" paper is an excellent article for those not familiar with how requisite concepts apply to talent pool management. Olivier describes the "working journey" that characterizes the process of moving through progressively higher levels of capability. The potential impact on society from effective talent pool management is also given attention and suggests how national human resource policies can affect the development of a nation's talent pool.

Managing large talent pools in a requisite system can be extremely time-consuming. To assist in what could be a monumental task in a large organization, **Donald V. Fowke**, a former CEO turned consultant, has developed a web-based talent pool management system that allows managers worldwide to follow the progress of their subordinates. Not only does the system ensure uniform treatment of all managers, it provides opportunities for feedback and discussion of personal capability assessments. The efficiency of the web-based system also involves the MoR's, who are a critical aspect in talent pool management.

From Potential to Performance

Judith Hobrough and Peter Taylor

with input from Russell Connor

- The matching of individual capability with current and future levels of work is likely the most important strategic human resource process in an organization.

- How to recognize the symptoms of mismatch between individual capability and level of work required.

- High performance is not the same thing as potential.

- Using an individual's past and/or current performance as the indicator of future performance ignores the complex nature of future capability.

- Individual levels of capability change over time in a predictable manner.

Effective current performance is not necessarily a good indicator of a readiness to move to a more complex role. When effective performance in current role is used as the only criterion for promotion it can lead to people being over-extended. This phenomenon of over-promotion is aptly described in The Peter Principle[1] *and refers to people being promoted until "they reach their level of incompetence"—an old adage but still true today.*

Ask chief executive officers what they require from their human resources function and their responses will include:

- Be a strategic partner for the business.
- Provide the basis for sustained high performance.
- Provide a pool of talented people who can deliver excellent performance.
- Develop effective leaders equipped to manage their people and their performance.
- Implement policies that have integrity and are robust.

Yet many years after CEOs started to ask for these things, there is still a lack of clarity about how to develop high performance and what is meant by potential. There is often a reliance on fads and fashions, quick fixes and easy options rather than focused solutions to real problems. Often, these solutions "look good" and work for a while, but prove to be superficial and do not stand the test of time.

Performance management is an area where HR functions could provide the lead, yet relatively few organizations have processes in place that nurture or enhance performance. In April 2005 e-reward.co.uk[2] concluded that, of the 181 organizations responding, covering over one million employees, 96 percent had performance management systems; 32 percent judged that their impact was insignificant or "not known," 50 percent believed that staff were more de-motivated than motivated by the process, and 40 percent believed that there was no evidence that performance management improved performance. While the e-reward survey was conducted in the UK, it would not be surprising if similar results were found in other companies operating within an Anglo-American model, given the consistency of similarities within other management practices both in the US and other parts of the globe.

With the increase in global competitive pressures and the demand for world-class talent seemingly insatiable, it has never been more crucial to fully appreciate employ-

---

1   Peter, L. *The Peter Principle.* William Morrow & Company:1969.

2   www.e-reward.co.uk

ees who have the capability and/or potential for world-class performance. The purpose of this article is to introduce a framework and set of ideas that enable senior executives, whether in line or functional roles, to come to grips with the concepts of capability and potential. These provide the foundations for high performance.

Definitions, Scope, and Limitations

What do we mean by high potential?
- Is it just about excellent performance?
- Is it about impressive technical skills?
- Is it static or dynamic?
- Or is it something more elusive?

In making judgments about high potential, we are making predictions about a person's growth into the future based on a particular point in time. It is, therefore, important that we think about the individual from a broad perspective from which current performance and technical skills are just two components of a more complex picture. While current capability can encompass existing knowledge, skills, experience, and track record (with some caveats about the degree of match to the current challenges of a role), it also encompasses another essential factor: the individual's ability to handle ambiguity and deal with complexity and uncertainty, and to be able to make decisions when the information is not readily available, i.e., "when the individual cannot know what to do."

As people move into senior roles, previous knowledge, skills, and experience become less significant than their ability to make judgments in the face of uncertainty and ambiguity. The debate about whether executives can move from one industry sector to another without past experience has gone back and forth for years. (It is acknowledged however that a number of other factors come into play here, not least of which is the cultural context). The ability to make appropriate judgments when it is not always possible to have all the supporting data is essential for successful performance. This view is not new.

In the "Nichomacean Ethics" Aristotle described three kinds of knowledge: *phronesis, episteme* and *techne*. The first kind of knowledge, *phronesis*, is practical wisdom. It is knowing what to do and how to do it, at the right time and with the right people, with the right mix of persuasion and challenge, and the right sense of what to leave unsaid and undone. When analysis is not sufficient, there is no technique that we know will work and so we must draw on inner resources to make a judgment. Practical wisdom can be supported by the second kind of knowledge, *episteme* (intellectual knowledge), which emerges from analysis and theory and of which we can be certain. The third kind of knowledge, *techne*, is about how to do things with a view to an outcome in which the person or the materials are changed in some way. In essence, it is about delivery. When we provide *techne*, we may feel competent and proud that we have mastered an art. For Aristotle neither *episteme* nor *techne* were sufficient for the complexities, ambiguities, and unpredictabilities of human affairs. Their cloudiness and potentiality require *phronesis*.

Aristotle used another concept, *sunesis*, often translated as understanding or perceptiveness.[3] The concrete etymology is about "joining the dots" (sun is same as syn, i.e., "together" as in synergy). So *sunesis* is "reading" the context to create the landscape for decision. For Aristotle, *sunesis* was the prelude to *phronesis*. It may well be that today when we talk about identifying capability, the capacity to scan and construct context, we see *sunesis*. We will return to this later in this article.

The words "capability", "potential," and "performance" are used in business conversations every day, and underlie such questions as, "Will he or she make the grade?" "Have they got what it takes to really make a difference?" "What is our bench strength?" and "Can we raise our game to compete with the best?" Because they have become common currency in this way, the real meaning of these words has become blurred.

This blurring of definitions is apparent when high performance is used as the only selection criterion when it comes to promotion. Performance is not the same thing as potential. Effective current performance is not necessarily a good indicator of a readiness to move to a more complex role. When effective performance in current role is used as the only criterion for promotion, it can lead to people being over-extended. This phenomenon of over-promotion is aptly described in *The Peter Principle*[4] and refers to people being promoted until "they reach their level of incompetence," an old adage but still true today. A fundamental challenge for managers in all organizations is to distinguish between current performance and future potential. A key question here is "potential for what type of challenge?"

---

3   The description of Aristotle's work is taken from a paper written by Dr. G. Stamp, June 2004 and is part of an ongoing discussion on the links to the Career Path Appreciation, a process for identifying potential in individuals.

4   Peter, L. *The Peter Principle.* William Morrow & Company:1969.

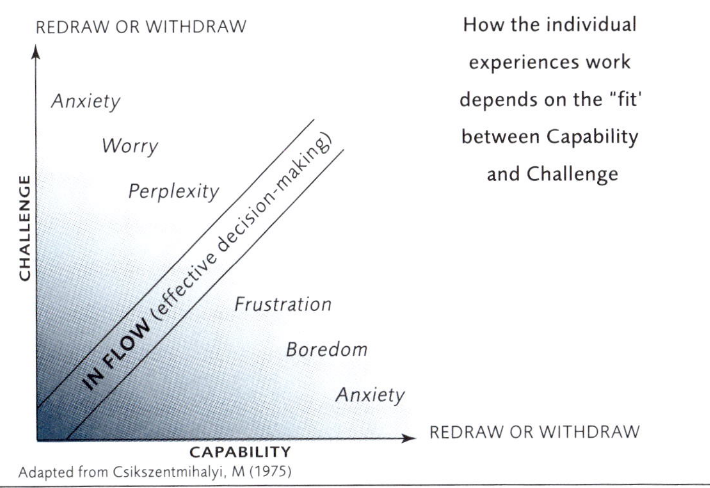

FIGURE 5.2.1: CHALLENGE AND CAPABILITY

An integrated framework enables the concepts of capability, potential, and performance to be clearly defined. Simply put, *capability* is the ability of someone to handle particular levels of complexity and ambiguity, and *potential* is the future capability of someone to work at a particular level. Sustained high *performance* is a record of someone making consistently sound judgments at the level of work required resulting in the achievement of goals and objectives. Judgment has two distinct factors; the outcome (what actually happened) and how the decision was made.

In Flow: The Match Between Capability and Challenge

We know that when people are "in flow," i.e. the challenges of their role matches the capability they bring to that role, decision making comes naturally. Even if people do not have the answers at their fingertips, they feel that they have the mental resources to find the answers. As Figure 5.2.1 shows, there are also important psychological consequences of moving out of flow. These can have significant business impacts as important decisions are either made in haste without due consideration or are inappropriately delayed.

Whether individuals are in or out of flow can have significant implications on the quality of their performance. When people are underutilized, their energy is channeled into finding meaningful work. They may cross over the boundaries of their roles, finding things that interest them, and often interfering with other people's work. Their performance may drop. We have experience of people's performance dropping as they "grow out of their role," yet their employing organization insists that they will not be promoted until their performance improves and a stalemate ensues. In extreme cases, people can stop believing in their own capability. When people are promoted into a role that is too big too soon, the consequences are similar except that they pull in the boundaries, often leaving out those elements that are important to that particular role. With senior appointments, the impact of this may not be known immediately, something a number of organizations have experienced over the years.

Therefore, we can hypothesize that the better the match between capability and performance, the better the performance. Being able to match people's growing capability to increasing challenges in work is essential for the well being of both individuals and organizations.

Spotting Potential

A widespread attempt to spot those with the potential for further development is inherent in the development of competency frameworks. Such frameworks attempt to identify the behaviors that would indicate success in a particular organization. In theory, they should flow from the strategic goals through the business drivers into the behaviors required to deliver these goals. These frameworks were established to provide a common language and a basis for determining what "good" looks like.

However, the behaviorally based "one-size-fits-all" approach of many models ensures that the competencies never quite suit the specific circumstance in the way that was intended. For example, the requirement to demonstrate competence in "Building External Relationships" is very different if one is managing a production unit rather than running an international strategic business unit.

Most competency frameworks, however, omit vital ingredients, because they are the ones that are difficult to describe, identify, and measure. Even seasoned senior executives are rarely able to articulate the thinking process involved in making far-reaching decisions or the perceptual skills involved in defining and seizing opportunities. While often valuable in identifying development needs, competency frameworks rarely get to the nub of "high potential."

Other processes used to identify those with high levels of potential include development/assessment centers. Exercises are designed to provide people with the opportunity to demonstrate their thinking around challenges that the organization expects individuals to be able to manage. There are varying degrees of success with these centers depending upon the robustness of the frameworks that are used and the ability of the exercises to differentiate and measure what they set out to measure.

Individuals themselves, however, give us clues if only we realize what they are indicating. Here are some behavior patterns that people with high potential often exhibit from an early age:

- a habit of growing out of each job faster than average
- getting bored quickly once they know how to do something
- seeing the context of their work more quickly than their peers
- grasping the bigger picture, being more aware of external factors like markets, competitors, suppliers, technology development, and what trends are indicating connections and new possibilities
- questioning assumptions and being more ready to deal with greater ambiguity than their colleagues
- challenging existing rules and experimenting with new methods
- being critical of "establishment thinking" and proposing alternative options

As will be seen in this article, there are processes that enable us to explore with individuals, within a structured framework, how they frame their world, including the nature of the judgments they make and the information and scanning that they undertake in order to come to a view about what needs to be done. It is possible to establish the complexity and ambiguity that an individual can handle at any one moment in time, and from that make predictions about his or her potential growth. It is important to establish the difference, if any, between one's current work and the capability one brings.

Experience shows that in many organizations, particularly at middle and senior management levels, individuals often have more capability than their role requires. This is particularly so in organizations characterized by high levels of technology and specialist knowledge. What is often missing is the range of other skills required to be able to convert capability and potential into performance. Unless fully understood and developed, this is a wasted resource for the organization.

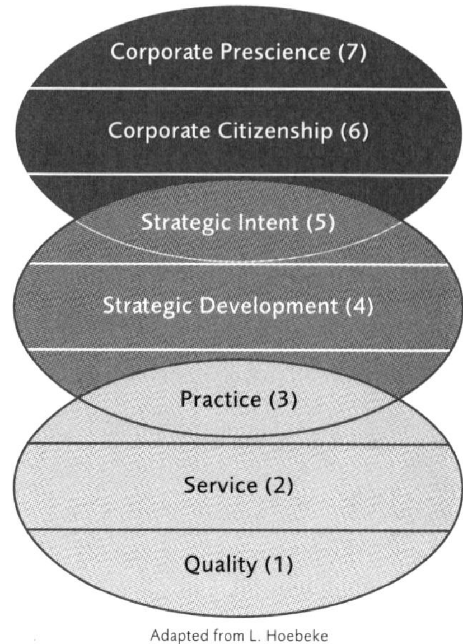

FIGURE 5.2.2: DOMAINS OF WORK

Appreciating Potential

Within organizations, it may help to ground the meanings of concepts such as capability and potential by asking the question, "Capability and potential for what?" What is the work that needs to be undertaken? In this way, the definitions become focused and applicable to challenges in the workplace in a way that is not static.

Understanding the Working Context

As we know, the challenge as we move up in any organization changes from dealing almost exclusively with the "here-and-now" to handling more complex issues and associated levels of uncertainty, as well as much longer timeframes.

Over many years, *bioss* has developed a framework that is helpful in identifying the "what," or how the work changes as one moved through organizations.[5] The model provides an objective measure of work complexity with the themes of work

---

5   See *Matrix of Working Relationships* and *General Theory of Bureaucracy* in reference list.

FIGURE 5.2.3: TWO SIDES OF THE SAME COIN

(quality, service, practice, *et al*) identifying the different types of work found in organizations. The descriptions of work are matched with descriptions of the personal capability required at each level to successfully carry out that work. The model sets a framework for understanding how each level adds value to the levels above and below. (See Figure 5.2.2.)

Traditionally succession planning has identified particular candidates for a particular role. When changes in the organization necessitated changes in roles the whole planning process needed to adjust. By thinking about work from a complexity basis, the succession planning processes can be more dynamic and agile.

The Other Side of the Coin – Capability

This integrated and robust model integrates work and people as if they were two sides of the same coin. (See Figure 5.2.3.)

Each level of work has its corresponding theme of capability. In order for someone to fully comprehend a particular level of work challenge, he or she must be able to "pattern and order" his or her experience and perceptions as a basis for making sense of their world and acting in it with purpose and intent.

"Patterning and ordering" involves taking in information and making sense of it, generating and choosing between alternatives, and then living with any remaining uncertainty. This may well be what Aristotle refers to as *sunesis*. A consequence of decision making at higher levels is no longer being able to "know" whether this was the right choice. As the size of the role increases and becomes more complex, the time before one can say for sure that "that was the right decision" increases. At senior levels it can take years. The decision by a forklift truck driver to turn left or right may be critically important, even to human life, but the outcome is clear almost instantly. In contrast, the decision of a CEO to change the entire strategic direction of his or her company may take six or seven years before the full impact can be stated with any certainty and the judgment regarding the success or failure of this decision can be made.

Individuals' capabilities to handle increasing levels of complexity and ambiguity grows throughout their lives and their growth path can be identified and, based on research studies, extrapolated into the future. We know that individuals vary in their ability to handle complexity and ambiguity in decision making and that this capability grows and develops at different rates. These development curves are illustrated in Figure 5.2.4.[6]

Figure 5.2.4 illustrates the development curves for two different individuals.

Person A enters the organization with the inherent capability to work at quite a high operational level and could be fast tracked. He or she will make a transition into level IV in his or her mid to late 20s, into level V during his or her mid 30s, and into level VI during his or her mid to late 40s

Person B would make the transition into level III (practice) during his or her 20s to early 30s and make an excellent contribution to operational roles for the rest of his or her career. Although he or she will transition into strategic development (level IV) during his or her mid 40s, it is unlikely that he or she would ever comfortably generate the "what" that is required at that level. He or she would, however, make a substantial contribution to that work from an innovative practice perspective.

The opportunity to find the emerging future business leaders rests on being able to identify those that are able to handle uncertainty and ambiguity, to make sense of this for themselves and others and to do so ahead of their peers.

A central tenet of this approach is that *capability is never static*. It grows at various paces and in various places. It crosses transition points (when people move from one level of capability to a higher one) and it is one of the dynamics of our lives. Our research identifies transitions in capability as key events in people's lives, times when they will make major changes in their personal and working lives. For example, it is often during these periods that people take additional education and qualifications. Clearly, transitions do not occur overnight and can take two or three years, during which time people are reaching for a new way of thinking, often to

---

6   The curves are approximated for the purpose of this diagram they should not be taken as an exact replica of the development curves.

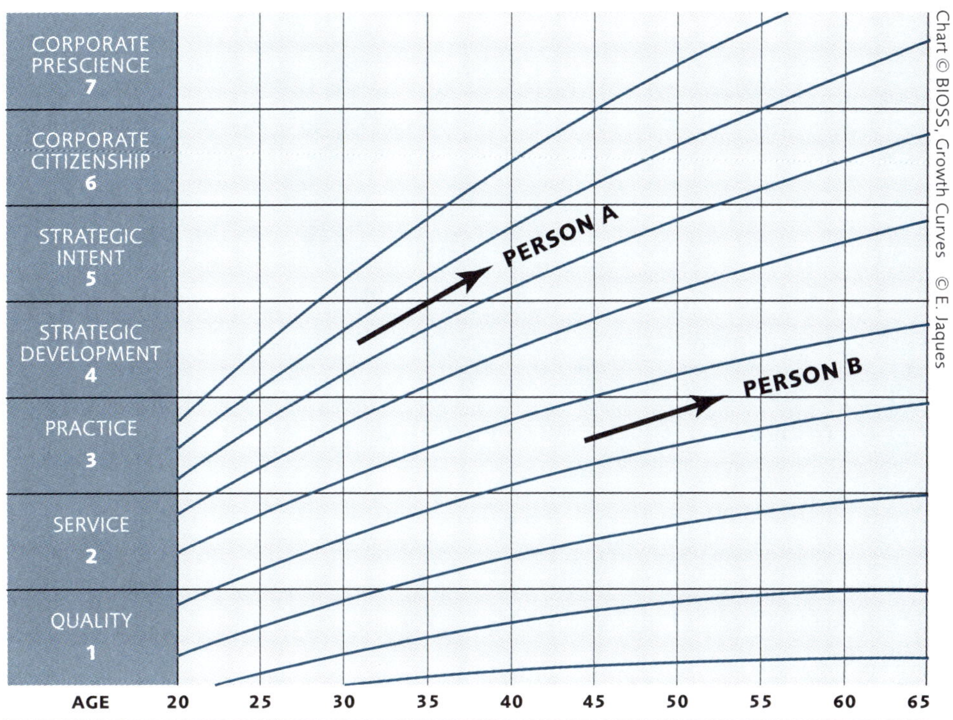

FIGURE 5.2.4: GROWTH CURVES FOR PERSONS A AND B

Based on and adapted from work by Elliott Jaques, in *Requisite Organization. 1989.*.

fall back down again. If the context for this transition is not supportive, individuals can experience great stress and uncertainty. Therefore, it is necessary to understand that when identifying capability and potential, there are different indicators that are relevant to different groups depending on their age. Identifying the potential in a graduate population is different to that of an emerging talent pool, or to that of senior managers who are moving into strategic roles.

Converting Potential to World-class Performance

When we refer to capability we are referring to the center piece of the capability potential jigsaw, i.e., the judgments that people make. However, having capability to match the challenges of a role is the necessary, but not sufficient, ingredient. The emphasis on such factors as emotional intelligence is an example of organizations trying to find the "holy grail." How this capability finds "its voice" is, therefore, de-

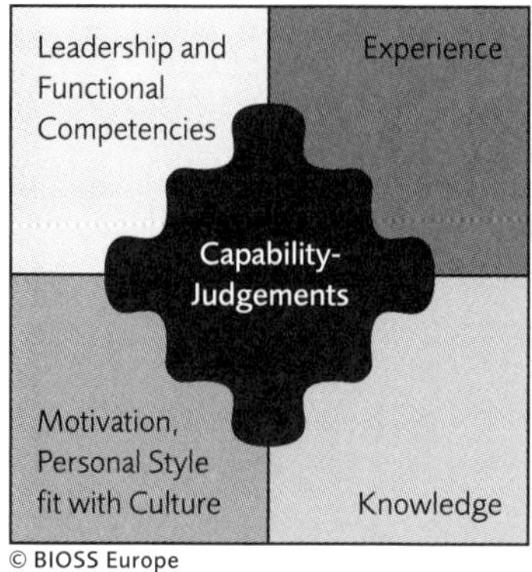

FIGURE 5.2.5: THE JIGSAW OF POTENTIAL

pendent upon a range of other factors including the necessary knowledge, skills, and experience of which competencies are one part. The various elements do, of course, include career aspirations of individuals and are part of the motivational piece of the jigsaw. How we see ourselves, how we believe others see us, and the need to balance the various elements of our lives is very important.

Figure 5.2.5, the jigsaw diagram, provides a framework for thinking about the conversation of capability into effective judgments. As mentioned above, having the capability to handle the complexity of a particular role is important, but how this capability is converted is also crucial. Several things come into play here that range from experience to the quality of interpersonal skills.

Often people are identified with the capability to work with a particular set of challenges, but they lack the ability to convert this into effective performance for any number of reasons, some of which are highlighted above. This is referred to as "raw" or "theoretical" potential. One theory is that high performance requires synergy between *sunesis* (capacity to engage with complexity) and the decision that is right for the moment, *phronesis*.

Without the capability in the first place, people are unlikely to be able to assimilate and use the learnings gained through development. All things being equal, people can be fast-tracked to gain the necessary skills and experiences.

In addition, the "climate" provided by the company or the context set by the boss is critical. Although a great deal has been written on personal motivation, in fact most people working in organizations want the following:

- to be clear about what they are expected to do and how what they do fits in with the organization's goals and the work of others
- to be given the space to bring their judgments to bear on the work in a way that maximizes their potential
- to know how well they are doing and for their contributions to be recognized and valued
- to know where they are going and their career opportunities for growth

bioss is clear that a defined and robust framework for understanding both the complexity of work and the capability of the individual has to underpin performance management. One key element of sustained high performance suggests that there needs to be a match between the work challenge (level of complexity) and the individual's capability to handle it.

Conclusion

It is clear that the levels of work complexity and capability model provides a robust and integrated framework upon which to identify the potential of individuals to handle increasingly complex work. It is therefore possible to target development and provide individuals with the knowledge, skills, and experiences they require to maximize their potential.

As David Ulrich noted in *Harvard Business Review*[7] when writing about the need for a robust framework, "It is relatively unimportant which framework an organization uses to define the company's architecture, as long as it's robust." He also noted that it needed to be clearly articulated because without clarity, managers can become short-sighted about how the company runs and may lose sight of strategic implementation and what stands in its way.

There are very few models that use the same premise to look at both the work that needs to be done and the capability needed. This seamless way of looking at the different types of work challenges found in organizations and the individual capability to pattern, order, and make sense of this enables organizations to do the following:
- develop very clear understandings of the real challenge facing them and how each and every role adds value

---

7   Ulrich, D. "A New Mandate for Human Resources" *Harvard Business Review.* 1998.

- evaluate an individual's current level of capability
- match the individual capability to the work at that level and map capability across the organization
- predict future growth in capability for both individuals and the organization
- develop focused succession and development plans

The core of effective performance depends upon the ability of organizations to clearly articulate the work needed to deliver their strategic goals combined with the ability to identify individuals who are able to match these demands.

ABOUT THE AUTHORS

Peter Taylor's consulting work focuses on the development of people and organizations as well as change management. His work has extended across reviewing strategies, changing structures and systems, and evaluating the competencies, qualities and capabilities of people. He has served as HR director of a large financial service's subsidiary organization. As a manager, he gained first-hand knowledge of introducing career and performance management systems. With extensive experience using the EFQM Excellence Model, Taylor led a team that won the British Quality Foundation annual quality award.

With a Masters in Management Development through Salford University, he is a Chartered Member of the Institute of Personnel and Development. Qualified in the interpretation of psychometric tests and questionnaires, he is a Master Trainer in Team Management Systems, Deputy Managing Director of the *bioss* European operations, and a practitioner of Career Path Appreciation (CPA).

A graduate of Brunel and London University, **Judith Hobrough** is a consultant within the area of people and organizational development. She has extensive international experience as well as experience in the management and implementation of projects in both the private and public sectors. Her work involves helping organization to design the most effective structure to achieve their corporate objectives, developing human resource strategies, redesigning roles, identifying level-specific competencies and systems, as well as matching people to work roles. A key aspect of her work is concerned with the area of talent management and all that is entailed in the identification and development of potential together with effective supporting processes.

Hbrough is a Chartered Psychologist and a member of the Occupational Division of The British Psychological Society. She sits on the Board of bioss International and is MD of their European operations. She is a practitioner and trainer in Career Path Appreciation (CPA).

Individual Capability and Our Working Journey

Andrew Olivier

WHAT'S IMPORTANT

- The longest task an individual has is managing his or her own life goals and career. How we experience our own journey, how we discover our own potential, how we manage to use as much of our potential as we can are the keys to career development and life satisfaction.

- The CEO and executives need a sensitivity to the "Working Journey"concept, an empathy that individuals be all that they can be by helping them find fit between their capability and work role, and understand when they need to move to the next job.

Our Working Journey is public, for others can observe and judge our capability in action and where our decisions impact the journeys of others. It is also a private journey, for it is yours to travel and no one else can do it for you. To understand how to manage it, we need to understand how our capability shapes its path and creates certain changes.

For many executives, one of the best ways to learn the concepts of requisite organization is to apply them to their own individual work life experience, what I have come to call the *Working Journey*. This article is about how the growth of our individual capability drives our Working Journey and the impact this has on talent pools. I will show you how to understand your own transitions from one level of capability to another. You can use the same methods and ideas to manage other talent pools of any size, whether within your team, site, organization, region, or nation.

Capability and capacity have already been defined in other articles in this book, which reviews the work of Elliott Jaques and others in the area of requisite organization (RO). While much of Jaques's work focused on designing effective organization structures and systems to manage the enterprise and plan for leadership succession, a different group led by Gillian Stamp at Brunel University developed expert methods to assess capability. Her work, with its focus on understanding individuals' career paths and fit by following their career progression over the years, led to seeing the capability growth in individuals over time. It brought humanity to the RO approach, a humanity that provides powerful explanatory support to the individual and deepens the manager and manager-once-removed (MoR) understanding of key employees.

Our Working Journey is public, for others can observe and judge our capability in action and our decisions impact the journeys of others. It is also a private journey, for it is ours alone to travel. To understand how to manage it, we need to understand how our capability shapes the path and creates certain changes.

Capability, the Engine of Your Working Journey

Elliott Jaques's research shows that individuals process information differently and that this ability grows and evolves *predicatively over time*. It is this predictive aspect that has provided greater insight into career management, appreciating change in a Working Journey, and allowing organizations to allocate and manage human capital over time.

Jaques's array of time horizon growth curves maps the growth of our capability over time according to nine growth modes. This allows us to predict when someone will make a transition into a new order of complexity in his or her Working Journey.

Our cognitive capability drives our need to actualize, and thus powers our search for the kind of work or opportunities that let us fully use it. The greater our future capability, the more we actively seek change, the more we seek out new environments, and the more we influence the journeys of others. This can both be a blessing and a curse!

Jaques's framework underpins the capability assessment instruments that use the growth curves as a basis. Knowing the location of an individual on the growth curves (i.e., an individual's mode) allows one to predict his or her growth rate over time. Jaques was firmly opposed to commercialization of these methods of assessments and preferred organizations to do capability assessments themselves, favoring a process known as talent pool calibration or gearing, in which managers and MoRs judge their subordinates' capability. However, this is often not aimed at personal development or individual awareness, but rather effective talent pool management.

Flow: When Your Capability Matches Your Work

The aim of understanding the work required as well as the individual's capability is to match the two together, providing the conditions for being in what Csikszentmihalyi called "flow."[1] Flow occurs when you lose yourself in what you are doing, a hobby, a task or a job, forgetting even the passing of time with the enjoyment of what you are doing.

Csikszentmihalyi's characteristic of flow also describes the state when your level of cognitive capability matches the level of work required by your role and the role engages your sense of purpose, knowledge, and skills. You are cognitively engaged, interested, allowed to experiment, have accountability and responsibility, and are recognized, rewarded, and fulfilled. When you are underutilized, have more capability than the role requires, or over-extended, not having the level of cognitive capability to cope with your role, you move away from flow.

This movement is on a continuum. If over-promoted or in a role beyond your level of cognitive capability, you move from flow to perplexity, not knowing how to respond or which signals are relevant or what decisions to make; then worry, waking

---

1   Csikszentmihalyi, M. *Flow: The psychology of optimal experience.* New York: Harper and Row, 1990.

up in the early hours of the night still churning in your mind; and finally, into psychological anxiety. If the situation is not addressed, this can lead to depression. (See Sidebar 1 for an example of being out of flow because of over-promotion.)

Being undcrutilized is similarly debilitating. When your role is smaller than your current level of cognitive capability, what used to be flow becomes boredom because of not being fully engaged in your work. Farther from your level, it becomes indifference, not caring about your performance or goals. Farther still from a good fit, it can lead to psychological anxiety. Again, if the situation is not addressed, depression can result.

Both ends of the continuum represent potentially serious situations. Being underutilized or over-extended for prolonged periods may cause people to resort to substance abuse, depression, and withdrawal, loss of energy for life and a host of other related symptoms.[2]

Promoting a person into a role before he or she has the necessary cognitive capability is setting that person up to fail. These failures can cost the organization dearly, as well as damaging the individual's Working Journey. Likewise, leaving individuals too long in a role when they have excess cognitive capability means they are at risk of leaving, and/or becoming increasingly bored and a liability to the organization.

Mismatches can lead to debilitating anxiety in the individual, which is why you and your organization must watch your transitions from one level to another. However, ultimately it is your Working Journey and you alone are accountable for it.

Work and capability matching is a necessary (but not sufficient!) condition for flow on the job. It is a time when our well-being at work seems to flow into our personal journey as well, when everything moves easily, success comes almost effortlessly; it's a golden time. The challenge is to work with this shifting kaleidoscope and ensure that, as far as possible, you are doing the right work at the right stage of your life. This makes it vitally important that you understand and plan for your transitions.

Passages, Transitions, and Your "Call to Adventure"

Transitions refer to that point in time when cognitive processes shift from one way of looking at and processing the world to another, when we move from one level of complexity to the next. As with most transitions, these times can be confusing and stress-

---

2   Stamp, G., and Stamp, C. (1993). "Well-being at Work: Aligning Purposes, People, Strategies and Structures." *International Journal of Career Management*, Vol.5, No 3.

ful, exciting and illuminating, damaging or highly fulfilling, depending on your work and life context. Often transitions are marked by proactive change: leaving a company, changing career direction, or ending relationships as different work and creative challenges are sought. Failure to find work or expression at the next level can result in increasing frustration and anxiety; a former high achiever can lose self-confidence and reputation. By ignoring the transitions of its employees, the company stands to lose both the high potentials and the time and resource it costs to replace them.

These transition periods are fundamentally important times for us. They represent a "Call to Adventure" (a concept borrowed from Joseph Campbell's 1971 work) in which we are all called upon to make a heroic journey, a pilgrimage or quest.[3] We feel dissatisfaction with where we are, with our work and lives, losing that joy in our work that comes with flow, but do not have a clear picture of where go. The Call to Adventure begins subtly, and if ignored, grows increasingly strident. Some ignore it, making a trade-off with other values; some accept the Call with alacrity; and some may not even notice it, easily stepping up their current work to meet their grow-

---

3 Campbell, J. *The Hero with a Thousand Faces.* Bollingen Series XVII. Princeton University Press, 1971.

ing capability. But for many the urge to find flow and actualize becomes so strong that the call is answered. We embark on a new journey within the greater Working Journey of our lives.

The search begins to find Csikszentmihalyi's "flow" and Campbell's "bliss," that place where what we do feels right, feels good, and has intrinsic recognition and reward. We seek again that time of synchronicity, energy connections, and abundance—a golden time. We seek mastery of the new challenges that the transition has brought. On this sometimes perilous journey, success is not guaranteed. Setbacks and failure are often important teachers.

Each journey ends with a return. Campbell postulates that we see a new being emerging, a very different individual to the one who started out, so hesitant and unsure. Returning, we are bearing new skills, garnered wisdom, and tales of adventures. Each of these journeys and transitions may vary in number and duration, depending on the mode, but few journeys are shorter than 6 years and some may last 20 or more years. They are fundamental drivers in our lives. For those who will transition more than once, each new transition is another Call to Adventure, a new chance to voyage and recreate oneself.

Talent Pools

As our capability develops, we transition and seek new roles for challenges and mastery. This simple fact also has major implications for groups striving to capitalize on the potential and capability within their talent pool. There are many different types of talent pools, of course, and we occupy one or more at any given time. There are national talent pools and within that there are multitudes of configurations: corporate talent pools, industry talent pools, entrepreneurial talent pools, sporting talent pools, and so on. However, most of us perform most of our choreographed work within organizational talent pools.

Organizations are keen to identify future leaders and top executives create succession plans or leadership pipelines to grow future managing directors and CEOs from within the organization. Fundamental to this mission is to identify those individuals who may develop the capability to work at a level V or strategic intent perspective. Jaques's growth modes provide this insight and this potential capability can be identified in individuals as young as their early 20s.

For those tasked with managing the organizational talent pool, there are a few basic principles that require explanation.

Transitions

People should be moved to experience a new work level during or shortly after a transition. This requires knowing who is able to operate at what level, when this will shift, and what appropriate development is in order so that they can operate effectively at the new level.

Although people pipelines focus on leadership succession, transitions should be watched at all levels. Most organizations will have people at levels I and II who are capable of working at the next level, as Mary's story illustrates. (See Sidebar 2.)

Both people pipelines and transitions require an in-depth understanding of the tasks and the individuals, both currently and what they may look like in the future. Understanding the individual's potential and the evolution of the role and structure of the organization is crucial to managing the transition effectively.

Simple Supporting Systems

Overviews of talent may take the form of a matrix that maps potential and performance, or another form of coding that records the relevant information. Whatever the system, it facilitates the managers' decisions around talent allocation and development, which means that the information needs to be easily understood and laid out concisely.

People Pipelines

Actively manage your people pipelines to ensure that a flow of talent is created and managed for the different work levels. Talent pool candidates may need to be grouped into disciplines or job families for direct succession routes.

One level VI global company, comprised of four level V strategic business units and a host of other related financial entities, struggled to establish how the corporate center should add value to the organization. Some business units used requisite organization concepts and some did not. Support functions were sometimes cen-

2. NATIONAL CALL CENTER EMPLOYEE

"Mary" joined an organization as a trainee in a national call center. Her group received intensive training and had its capability assessed as part of an experiment. The call center manager battled a 30 percent turnover rate and low engagement scores, as well as a declining market share. The experiment assessed the cognitive capability of top performers, non-performers, and a control group.

Capability appeared to be a key factor in performance. Successful call center operators relied on the full range of skilled quality work (level I), and also had the capability to move into level II within the next five or so years. They were mode III individuals within a specific age grouping. Those who were poor performers were a mix of individuals who could not cope with the level required as well as those who were underutilized by it.

Mary was a mid-mode V and already well into high level II. This fact indicated that she would not find fulfillment in an already stressful environment, and indeed she did not. The national call center manager used the capability assessment information to fast track her to team leader. A year later she helped set up a new call center, and she is now a national sales manager.

---

tralized and sometimes not; for example, some entities had their own training and leadership academies, while others did not.

The company identified the corporate center's unique added value as the preparation of leaders for the passages from level III to IV, IV to V, and V to VI. The focus of the corporate core, therefore, shifted to managing the people pipeline and the focus of development became what was required to be successful at the next level.

James Strong's story (see Sidebar 3) illustrates a salient point: high-potential individuals move around and, while they are in your company, talent pool managers need to know, track, and develop them effectively. They are the drivers of the future organization. High-mode individuals are also a key national resource. A nation needs to ensure that high-potential talent is attracted and sometimes repatriated back to the country to ensure its viability.

James Strong joined the Australian Army at the age of 16. When he left the Army at 19, he was already cognitively comfortable with level III work. His leaving was often put down to "discipline difficulties," though clearly he was able to operate at a level far beyond that expected by the Army. He was bored and out of flow.

James joined the mining industry and was rapidly promoted to a leadership role while he continued studying law. At 39, he left the mining industry and moved to Canberra as an industry lobbyist. In his early 40s, he took on the role of privatizing a state airline. This was a golden time, a time of "flow," and he loved leading from the front. He received widespread acclaim for his success as CEO. At 45, he was managing partner of a national law firm, only to discover again that he was bored. After completing his brief, he became CEO of Quantas Australia's iconic airline. Here he headed the most rapid growth phase ever experienced by Quantas, firmly establishing it as a leader in its industry. He retired in his late 50s.

James is now chairman of a number of blue chip companies, such as IAG, Australia's largest general insurer; Woolworths, the highly successful food retailer; and Rip Curl, a surfing lifestyle company operating globally, as well as chairman of the Australian Council for the Arts.

What is interesting is that James made dramatic career changes at all his transition points. His Working Journey is characterized by occupying multiple talent pools, multiple transition points, and many Calls to Adventure, not all of them easy to heed. He recalls that letting go of the CEO "monkey" as he transitioned into level VI was the toughest thing to do.

Entrepreneurial Talent Pools

High-mode individuals enjoy creating uncertainty in their Working Journeys by deliberate perturbation. Transition points cause fundamental changes and the entrepreneurial career path illustrates this well.

A study was conducted over a six-year period of 40 entrepreneurs in Southern Africa, all operating in highly volatile environments. Crime, widespread poverty, lack of skills, economic sanctions, and protectionist government policies had hindered business formation and growth. All were successful and first-time business owners. Company sizes varied from 20 employees to almost 40,000, structures varied from national to multinational, and ages of the businesses from 4 years to more than 40 years.

All of the entrepreneurs were high-potential individuals with growth modes from mode V to VII. More than 50 percent came from corporate backgrounds and had left their organizations in frustration, often while working in high level III roles. All were in a phase of personal transition between work level III and IV or were under-utilized in high level III positions with no career move in sight. Some tried to utilize their capability and reduce their frustrations by registering for higher degree studies, such as MBAs. The theses they wrote served as seeds for many entrepreneurial ideas that became successful. This was the time that they started their businesses.

The transition into level IV seems to be a critical period and is the time when people most leave an organization in search of greener pastures. From an entre-preneurial and organizational growth perspective, each time they personally transitioned work levels, they ratcheted their company's growth with them.

Conclusion

In conclusion, I have hoped, in the course of this article, to examine the implication of our individual capability on our Working Journeys and on the talent pools in which we swim. This information needs to be more accessible to our employees and to us in order that we plan our journeys and equip ourselves for the road ahead. To those who manage talent pools, this enables understanding the complex interplay of factors to manage for individual wellbeing and organizational performance.

ABOUT THE AUTHOR

Andrew Olivier has had an eclectic career. He is a decorated marine officer, has worked in the corporate world, built a software company, and had two management consultancies. The Southern African management consultancy in 1998 changed its name to bioss South Africa and in Australia, was bioss Australia. Olivier works in-dependently and discretely with high-potential individuals, many of whom are well known public figures, advising and coaching them on their journeys and their lega-cies. He enjoys fine art and owns an art gallery. In 2003 he published *The Working Journey* and is currently working on a new book. He has a strong interest in fighting global poverty and is looking at ways of helping micro entrepreneurs in developing countries.

3

Implementing a Web-based Requisite Talent Management System

Donald V. Fowke, FCMC

WHAT'S IMPORTANT

- This talent management succession planning system provides the structure and discipline within which managers can make judgments and decisions and initiate actions needed to supply the talent needed for growth as well as to support individuals in developing their own capability.

- The system integrates requisite organization concepts of structure and development into the only known web-based, user-friendly, support for RO's best management practices.

- It stresses the all-important manager-once-removed concept and describes how processes are designed to overcome the common stumbling blocks to keeping vital information up-to-date, overcoming distortions in judgment, and providing effective feedback as part of on-going dialogue.

It takes time and experience to develop the skill to distinguish between someone who isn't suc-
ceeding because he or she lacks skilled knowledge and experience from someone who just isn't
capable. We found you just have to keep working at it.

This story of an evolving talent management and succession process is told through the voice of the vice president of human resources (VP HR) of Owen Chemicals, a disguised composite company that allows telling the tale to include the richness of experiences in implementing this web-supported system in a variety of settings. Following are the concerns of those involved as pertains to their particular roles in the company. Their specific concerns will be discussed in this article.

CEO: "I need to know where my business unit heads will be coming from seven years from now."

Vice President: "Our young engineers are getting into middle management without having the necessary basic skills in people management."

General Manager: "We need bosses, and bosses' bosses, to come to a meeting of the minds about what young managers and professionals need to develop fully. It's tough when everybody is moving around the way they do."

High Flyer: "You know, career visibility is important. I need to know that how I'm doing and what I want to do is on the screen of the powers that be. If not, I'll go someplace where I'm seen."

VP HR: "Our tendency in appointment has been to grab the closest warm body and get on with it. To have managers consider a broader group, including people they don't know, they need a simple way of getting the information, which should include track record, judgments on potential, and developmental needs."

COO: "I've got accountability for nine direct reports. And I've got manager-once-removed accountability for 47 others. I can't stay on top of this unless I've got all the information at my fingertips when I need it, including salary and incentive options."

VP HR: We have a new CEO. And this was the first thing he put to me. It was serious, because he came with a very ambitious mandate to grow the company. I'm happy to report I could give him pretty good answers because our Global Talent Management System puts them at my fingertips. The next day I gave him Figure 5.3.1, and we spent an hour talking about the developmental experiences needed to prepare the most promising candidates. What he was looking for, of course, were managers who would be or become capable at stratum V, were motivated, and who

Owen Chemicals
Forecast Executive Talent 2005 - 2017

	2005	2009	2013	2017
7.3				
7.2			1	
7.1		1		1
6.3	1		1	2
6.2		1	1	1
6.1	1	1	2	4
5.3		2	1	6
5.2	3	1	10	8
5.1	7	9	6	6
4.3	11	16	14	13
4.2	16	10	10	6
4.1	7	4	2	2
	46	45	48	49

Chief Officers, Group VPs

2005 Top Executives

		Stratum
Morton	Frederick	6.3
Harvey	Shirley	6.1

2009 Top Executives

		Stratum
Morton	Frederick	7.1
Harvey	Shirley	6.2
Reynolds	Robert	6.1

2013 Top Executives

		Stratum
Morton	Frederick	7.2
Harvey	Shirley	6.3
Reynolds	Robert	6.2
Carlyle	Terry	6.1
Stacey	Francis	6.1

2017 Top Executives

		Stratum
Harvey	Shirley	6.3
Reynolds	Robert	6.3
Carlyle	Terry	6.2
Stacey	Francis	6.1
Barber	Lloyd	6.1
Tremblay	Alain	6.1
Herbert	Albert	6.1

Business Unit or Equivalent

2005 V Capable: Business Unit President or Equiv.

		Stratum
Lavery	Kenneth	5.2
Gagnon	Lisanne	5.2
Carlyle	Terry	5.2
Fortier	Dennis	5.1
Cameron	Angeline	5.1
Chan	Ian	5.1
Voight	David	5.1
Roberton	John	5.1
Kilburn	Dale	5.1
Morton	Marion	5.1

2009 V Capable: Business Unit President or Equiv.

		Stratum
Lavery	Kenneth	5.3
Carlyle	Terry	5.3
Cameron	Angeline	5.2
Roberton	John	5.1
Kilburn	Dale	5.1
Burton	Lesley	5.1
Garland	Eric	5.1
MacDonald	Sarah	5.1
Briant	Andre	5.1
Darryl	Daniel	5.1
Arbuthnot	Dianne	5.1
Pratt	Pauline	5.1

2013 V Capable: Business Unit President or Equiv.

		Stratum
Lavery	Kenneth	5.3
Cameron	Angeline	5.2
Roberton	John	5.2
Kilburn	Dale	5.2
Burton	Lesley	5.2
Garland	Eric	5.2
MacDonald	Sarah	5.2
Briant	Andre	5.2
Darryl	Daniel	5.2
Arbuthnot	Dianne	5.2
Clarkson	Rick	5.2
Pratt	Pauline	5.1
McMillan	Timothy	5.1
Carson	Victoria	5.1
Chanson	Theresa	5.1
DuBarry	Dianne	5.1
McCusker	Herb	5.1

2017 V Capable: Business Unit President or Equiv.

		Stratum
Lavery	Kenneth	5.3
Cameron	Angeline	5.3
Burton	Lesley	5.3
Garland	Eric	5.3
MacDonald	Sarah	5.3
Clarkson	Rick	5.3
Roberton	John	5.2
Kilburn	Dale	5.2
Briant	Andre	5.2
Darryl	Daniel	5.2
Arbuthnot	Dianne	5.2
Pratt	Pauline	5.2
Jean	Dianne	5.2
Rilkoff	Mike	5.2
McMillan	Timothy	5.1
Bradford	Terrance	5.1
Standish	Richard	5.1
Giguere	Mark	5.1
Woodbury	David	5.1
Carrier	Damien	5.1

FIGURE 5.3.1

we could assure had the necessary skilled knowledge and experience to run a business unit.[1]

You'll notice that we make a clear distinction between "potential" and "experience." In the beginning our managers tended to mix the two up, thinking that if someone had the experience they surely would have the potential. This is nonsense of course, and it leads to the "Peter Principle" where people are promoted to their level of incompetence. You can document experience. Assessing potential is harder.

He could have very good confidence in the data, because it represents judgments by each candidate's manager and manager-once-removed, the boss' boss so to speak, as you can see in Figure 5.3.2.

That was not always the case. When we started with talent management five years ago, we relied heavily on expert interviews by our consultants to assess current potential capability. This got us started in a practical way, and as our managers worked with ideas of distinct strata for managerial work, they got to be pretty good at distinguishing, for example, between somebody capable at stratum III high or stratum IV low. You can see in Figure 5.3.2 how these judgments are recorded in our system.

One should not underestimate both the importance and difficulty of getting managers competent in this area. It has taken us a couple of years to help our managerial team understand the seven strata in our company and, through "gearing" sessions, learning to distinguish between those who could do the job and those who couldn't. Part of the problem is that managers are often not comfortable about making judgments about people in front of their peers. And changing this requires developing the confidentiality norms in the group so that what someone says about a person stays in the room. At a technical level, it takes time and experience to develop the skill to distinguish between someone who isn't succeeding because he or she lacks skilled knowledge and experience from someone who just isn't capable. We found you just have to keep working at it.

We know that high-potential talent needs to be identified early. Men and women who will be business leaders at stratum V and above need to make the turn from front-line manager at stratum II to manager of managers at stratum III before age 27. And they need to be able to assume general management roles in stratum IV before age 43.

Vice President: "Our young engineers are getting into middle management with-

---

1   The concepts of strata and developmental path used are inspired by Cason and Jaques, *Human Capability*, Cason Hall Publishers, Gloucester MA, 1994.

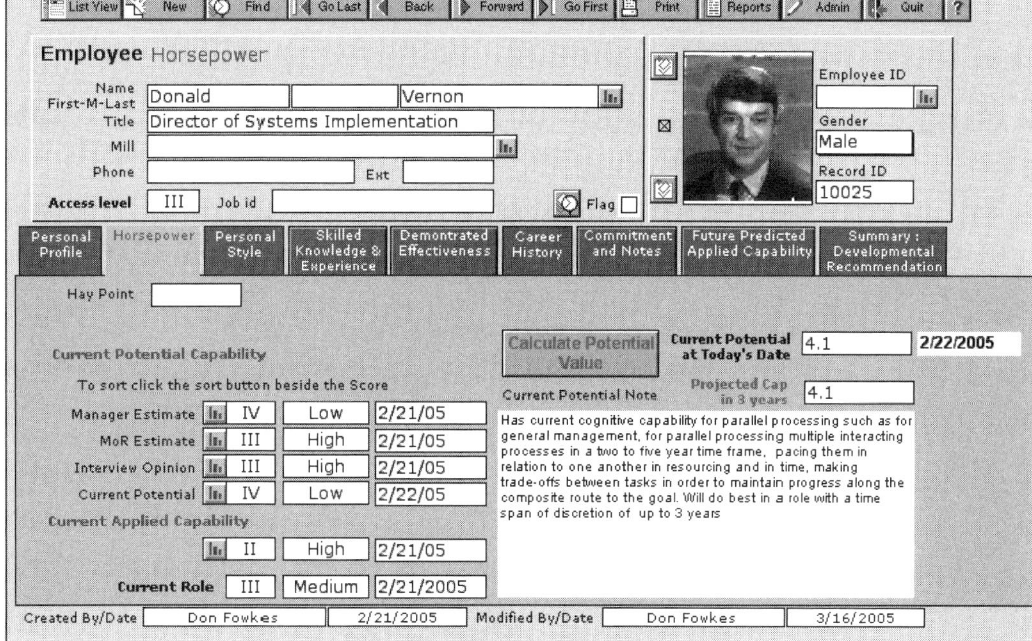

FIGURE 5.3.2

out basic skills in people management."

The literature about developing leaders is clear about the importance of managing "turns." Making a turn is moving from one managerial stratum to the next. Stephen Drotter, for example, distinguishes among mastery potential, the ability to do better at the same level of work; growth potential, the ability to do bigger jobs at the same level in the near term; and turn potential, the ability to move to a higher stratum in three to five years.[2]

We have many engineers who start at the company doing technical work. They aren't necessarily the best people-people, but they are promoted to senior management. It is critical to provide them with the necessary skilled knowledge, training, and experience to manage people. That is why we make such a point of having managers routinely assess subordinate skills in the managerial practices, as you can see in Figure 5.3.3. So when our system alerts, as it does in Figure 5.3.2, that an individual is coming up on an important turn, we pay close attention to his or her ratings

---

2   Charan, R., Drotter, S., and Noel, J. *The Leadership Pipeline: How to Build the Leadership Powered Company*. San Francisco: Jossey-Bass, 2001.

List View | New | Find | Go Last | Back | Forward | Go First | Print | Reports | Admin | Quit

Employee Skilled Krowledge & Experience

Name First-M-Last: Donald | Vernon
Title: Director of Systems Implementation
Mill:
Phone: | Ext
Access level III | Job id | Flag

Employee ID
Gender: Male
Record ID: 10025

Personal Profile | Horsepower | Personal Style | Skilled Knowledge & Experience | Demonstrated Effectiveness | Career History | Commitment and Notes | Future Predicted Applied Capability | Summary : Developmental Recommendation

Professional Qualification: MCSE
Degree: Commerce
University: U of Saskatchewan
Graduation Year: 1987
Other Degree:
Other University:
Other Graduation year:
Other Training:
Bilingual:
Trades:

Managerial Skills

Managerial Skills	Future Predicted Applied Capability	Summary : Developmental Recommendation
Setting Context	3	2/21/2005
Recruiting	2	2/21/2005
Team Development	4	2/21/2005
Assign Tasks	3	2/21/2005
Coach Subordinates	4	2/22/2005
Evaluate Performance	2	2/21/2005
Develop Subordinates	2	2/21/2005
Recommend Deselection	1	2/21/2005
Assess Potential of SoR	2	2/21/2005
Mentor SoR	3	2/21/2005
Career Development of SoR	2	2/21/2005

Management System Training

One Day Intro: | Values Training:
Three Day Intro: | Site Impact Training:

Created By/Date: Don Fowkes | 2/21/2005 | Modified By/Date: Don Fowkes | 3/16/2005

FIGURE 5.3.3

on the managerial practices. We've learned that these skills need to become second nature, and the best time to get it right is before the turn from stratum II to stratum III. For a young engineer doing a first supervisory job at level II, we need his or her immediate superior at level III to coach intensively on the managerial practices. And we insist that the manager-once-removed (at level IV) ensure that those skills are developed before we move them on.

General Manager: "We need bosses, and bosses' bosses, to come to a meeting of the minds about what young managers and professionals need to develop fully. It's tough when everybody is moving around the way they do."

One of the principles of requisite organization is that the manager-once-removed is an important key to the development of leadership talent. We found leadership development perhaps the hardest thing we had to learn to do as a company. At very senior levels, the manager-once-removed scope can feel overwhelming. A group vice-president, for example, may have as many a seven business units reporting to

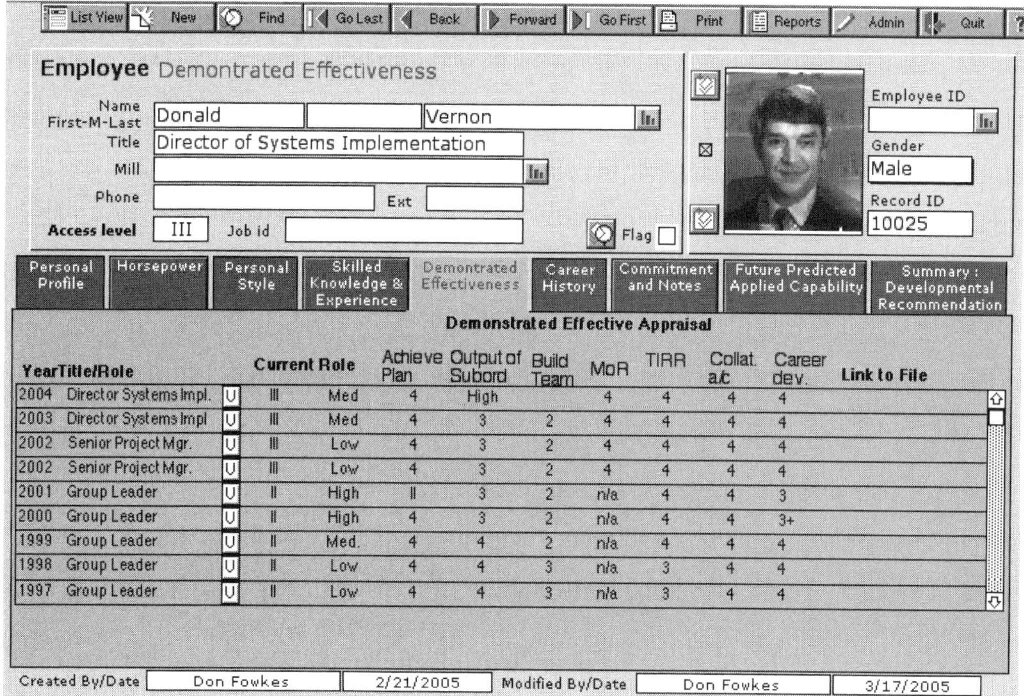

Employee Demontrated Effectiveness

Name First-M-Last: Donald — Vernon
Title: Director of Systems Implementation
Mill:
Phone: — Ext
Access level: III   Job id   Flag

Employee ID
Gender: Male
Record ID: 10025

Personal Profile | Horsepower | Personal Style | Skilled Knowledge & Experience | Demontrated Effectiveness | Career History | Commitment and Notes | Future Predicted Applied Capability | Summary : Developmental Recommendation

Demonstrated Effective Appraisal

Year	Title/Role		Current Role		Achieve Plan	Output of Subord	Build Team	MoR	TIRR	Collat. a/c	Career dev.	Link to File
2004	Director Systems Impl.	U	III	Med	4	High		4	4	4	4	
2003	Director Systems Impl	U	III	Med	4	3	2	4	4	4	4	
2002	Senior Project Mgr.	U	III	Low	4	3	2	4	4	4	4	
2002	Senior Project Mgr.	U	III	Low	4	3	2	4	4	4	4	
2001	Group Leader	U	II	High	II	3	2	n/a	4	4	3	
2000	Group Leader	U	II	High	4	3	2	n/a	4	4	3+	
1999	Group Leader	U	II	Med.	4	4	2	n/a	4	4	4	
1998	Group Leader	U	II	Low	4	4	3	n/a	3	4	4	
1997	Group Leader	U	II	Low	4	4	3	n/a	3	4	4	

Created By/Date: Don Fowkes — 2/21/2005   Modified By/Date: Don Fowkes — 3/17/2005

FIGURE 5.3.4

him or her. The number of subordinates once removed could easily number 40 or 50 stratum IV or high stratum III managers.

We have gearing sessions, where our corporate executives and business unit presidents review talent together. I know this is the way Jack Welch insisted on doing it at General Electric. To the degree we have been successful with this, it has improved our executives' understanding of what we are measuring, such as current potential capability, as opposed to how it is being applied right now, as well as what that long-term potential might be. I'd consistently recommend we do more of it.

Practically speaking, however, our executives are too much on the move internationally to be able to do enough of this. We have learned to do this on the fly through our Global Talent Management System, which is now web-based and therefore accessible from anywhere in the world. For those who like to work on long international or cross country flights, we make a disk-based version of their talent pool available to them.

The key to this, of course, is having all the information available in the same place in electronic form, as in Figure 5.3.4.

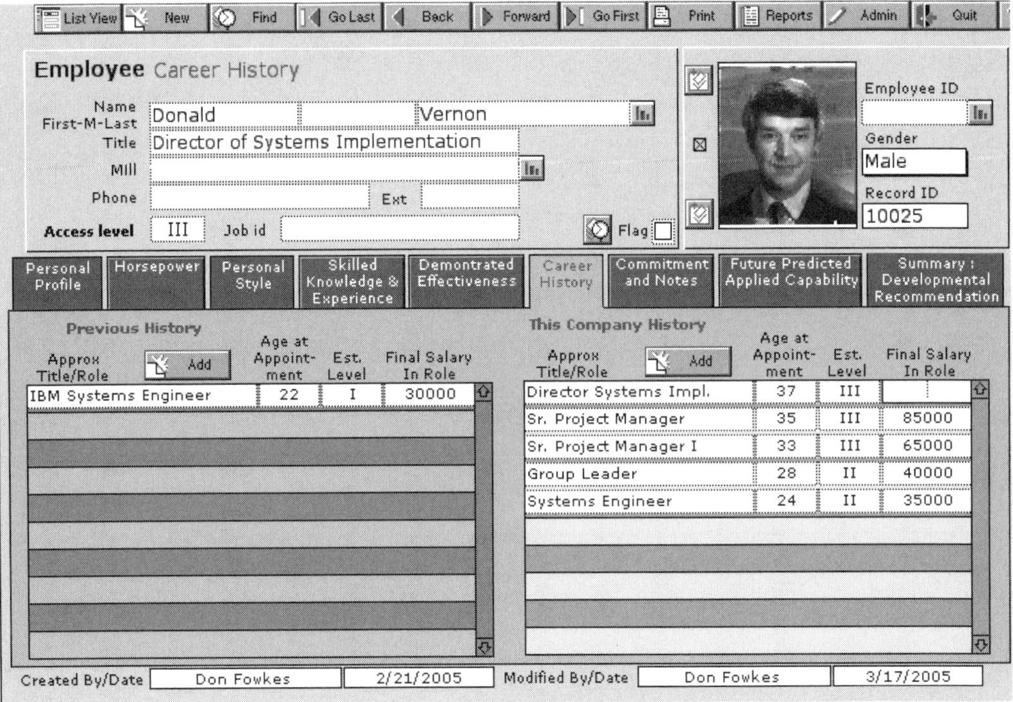

FIGURE 5.3.5

No more papers or forms that they need to lug around, which of course they won't do. So the Global Talent Management System incorporates historical effectiveness appraisal data, so that both managers and managers-once-removed can see how individuals have done in each job they've had with the company. This is important, because track record is a very good predictor of potential, and we need to balance our sense of potential with measures of actual performance. The file also contains information on work history in previous employment, which is helpful in forming an opinion of what gaps need to be filled, as in Figure 5.3.5.

Overall, we want the managers and managers-once-removed to agree on something we call "future predicted applied capability." This is a considered opinion, taking into account all of the data including forecasts of mature potential capability. We want agreement on how far the individual is likely to rise in this company, as indicated in Figure 5.3.6. Through cyberspace, we get independent readings from managers and managers-once-removed, and very often there is close agreement because our executives have become increasingly skilled as they have worked with the

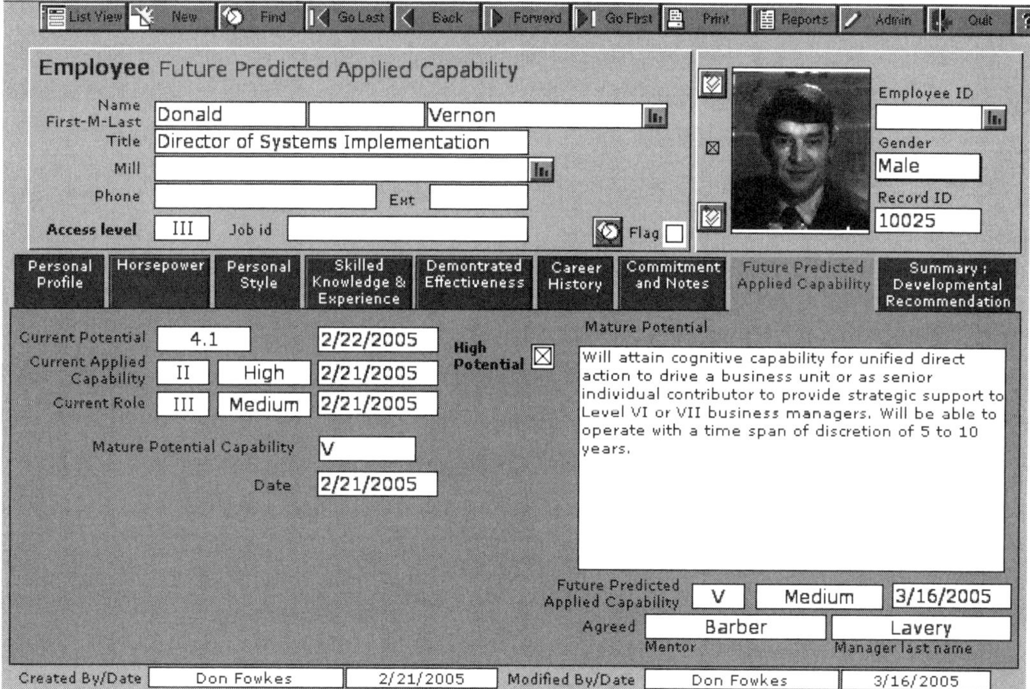

FIGURE 5.3.6

system. Of course, where there is disagreement we need to go back to them to sort it out, sometimes by email or by phone, and sometimes by sitting down together to hash it out.

Every year we want the manager and the manager-once-removed to agree on a developmental plan for the individual. We ask the individual to take the initiative in this because our philosophy is that people are accountable to take initiative for their own development.[3] So, the first ideas to appear in Figure 5.3.7 are entered by individuals, in terms of the experience they feel they need and the kind of educational programs that would help them as individuals.

Because the manager-once-removed is accountable for the long-term development of the people who work for his or her direct reports, this person has a key role in this area. He or she can take a point of view that may make it tough for the manager short term, but is beneficial in the long run. He or she has access to roles

---

3   Editorial note: According to Jaques's and Brown's model, the manager is accountable for development of an employee for his or her current role and the MoR is accountable for his or her development for future roles)

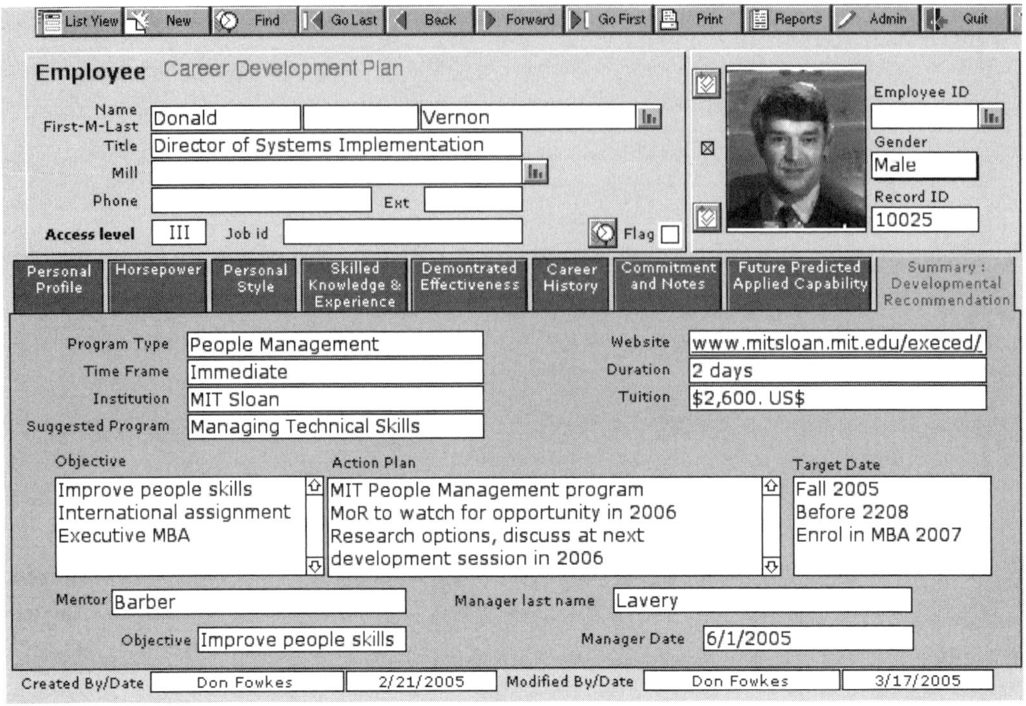

FIGURE 5.3.7

in other operating units or other businesses that might provide needed rounding. In the end, of course, we want a meeting of the minds. In practice, the most back-and-forth, and face-to-face discussion usually takes place around the highest potential people, as it should.

High flyer: "You know, career visibility is important. I need to know that how I'm doing and what I want to do is on the screen of the powers that be. If not, I'll go someplace where I'm seen."

One of the really important HR jobs here is keeping the Global Talent Management System files up-to-date and the processes moving. At corporate headquarters, we are accountable for managers in stratum IV roles and higher, which means plant managers, and equivalents in other functional areas. We rely on business unit HR to handle stratum I to III. Their work is very important, because they are the source of the talent stream we count on for the future.

We have a profile for each individual updated each year, like that in Figure 5.3.8. This snapshot is produced from our system, and is a good summary. We make this

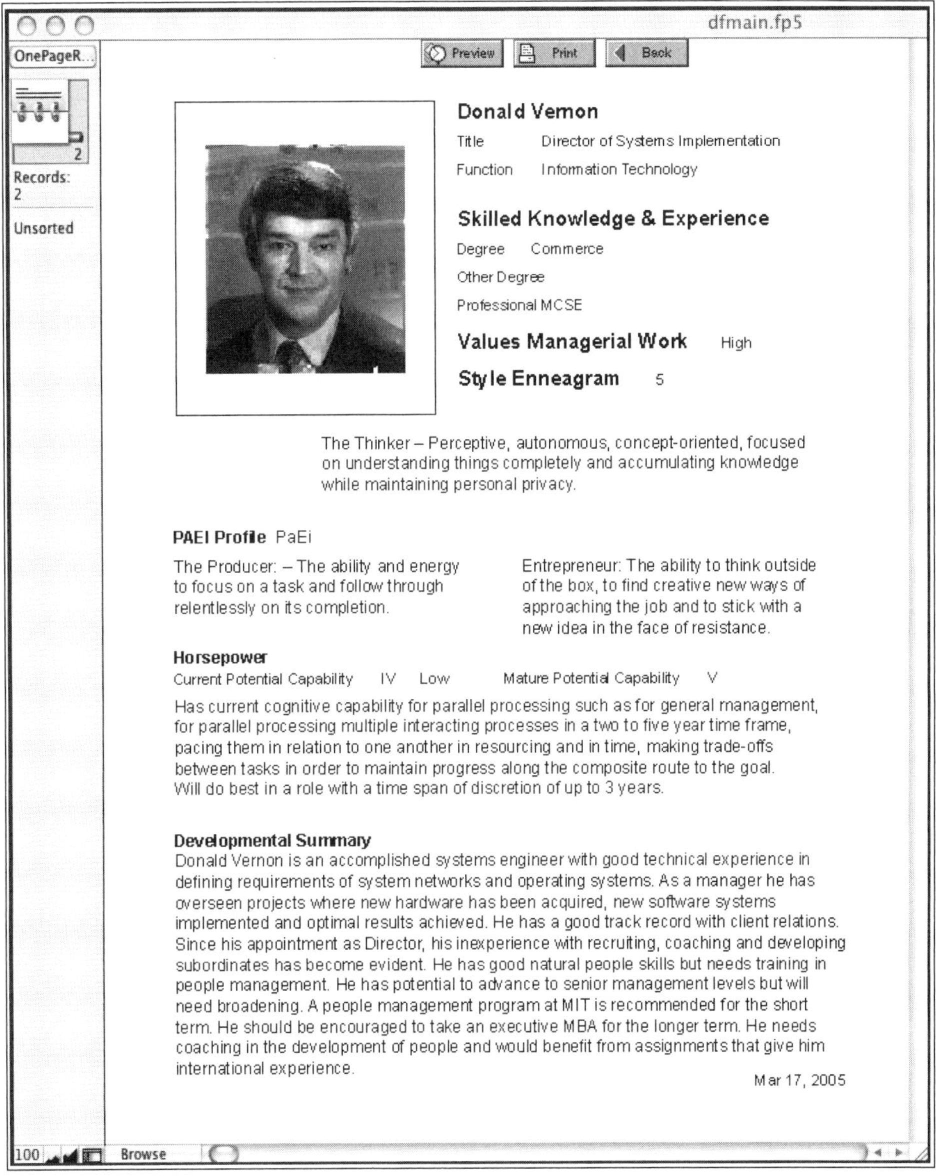

FIGURE 5.3.8

profile available to each individual every year. When we started out, our consultant insisted on having each individual review the profile for material errors before letting managers see it. We think it is important that the system be transparent, that people know what their file says about them. You'll notice that Figure 5.3.8 shows "mature potential" clearly. What this reveals is how far we think the person can go: what stratum they can eventually reach. Some companies keep this opinion hush-hush, because they are afraid of de-motivating people by telling them there are limits to their potential. Our experience has been that people usually are realistic about this. We like to be able to say, for example, someone has growth potential in stratum III and that he or she will likely have turn potential to a general management role in stratum IV by age 50. Then we and the individual can focus our attention on what skilled knowledge and experience are needed to actualize this, and how we can work together to make it happen. We think this is better than fostering unrealistic ambitions, or beating around the bush.

Sometimes people disagree with what we say about their potential, and we think it important to keep an open mind. We follow the practice of reviewing this every year. In some cases we will get third-party assessments done to sort out differences.

The profile makes for a talking point with the manager-once-removed. Managers-once-removed try to touch base, however briefly, with every subordinate-once-removed during the year. They tend to do this as they move around the company in the normal course of business, or maybe at annual offsite meetings.

For high-potential talent, managers-once-removed and managers sit down together with the individual for a good discussion. This ensures that good feedback is given from the immediate boss, and the boss's boss has firsthand exposure to the individual, and the individual can be assured that the manager-once-removed is looking out for him or her, and considering options in other divisions or units that may fit with the development plan.

Individuals keep their file up-to-date, with courses they take etc., and importantly with the first draft they make of their developmental plan. Individuals need to take initiative in making what is in the plan happen, to the degree they are within their authority. Superiors and HR need to open the way for other things.

Overall, this system keeps people from getting lost and overlooked, and we have a good track record of keeping the talent we want and need to support our future growth.

VP HR: "Our tendency in appointments has been to grab the closest warm body and get on with it. To have managers consider a broader group, including people they don't know, they need a simple way of getting the information, which should include track record, judgments on potential, and developmental needs."

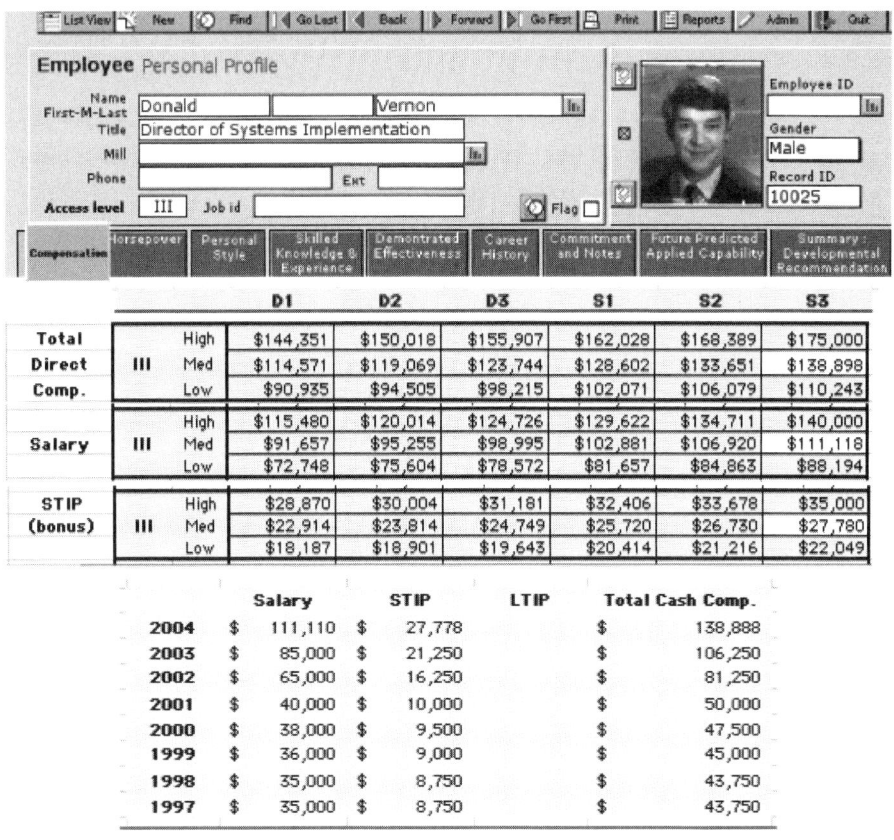

			D1	D2	D3	S1	S2	S3
Total	III	High	$144,351	$150,018	$155,907	$162,028	$168,389	$175,000
Direct		Med	$114,571	$119,069	$123,744	$128,602	$133,651	$138,898
Comp.		Low	$90,935	$94,505	$98,215	$102,071	$106,079	$110,243
Salary	III	High	$115,480	$120,014	$124,726	$129,622	$134,711	$140,000
		Med	$91,657	$95,255	$98,995	$102,881	$106,920	$111,118
		Low	$72,748	$75,604	$78,572	$81,657	$84,863	$88,194
STIP	III	High	$28,870	$30,004	$31,181	$32,406	$33,678	$35,000
(bonus)		Med	$22,914	$23,814	$24,749	$25,720	$26,730	$27,780
		Low	$18,187	$18,901	$19,643	$20,414	$21,216	$22,049

	Salary	STIP	LTIP	Total Cash Comp.
2004	$ 111,110	$ 27,778		$ 138,888
2003	$ 85,000	$ 21,250		$ 106,250
2002	$ 65,000	$ 16,250		$ 81,250
2001	$ 40,000	$ 10,000		$ 50,000
2000	$ 38,000	$ 9,500		$ 47,500
1999	$ 36,000	$ 9,000		$ 45,000
1998	$ 35,000	$ 8,750		$ 43,750
1997	$ 35,000	$ 8,750		$ 43,750

FIGURE 5.3.9

This has maybe been the toughest thing to implement. It requires managers to be willing to bend their urgent priorities a bit to get a solution that is better for the company as a whole. The key to it has been HR managers developing computer skills and spending the time sifting through the files, so that an array of alternative candidates comes up. To the degree that we have lead time with retirements or known moves, this allows us to make use of emerging vacancies to take staffing actions that are better for the people in the system and best for the company. Our better HR managers take their laptops into the boss's office, plug it into the on-line system, project it onto the wall, and run through a series of options.

COO: "I've got accountability for nine direct reports. And I've got manager-once-removed accountability for 47 others. I can't stay on top of this unless I've got all the information at my fingertips when I need it, including salary and incentive options."

It will be clear that we had the COO's concerns in mind when we put the system together the way we did.[4] As a matter of fact, we are still working with an awkward interface with the payroll system, but we are gradually getting to full integration.

Most recently, we have implemented a compensation module, based on "felt fair" pay structures. Now managers can make salary adjustment, short-term incentive and long-term incentive recommendations right in system, in the full context of all the information about individuals, as indicated in Figure 5.3.9.

Overall, we have a living, evolving system that provides the structure and discipline within which managers, from frontline to CEO, can make the judgments, take the decisions, and initiate the actions needed to build our inventory of talent, globally.

Of course, we didn't arrive to this happy state overnight, or all at once. We have been working at it for about seven years now. We started with clarifying the levels in our organization in terms of strata. We did this in rough terms, recognizing that we were a stratum VII company made up of a dozen or so stratum V business units. Within each of these we could see stratum IV general managers and senior functional jobs, supported by what we call directors at stratum III. Then we have frontline managers at stratum II. And as the company got bigger we had created group vice presidents at stratum VI. We didn't worry too much about a finer grid within strata, nor did we try to get the gaps filled or compression relieved. We left that for later.

We hired a skilled consulting firm to create the initial profiles of our stratum III+ people. Our goal has been to have our own managers skilled at making new profiles and keeping the talent pool up to date, but we couldn't start there because our people didn't have the skilled knowledge and experience to do it. We asked our consultants to feed back the draft profiles to individuals and to provide packages of profiles to each manager and manager-once-removed. And we asked our consultant to coach our managers on how to use the profiles, give the feedback, and get a good dialogue going. Then we insisted that our managers do the job of coaching as managers and mentoring as manager-once-removed.

4　The Global Talent Management System is implemented in Filemaker Pro.

It took maybe three years of iteration to get this about right across most of the company, breaking down reluctance to have candid discussion, building skills in giving feedback and interaction, and using gearing sessions when we could get them to get some consistency in our understanding of strata, skilled knowledge, and experience, the importance of style, and so on.

The results have been quite successful. We have developed a talent management succession planning system that provides effective feedback as part of the on-going dialogue, which is integral in developing the talent needed for the continued growth of the company.

ABOUT THE AUTHOR

Donald V. Fowke, FCMC is an experienced consultant in strategy, organization, and people development using the concepts of global organization design. He has assisted in defining business strategy and plans for companies in a variety of industries, designed organization structures, and change management programs to ensure implementation and follow-through on the strategy, assessed executives, and managers against the needs of the new roles, implemented talent pool systems. He has designed compensation incentives and "felt-fair" rewards throughout the organization.

Fowke holds a B.E. in mechanical engineering and a diploma in business administration from the University of Saskatchewan and an S.M. from MIT's Sloan School of Management. He was visiting scholar at the Graduate School of Public Policy at the University of California at Berkeley. He was chairman and chief executive officer of Hickling-Johnston Limited for ten years and managing director of William M. Mercer Limited for five. He is a professional engineer and a Fellow of the Institute of Management Consultants of Ontario. He was, for 12 years, a member of the Young Presidents' Organization, and is currently a member of the World Presidents' Organization.

PART SIX

The Dynamics of Implementing the Levels of Work Approach

The Dynamics of Implementing the Levels of Work Approach

Many are curious about the CEOs and organizations that elect to use part or all of requisite organization theory. Some have speculated that organizations where managers have technical training such as engineering or medicine are more attracted to the theory. Others say it's the capability and psycho-graphics of the CEO. **Glenn W. Mehltretter, Jr.** and **Michelle Malay Carter** introduce us to an intriguing new explanation of the leader and organizational characteristics related to varying interest and application of RO concepts in their article "Assessing Requisite Readiness."

Many executives take action on strategy, organizational design, staffing, and management system issues by following a colleague's success, a bench marking activity of best practices, an article or book they have read or perhaps take the recommendations of a well-recommended consulting firm. Often they may act on direction without really understanding the theory or evidence behind what they are doing. Is it just a fad? How solid is it? Do I understand it well enough? **Herb Koplowitz,**

Ph.D, a senior management consultant and a registered psychologist grounded in developmental theory and the philosophy of science, had the privilege of intellectual comradeship with Elliott Jaques over more than ten years. His own curiosity and questioning dialogues with Dr. Jaques on what in requisite organization was science and what was something else led to his stimulating article, "How Solid Is Requisite Organization?"

In his 2002 Keynote address to the Midwinter Conference of the Society of Consulting Psychology, Elliott Jaques first used the term "organizational engineering" to designate the field of organization and human resources management. This new term reflected the mature result of the evolution of the organizational problem-solving side of requisite organization theory. It is true that the term carries some unfortunate connotations, like the apparent lack of concern for human values such as mutual trust, personal achievement, job satisfaction, fairness and collaboration. **Harald Solaas**, an HR consultant and professor at the Universidad de Belgrano, in his article "Organizational Engineering and the CEO," writes about how he deals with a CEO's concerns about implementing requisite organization. The article notes that "organizational engineering" is really the engineering of mutual trust in human work organizations.

Assessing Requisite Readiness

Glenn W. Mehltretter, Jr. and Michelle Malay Carter

WHAT'S IMPORTANT

This article examines two developmental models that will help you:

- Learn how a CEO's current values stage and cognitive capacity influence the decision to implement all or part of requisite organization.

- Learn how to assess an organization's developmental stage and use this information to inform strategy decisions and the change management process.

- Learn how to assess whether an organization is ready for a total requisite organization implementation.

- Learn the points to consider when assessing whether certain parts of the requisite organization model will be congruent with an organization's current level of development.

In this article,[1] the authors explore why only a handful of organizations have adopted the full gamut of requisite organization (RO) principles and practices as their managerial leadership model despite RO's longstanding scientific validity and undeniable practicality.

The authors contend that, quite simply, the model is a solution before its time. As the business world develops, RO will become increasingly attractive to those wishing to take their organizations to the next level.

We live in a developmental universe. Levels, stages, and hierarchies abound with less complex ways and forms giving birth to more complex ways that transcend and include the former. Elliott Jaques found this to be true of both work and human capacity for work.

Jaques categorized work into strata, each stratum more complex than the former. Further, he discovered a complementary truth that human capability to perform work matures throughout adulthood. As one matures, he or she becomes capable of performing higher levels of work.

Work, as defined by Jaques, is the exercising of judgment and discretion to solve problems. As one's cognitive capacity matures, he or she is able to mentally manage more data, more variability, and higher-order models when searching for solutions.

Just as cognitive development can be mapped, values can be categorized into stages that grow in complexity, a common model being Maslow's Hierarchy, which ranges from an infant's concern for survival to the mature adult seeking self-actualization.

Cognitive and values development are just two pathways humans traverse. One's individual development progresses through multiple lines simultaneously to include moral, interpersonal, spiritual, and affective. Add to this that not only do individuals develop, but so do organizations, cultures, and countries, and it is evident that the unfolding nature of our universe permeates our lives. Consequently, when interacting with others, we take into account each other's level of development. For

---

1   © Copyright 2006 PeopleFit. Opinions expressed in this paper are solely those of the authors and do not necessarily reflect the opinions of the editors or the Global Organization Design Society as a whole.

instance, a mother does not feed her infant a steak dinner, but will offer a spoonful of mashed potatoes.

It is in this vein that the authors contend that for an organization to adopt the full breadth of RO principles and practices, the organization and its leadership must be at a minimum level of fairly sophisticated development in three areas: 1) leader capacity relative to strategy level, 2) organizational values stage (also referred to as developmental stage), and 3) skill competencies relative to values stage. Therefore, data gathering in these three arenas, leadership capacity, values, and skills, will allow organizational leaders and requisite practitioners to judge an organization's requisite readiness. The remainder of this article will examine these factors in relationship to readiness for RO.

Leader Capacity Relative to Strategy Level

Research suggests that in order for a leader to bring about transformational change within an organization, he or she must possess cognitive capacity one level beyond that which is requisite for his or her current role.[2] This excess capacity is necessary to step outside what is, then plan for and execute the transformation. Excess capacity is what makes some leaders yearn to take their organization "to the next level" for that is where they presently reside.

RO is a total systems model. According to the model, one must reach stratum V cognitive capability in order to be able to conceptualize a total system. Therefore, for an organization to transform from one operating model to a requisite, total-system model, the authors hypothesize that a stratum VI capable leader at the helm of a stratum V business is ideal.

A stratum V capable leader running a stratum V business can bring about growth and *incremental* change, but he or she will not succeed at bringing about transformational change, as it takes capacity one level beyond the level of the current business. The authors assert that barring external pressure, a self-aware stratum V leader of a stratum V organization will not seek to transform the organization to another higher-level model as this process will prove to be over his head and beyond his grasp—a formula for personal failure.

---

2   Mehltretter, G. W. *The Contribution of Complexity of Mental Processing and Stage of Ego Development to Transforming Leadership.* University Microfilms No. 9621946, 1996.

The authors are currently engaged in a total RO transformation with a stratum VI capable leader running a stratum V organization. The leader of this organization partnered with the authors to apply portions of RO for a decade before committing to undertake the transformation of his entire business unit. During the latter part of that decade, he matured from stratum V capability to stratum VI. This evidence supports the two aforementioned hypotheses: excess capacity is needed for transformation and to implement a total-system change, a stratum VI leader at the helm of a stratum V business is ideal.

Additional evidence supporting the need for excess capacity can be found in a review of the total quality movement. During the 1980s and 1990s, about 20 percent of organizations that attempted to adopt a total quality mode of business were successful at a transformative level. The authors' data from extensive talent pool evaluation work suggests that about 20 percent of employees within managerial hierarchies have capacity one level above their current role. If this is true for CEOs, then 20 percent of the attempting organizations had leaders possessing the excess mental horsepower to make the transformation. In addition to leadership cognitive capacity, organizational values stage is likely another contributing factor to the total quality boom. This factor will be examined next.

Organizational Values Stage (or Developmental Stage)

The developmental nature of values has long been understood. The authors will use the Spiral Dynamics model, originated by Dr. Clare W. Graves and expanded upon by Don Edward Beck and Christopher C. Cowan,[3] to discuss their observations regarding developmental stage and requisite readiness. While Graves' model is featured in this article, Brian Hall's model,[4] which aligns closely with Graves' model, has also influenced their thinking.

Developmental stages can be thought of as *worldviews*, i.e., the set of values one applies in viewing and understanding the world.

Beck's and Cowan's work explores these worldviews in depth. Ronnie Lessem says the following about Beck and Cowan's developmental stages.

---

3   Beck, D. E. and Cowen, C. C. *Spiral Dynamics: Mastering Values, Leadership, and Change.* Malden, MA: Blackwell, 1996, 2006.

4   Hall, B. *Values Shift: A Guide to Personal & Organizational Transformation.* Rockport, MA: Twin Lights, 1994.

BLUE Truth	ORANGE Prosperity	GREEN Communitarian	YELLOW Systemic
→→→**TRANSCEND AND INCLUDE**→→→			
• Only one right way	• Compete for success	• Seeks inner peace	• Big picture views
• Sacrifice for purpose	• Goal-oriented drives	• Everybody is equal	• Integrative structures
• Orders from authority	• Change to progress	• Everything is relative	• Naturalness of chaos
• Do right, obey rules	• Material gain/perks	• Harmony in the group	• Inevitability of change
• Adhere to tradition	• Bottom-line results	• Reach consensus	• Highly principled
• Promote via seniority	• Experiment to win	• Collaborate	• Knowledge-centered
• Cautious and careful	• Successful win spoils	• Accept any input	• Competent get spoils
• Conserve	• Consult experts	• Communal spoils	• Self-directed
• Righteous earn spoils	• Upwardly mobile	• Explore feelings	• Takes each as is
• Rewards to come	• Image-conscious	• Belonging, acceptance	• Does more with less
• Guilt and punishment	• High-tech, high-status	• Participative activity	• Power is dispersed
• Know-your-place	• Wants to prosper now	• Social safety nets	• Life is learning
• Moralistic	• Leverages influence	• Politically correct	• Intrigued by process

Adapted from *Spiral Dynamics: Mastering Values, Leadership, and Change*

TABLE 6.1.1: DEVELOPMENTAL VALUES STAGE (PARTIAL LIST)

Each...reflects a worldview, *a valuing system, a level of psychological existence, a belief structure, an organizing principle, a way of thinking or a mode of adjustment. It represents, firstly then, a core intelligence that forms the systems and directs human behavior. Secondly, it impacts upon all life choices as a decision-making framework. Thirdly, each* worldview *can manifest itself in both healthy and unhealthy forms. Fourthly, such a* worldview *is a discrete structure for thinking, not just a set of ideas, values or cause. Finally, it can brighten and dim as the Life Conditions (consisting of historic times, geographic place, existential problems and societal circumstances) change.*[5]

Beck and Cowan use colors to differentiate one worldview from another. Although Beck and Cowan have identified seven stages, this article focuses on the third through sixth—blue, orange, green, yellow—as they represent the levels of development that characterize first world organizations.

The table above, adapted from *Spiral Dynamics*, summarizes the values that permeate the various levels.

---

5   Beck, D. E. and Cowen, C. C. Spiral Dynamics: Mastering Values, Leadership, and Change. Malden, MA: Blackwell, 1996, 2006. pp. 4-5. We changed the word "v-meme" to "worldview"

Skill Competencies Relative to Values Stage

As organizations face increasing challenges, they must progress through these stages of development to survive, and the models they adopt as templates to realize their higher-order strategies become more complex. Thus, the individuals within these organizations must acquire knowledge and learn new skills in order to "live out" higher-order, more complex values and strategies.

A mindset shift will not suffice. Organizations cannot plan their way to the next level of development, create fancy slogans, print posters, and wait for the change to occur. If the CEO and a core group of the executive team have not developed their value set to the place that this latest solution demands, excessive "talking the talk" will not give way to "walking the walk," as was likely the case with many of the unsuccessful total quality initiatives.

In order for execution to occur, a mindset and authentic value shift must be accompanied by the skill development necessary in order to "live out" the new mindset. Moreover, this skill development must take place at all levels of the organization. Many well-intentioned organizations spend millions on training their non-executive staff only to find it does not "stick" once the employees return from training. A mindset shift and skill development will only be effective if organizational systems, structure, policies, and practices are aligned to facilitate the shift. Creating systems and infrastructure to support the new value set is a key part of the skill development necessary at the executive level. The authors' experience bears that even with serious commitment to new ways, old habits die hard. Frequently opportunities for practice, feedback, and reinforcement of new skills are necessary. The learning curve is messy and awkward.

Then, as the developmental universe would have it, just as an organization begins to master skills and conquer the issues of its current level, a sense that there is something more to the picture will arise. Moving to the next level brings increased capacity and the ability to resolve the issues created by the previous level; however, new levels subsequently create new issues that only the next order of thinking will be able to contain, and the stretch toward this new way of living and thinking will begin. This satiate-and-stretch cycle repeats at higher and higher orders. Although the movement is primarily forward, instability and stress can cause an organization to regress to lower levels.

A historical review of United States industry demonstrates several iterations of this satiate-and-shift cycle. Post World War II was blue-centric with an emphasis on following rules, paying dues, and working up the ladder via tenure. In return for being loyal and following the rules, organizations offered lifetime employment and hefty pensions. During this era, organizations focused on stability and order. Bureaucracy and excessive layers abounded. Change and risk-taking were avoided. The existence of labor unions is consistent with this worldview. Governmental regulation was common as evidenced in the utility and airline industries.

As the US began to face global competition in the 1970s and 1980s, the need for a shift in values arose out of a change in life conditions. Those heavily entrenched in a blue worldview were shocked and dismayed as Americans began driving Japanese-made cars. A small cohort of Americans was emerging that was no longer interested in sacrificing for the greater good (of the US in this case), a blue value. Instead, this cohort was interested in better, faster, cheaper, orange values. As more individuals stretched toward orange, the organizations they populated began to reflect this reality as well. Yet, not all organizations responded to the changing marketplace and culture. The authors are currently working with a regulated utility company still entrenched in the blue worldview. The organization foresees imminent deregulation and understands that adopting an orange value system is necessary for it to compete in an open market.

As has been said, when the student is ready, the teacher will appear. In the 1970s and 1980s when blue organizations began to experience the limitations of their worldview and were suffering an inability to adapt and compete, they began searching for tools and templates to take them to the next level, orange. Out of these conditions arose the total quality movement of the 1980s and 1990s. A majority of the tools found in this model embrace bottom-line results, continuous improvement, and increasing quality. *Management by Objectives*, *In Search of Excellence*, and *The One Minute Manager* are consistent with orange values. Privatization and deregulation occurred in the utility and airline industries as competition became the answer of the day.

Orange values and all value stages have a healthy time and place within organizations, but each may also manifest in ominous ways. For example, when number-crunching becomes an organization's primary focus, employees become simply another resource to be used and discarded in an effort to reach "the goal." When bonus programs and commission sales systems pit employees or departments against one another, the system can become toxic. This toxicity was evident during the 1990s as organization after organization fell prey to scandalous behavior and/or bankruptcy.

About this time, uneasiness began to resonate in some organizations. Many pined for the good old days of blue values. However, this yearning was misplaced, as blue solutions could not meet the more complex demands of the current conditions, and the stretch toward harmony-centric green values began in the leading-edge cohort of organizations.

During the 1990s, an uprising of political correctness, diversity initiatives, wellness programs, interpersonal skill development, and work-life balance began to appear as people sought to heal themselves from the burnout they had suffered at the hands of orange values. Executives worked with coaches to process emotions, to negotiate win-win solutions, and to become sensitive to the needs of others. Executives were called upon to be stewards and servants, not movers and shakers. Organizational development consultants called for dialogue, conflict resolution training, and appreciative inquiry as a means for enhancing communication, facilitating sharing, and creating learning organizations. Tolerance abounded; all views were heard; decisions were made by consensus. Underdogs were surrounded by helpers. Employees were called upon to be open, cooperate, and collaborate. Consequently, the skills they developed in the orange worldview, although useful and necessary, were now inadequate to "live out" green values.

Newly green organizations found themselves bloated from overly ambitious acquisitions undertaken during the orange stage and began to shed non-core businesses. After returning to their cores, companies began pursuing strategic alliances—viewing former competitors as potential partners. Outsourcing became a key strategy. Like hand in glove, the green skill base was particularly critical to managing these alliances. For a while, all felt right as the benefits of this tight-knit, harmonic, egalitarian world were reaped. Some leading-edge organizations are still experiencing this place of contentment.

However, a parallel reality is in play during this harmonious time. When operating under green values, systems and structure are generally downplayed or even dismantled. This hard-won freedom eventually becomes a liability as the green organization struggles to balance competition, caring for people, managing its business, and interacting with partners and vendors all at the hands of long-atrophied systems. Eventually green organizations find the cost of caring for people is too great. The collective process consumes too much time and the price of keeping everybody happy exacts its toll on the bottom line. Change must occur or bankruptcy will.

The authors of *Spiral Dynamics* and the authors of this article agree that RO in its complete, total-system form is a solution appropriate for a yellow environment, the stage beyond green. The authors speculate that nearly all US organizations currently "reside" in the blue, orange, or green stages, with the overwhelming majority still firmly rooted in orange. Canada and some northern European countries seem more strongly rooted in the green value set with more collective systems like national healthcare and more redistribution of wealth via higher taxes, and thus their organizations reflect a greener value set. This is likely why RO has a stronger following in Canada than the US as Canada has a value set closer to that of RO.

The authors believe that this understanding of the yellow values embedded in the RO model answers the authors' initial question: Why have only a handful of organizations adopted the full gamut of RO principles and practices as their managerial leadership model? Quite simply, the sophistication level of the RO model provides an action strategy slightly ahead of the challenges faced by most of today's organizations. They do not adopt it, because they do not yet see the need for it. As organizations continue to satiate-and-stretch, more will seek the RO model as the most congruent and logical way to pursue their yellow values.

In the words of Beck and Cowan, "An individual, a company, or an entire society can respond positively only to those managerial principles, motivational appeals, educational formulas, and legal or ethical codes that are appropriate to the current level of human existence."[6]

Thus, the authors assert that attempting a *total RO implementation* within organizations with lower levels of development will not succeed due to incongruent mindsets, skills, and systems. For example, incentive compensation can play a positive role in an orange organization pushing for bigger, better, and greater ways. The skills developed around incentive pay in the orange worldview may be a next logical step beyond the entitlement, tenure-based value system that pervades the blue stage. However, incentive pay is not appropriate in a yellow-value environment, as it interferes with cross-functional alignment, a core yellow value.

---

6   Beck, D. E. and Cowen, C. C. *Spiral Dynamics: Mastering Values, Leadership, and Change.* Malden, MA: Blackwell, 1996, 2006. p. 29.

Similarly, although total quality was mostly packaged and sold using orange-worldview buzzwords, such as continuous improvement, efficiency, and effectiveness, according to Beck and Cowan, some key elements of Deming's philosophy were higher-stage concepts. Deming's call for the removal of fear and appraisal-type ratings of people is one example. Interestingly, these points, which strongly conflict with the orange value of competition, were largely ignored during the total quality explosion. Thus, some would argue that total quality, implemented in its complete form, is a yellow-worldview solution as well.

Hence, endless debates about best practices and the "right" way to do things are a waste of time. Solutions must be considered in light of current life conditions, as different conditions call for different solutions.

Does this mean that RO has no place in organizations that have not yet developed to the yellow worldview? No. The authors' consulting experience bears that certain requisite tools and teachings can be contained by organizations that have not yet reached a yellow stage of development. Matching RO tools to developmental stages is a subject for future research.

Can Levels Be Skipped?

A natural question that follows the preceding argument is: Can levels be skipped? If an organization decides it wants to become requisite, can it leap over intervening levels to get to yellow? It appears that just as a baby who does not crawl before walking will encounter depth-perception deficiencies later, people and organizations that miss pieces of development along the way will be incapacitated in some manner at a later stage. Beck and Cowan assert and the authors' experience bears that it does not appear that organizations can skip levels of development without consequences. Hence, some organizations may discover the need for remedial skill building in order to "live their values."

For example, the authors' are currently working with a client who has had success in implementing a series of requisite practices and polices over the course of the last year. However, the organization is finding it more difficult to facilitate collaborative cross-functional working relationships, one of the more complex, higher-order RO endeavors.

Observing the leadership team at work reveals deeply entrenched orange-stage behaviors to include interrupting, ignoring, and competitiveness between functions. This orange value system facilitated its ability to grow and compete in the marketplace until now, but it is no longer serving the team as it attempts to move to the next level. It appears a concerted effort in green-value skill building, collaboration, negotiation, listening, and conflict resolution, will be necessary for this client to embrace yellow-stage processes.

Conclusion

RO is not *the* solution. It is *a* solution for the discontented green organization with a leader possessing capacity beyond his or her role, looking for a model that will allow him or her to both care for his or her people and get work done. The system integration and cross-functional collaboration combined with managerial accountability and authority outlined in the RO model facilitates this best-of-both-worlds desire. It is the *requisite* solution for this set of life conditions; that is, as called for by the nature of things.

RO practitioners and interested executives will do well to assess organizations in three key areas: 1) leader capacity relative to strategy level, 2) organizational values stage, and 3) skill competencies relative to values stage, and then offer teaching and tools that will tend to the organization's current life conditions. Many requisite tools and practices can be embraced within blue, orange, and green organizations. Its application is not limited to yellow-worldview organizations.

Looking to the future, it is not a question of *if* requisite organization in its full form will become widely adopted, it is *when*. When will a cohort of organizations begin moving toward a yellow stage and quite naturally embrace this well-crafted yellow solution? The authors believe this will occur over the next few decades.

Final Thoughts on Jaques's Legacy

Human nature is such that people at higher levels of development often respond to those at lower levels of development with paternalism and condescension while thinking: those poor people; they don't know what they don't know. Similarly, when humans are confronted with people several levels of development beyond themselves, they tend to respond with fear and vilify the "fringe" person or group with responses such as: "Those heretics; how dare they disparage all we hold dear?"

Elliott Jaques, a man before his time, was often vilified. It is sad and ironic that social justice was of great concern to Jaques. The authors believe that eventually, it will be clear that the value set embedded in RO is one deeply committed and enhancing to human dignity and well-being at work, and consequently, Jaques will earn his place in history as the passionate humanitarian the authors knew him to be.

ABOUT THE AUTHORS

Dr. Glenn W. Mehltretter, Jr. is founder and president of PeopleFit® management consulting firm founded in 1981. A researcher, consultant, and executive coach, he travels internationally to speak about the tools and processes he developed to apply RO theory in the areas of organizational design, strategy, and talent management. He regularly provides training to RO consultants in his cutting-edge work in assessing cognitive capacity.

His firm has accumulated more than 5,000 data points in matching people to roles and that data was the basis for the creation of the PeopleFit Integrity Index, a benchmarking measure for effectiveness in deploying human resource talent.

Michelle Malay Carter, a consultant with PeopleFit, has 15 years of experience in training and organizational development, as well as several years' experience in marketing and communications.

An author and speaker, her writing has been featured on HR.com, and she served as a visiting lecturer at NC State University.

Her graduate thesis related her experiences using requisite organization principles to create a selection and succession strategy within a national sales department.

She holds a B.S. in Journalism/Advertising from Kent State University, an M.A. in Organizational Development from NC State University, and a certificate in OD from UNC-Charlotte.

How Solid Is Requisite Organization?

Herb Koplowitz, Ph.D.

My dear Wormwood,

...(A) few centuries earlier ... the humans still knew pretty well when a thing was proved and when it was not; and if it was proved they really believed it. They still connected thinking with doing and were prepared to alter their way of life as the result of a chain of reasoning. But what with the weekly press and other such weapons we have largely altered that. Your man has become accustomed, ever since he was a boy, to have a dozen incompatible philosophies dancing about together inside his head. He doesn't think of doctrines as primarily "true" or "false", but as "academic" or "practical", "outworn" or "contemporary", "conventional" or "ruthless". Jargon, not argument, is your best ally in keeping him from the Church. Don't waste time trying to make him think that materialism is true! Make him think it is strong, or stark, or courageous- that it is the philosophy of the future. That's the sort of thing he cares about.

—C. S. Lewis[1]

If you are an executive considering use of requisite organization, the solidity of RO is important for three reasons.

1. You must assure yourself that RO will help you effectively implement your strategy in an efficient and trust-building manner. There is no shortage of theories, models, and guidelines for structuring, staffing, and managing, and you need to have confidence that the choice you make is solid.

2. You need to understand how you can modify the approach without losing its benefits. This will require you to understand what makes the approach solid.

3. You are likely to come into disagreements with others in your organization about your new ways of designing and managing your organization. To address their concerns, you must have an understanding of what gives RO its power

This article describes a way of understanding RO that will help you test the approach for yourself, adapt it to your circumstances, and meet the concerns of others in your organization. The core of the article is focused on the understanding of RO as a discipline comprising three levels, each serving as the foundation of the next:

1. The *language* is the system of concepts we use to understand the work world.

2. The *science* tells us, in terms provided by the language, what is true about the world of work.

---

1   Lewis, C. S. *The Screwtape Letters.* San Francisco: Harper, 1942. pp. 11-12,

3. The *engineering* comprises templates (e.g. give each employee a manager one stratum higher) and methods (e.g. the time-span interview) grounded in the science for solving real-life problems.

I shall describe each of these and show how distinguishing among them can help you navigate these potentially troubling waters.

The Three Levels

Language

The language is the system of concepts we use to make sense of and describe organizational issues. It is the conceptual aspect of what Thomas Kuhn (1962) called a "paradigm".[2] Our language influences what we pay attention to and how we diagnose organizational problems. Much of management literature focuses on culture and personality, and many executives try to fix organizational issues by building a sales culture or by hiring people of a certain personality type. They make sense of the situation they are in by calling it a "cultural problem" or a "personality problem." The concepts used specifically in RO focus on trust, work, and the ability to do work and lead to diagnoses centered on accountability and capability. They lead to making sense of a situation by calling it an "accountability problem" or a "capability problem." RO's language includes the following elements:

- *Work.* Work is the exercise of judgment and discretion while engaged in a task.
- *Complexity of work in a role.* One role can be said to require more complex work than another.
- *Potential of an individual.* We can say of two people that one of them can do more complex work than the other. We call this property "cognitive capacity" also referred to as capacity for information processing (CIP) and mental complexity.
- *Responsibility vs. accountability.* Holding someone accountable is different from that same person's feeling responsible.
- *Applied capability.* Applied capability is what an employee will do, and it is determined by cognitive capacity, skills and knowledge, and values (motivation).

---

2   Kuhn, Thomas. *The Structure of Scientific Revolutions.* Chicago: The University of Chicago Press, 1962.

(This assumes that the individual is not hindered by alcoholism, uncontrollable rage, crippling anxiety, etc.)

The language determines what data we look for and how we make sense of the data we observe. It is the lens through which we view organizations and people at work in them.

All those who write about the workplace have their own language, which is often not noticed if common terms, like "employee," "skill," and "manager," are used, even though these terms may carry a specific meaning within the approach. Significant terms in the index of *Requisite Organization*,[3] from "accountability" to "work" are absent from the index of *Good to Great*.[4] But the latter includes "core ideology," "level 5 leadership," (within Collins' model of five approaches to leadership, unrelated to stratum)and "passion," all absent from the former. Clearly, Jaques and Collins look for and see very different issues, strengths, and problems when they look at the same organization.

Two RO concepts in particular can be problematic to an executive.

1. *Cognitive capacity.* This is an employee's raw ability to handle complexity. Most managers find this concept helps them understand issues in their own career and problems they have had with subordinates. But a few managers believe that all people have the same potential. They understand capability to be all about effort, skill, and knowledge. They believe that anyone can acquire the skill and knowledge to solve any problem if they just try hard enough. If you talk about a subordinate of theirs who obviously tries hard but continues to fail at some complex task, they will say, "Yes. I just have not been able to find out how to explain to them how to do this task." They will not say, "Oh, I get it. Sandy lacks the cognitive capacity to handle a task of this complexity."

2. *Subjectivity.* Some aspects of the work world are objective; one can count the number of employees in a unit, measure the output of a machine, and calculate the profit of a business unit. RO is based on the concept that some aspects of the work world are inherently subjective. Managers judge the following:

- Their own satisfaction with a subordinate's performance,
- How big a given role needs to be, and
- Whether to discontinue a given product.

---

3   Jaques, E. *Requisite Organization: A Total System for Effective Managerial Organization and Managerial Leadership for the 21st Century.* Arlington, VA: Cason Hall and Co. Publishers, 1996.
4   Collins, J. *Good to Great.* New York: HarperCollins Publishers Inc., 2001.

Of course, managers consider all the relevant objective data they can gather, but no formula turns those data into a decision. The language of many managers, however, includes a belief that everything can be made objective. They would remove managerial judgment from significant decisions through intricate bonus formulas, point systems to determine the size of a role, and complex ROI calculations to determine whether to discontinue a product. Point out to such managers that raters routinely fudge the job evaluation figures to ensure that the end result is consistent with their own judgment of the size of a role and they will say, "That just shows that the job evaluation system doesn't have the formula right." They will not say, "Oh, I get it. Some things are just subjective and must be arrived at through judgment."

The first test of the solidity of RO is whether its concepts make sense to you. If it does not make sense to you that one role may have more or less complex work than another, or that one employee may have more or less potential than another, or that some issues in the work world cannot be decided objectively, then the language will not feel solid to you. As that language is the foundation of the science and the engineering, you are unlikely to be comfortable with RO engineering templates and methods.

Consider the drawing that can be seen either as a picture of an old woman or a young woman. How do you show others the young woman? You may explain, "This line is her nose, this is the edge of her scarf. See? It's a drawing of a young woman." You cannot prove that this is truly a picture of a young woman or that it is really an old woman. Similarly, when you explain an employee's failure as the result of insufficient cognitive capacity, you are not proving that it is wrong to view capability in terms only of skill, knowledge, and effort. Rather, you are helping managers make sense of employees' problems in a new way. The value of cognitive capacity as a concept is not its truth, but the help it gives us in making sense of the work world. Over time, the manager may come to see that cognitive capacity helps them understand situations that had previously resisted their attempts to make sense of. Over time, practices like talent gearing, grounded in the concept of cognitive capacity, may prove useful to managers and they may see the world through a different lens. Until that happens, they will follow procedures because they are required to not because they expect them to be helpful. You may require them to take part in talent-gearing sessions and to make use of other managerial practices grounded in cognitive capacity, but they will only change their way of understanding the work world over time as they come to see how RO helps to them understand situations they have no other way of understanding.

Science

Science is the system of facts, e.g. causal relationships, that describes objective reality. Science is about objective truth, the aspects of reality we all see in the same way. You and I may disagree about how beautiful a painting is, but we should agree on how long and wide it is. We may disagree on whether we like Sandy, but if we disagree on whether Sandy is stratum III capable then at least one of us is wrong. And we can examine the evidence and agree as to whether Sandy's cognitive capacity has matured along the path predicted by the progression charts.

Language gives us the terms that the science is expressed in. So the science in RO is about trust, work, and capability rather than about what creates passion, what makes someone a level 5 leader, or what level 5 leadership accomplishes. Some of the facts in RO's science generate little controversy:

- Complexity of work and capability are both stratified. People generally accept, value, and benefit from guidance and ongoing accountability more from someone a stratum more capable than themselves than from someone at their own level.
- People will fail at work beyond their own level of capability and will generally be bored in work at below their own level of capability.
- Treating people with disrespect lowers trust.

Some of the science in RO is not immediately obvious and even runs counter to conventional wisdom.

- You can tell how big a role is and what it should be paid just by finding the length of the longest task in it. (Conventional wisdom is that it takes complex analysis to determine the size of a role and that one must consider factors such as the amount of risk entailed, the number of people managed, etc.)
- Good teamwork depends on coordination of the work of the team members. (Conventional wisdom is that teamwork comes from consensus about team goals and from members' understanding and liking each other.)
- Cognitive capacity matures according to the progression curves. (Conventional wisdom is that there are things we can do to make people smarter—not just more skilled or knowledgeable, but more able to handle complexity.)

If you find RO's science credible, you will likely feel on solid ground with the approach. If others in your organization have difficulty with the science, they can be persuaded with evidence because these are matters of fact. I have more than once done time-span interviews, partnering with an internal HR person who was skeptical that a role can be measured simply by finding the length of the longest task in it. At the end of the first day of joint interviewing, my internal partner will often say, "When you told me about time span this morning, I did not believe it would measure the size of a role. Now that I've seen it in action, I am convinced that it does measure a role."

Engineering

Most of the management literature is about what might be called "craft," where designs are justified by precedent or best practices. (See the distinctions drawn by Harald Solaas later in this book.[5]) *Good to Great*, perhaps the best-known recent study of craft, yields very valuable information on what templates and methods have been used in great companies, but does not research the underlying psychology of level 5 leadership. Like craft, *engineering* has methods and templates for solving real-life problems, in this case, the problems of effectively pursuing strategic targets in an efficient and trust-building manner. In contrast to craft, engineering is grounded in science. Each RO template is justified by scientific fact.

- Give employees a manager one stratum above them: managers at the same stratum as their subordinates will not add managerial value and subordinates may resent taking direction from managers who feel more like peers.
- Give each employee one manager: An employee with more than one manager will be pulled in too many directions and will lose trust in the organization.
- Define *employee* as someone who, in exchange for a salary, is accountable for a) working with full commitment on tasks assigned by the manager, b) giving the manager his or her best advice, and c) staying within policy: If you make employees accountable for their own output (e.g. by giving them bonuses for their output) you make it difficult for their managers to get them to do work that is not bonused.

---

5   Solaas, H. "Organizational Engineering and the CEO." *The Executive's Guide to Organization Design, Levels of Work, and Human Capability.* Shepard, K., Gray, J., and Hunt, J. (eds.); pending publication, July 2007.

The scientific basis of each template allows us to know why the template works, the conditions in which it works, and how we might modify it under different conditions. For example, you may find that you have a manager at stratum IV with a subordinate at stratum II. The engineering templates recommend a one-stratum difference between managers and subordinates, but before adding another layer at stratum III, ask yourself what problems the science predicts will result from your current structure:

- There will be poor manager-subordinate communication, because the manager speaks in terms too abstract for the subordinate to understand.
- The manager, being bored with discussions regarding stratum II concerns, will not coach well.
- The subordinate will not know what to do nor whether he or she has done it well, because the manager lacks the patience to discuss such matters at the level required.
- The stratum IV manager does not do stratum IV work because he or she is bogged down. The manager must do the stratum III work and may find it easier to do some of the stratum II work than to explain to subordinates the work that must be done.

Thinking about the scientific assumptions behind a template allows you to determine whether those assumptions apply in your case.

- Is there good communication between the stratum IV manager and stratum II subordinate, because the manager is particularly skilled at explaining matters two strata below?
- Is there little work to be done at stratum III in that area?

In this case, the marginal gains in effectiveness and efficiency from hiring a manager at stratum III may not justify the additional costs.

Because craft is grounded in precedent, it gives us little guidance as to how to modify templates. From a craft approach, we may have some sense as to how Wal-Mart structures its logistics department, but we may not know which aspects of that approach need to be modified for our organization. In contrast, the science underlying RO's engineering helps predict the consequences of following, adapting, or violating RO templates.

Two other considerations should affect your decision whether to modify RO templates. First, the RO templates are uniquely complete and integrated. They cover structure, staffing, management, compensation, talent pool development, and team-work, and the templates in each area are consistent and interdependent with those in all of the other areas. If you modify the compensation template, for example, by offering output-based bonuses, you need to recognize the impact this will have on other templates; it will be difficult to hold managers accountable for their subordinates' outputs if your compensation system entices the subordinates to focus on bonused outputs and therefore to lose focus on other accountabilities.

The second consideration is that the value of the templates depends on certain assumptions that may not apply to your situation. Three are particularly salient:

1. All of the templates are in place. Having a manager and subordinate at the same stratum may not itself present much of an additional problem if none of your managers are well trained in task assignment, coaching, and the other managerial leadership practices and if you have no intention of providing such training soon.

2. Strategy and good management require the same structure. As in our example above, your strategy may call for a stratum IV and a stratum II employee in a certain department where there is little stratum III work. Particularly in small companies, it may be impractical to have all of the roles required for ideal management.

3. You are concerned with building the good society as well as with maximizing profits. Some of the RO templates are more designed to be consistent with a fair society than to maximize effectiveness, efficiency, and trust within your own organization. Following the felt-fair pay templates may require you to pay more for certain roles than the local market requires and that may put you at a competitive disadvantage. You must decide how to handle conflicts between building the profitable company and building the good society.

The test of a language is, "Does it help make sense of the data we have?" and the test of science is, "Is it true?" The test of engineering is, "Is it useful?" The final test of the solidity of RO is whether its engineering helps you create and develop an organization that effectively pursues and adjusts strategic targets, does this efficiently at lowest cost and in least time and is trustworthy, ensuring employees they will be treated respectfully. You are unlikely to test this rigorously. You can, however, play out scenarios to judge whether any other approach would be of greater help in addressing the issues you are facing. Figure 6.2.1 summarizes the features of language, science, and engineering.

LEVEL	PURPOSE	CONTEXT	RO EXAMPLES	RELATIONSHIP TO LEVEL ABOVE
Language	Help make sense of issues	• Concepts • Relationships among concepts	• Cognitive capacity • Applied capability = cognitive capacity + skills and knowledge + values	
Science	Describe objective truth	• Causal laws • Facts	• Felt-fair pay curve • There are four processes for information	Facts and laws of science are expressed in terms from the language
Engineering	Solve real-life problems	• Templates • Methods	• One level/stratum • Talent pool assessment process	Templates and methods are justified by laws of science

FIGURE 6.2.1: FEATURES OF LANGUAGE, SCIENCE, AND ENGINEERING

Implications

A major focus of this article has been helping you test the solidity of RO and meet the concerns others in your organization may have about it. My advice has been that you start by clarifying the nature and purpose of any statement that is controversial. Determine whether it is a statement of

- *Language*: helping you make sense of the world of work,
- *Science*: telling you what is true about that world, or
- *Engineering*: helping you solve organization problems.

If others in your organization are uncomfortable about aspects of RO, you can try to help them a) see how the new concepts help make better sense of workplace issues, b) understand the evidence behind the science, and c) appreciate the usefulness of the templates.

The second focus was on modifying the engineering templates and methods. The goal is not to follow the templates as closely as possible but to optimize effectiveness, efficiency, and trustworthiness. When using an RO template or method, check to see whether the scientific assumptions underlying it apply in your situation.

You may be one of the many executives who find RO gives them solid ground to stand on when making structural, staffing, and managerial decisions. Being clear in your thinking about it, being aware of the different levels of the discipline, will make it a more powerful and useful tool for you.

Herb Koplowitz, Ph.D., president of Terra Firma Management Consulting, works primarily as a consultant to consultants. His deep understanding of requisite organization helps human resources and organization design consultants make the best application of the approach within their organizations. He helps consultants in other fields ensure their advice is implemented; he helps their clients develop the structure, staff, and management practices required to do what the professional recommends. He has helped organizations in every sector build trust and become effective and efficient through appropriate structure, staffing, and management practices. Koplowitz has worked with requisite organization for 15 years and has trained and lectured on it in the US, Canada, Jamaica, South Africa, and India. His practice in requisite organization is informed by a 12-year professional relationship with Elliott Jaques and earlier studies in mathematics, philosophy of science, cognitive development, and general systems theory.

Organizational Engineering and the CEO

Harald Solaas

WHAT'S IMPORTANT

- A CEO can benefit from the power and payoffs that requisite organization's modern social engineering can bring to organization development.

- Most companies attempt to solve organization and human resources problems by copying others or by trial and error. Both processes can work, but often produce costly failures.

- These same companies often act differently when dealing with technical problems because the applied art of engineering allows them the efficiency and economy of devising realistic solutions and testing them experimentally rather than in practice. Risks and costs are greatly reduced.

Nature, to be commanded, must be obeyed.

—Francis Bacon

Craft and Science in Organizational Development[1]

Years ago, my partner and I had an interview with the CEO of the local Argentine branch of an international company who was looking for consulting help. Point blank, the CEO said, "I am evaluated by my principals for the bottom-line results I get. What can you do to help me with this?"

In my recollection, my partner and I were resourceful enough to come up with a reasonable answer, but the significant thing is that now I cannot even remember what it was. So it must not have been terribly conclusive. This was in the days before I adopted RO theory and practice. If I were now confronted with the same situation, my answer would be quite different. It would go something like this.

What I can do for you is assist you in building an organization in which:

- Your organizational structure will fit strategy and will be highly economical.
- The talents and capabilities of people will have the best possible fit to the needs of the company.
- Most people will earnestly try to do their best.
- Managers will be naturally regarded as leaders.
- Trust, collaboration, and integrity will prevail.
- People will not want leave the company.
- Good applicants will seek to join your company
- Many chronic conflicts and tensions you now have will somehow not be there any longer.

And as an outcome of this process, you and some people in your managerial team will have acquired the skilled knowledge needed to support this in the future and to replicate it in new contexts.

To do this, you would have to understand my proposal and use it to make your

---

1   Acknowledgement: In the attempt to single out requisite organization theory in the organizational field, I have amply used the valuable distinction of conceptual framework, science and engineering developed by Dr. Herb Koplowitz. This is the best way I have found to explain its practical value to the executive. See preceding article, Koplowitz, H. "How Solid Is Requisite Organization?"..

own plan and work hard at it. Now, would that improve your bottom line? That is a question only you can answer.

This is a fair answer that specifies what I truly can and cannot deliver and under what circumstances. This somewhat blunt executive might think he or she has heard many things of this kind before, and press me to justify why I am so confident that I could deliver what I say I can.

Then I might relate success stories. I might refer to my own experience and to several well-documented cases of successful applications, all of them showing results in line with my promise above. And, yes, bottom-line results too, very good ones, and also fine results with other hard indicators, such as market share, business expansion, indexes of efficiency within the industry, cost reduction, and so on.

Still, at this point I would feel I have not yet told him or her the reasons I know I will deliver. I am aware that other consultants working under different inspirations than RO could manage to put up an equally impressive and credible story. I have not yet made my approach specific. I have not yet gotten through to the executive what the real foundations of my work are.

If this CEO were inquisitive enough to ask and patient enough to listen, and I could relay, of course, appealing to his or her present knowledge of applied arts based on science. It would go something like this:

Developing organizations is an applied art. Every case is unique and requires specific comprehension and the creation of innovative solutions. That is the art side of it.

Now, an applied art is based on craft, that is, on precedents of previous success. But it can also be based on science, like modern medicine or engineering, and that makes all the difference.

Craft consists of trying to solve problems by doing what worked well in the past for others, in other places and circumstances. It is highly useful, and can sometimes be the most practical way to solve a management problem. In our current times, organizational development interventions are by-and-large based on craft. Some are successful, but this practice carries all the limitations and hazards inherent to craft, such as:

- It is not very good at solving new problems.
- The cost of errors can be extremely high, as the only means of testing is actual practice. As an experienced company officer, you may have seen this in the form of promising and highly touted innovations that seem to vanish within

a few years. Sometimes they leave behind considerable discontent and skepticism, because they are simply unreal.

- It gives you no action principles, only ready-made solutions. Benchmarking, for instance, often involves learning from others a few best practices key metrics. Its major shortcoming, however, is that it can never completely identify what made them work well for others.
- It does not let you grasp problems, because it does not provide knowledge on their root causes.

What I can bring to you is the "organizational engineering" approach; that is, an applied art based on science in the field of psychology, rooted in the nature of human beings and the psychology of their problem-solving (work) capabilities. By using this approach:

- New problems can be analyzed, and sound hypotheses on root causes developed.
- New solutions can be first tested in principle, rather that in actual practice, at minimal cost.
- Knowledge of root causes, not obvious but based on scientific discovery, let you understand your problems before you devise action measures.

Just think of modern scientific medicine, as compared to pre-scientific medicine four centuries ago. Think of antibiotics versus herbal concoctions, or of modern surgery versus the bloodletting done by barbers.

Now, what are these scientific bases? They are few, as they were at the beginning of modern physics, but decisive:

- Human capability is discontinuous. The processes people use to solve work and life problems vary in quantum steps. This is why collective human work in all times and places is naturally structured in discontinuous strata.
- Complexity of processing required for solving work problems increases with the complexity of work roles.
- People have acute, vivid, and accurate senses of variables pertaining to the world of adult work, such as the level of work in their jobs, fair pay for the work they do in them, their own and other's innate capability. These are innate, and cannot be changed by external influence.

These assertions are supported by objective metrics, which are used on actual RO applications. On these bases, fine pieces of organizational engineering have been developed. Let me give you, as an example, a phenomenon that has received enormous attention for more than half a century now: that of managerial leadership. There are many authors and lots of books, but no consolidated, proven, and consensually accepted basis for action. There is no development that can give you a reliable guarantee that it is going to work. There is, however, an engineering of leadership. Let me describe its main components, which comprise both art and science:

- Above all, adult people want work commensurate with their capability and fair economic recognition for it—a point on human nature.
- A manager's job should be one, and just one, stratum of complexity above that of his or her subordinates, so he or she can add value to the work of subordinates, thus helping to satisfy the first of the two needs above—a point of structure.
- Then both roles of manager and subordinate should be filled with people of the right capability. This requires a requisite system for evaluating individual capability, and a good internal selection process—a point of HR systems.
- Managers should be made accountable for the results and for the effectiveness of their subordinates, and for following managerial leadership practices.
- Subordinates should be made accountable for their effectiveness (doing their best), not for their results—two points of HR policy.
- Managers need certain minimal authorities to assign work, evaluate effectiveness, veto appointments, deselect ineffective employees, and decide on pay within policy—points of HR policy, managerial leadership practices.
- To support these, certain requisite HR systems must be in place, at least evaluation of effectiveness, job grading, and compensation—points of HR systems.

Get all this in place and then yes, you will predictably have healthy and effective leadership throughout your organization, with very limited risk of failure. It is fortunate that many organizations have received the benefits of this engineering of leadership. For one, T. Owen Jacobs of the Army Research unit said one of Elliott Jaques's main influences was moving the Army away from an individual focus to looking at contextual factors and building leadership systems.

Does this look too complex compared to the classical simplicity of attempting to identify personal traits of leaders or leadership behaviors? Well, the search for the philosopher's stone was simpler than modern chemistry. Engineering is as simple or as complex as reality demands.

Frequent Concerns of CEOs

The CEO, whether thorough and reflective or not, would certainly have other questions. For instance,

"Is this a big organizational overhaul you are asking me to get into that will take a lot of time, make people anxious, and raise an awful lot of expectations?"

What I can do for you is listen to what you need and provide specialized knowledge that will give you a grasp of the situation in your company that you do not now have. If you allow me to interview, observe, and learn about your company, I will give you explanations of your concerns that are not obvious, because they come from research, not just from common sense and experience. And, I will tell you why these explanations are sound.

Is what you want a big overhaul or a limited intervention? That depends on one hand on the nature of the problem and on the other on what you decide to do with it. I'll help you diagnose the problem, and then you may decide to solve it, to leave it as it is for the time being, or even to leave is as it is but learn how lo live better with it. Now, what is your main concern about your organization?

"I want to keep on growing, but I don't know whether I have the people I need."

I can offer a plan for assessing raw capability of all your staff relative to your present and future structure needs. This can be done fairly quickly and without need of modifying any of your present structures and systems. The result will be a map that tells you who is or is not a candidate for which roles from a raw capability point of view and what outside recruitment needs you have. This is a viable limited intervention.

"I'm worried about the quality of our selection processes. HR people make a big fuss and present fat reports, but we don't seem to be getting what we need. Too many failures."

Let me explain the three-factor selection method. It is based on scientific knowledge on human capability, and I can provide a valid method to measure it in your applicants and relate it unequivocally to the level-of-work in the roles you are selecting for. It includes two other factors based on sound selection experience, and leaves out many variables about the applicants that are costly to investigate and of unproven predictive value. In addition to being a good predictor, it is far more economical than what you now use. This is another viable limited intervention.

"I am interested in what you said about leadership. Can you offer a simpler version? Can you give my managers some training on how to be better leaders?"

Well, you have surely grasped from what I said that I am talking about a leadership system. Good managerial leadership is not the affect of something individuals have, either innate or acquired, but of a managerial system. If I taught this system to your people, I would be telling them about good practices they cannot affect, because the policies and the systems are not in place. If I did this, I would be falling back into the classical make-believe leadership development. If I am successful, your managers will come to your office and tell you how great the training was, and then they will go back to their old routines after a nice, refreshing break. That would be poor engineering. I did that in the past, but I don't do it any longer.

"I have chronic squabbles between sales and product development/sales and credit analysis/production and sales/product development and marketing, etc."

"I am getting a lot of restlessness about our compensation systems."

"We have good pay levels and benefits packages, but all the same good people leave the company."

"Somehow people seem never to understand what really needs to get done."

"I need to raise ethical awareness and standards in this company."

"I would like to see more teamwork around here."

Considerations are pretty much the same as for the leadership system above. With your support, I can provide some precise and economical methods to collect data and analyze key aspects of your management system that are missed by other approaches, and I can work with you and your staff to collect and analyze the data in a way that will enable you to do it yourself in the future. And, based on our review of this data, I will be able give you sound conjectures on the root causes of your problems. Then you can move on and be well equipped to the action stage.

"Can I try it first as a pilot?"

Prototyping is a part of good engineering. What you test are action principles based on hypotheses, not just hopeful ideas. This leaves good learning for the larger scale application stage. And cost is limited. Yes, you can try it as a pilot.

"I need to make my contact people more client-oriented."

"I need to raise quality awareness."

I can tell you right off what *not* to do: don't make a parallel "organizational scaffold" of internal diffusion campaigns, client service, or quality committees and training courses. Go through your present system of managerial accountability.

"I need to improve results. I want a program of incentives based on results."

It is possible to anticipate some effects of a program of this kind. In the short term, you may get some results in line with what you want. However, there will be other less desirable effects. You may be confronted with breakdowns in critical cross-functional relationships or other required behaviors that are not bonused. By taking responsibility for evaluation of effectiveness away from managers, you will be inevitably undermining one of your most precious assets, managerial leadership. You will find people who maneuver to get incentives without adding real value to the company, or who plainly cheat. Apparently unrelated problems of discontent and mistrust will become common currency. You will find yourself in situations in which you have a clear feeling that you are over or underpaying, and you will be caught in your own scheme.

I can offer some objective data on how people feel about the money they get for their work. This may clarify your choice of whether you want to appeal to greed or to fairness, and how a simple system of fair pay could be implemented. Of course, it may well be that your present compensation system does not help bring about good results. I suggest we have a look into it.

RO-based Practice as an Enabler for the CEO

A plausible answer to the question "What can RO-based practice do for the CEO?" would be that it enables him or her to do in the field of organizational development something that is already familiar to him or her in other areas, such as that of production technology. It enables the use of scientific knowledge for purposes of prediction and control.

In enterprise, as in all human endeavors, problems keep on appearing in new forms all the time, and it takes imagination and creativity to devise solutions for them. At inception, these solutions are by their very nature untested, and the majority of them are bound to be either discarded or survive only in highly modified versions.

As a rule of life, new attempted solutions are tested in the real world. Those that produce desired outcomes survive, and most are discarded or recycled until they become viable. This is an ultimately effective, but slow, clumsy, and, above all, very costly process, like that of natural selection. This is the model for generating useful knowledge based on craft.

Humans, however, have availed themselves of a unique approach, small within the whole quest of solutions for real-life problems, but nevertheless of dramatic consequence: that of technology based on science.

Innovative solutions that ultimately result in technological advances are, when first hatched, based on mere unwarranted intuition, and just as prone to failure as any other prospective solution. However, scientific knowledge makes a big difference in their hazard-strewn path to effective, proven technology. Most bad prospects are killed in the bud, in the field of ideas (inherent hypotheses consistent or not with previous scientific knowledge). Then, experimental testing can be planned, which is a second screening, and finally prototypes can be built and tested. The few survivors of this quick, painless, and highly economical process have few chances of becoming costly failures in the real world.

In our current times, organizational solutions are by-and-large first accepted by their power to make sense within the existing framework, rather by than their correspondence with reality. Few survive, and the slow and uncertain elimination process involves lots of waste and disappointment.

RO theory changes this scene. When confronted with a new organizational behavior problem, a CEO and his or her staff may think up solutions and test them quickly and inexpensively, in the style that is currently accepted as normal good practice in production technology. The results are equally momentous and satisfying.

ABOUT THE AUTHOR

Harald Solaas is an organizational consultant who lives and works in Argentina. He has conducted a variety of organizational programs in a wide range of industries and in governmental administration, both in Argentina and in several other Latin American countries.

He earned his degree of Psicólogo Laboral (industrial psychologist) at the Universidad Nacional de La Plata in 1967. He performed as a company HR officer in several companies for many years after graduation. His most significant experience was in the local Argentine company of the SHELL Group.

Solaas adopted RO theory as the theoretical and technical foundation for all his work in 1995. Between 1997 and 2000, he participated in a large project upon which

Dr. Elliott Jaques acted as a consultant. In the course of this project and afterwards he kept an intense exchange of theoretical and technical material with Dr. Jaques.

Solaas has taught in several universities in Argentina, and currently holds the Chair of Análisis y Diseño Organizacional at the Universidad de Belgrano, Buenos Aires. For the last 11 years, his efforts have been focused on making the benefits of RO practice more widely known and available to working organizations of all kinds.

Development and Diffusion of Levels of Work Concepts

Development and Diffusion of Levels of Work Concepts

Nearly 60 years ago, revolutionary management ideas began to emerge in post-war Britain. Fortune and chance brought two brilliant and extraordinarily different men together for a long and fruitful collaboration. Wilfred Brown and Elliott Jaques worked together in one of the longest social experiments in the history of the world at Glacier Metals Company, and then Brown sponsored Jaques in interdisciplinary social analytical research at Brunel University and in the diffusion of the ideas throughout the UK and the world. Our author, **Alistair Mant**, knew both Wilfred Brown and Elliott Jaques and through his experience at the Tavistock Institute and as a management consultant gives us a rare perspective on the values these men held, their personalities, and the nature and meaning of their exploratory work that has emerged over the years as a major new management paradigm. Mant's article "Wilfred Brown and Elliott Jaques: An Appreciation of a Remarkable Partnership" is particularly important in that the number of individuals who worked with Jaques and Brown when they were together at Glacier is unfortunately diminishing.

Many executives are diligent in their search for best practices to use in improving their organization's performance and are frustrated as they encounter the endless management fads in business magazines and bookstores, thousands of often arcane and theoretical articles in the academic journals, and consultant promises based on questionable or scant experience or research. Some continue in the hope of finding best practices that are grounded in the best applied science. These executives demand that a candidate approach be normative rather than merely descriptive, be systematic rather than partial, has rigorously defined concepts that have been tested and validated, has implementation methods and tools that have been tested and refined, and enables situational understanding of implementation contingencies. In his article "Requisite Organization: Theory and Validation." **Kenneth C. Craddock**, arguably the ranking authority on the literature pertaining to requisite concepts, describes the roots of the levels of work and human capability approach and its development in academia first in the UK and then in universities and related use around the world. His article is based on his comprehensive 4th edition, *Requisite Organization Annotated Bibliography*, now posted on the Global Organization Design Society's website.

The epilogue provides direction on how to learn more about this approach and how to proceed to learn and to work in your organization. It also describes the role of the Global Organization Design Society in supporting your learning and the spread of awareness and skill in this field around the world. And finally the epilogue describes what you can do to support the Society's work while at the same time helping yourself and your organization.

 1

Wilfred Brown and Elliott Jaques: An Appreciation of a Remarkable Partnership

Alistair Mant

WHAT'S IMPORTANT

- This article demonstrates the unique partnership and commonalities of Wilfred Brown and Elliott Jaques.

- It gives an inside perspective on their roots, development, personalities, and work.

- It discusses their mutual belief in fairness, with Brown emphasizing technology and democratic philosophy and Jaques demonstrating great depth in understanding human psychology.

- It reveals their strongly humanistic roots in terms of the idealism of industrial democracy and in their profound understanding of being human.

A rock pile ceases to be a rock pile the moment a single man contemplates it, bearing within him the image of a cathedral.

—Antoine De Saint-Exupery, 1900-1944

My task here is to explain to devotees of Elliott Jaques's work how his 37-year friendship and professional collaboration with Wilfred Brown shaped that work. One cannot understand Jaques without a grasp of the Brown element. It was as if their great brains were fused together in their work. I knew them both, having worked for most of the 1970s at the Tavistock Institute in London. But I knew Wilfred Brown better, having played a great deal of golf and written a book with him.[1] For those who understand these matters, Brown had been a scratch golfer in his youth and was still dangerous in his late 60s. When he was ennobled in 1964, he took the title Lord Brown of Machrihanish (the name of his beloved golf course near his cottage on the Kintyre Peninsula in southwest Scotland).

The Partners

Few partnerships in history rival this for fruitfulness. Arguably, the association with Brown was the making of Jaques. Of course, following the tenets of Stratified Systems Theory (SST), Jaques would have made his mark somehow or other. But the circumstances of immediate post-war (World War II) Britain provided an almost perfectly complementary interest, knowledge, and access to power on the part of these two men.

This kind of partnership, between a major thinker and a major player, generally involves a great thinker gaining access, via a player/collaborator, to a great field of study in the real world of events. This tends to relegate the latter to also-ran intellectual status. Wilfred Brown, in his special way, was just as clever as Jaques about the work they did together.[2]

The Tavistock Background

The basic facts are well-known. In 1948, the newly-formed Tavistock Institute of Human Relations in London had morphed out of the old Tavistock Clinic for

---

1 Brown, W., Hirsch-Weber, W., and Mant, A.; *Bismarck to Bullock; Conversations about Institutions in Politics and Industry in Britain and Germany.* Anglo-German Foundation, 1983.
2 Frankfurt, H. G. *On Bullshit.* Princeton University Press, 2004.

Medical Psychology (set up after World War I to treat and to better understand shell-shock and related traumas). The Institute was meant to bring the remarkable insights gained during World War II into the broader community, but in particular to post-war business and industry. Those insights centered mainly on the nature of effective leadership, managerial selection, and teamwork.

The post-war British government supported this development, but it was the Rockefeller Foundation that put up the initial grant money for the new Institute in 1946. It was incorporated in 1947 and the great Glacier Metals project, on which Jaques cut his action-research teeth and on which he would work for 17 years, was one of its first projects in 1948. But Glacier Metal only became a part of the Tavistock's initial program because of the determination of its remarkable 40-year-old chief executive Wilfred Brown.

Over time, this skepticism about the Tavistock's psychoanalytical orientation on the part of the established academics was paralleled by nervousness on the part of a resurgent British business community. Britain was broke by the end of the war, but making money from business wasn't so difficult in the post-war rush for growth. Numerous studies have shown how British business dashed for easy growth without ever revisiting or reforming its worst traditional practices. Marshall Aid money poured into Britain as well as Germany after the war (twice as much as it happens), but nowhere did it lead to the fundamental rethinking that occurred in Germany, especially as to labor relations.

Skepticism and Bullshit

This skepticism on the part of both the academic and the business communities is an important accompaniment to the Jaques-Brown story. Those people around the world who regard the Tavistock canon, "Stratified Systems Theory" and "requisite organization" as nothing less than blindingly obvious truths are generally puzzled that others (the great majority) don't get it. This is an important phenomenon to understand if we hope ever to spread these important insights more widely. The simple view is that most academics are distrustful of anything other than hard science and most business people are defensive in the face of any evidence that suggests they have got it all wrong. The Glacier study therefore attacked the establishment on two powerful fronts at once.

For the purposes of this paper, I propose to construct the events from 1948 to 1985 (the year of Wilfred Brown's death) in the following way: the intellectual alliance of a Canadian and a Scot (together representing clarity of thought and authority) against the massed ranks of American and English bullshit. (Here I employ the term *bullshit* in the same precise sense as Professor Harry Frankfurt in his famous Princeton monograph *On Bullshit*.[3]) In this version of history, those in the adjoining dominant cultures of America and England do not tell "lies" about themselves or about the glib consultants they employ, they have simply come to believe in the unrelieved diet of bullshit, emerging from the business and management academy.

This view of history casts Jaques and Brown as clearly superior intellects, drawn by their off-center position in the power nexus (not American; not English) to point out that the emperor isn't wearing any clothes. Both men were famed for not suffering fools gladly and neither bothered much with diplomacy. So they got along fine. Brown was nine years older than Jaques (who was only 31 when the Glacier project began.) The seminal *Changing Culture of a Factory* was his Harvard Ph.D. on Glacier, submitted in 1951.[4]

Thought Leadership

As the Glacier project proceeded, Jaques and Brown increasingly detached themselves from the Tavistock "human relations" and "group relations" movements. It was not that they were unmindful of interpersonal relations or group processes, but rather that they came to understand the higher importance of authority, role clarity, accountability, and power—in short, managerial leadership. Harry S. Truman probably captured the predominant post-war American view when he said: "a leader is a man [sic] who has the ability to get other people to do what they don't want to do—and like it!"[5] This captured well the pragmatic post-war American view that the key element of leadership is persuasiveness, backed up by sincerity.

In the post-war years, wherever American thinking about management led, England meekly followed. When parts of American academia turned against the Glacier/Tavistock view of reality, much of the English management movement

---

3   Frankfurt, H. G. *On Bullshit.* Princeton University Press, 2004.
4   Jaques, E. *The Changing Culture of a Factory.* London: Routledge, 1951.
5   Mant, A. *Intelligent Leadership.* Melbourne, Australia: Allen & Unwin, 1999.

followed suit. One goes to England for eloquent charm (B.S., if one insists), but one goes to Scotland for strict role clarity and precise accountability. (In Scotland they say: "the only time you need an agreement is when there's a disagreement." In other words, get it in writing—what the English might regard as red tape.) Brown understood the importance of formal arrangements—something the "human relations" and "group relations" schools were then retreating from. In the course of time, Jaques became a constitutionalist too, just like the managing director. Jaques had had a deep education, but it wasn't broad. Brown, who never went to university at all, probably taught Jaques international history.

For Jaques, the formal break with the group relations movement came in 1952 when he quit the Tavistock, leaving behind a few eminent colleagues who felt, rightly or wrongly, that their contribution to the Glacier work had been marginalized. As a founder member of the Institute, Jaques's departure represented quite a schism in the Tavistock ranks. Not for the last time, Brown paved the way for Jaques's career development by providing a job at Glacier. By this time, Jaques had already grasped the importance of the time dimension as a measure of role responsibility and individual capability—an early example of his great skill in listening to other people.

It's likely though that Jaques's great concern with fairness had something to do with Brown's influence. Brown was old enough to have witnessed the slum conditions in Glasgow after World War I, and had already formed a political view on the centrality of work and employment in human dignity. Brown hated the idea of unemployment and saw it as the joint responsibility of employers and government to ensure it never took hold. It was enough to make him a lifelong socialist in a somewhat conservative family. The Brown family interests had been severely damaged by the bankruptcy of Clydeside shipbuilders in the 1920s. Brown brought to Jaques a profound understanding of history, and especially political and constitutional history.

Wilfred Brown: The Man

We know what these two warriors shared in common a fierce intellect, a deep-seated and passionate concern for justice (fairness), and a prevailing impatience with any shilly-shallying. This latter characteristic of both men (the impatience) was commonly misinterpreted by others as arrogance. Both of them tended to give other people a hard time if they seemed to be confused or waffling. But what were the key differences, from which they drew their complementarity? It seems Brown was more firmly rooted in secure family and community. Jaques's family origins are obscure and apparently less ordered and happy. The Browns weren't rich, but they were solid, well-respected and clever.

Wilfred's father ran an electrical wholesaling business, and young Wilfred was always technically gifted. Most people at Glacier believed that if he had gone to university he might well have ended up as a distinguished scientist in one field or another. It was certainly important for Glacier to have a managing director who understood something of science and technology, given it was the biggest manufacturer of plain bearings in Europe at the beginning of the study.

So, although young Wilfred was sent to a minor English public (i.e., private) school in Blackpool, there wasn't the money to support university. He went straight to work and ended up in Glacier at the age of 24. He was an enterprising young man and a superb salesman. Also, not irrelevant, he was a scratch golfer, no bad thing if the boss and his daughter are mad on the game too. The short version of the story is that he married the boss' daughter in 1934 and she died in childbirth in the following year. Within a further year, both her parents died also, leaving Wilfred Brown's sister-in-law the major shareholder and the company (which had originated in the deep south of the US) somewhat rudderless in the next three years.

Brown: The Politician and Political Scientist

War was now approaching fast and Glacier, a crucial supplier of plain bearings to the war effort, needed a new chief executive. Technically, Wilfred Brown, still in his 20s, was too young and he had become attracted to the newly-formed Commonwealth party. Its main aims were common ownership of wealth, a revitalised democracy, equal opportunity, colonial freedom, and organization for world unity. (Sir Stafford Cripps did his best to persuade Brown that any incoming Labor government would need at least a few members running firms in order to offer practical advice to government).

However, by 1937 Brown had assumed the chairmanship and chief executive role at Glacier Metal. He was then 29. The demands of wartime production represented a baptism of fire for a brand-new, and very young, CEO. He married Marjorie

Skinner (his wife and partner for the next 46 years) in 1939. From the start, Brown was determined that the principles of social justice should determine the managerial leadership of the firm. Brown was a passionate believer in democracy in general and in industrial democracy in particular. He believed passionately that people at work had exactly the same need for political representation of their interests as *employees* as they did in their role as citizens in the body politic.

He also knew that the workers always had the potential *power* to bring the entire system to a halt if they chose, therefore, he reasoned, they must be brought within the constitution in exactly the same way that the lawless English mobs were tamed by the successive Reform Acts of the 19th century. Within 50 years or so, the English mob had become the sober and virtuous late Victorians. Their genes, he argued, had not altered but their interests were now properly represented in the parliament. The problem was therefore structural. It was Brown's great vision to replicate that process of political inclusion within the firm. That meant Glacier needed to develop a constitution and to replicate the great organs of the state in the firm—a representative legislature to make the laws (the works council), an executive branch to execute policy (management), and an independent judiciary to adjudicate in case of abuse of power (the appeals procedure).

Achieving that goal was not a simple matter. In the *Glacier Project Papers*, Brown confessed (with his customary frankness):[6]

> *Between 1939 and 1947, as a Chief Executive, I followed the "psychological" mode of thought about organisation. By the end of that period I had managed to get the executive, representative and embryo legislative systems hopelessly confused. The result was a dangerous weakening of the authority of managers and no consequential feelings of freedom or satisfaction on the part of other members of the Company. (p. 158)*

All this taught Brown the central importance of the manager's authority to manage (this was no wishy-washy view of industrial democracy). He disdained the idea that workers want or need to participate in decision-making. That, in his view, was the province of the manager and, he believed, most of the workers wished their bosses would get on with it—and competently. But policy formation, especially when it affects the workers' interests, is something workers do need to have a stake in, through some form of representation. Brown's view was that leaders should find out where the realistic power blocs exist, and then organize them into a constitutional frame-

---

6   Brown, W. and Jaques, E. *Glacier Project Papers.* New Hampshire: Heinemann, 1965.

work. Otherwise the managers will always be at their mercy. Brown understood power; his quest was to channel it into *legitimate authority.* He even persuaded the Glacier managers to form a union to represent their collective interests when it seemed likely their salary differentials with the workers were to be eroded.

Brown understood that Britain had largely showed the world how to create the civil institutions of democracy, but had failed utterly to install the parallel institutions in the industrial and employment sphere. He knew also that Germany, despite its travails of political democracy since unification in 1871, had started to pay attention to industrial democracy in the mid-19th century. He knew, for example, that the so-called "Frankfurt Parliament," born of the revolutionary period 1848-49, had drawn up provisions for local, district, and regional works council organizations. The irony is that the professionals who formed the "parliament" thought the British were forging ahead in industrial democracy, based on the example of a few Scots and north of England industrialists and thinkers. Not so.

So, from the start, Glacier Metal was Wilfred Brown's test-bed for social and political experiment and a kind of action research project into social justice. Brown had installed sophisticated veto-power works councils in each of Glacier's six factories as early as 1941—seven years before the Tavistock team appeared on the scene. Jaques and his Tavistock colleagues were *useful* to Brown's grand scheme.

Social experiments aside, Glacier faced an array of problems after the War ended, including growing competitive pressures in an increasingly international market. The firm desperately needed a proper R&D capability—something Brown set out to fix as a top priority. Even more pressing was the problem of manufacturing licenses—government had stepped in to suspend patent protections for the duration of the war effort. After the war, Glacier was sued for damages for the infringement of patent rights. This was a time of crisis for Glacier's young managing director and it took its toll on him and his young family.

One outcome of the contact with Jaques was Brown's entry into psychoanalysis, something he found very helpful in dealing with the enormous pressures he faced. Skeptics argue that psychoanalysis is often helpful for those who don't really need it—rarely for those who do. Brown was an enormously creative individual hemmed in by responsibility.

It is noteworthy too that Brown (the hard-headed managerial technician) was in pursuit of fundamental principles of human behavior in formal political systems:

Jaques (the social scientist) was in search of the hard science within the social milieu—hence his references to physics in demonstrating the replicability of RO principles. Nothing else shows their remarkable complementarity better than this odd juxtaposition of science and social science. By the time Wilfred Brown lay struck by a stroke, speechless and dying in 1985, with Jaques frequently at his bedside, their differences had dissolved into simple friendship.

The Partnership

Brown continued to provide a context for Jaques's professional development. Brown immediately involved Jaques as an associate lecturer at the local Brunel College of Advanced Technology (where Brown chaired the governing body). When the College became the platform for the new Brunel University, Brown and the Vice Chancellor wanted to create a new integrated School of Social Sciences embracing Psychology, Sociology, and Economics (along the lines of Oxford's PPE degree). Jaques was duly installed as its first head of school. He stayed there until 1970. Meanwhile, Brown had become the University's Pro-Chancellor in 1966, and was instrumental in making Brunel an all "sandwich" degree university—providing study programs that intersperse study with periods of real work in industry.

By then he had successfully engineered the sale of Glacier to Associated Engineering, a major UK industrial group. Brown hoped that the industrial democracy institutions he and Jaques had created at Glacier would be resilient enough to expand after the transfer of ownership. He was disappointed when that proved not to be the case. However, some of the best Glacier managers and labor relations professionals were snapped up in the following years by incoming Japanese firms (which knew all about the ability-based Glacier project).

Meanwhile, Brown had become a government minister in the Board of Trade (his Life Peerage allowed him into government ministry as a member of the House of Lords). The then Prime Minister Harold Wilson appointed him Chairman of the Docks Modernization Board, which duly did away with restrictive practices in the workplace by guaranteeing a minimum wage. The new Labor government knew that it needed a practical socialist businessman to steer industrial legislation through the House of Lords.

However, Brown, understanding that the iron rules of power obtain at the national level as well as in the enterprise, saw that the House of Lords was an anachronistic institution in the sense that the power blocs it represented (the landed gentry, the clergy and so on) were largely irrelevant in the new world of business competitiveness. The union movement, for example, had no realistic stake in the national decision-making process. This tended to render them collectively irresponsible. Brown wanted to abolish the House of Lords and replace it with a "House of Occupations" in order to constitutionalize the main occupational power blocs (thus leaving geographic representation to the House of Commons).

This radical idea symbolizes Wilfred Brown's and Elliott Jaques's greatest bond, their shared passion about *fairness*. Much of Jaques's professional life was devoted to the search for a fair way of rewarding the central activity of human life—productive work. Brown simply took the principle to its logical national level. If work is central to the human experience, then government has a duty to ensure that our deep understanding of what is right and proper is reflected in the national system of rewards. Ever the institution-builder, Wilfred Brown looked for the means of achieving that at the national level through new institutions. Today, British labor unions are increasingly enfeebled. The gap between the rewards of barely-accountable captains of industry and their insecure and underpaid employees continues to grow, latterly under a "socialist" government. Nobody thinks it is fair.

When he finally left government, Wilfred Brown waited for the board membership offers to pour in from big business. But by that time his uncompromising intellect had made its mark in the boardrooms of London and, of course, in the House of Lords. For the City of London—the heart of finance capitalism—one needed charm and a talent for dissembling. The offers never materialized.

And that is the point. Brown was about clarity, precision of concept, formality, and the centrality of authority as liberating factors. English business was instead embarked on a long journey into reassuring bullshit. British business has yet to begin to attend to some of the fundamentals exposed by Brown and Jaques and to build industrial and employment institutions parallel to its great civil institutions. We all still await a grasp of the principles of industrial democracy in English-dominated business.

Alistair Mant was a consultant and senior social scientist at the Tavistock Institute in London in the 1970s, having migrated from the IBM Corporation. At Tavistock, he met Elliott Jaques and through the Institute, he also worked with Wilfred Brown. In recent years, he has specialized in the study of the gray area between the private and public sectors, and especially in public-spirited corporations and businesslike government. This is the arena in which Jaques and Brown built their collaboration. The Glacier Metals project was essentially a deep exploration of the possibility of decent and dignified behavior in a highly competitive world.

Alistair Mant acknowledges a debt to these two leaders, and especially to their understanding that it is always fruitless to set out to circumvent the laws of nature. At Glacier this meant determining the natural properties of humanity (the need for fairness, justice, formality, and an appreciation of wisdom) in big and complex employment systems.

Alistair Mant's book *Intelligent Leadership* explores this "socio-technical systems" terrain in more general terms. For the past 12 years, he has been strategy advisor to the UK Employers' Forum on Disability, the world leader in linking big business with the interests (including employment) of disabled people.

Requisite Organization: Theory and Validation

Kenneth C. Craddock

WHAT'S IMPORTANT

- There was enormous intellectual excitement generated by requisite organization theory when it first emerged.

- In the late 1960s, the Japanese adapted parts of the theory.

- Academic debates in the West drove the theory out of consideration at the end of the 1960s. Replications of Jaques's and Brown's theories were strong, but came only in the 1970s.

- The further development of the theory by Jaques came from major 12-year engagements at CRA (now Rio Tinto) in Australia and in the US Army.

- The theory is now being applied with vigor in many countries and many aspects of modern Japanese management now being introduced in Japanese facilities around the world appear to incorporate important aspects of Brown's and Jaques's work.

The basis of this organizational theory, now called requisite organization, was developed initially by Elliott Jaques and Wilfred Brown at Glacier Metal Company in the UK (1948-1965). Elliott Jaques (1917-2003) was a Canadian by birth and earned two doctorates, an MD from Johns Hopkins (1941) and a PhD in social relations from Harvard (1951). He wrote some 20 books and over 80 articles.

Wilfred B. D. Brown (1908-1985), on the other hand, came up intellectually through a practical but acceptable British route. Chairman and Managing Director (CEO) of the Glacier Metal Company, Ltd. in the UK (1939-1965), he sponsored the development of this organization theory, including works councils, and also contributed extensively to it. He wrote seven books and several dozen articles on the theory.

In 1965 Lord Brown sold Glacier Metal, by then the largest plain-bearing manufacturer in Europe, to Associated Engineering (AE). He joined the government as a Minister of State at the Board of Trade (1965-1970). At this time he also became Pro-Chancellor of Brunel University (1966-1980), a top administrative position rather than an academic one.

Jaques then became head of a new graduate school of social science at Brunel University. In 1967 he founded a research and consulting institute affiliated with the School of Social Sciences that advised government and non-profit organizations (Brunel Institute for Organization and Social Studies, BIOSS). Jaques came to the US in 1980. He continued his research and consulted primarily with organizations in Australia and the United States in the 1980s and in Argentina and Canada in the 1990s. He also consulted with academics, consultants and researchers at Nottingham, Berkeley, Southern Illinois, Harvard, Cranfield, Minnesota, George Washington, and Buenos Aires.

---

1   *The Prince, Book VI.* Bondanella, P. and Musa, M. (trans.) Oxford, 1985.

The Theory and Its Place

There were almost no UK business schools in the 1940s and 1950s. As Jaques and Brown were starting, they reviewed the writings of academics on business and found these not helpful and not realistic. Both men realized they were on their own, and so began research anyway under the press of time and business.

This organizational theory had several names as it developed through different stages. In the UK it was variously known as time-span of discretion (TSD), equitable payment, rank theory, social analysis, the Glacier Project, and levels-of-work (LoW). Later, in the 1980s and 1990s, it was known in Australia, United States, Canada, and Argentina as stratified systems theory (SST) and as requisite organization (RO). To be sure, the latter versions were more complete and scientific. Even so, these changes in name were confusing.

If this essay was organized chronologically, it would reveal the history of the theory: its propagation in the 1950s; its waxing as an attractive management theory in the mid-1960s; its adaptation in the late 1960s by the Japanese *keiretsu* (pronounced as in "weigh," a set of companies with interlocking business relationships and share-holdings); the rejection by many Western academics at the end of the 1960s; the powerful validating studies published in the 1970s; the thin stream since of dissertations, theses, and articles on five continents confirming the theory; its adoption by organizations across the world (including propagation by the Japanese) in the 1990s; and the continuing belief of some academics that there are no data to support Jaques's and Brown's theory.

According to Peter Drucker, management has been dominated across the 20th century by Frederick W. Taylor. This may be an overstatement, but subsequent theories had to define themselves with respect to Taylor's ideas. Taylor used static concepts from Newton's physics to extend Adam Smith's theory of the division of labor. His approach created the mass assembly-line. (The Europeans call this "Fordism.") It is not scientific, although it was as scientific as anything in 1900. It intensified effort-wage bargaining, because first the workers and then the managers/engineers in the 1920s recognized there was no science in time and motion studies (Abruzzi 1955)[2] Above all, Taylorism denied discretion to the workers and they often rebelled.

---

2 Please Note: All references are to *Requisite Organization - Annotated Bibliography* (2007, 4th edition), which is available for download at GlobalRO.org. This chapter is adapted from the Introduction (Part I).

In contrast, Jaques and Brown showed when and how to combine elements of labor back together within individuals to form wholes at each level. In the UK, Jaques's discoveries, that discretion was an essential part of every employee's role and the level of trust was a key to every workplace, took hold in part due to Oxford don Alan Fox's 1974 book, *Beyond Contract*. Discretion (judgment) was what the employee brought to the work. High trust was necessary to allow that discretion to be used. Contracts between principal and agent were not enough.

Outside the UK, Chester Barnard, former CEO of New Jersey Telephone turned management author, endorsed Jaques's first book on it in several ads (Jaques 1956). Cornell Professor Henry A. Landsberger used Parsons (1958) and Jaques's TSD and hierarchy level (1956) to develop a scheme of horizontal decisions, work-flows, conflicts, and legitimate dilemmas at every managerial level (1961). (This was replicated by Mark Kriger in 1983.) Berkeley graduate, Robert Blauner, showed worker alienation was not a Marxist concept but was due largely to the thwarting of discretion (1964). Australian Professor F. Kenneth Wright linked Penrose's theory of the growth of the firm to Jaques. Structuring the firm into requisite strata ensured the optimal assignment of the talent available and provided strategic capability at the top (1964). Harvard economics Professor Harvey Leibenstein separated "managerial capacities," and "discretion and judgment" as causes for the firm's failure to reach the ultimate limits of output from given inputs. In creating managerial "X-efficiency," he asserted that incentives would improve productivity per man yet have little influence on the growth of the firm (1966). Harvard business Professor Pearson Hunt viewed the theory as an argument in favor of corporate decentralization (1966).

Six discoveries marked the development of Jaques's theory from mainstream research on organizations: the "social analysis" methodology (Rowbottom 1977), which began in the late 1940s and extended over 15 years; the recognition of linked "managerial authority and accountability" around 1950 (Jaques 1951); the discovery of "time span of discretion" (TSD) in 1953; the discovery of "felt-fair pay" (FFP) the next year (Jaques 1956); strata based on differential behavior (Jaques 1961), and, the discovery of "levels of abstraction" in work roles by Dr. D. John Isaac, Jaques, and their Brunel colleagues (Jaques et al 1978).

Professor Harold Koontz named the then-current academic situation "the management theory jungle" (1961). This article led to Koontz the next year holding a Symposium at UCLA and his 1964 book was based on it. Among other luminaries,

Koontz invited Brown to speak on the need for well-defined management terms grounded in experience of the work place. Brown spoke on "contraction," the meeting the CEO held with all his reports—all at once (replicated by Davis in 1968). There Brown confronted Herbert Simon on the issues of common definitions of terms and the need for a testable theory. The crowd is reported by Emeritus Professor Anthony Raia, an attendee, to have sided with Simon. It favored multiple theories. As Koontz put it, for many academic theorists "the roadblock to understanding is unwillingness" (1961, p. 185). In other words, the academic world at that time gave publication and distinction to any who developed their own theories and nothing to those who pursued common definitions. In 1965 both Jaques and Brown were invited to speak at a conference on their theory at Southern Illinois University.

At Brunel (and BIOSS) during the 1970s the theory was used as the basis for several research streams. Isaac had established multi-modal distributions and with Gillian Stamp established a matrix of levels of complexity that modeled continuities and discontinuities between levels. Career Path Appreciation (CPA) was the work of Stamp with considerable support from Ian Macdonald and Carlos Rigby. Others focused on the public sector at various role levels and on the levels of purpose and values that guided the enterprise.

Gillian Stamp became head of BIOSS in 1985. Stamp was invited to see if CPA could be used in the mining industry to develop black South Africans and brought requisite theory to that part of the world. Also, Aldo Schlemenson got his doctorate at Brunel in entrepreneurial endeavors, returned to Argentina, and published it in Spanish. It soon began to catch on.

From Tinkers to Evers to Chance (From UK to Japan to US)

In the late 1960s, the Japanese shifted their focus to the individual worker's ability, making the manager-once-removed (not the superior) accountable for his or her assessment, and the matching of the individual to the role. A Nikkeiren (Japan Federation of Employers' Associations) study group visited the Glacier Metal Company (Moreton in Wright 1997 BBC). In 1969, the Nikkeiren officially adopted an "Abilities First" approach to evaluations Japan-wide that incorporated Glacier concepts. Within a decade all the *keiretsu* had been re-organized according to these principles. In 1981 this approach was extended to the US through Toyota's

NUMMI plant, a joint venture with General Motors to build vehicles in California. That experiment showed this approach worked just as well with US workers as with Japanese.

The Japanese had developed the "age-wage profile" in 1927 (Koike 1997). When they saw the "maturity growth curves" in this capability theory, the similarity must have been apparent to them (Jaques 1956: trans. 1968; Brown and Jaques 1965: trans. 1969). The two charts displayed the same data in the same visual arrangement and the curved bands are almost identical. In each, the worker's increasing ability/effectiveness is indirectly reflected in the increasing wage earned by the worker. (The Japanese did not use time-span directly.) This theory appears to have confirmed the right path and showed how the elements extended across the organization. But they soon discovered Western firms did not collect these data on their employees.

In 1974, Haruo Shimada received his Ph.D. at University of Wisconsin, Madison, on a comparison of Japanese and American "Age and Wage Profiles," and it was immediately published in the US by the National Technical Information Service (NTIS). The next year he published it as an article in Japanese. This article was cited by Kazuo Koike, Professor at Hosei University, when he detected a new and different approach by Japanese managers to the workplace (1978). Koike conducted many studies over 25 years documenting these changes. Shimada is now at Hitotsubashi University, with Hirotaka Takeuchi and Ikujiro Nonaka, the authors of the 1995 best-selling book, *The Knowledge-Creating Company*. They cited Jaques's 1979 *Harvard Business Review (HBR)* article as the centerpiece of their innovation structure.

Shimada published a chapter in MIT-Sloan Dean Lester Thurow's 1985 book, *The Management Challenge: Japanese Views*, noting the Japanese had exported these strategic human resources management systems at NUMMI. MIT produced several books on the automotive industry and "lean manufacturing" that were best-sellers. Toyota, meanwhile, went the other way—toward uncertainty and change and "human ware"—to drive improvements (Koike 2002). Toyota, like many Japanese firms, also vertically combined Deming's improvement cycle and Jaques's time-spans to ensure objectives were attained ahead of the competition (*hoshin kanri*) (Hunt 1966, Kriger and Barnes 1992, Kondo 1998). The impact crushed the three Detroit-based automakers in 2006.

These Japanese practices were reported in Western media, including the *HBR*, but aroused little interest in academia. Of far more interest in the 1980s was the way activities of the Ministry of International Trade and Industry (MITI), lifetime employment (*nenko*), and the fable of "Japan Inc." violated neoclassical economic assumptions (Johnson 1988).

In Japan, unlike in the West, this human capability theory was used to match highly skilled people to highly sophisticated machines and the focus was on assuring long-term commitments, roles, and responsibilities through lifetime employment (*satei, nenko*) (Hayes 1981 *HBR*). Organizationally, the company strategy was linked to operations directly through each managerial level. Top management ensured strategic consistency of operations through planning at every level. One key was to avoid false choices by setting "time spans" that blocked the reassertion of short-term flexibility over the long-term objectives (*hoshin kanri*) (Wheelwright 1981 *HBR*).

Education for Management

In 1959 two high-profile studies of graduate business education in the US came to the same conclusion: we must shift away from undergraduate vocational training and toward graduate level business education due to an anticipated increase in the complexity of business. The Harvard Business School (HBS) curriculum offered an academically valid alternative to the trade school training offered elsewhere. It also offered the case method (taken from the law school) and an ongoing case publishing house. Other US business schools soon fell in line, pursuing HBS as a model.

Glacier Institute of Management (GIM) was begun in 1961. It offered a different business education model, similar to today's executive education. It was based on the Glacier experience rather than the MBA offered by HBS. When Jaques moved to Brunel, it looked as if the Glacier model would be used in starting a new business school. The goal of HBS became to retake the intellectual initiative from the resurgent British (of course, they were not all Brits but they published there): Burns and Stalker, Woodward, Rice, Emery and Trist, Brown, and Jaques.

HBS funded its own research program, sponsoring at least seven PhDs. Edna Homa was directly focused on testing Brown's and Jaques's theory. Laurent Picard used TSD as part of a basket of measures. The others used the theory in a variety of minor ways. HBS successfully retook the initiative with the publication of Lawrence and Lorsch's contingency theory in 1967. (But contingency theory was not as promising a research direction as first thought. Researchers realized Lawrence and Lorsch had placed uncertainty in the wrong spot, in the environment rather than inside the managers (Downey 1974, Milliken 1985).)

Support for the Theory

By the early 1970s the supporting academic research on Jaques's and Brown's theory had slowed to a trickle. The BiOSS intervention at the National Health Services was seen as bogged down in bureaucracy and ineffectual. The annual rate of Ph.D.s was half that of the 1960s. The theory was seen as a fad whose day had passed.

But over the decades a thin stream of evidence supporting Jaques's and Brown's theory trickled in. They appeared as articles in academic journals and professional/practitioner reviews, as books and chapters, and as government publications. These results taken together constitute a substantial body of cumulative knowledge. Over 2,000 studies were done directly using this theory, plus 1,200 mainstream results supported it for an academic total of 3,200. Of these, 1,100 were published in peer-reviewed journals. This research included 300 articles in first-tier (A-level) journals required for tenure at elite schools.

Some 80 doctorates have been earned on Jaques's and Brown's organization theory (1962-present). Doctorates were earned at 44 schools. Twenty doctorates were earned at elite universities: Berkeley, Cambridge, Cornell, Harvard, London, Michigan, Monash, Oxford, UCLA, and Yale.[3]

These books, dissertations, and articles are spread across many topics. The academic disciplines of the first-tier articles include management (and organizations), economics, psychology, industrial relations/human resources management/labor economics, sociology, and operations/decision analysis/information systems. This variety is a double-edged sword. The lack of prominence in any single topic is one reason Jaques's and Brown's theory does not have a high profile. It has been applied across many types of organizations: private sector, family business, non-profit, voluntary, religious, and government. This, however, also shows its robustness.

Schools where the Brown and Jaques's theory has had sustained research include: Berkeley (1961-1976), Nottingham (1962-1977), Buenos Aires (AR) (1962-present),

---

3   I included a dissertation in the Annotated Bibliography if the author used, validated or extended this theory or else applied its measurement instruments or analytical frameworks in the research section. A discussion in the literature review section was not sufficient for inclusion.

Brunel (1965-present), Cranfield (1967-present), IIM Ahmedabad (India) (1968-1981), London School of Economics (1982-present), Southern Cal (USC) (1982-present), Carlisle (1983-present), George Washington (DC) (1985-present), ITBA (AR) (1990s-present), and Deakin (AU) (1990s-present).

Theory Exposes Data Lapse

This management practice was (and is) a challenge to many concepts in organization theory. It directly challenges much of the accredited curriculum of US business schools (and their imitators elsewhere). The main expressed objection by US and British academics at the end of the 1960s was the lack of supporting data. At that point, however, nine dissertations had been completed and a score of supporting studies had been published. These were simply ignored or dismissed by the critics, who focused only on the skeptical findings.

The real issue is much deeper. For half a century Western academics have persisted in collecting data that omits critically important framing information about people and organizations. They have failed to collect available data on the work level of the role and the work capability level of the individual. Their empirical data have been needlessly contaminated by these twin issues. (A parallel in marketing, for example, would be to conduct an external survey but fail to record the age and income of each customer.) As a result, these "empirical" studies must be reexamined.

Replicated Correlations

The average correlation today of the eight Ph.D. dissertations and four studies on time-span of discretion and hierarchy level is +0.87. The average for the four published studies and five dissertations that replicated time-span of discretion to felt-fair pay correlation is +0.89. Four studies and one dissertation have appeared on the felt-fair pay to hierarchy level correlation, averaging +0.915. (This last one needs more support, which is underway.) Several studies that generated low TSD:FFP correlations at +0.35 have been held forth as disproof of Jaques's and Brown's theory. Closer examination indicates three of four were limited to only stratum I non-managerial employees. The fourth may have encountered true chaos. Jaques's initial strong findings have been replicated and confirmed.

Thomas Kuhn raised the issue of credibility (1970). When would a reasonable person be convinced by a preponderance of this independently replicated evidence, allowing one to draw reasonable conclusions? First, TSD:FFP around 1973. Then, TSD:HierarchyLevel in 1976. Third, FFP:HierarchyLevel in 1979. The Progression Curves ("Age-Wage" Profiles) hypothesis would have become clear by 1974. Martin Richards examined the TSD alone, establishing that it was not the amount of risk that must be borne, but the length of time that it must be borne, just as Jaques claimed (1978).

Jerry L. Gray (unpublished, 2007) has indicated this still left the capability level of the individual to be inferred from the other two measures: time-span of discretion and felt-fair pay level. For the measurement of an individual's mental processing skills to be valid, they must be determined independently. Jaques published a study with Kathryn Cason in 1994 that showed how mental processing level was determined directly. It no longer had to be inferred.

This theory of human capabilities and work levels will allow the re-introduction of longitudinal panel data analysis into organization, management, and leadership studies. This in turn will enable precise measurements of the effects of various interventions and will allow true empirical testing of this and other theories in practice.

Corporate Universities

There were few business schools in Japan in the 1960s when Brown's and Jaques's organization theory was under consideration. The firms looked to General Electric's executive development program at Crotonville, NY (begun in 1956), as a model for how things were done. GE under CEO Jack Welch came to rely on a redesigned Crotonville for the means to spread new policies and new initiatives (including Brown's levels of management, under the rubric "career crossroads," and his "contraction") throughout management ranks. The Japanese purpose by the 1990s was not just total quality (TQ), but to educate managers as they ascended up the ladder. Their focus began with orientation and skills but as one rose, it shifted to leadership and strategy. This difference was picked up by Motorola, which set up its own corporate university. In this way, the corporate university became what it is today.

For example, Robert S. Kaplan, former dean of Carnegie Mellon's business school, HBS professor, and creator of the balanced scorecard concept, remarked to the

American Assembly of Collegiate Schools of Business in 1991, "Business schools completely missed the quality revolution," remained oblivious to time-based competition, and will have to lose market share to corporate programs to feel the "pain of irrelevancy" (Deutschman 1991).

US and Australia

CRA in Australia (now Rio Tinto) adopted it, initially under the leadership of its CEO/MD Sir Roderick Carnegie, with Jaques's consulting assistance, 1978-1990. Jaques also worked on this with Professor Catherine G. Burke of Southern Cal (USC). Australian Professor Stewart Clegg depicted this approach as an example of a postmodern organization, one that de-differentiates people (1990).

When the US Army adopted it, T. Owen Jacobs headed a major research project at the Army Research Institute, working in partnership with Jaques (1979-1994). Scores of studies by professors were published by NTIS as the project progressed. The book *Requisite Organization* (1989, 1996) came out of Jaques's transforming experiences at both places. Jaques became a visiting research professor at The George Washington University in 1989 at the invitation of Professor Jerry Harvey.

Canada and Argentina

Jaques was invited to Toronto by ACCORD, an association of organization development practitioners. Over the next eight years he trained hundreds of managers and consultants in multi-day seminars on the theory supporting Toronto and Canada to be a center of requisite practice.

Simultaneously, invitations originated in Argentina from Aldo Schlemenson, a former student at Brunel who was consulting and teaching there. Jaques gave many seminars for students, consultants, and potential clients. In Buenos Aires he became a ProfessorEmeritus (Hon.), at Universidad de Buenos Aires and at Universidad del Salvador.

Kenneth C. Craddock is a consultant specializing in requisite organization and in quality. From 1991 to 1993 he was an assistant to W. Edwards Deming at Columbia University, the man who gave statistical methods and quality to the Japanese. From the mid-1990s, he has researched the organization theory of Elliott Jaques and Wilfred Brown once he discovered it reduced each of Deming's Deadly Diseases of management.

He has authored an online *Annotated Bibliography* of works relating to requisite organization theory (downloadable from GlobalRO.org). This has identified the replications of this theory and their strong correlations. It has also doubled the number of dissertations done on this theory annually. The 4th edition brings these 3,200 academic citations down to the present and documents some firms publicly using the theory, including Avon Products, McKesson Healthcare, Inco International, JPMorganChase, General Electric, Honeywell, Group4Securicor, Newcrest Mining, Commonwealth Bank, Bluescope Steel, Nedcorp Bank, Algoma Steel, Baxi Group, Perrotts Group, Tata Sons, Wipro, and all seven Japanese *keiretsu* groups.

Craddock holds an MPA in management from the JFK School at Harvard and an M.A. from Columbia in history. He provides research support for companies looking for relevant RO precedents, consultants wanting research in RO literature, doctoral students seeking help in the field, and other business research.

Epilogue:
Building a Better Future Together

The Editors

People follow this path for a variety of reasons most often mentioning their organization's growth and profit. But in deeper, more personal conversations they will often describe how working in this new way is personally more productive and fulfilling, and have more fun working with their colleagues, and that they can see the positive changes in people at work that often carries over into better relationships at home and as citizens of their community. They know that this is a better way not only for profit now, but to sustain profitability, as well as to sustain long-term increases in trust, happiness, fuller use of each individual's potential and social well-being.

Let's help each other to go down this road together.

What You Can Do For Yourself and Your Organization

Whether you read every article straight through or read parts following your immediate interests, your next questions will probably be: "What are the best ways to explore this approach further?"; and, "What resources are available to help me?"

Granted we all have different learning styles, the CEOs and senior managers we have talked to reported frequent use of the following steps in their exploration and use of RO and often recommend them to others:

- Read more of the extensive literature about the approach including Elliott Jaques's *General Theory of Bureaucracy*, *Requisite Organization*, or *Executive Leadership*, or the several foundational books that are available for free download on the Society's website and increasingly available in web-based bookstores.

- Talk with other CEOs who have done it and invite them to speak to your senior management group. You will find a growing number of video clips of interviews with CEOs sharing their RO experience on the GO Society website, whichyou can play them for your senior team and discuss them together.

- Register on the GO website to receive notice of new resources as they become available.

- Attend one of the GO Society's world or regional conferences held at intervals in Argentina, Australasia, Europe, North American (often in Toronto), and South Africa. Conferences usually feature CEOs sharing their experiences and interests.

- Attend a public workshop on the levels approach sponsored by the GO Society in the regions, or Requisite Organization International Institute (ROII), at The Levinson Institute and increasingly by other major consulting groups.

- Retain a senior levels-based consultant with a proven track record in supporting successful implementations. Many senior consultants have contributed materials to the GO website and are members of our practice community.

- Staff your organization's executive HR role reporting directly to the CEO with a high mode individual who is fully capable at a level just below that of the CEO role. A stratum VII company, you should have an HR executive now capable at stratum VI. This is quite difficult. There is a wide-spread shortage of HR executives capable of this strategic work. If it is not possible to find one in the market, it's often necessary to transfer a capable executive to this function.

- Hire senior executives who have successfully implemented ROin previous roles, to provide RO project leadership. There are a number of ex-RO-experienced line managers working as external consultants who periodically play project leadership roles also as temporary or contract employees.

- After ensuring that your senior team members are all capable in their roles, one level below your own role, (this is often quite difficult to achieve and almost always requires external help) engage in an intensive educational program with this group, first with an overview, and then periodically as your group designs and implements the new systems over time.

- Use the GO Society's free resources--as well as this book--to educate managers throughout your organization.
- Persist in your personal efforts to transform your own behaviors to model RO managerial leadership practices that provide the glue to make a requisite system effective.
- Use requisite concepts to design your company's management system. (Don't call it Requisite Organization.) Call it "[Your Company's] Management System" based on your company's values and tailored to your strategic needs. Use it to build an effective managerial leadership development program to find and "grow" your organization's future leaders.
- Design new system components based on requisite concepts, ensure that they support your organization's values and strategy, and that they are well-linked and reinforce other key systems. You will find that your company will have fewer, simpler, more cost-effective, and mutually reinforcing systems. And these integrated systems will truly empower your managers and employees to develop trusting work relationships and to apply their full potential to their roles and the organization's goals.
- Use requisite concepts to invigorate / strengthen other improvement programs such as Quality, Six Sigma, Lean Six Sigma, or large IT Enterprise systems. When well designed, RO and these other programs are mutually reinforcing, springboarding positive results beyond expectations.
- Stay the course and avoid the chaos of wiring together various contradictory management fads.
- Keep in mind the guiding idea of the extraordinary power of an aligned systematic approach that aligns, strategy, structure, staffing and other management practices and programs. Fragmentary or piecemeal approaches are often dysfunctional, costly and unnecessarily confuse managers and waste their time.
- Adopt the manner of managerial reflection. Continue reading, reflecting, and networking, evaluating what you intend to achieve, how you try to do it and what you learned. Wilfred Brown, who sponsored the early development of

this method with Elliott Jaques, had little formal education but read widely, went through psychoanalysis,and kept a personal journal about his experiences in setting direction, developing and testing these new methods, and about his personal feelings and changes during the work. He set a good example for us all in how to be a reflective practitioner.

- Build and retain relationships with senior executives using this approach in non-competing companies to learn together with them.
- Gain energy and confidence by participating in the GO Society's growing community of practice—where collaborative learning and generous sharing are the norms.

What the GO Society Will Do to Support Your Efforts

The GO Society will:

- Continue to solicit important RO-related materials (books, articles, films, videos, recordings etc.) for free or low-cost access 24/7 on the web around the world. We will post materials in the language of the author on our website but will limit our print publication to materials already in English.
- Provide advice to guide reading in the field.
- Identify executives and other practitioners with RO experience to interview and post the videos on the web.
- Organize low-cost, web-based and face-to-face seminars in RO concepts and practice.
- Hold regional conferences to develop friendly and constructive relationships between practitioners and to provide venues for those new to the field to meet experienced folks and to learn the ropes.
- Support and grow the academic community, including those who teach, consult, and conduct research in RO-related matters.
- Encourage RO academics and other researchers to develop metrics and to develop studies to demonstrate before-and-after conditions in order to assess the impact of the RO intervention and to resolve problems of the past.
- Encourage researchers in all fields of management to strengthen their findings by
  - Ensuring research includes all appropriate levels of the organization. In the past, doctoral research has often been done by students who have had re-

search access primarily to strata I and II of an organization, and most research findings are relevant only for the levels studied.

  • Adding key RO variables to their research designs—level of the role, level of capability of the incumbent manager, and strength of the managerial leadership accountability system in place.

• Continue publishing the GO Reading Series of books and monographs (of which this is the first) to be available in both print and digital form.

• Develop metrics, tools, and databases to help users diagnose, benchmark, and evaluate progress.

• Develop a program to recognize outstanding contributions by practitioners and organizations to the field.

• Increase awareness of RO in the popular and business presses.

What You Can Do To Support the RO Community of Practice

• Share your RO-related experience by:
  • granting video interviews,
  • writing articles,
  • contributing endorsements and/or testimonials, and
  • speaking with other executives exploring the method.

• Support research on RO-related interventions in your organization by your own staff and grant access to academic researchers preparing case materials or doing research.

• Provide social and financial support to the GO Society. Specific financial support is needed for the Society's Bibliography project, telephone support to researchers and practitioners worldwide and development of the Society's web resources.

• Provide your organization's logo for use on the Society's web site.

Please write to us about your reactions to this book and your RO-related experiences. If you are willing to share your comments or endorsements with others, please include permission for us to publish your comments on the web or in print.

Address your comments to:
The Editors
Global Organization Design Society
32 Victor Avenue, Toronto, Canada, M4K 1A8
or email:
KenShepard@GlobalRO.org

The Global Organization Design Society was founded in 2004 to establish and operate a worldwide association of business users, consultants, and academics interested in science-based management to improve organizational effectiveness.

The GO Society fulfills its purpose by:

- Promoting among *existing users* increased awareness, understanding and skilled knowledge in applying concepts of Levels of Work Complexity, Levels of Human Capability, Accountability, and other concepts included in Requisite Organization and/or Stratified Systems Theory.
- Promoting among *potential users* of the methods, appreciation of the variety of uses and benefits of science-based management, and access to resources.

The GO Society supports the learning and development of current and future practitioners by:

- Holding world and regional conferences,
- Sponsoring public training workshops in the methods,
- Publishing books such as this one, and
- Maintaining a resource-rich website with related articles, monographs, books, and videos.

GLOBAL ORGANIZATION DESIGN SOCIETY

(A not-for-profit corporation incorporated in Ontario, Canada)

32 Victor Avenue

Toronto, Ontario, Canada M4K 1A8

Phone: +1 (416) 463-0423

Fax: +1 (416) 463-7827

E-mail: GOinfo@GlobalRO.org

www.GlobalRO.org

CONTACT INFORMATION

**RICHARD B. D. BROWN, B ENG.
MCIPD**
Chapel House, Coombe Lane
Sway, Lymington Hants, SO41 6BP, UK
PH: 0044(0) 1490 683382
Mobile: 07790 225 352
Email: rbd.brown@tiscali.co.uk

CATHERINE G. BURKE
University of Southern California
School of Policy, Planning
and Development
University Park
Los Angeles, CA, 90089-0626, USA
PH/FX: +1 (626) 573-0867
Email: cburke@usc.edu

CHARLOTTE M. BYGRAVE
Bygrave & Associates
3472 Ponytrail Drive
Mississauga, Ontario, L4X 1W1, Canada
PH: + 905 614 1965
FX: + 905 614 1965
Email: charlotte.bygrave@sympatico.ca

PIET L. CALITZ
bioss International Limited
Postnet Suite 146
Private Bag X782
Bedfordview, South Africa, 2008
PH: +2783 3001234 (mobile)
FX: +2711 4551677
Email: piet@bioss.com
www.bioss.com

MICHELLE MALAY CARTER
PeopleFit
6808 Garrison Ct.
Raleigh, NC 27612, USA
PH: +1 919 848 0527
Email: mcarter@peoplefit.com

E. FORREST CHRISTIAN
The Manasclerk Company
153 Harrison Blvd.
Valparaiso, IN, 46383, USA
PH: +1 (219) 381-4025
FX: +1 (928) 223-9273
forrest.christian@manasclerk.com
Skype/aim/yim/msn: manasclerk
www.manasclerk.com

STEPHEN D. CLEMENT
Organizational Design Inc. (ODI)
P.O. Box 9859
The Woodlands, Texas, 77387, USA
PH: 936 449 6503
FX: 936 597 4312
Email: sclement@organizational.com
www.organizational.com

KENNETH C. CRADDOCK, MPA, MA
530 East 84th St., 1F
New York, NY, 10028, USA
PH: (212) 628-2986 (h);
(212) 854-5767 (w)
Email: kcc6@columbia.edu;
KenCraddock@gmail.com

SHEILA DEANE
PeopleFit Australasia Pty Ltd
Suite 409, Princess Tower,
1 Princess Street,
Kew, Victoria, 3101, Australia
PH: +61 3 98528307
Email: deane@peoplefit.com.au

MAURICE DUTRISAC
Mastermind Solutions Inc.
www.mastermindsolutions.ca
PH: (416) 527 3536
Email: maurice@mastermindsolutions.ca
www.mastermindsolutions.ca

JULIAN FAIRFIELD
29 Moree street
Gordon, NSW, 2072, Australia
PH: +61 411850303
PH: +61 297001813
Email: Julian@abacusimports.com.au

JACK FALLOW
The Centre for Organisation
Effectiveness Ltd
Oakridge, Chiltern Hill
Gerrards Cross
Bucks, SL9 9TY, UK
PH: +(44) 1753 884874
Email: Jackfallow@btinternet.com

DONALD V. FOWKE, FCMC
New Management Network
12 Woodlawn Ave. W. Suite 301
Toronto, ON, M4V 1G7, Canada
PH: +(1) 800 387 2165
Email: fowke@vianet.ca

JERRY L. GRAY
Dean Emeritus and Senior Scholar
I.H. Asper School of Business
The University of Manitoba
181 Freedman Crescent
Winnipeg, Manitoba, R3T 5V4, Canada
PH: (204) 474 8434
PH: (204) 261 1624
Email:Jerry_Gray@umanitoba.ca

JERRY B. HARVEY
1544 Longfellow Street
McLean, VA 22101, USA
PH: 703 356 1245
FX: 703 790 5606

JUDITH HOBROUGH
bioss europe
33 St James Square
London, SW1Y 4JS, England
PH: +44 (207) 661 9387
FX: +44 (207) 661 9400
Email: judy.hobrough@biosseurope.com
Skype: Hobrough

JAMES G. (JERRY) HUNT, PH.D.
Paul Whitfield Horn
Professor of Management
Texas Tech University
Rawls College of Business Administration
P.O. Box 42101
Lubbock, TX 79409-2101, USA
PH: +1 806 795 4582
Email: jerry.hunt@ttu.edu

T. OWEN JACOBS
Executive Development Associates
13820 Holly Forest Drive
Manassas, VA 20112-3863, USA
PH: 703 730 7799
Email: toj1212@verizon.net

JANET LANGFORD KELLY
Zelle, Hofmann, Voelbel,
Mason & Gette LLP
9534 W. Gull Lake Drive
Richland, MI, 49083 USA
PH: (269) 209-6229
FX: (269) 629-5303
Email: janetkelly13@msn.com

HERB KOPLOWITZ, PH.D.
Terra Firma Management Consulting
307 Ontario Street
Toronto, ON, M5A 2V8, Canada
PH: 416 324 240
FX: 416 972 1354
Email: herb@tfmc.ca

GERALD A. KRAINES, M.D.
The Levinson Institute, Inc.
28 Main Street, Suite 100
Jaffrey, NH 03452, USA
PH: (603) 532 4700, ext. 227
FX: (603) 532 4750
Email: gkraines@levinsoninst.com
www.on-leadership.com

NANCY R. LEE
Requisite Organization Associates, Inc.
2016 Harbourside Drive, Suite 323
Longboat Key, FL, 34228, USA
PH: 941 387 0170
FX: 941 387 7607
Email: NMRLEE@aol.com
Skype: nancymrlee

IAN MACDONALD
Macdonald Associates Consultancy
Cedar House, Vine Lane
Hillingdon, Middlesex,
UB10 0BX, England
PH: +44 1895 255 758
Email: Ian.macdonald@maconsultancy.
com
www.maconsultancy.com

ALISTAIR MANT
Socio-technical Strategy Group
17 Florence Road
Brighton, East Sussex, BN1 6DL, UK
PH: + 44 1273 563780
FX: + 44 1273 563780
Email: alistairmant@hotmail.com

SARAH MCARTHUR

PO Box 84574
San Diego, CA, 92138, USA
PH: 858-300-7379
Email: sarahmc@sdedit.com
www.sdedit.com

PAUL MCDOWELL

25 Hammersmith Ave
Toronto, ON, M4E 2W3, Canada
Email: paul.mcdowell@resonanceconsult-
ing.org
www.resonanceconsulting.org

GLENN W. MEHLTRETTER, JR., MBA, EDD

PeopleFit
6808 Garrison Ct.
Raleigh, NC 27612, USA
PH: +1 919 848 0527
Email: gmehl@peoplefit.com
www.peoplefit.com

DWIGHT MIHALICZ MBA CMC

Senior Vice President,
Capelle Associates Inc.
First Canadian Place
100 King Street West, 37th Floor
Toronto, ON, Canada, M5X 1C9
PH: +1 416 847 0960
FX: +1 416 236 3044
Email: dmihalicz@capelleassociates.com
www.capelleassociates.com

JOHN H. MORGAN

Piñon Hills Community Church
2400 N. Butler Ave.
Farmington, New Mexico 87401, USA
PH: 505 325 4541
FX: 505 324 8221
Email: jmorgan@pinonhillschurch.com
www.TheJohnMorganCompany.Com

ANDREW OLIVIER

The Working Journey Pty Ltd
Email: Andrew@theworkingjourney.com
www.workcomplexity.com and
www.theworkingjourney.com

ATILIO A. PENNA, PH.D.

Atilio Penna and Associates
Consulting in Organization
and Human Resources
Tte. Gral. Perón 1479 piso 3 oficina. 6
Buenos Aires-Argentina, C1037ACA
FX: (54 11) 4371 8682/9028
Email: estudio@atiliopenna.com.ar
Skype name: Estudio Penna

GEORGE REILLY

George Reilly Consulting
573 Quarry Road
Carleton Place, Ontario,
Canada, K7C 4V4
PH: (613) 257-9065
Toll Free: 1-877-711-0131
Fax: (613) 253-1386
Email: georeilly@rogers.com

KEN SHEPARD, PH.D.

Canadian Centre for Leadership
and Strategy
32 Victor Avenue, Suite # 1
Toronto, ON, Canada, M4K 1A8
PH: +1 416 463 0423
FX: +1 416 463 7827
Email: KenShepard@CanadianCentre.com
Skype: kenshepard
www.CanadianCentre.com

HARALD SOLAAS

Harald Solaas y Asoc.
Av. Belgrano 2422 8 90
1950 Buenos Aires, Argentina
PH: 54 11 49435786
Mobile: 54 911 5958 7154
Email: harald@solaas.com.ar
Skype: harald.solaas

ILONA STAPLES

Graphic Designer and Artist
139 Craven Road
Toronto, Ontario M4L 2Z4, Canada
Ph: + 416 461 4445
Email: istaples@ica-associates.com
www.ilonastaples.com
www3.sympatico.ca/william.staples
wart@maconsultancy.com

KARL STEWART

Email: karl.stewart@maconsultancy.com
www.maconsultancy.com

PETER TAYLOR

bioss europe
33 St James Square
London, SW1Y 4JS, England
PH: +44 (207) 661 9387
FX: +44 (207) 661 9400
Email: peter.taylor@biosseurope.com
Skype: petertaylor4456
www.biosseurope.com

PAUL J. TREMLETT

President
COREinternational, Inc.
606-366 Adelaide Street West
Toronto, Ontario, M5V 1R9, Canada
PH: 416 977 2673 ext 11
Toll Free: 1 800 361 5282
Email: pault@coreinternational.com
www.coreinternational.com

MARK VAN CLIEAF

Managing Director
MVC Associates International
3001 N Rocky Point Dr. E.
Suite 200, PMB 2034
Tampa, Florida, 33607, USA
PH: Tampa 813-600-5259;
Toronto - 416-907-3832;
London, UK - 020 8432 6058
FX: 813-908-0196
Email: mark@mvcinternational.com
www.mvcinternational.com

GEORGE WEBER

Secretary General Emeritus
International Federation of Red Cross/
Red Crescent Societies
c/o 1815 Alta Vista Drive
Ottawa, ON, Canada, K1G 3Y6
PH.: +(001) 613 523 1770
FX: +(001) 613 523 7736
Email: gweber@cda-adc.ca

JOS J. WINTERMANS

200 Riverside Drive
Toronto, ON, M6S 4A9, Canada
PH: 416 762 7315
FX: 647 300 6570
Email: joswintermans@rogers.com

Index

Symbols